COLIN WOODARD

AMERICAN NATIONS

A History of the
Eleven Rival Regional Cultures
of North America

PENGUIN BOOKS

PENGUIN BOOKS
Published by the Penguin Group
Penguin Group (USA) Inc., 375 Hudson Street, New York, New York 10014, U.S.A.
Penguin Group (Canada), 90 Eglinton Avenue East, Suite 700, Toronto, Ontario, Canada M4P 2Y3
(a division of Pearson Penguin Canada Inc.)
Penguin Books Ltd, 80 Strand, London WC2R 0RL, England
Penguin Ireland, 25 St. Stephen's Green, Dublin 2, Ireland (a division of Penguin Books Ltd)
Penguin Books Australia Ltd, 250 Camberwell Road, Camberwell,
Victoria 3124, Australia (a division of Pearson Australia Group Pty Ltd)
Penguin Books India Pvt Ltd, 11 Community Centre, Panchsheel Park,
New Delhi – 110 017, India
Penguin Group (NZ), 67 Apollo Drive, Rosedale, Auckland 0632,
New Zealand (a division of Pearson New Zealand Ltd)
Penguin Books (South Africa) (Pty) Ltd, 24 Sturdee Avenue,
Rosebank, Johannesburg 2196, South Africa

Penguin Books Ltd, Registered Offices: 80 Strand, London WC2R 0RL, England

First published in the United States of America by Viking Penguin,
a member of Penguin Group (USA) Inc. 2011
Published in Penguin Books 2012

20

Maps drawn by Sean Wilkinson, Sean Wilkinson Design

THE LIBRARY OF CONGRESS HAS CATALOGED THE HARDCOVER EDITION AS FOLLOWS:
Woodard, Colin,————.
American nations : a history of the eleven rival regional cultures of North America /
Colin Woodard.
p. cm.
Includes index.
ISBN 978-0-670-02296-0 (hc.)
ISBN 978-0-14-312202-9 (pbk.)
1. Indians of North America—First contact with Europeans. 2. Indians of North America—Wars. 3. Indians of North America—Government relations. 4. Blacks—North America—Relations with Indians. 5. Whites—North America—Relations with Indians. 6. Regionalism—North America—History. 7. North America—Discovery and exploration. 8. North America—Relations. 9. North America—Race relations.
I. Title.
E98.F39W66 2011
970.004'97—dc22 2011015196

Printed in the United States of America
Set in Minion Pro Designed by Francesca Belanger

PENGUIN

AMERICAN

Colin Woodard is a writer, historian, and an award-winning journalist who has reported from more than fifty foreign countries and six continents. He is a correspondent for the *Christian Science Monitor* and the *Chronicle for Higher Education*, and his work has appeared in the *Economist*, *Smithsonian*, the *San Francisco Chronicle*, the *Washington Post*, *Newsweek/The Daily Beast*, and dozens of other publications. He is the author of *The Lobster Coast*, *The Republic of Pirates*, and *Ocean's End* and lives in Portland, Maine.

Praise for *American Nations*

***The New Republic* Editors' Picks: Best Books of 2011**
***The Globalist* Top Books of 2011**

"Mr. Woodard's approach is breezier than [David Hackett] Fischer's and more historical than [Joel] Garreau's, but [Woodard] has earned a place on the shelf between them."
—*The Wall Street Journal*

"Compelling and informative."
—*The Washington Post*

"[*American Nations*] sets itself apart by delving deep into history to trace our current divides to ethno-cultural differences that emerged during the country's earliest settlement."
—*The New Republic*

"Provocative reading."
—*News and Observer*

"Fascinating . . . Engrossing . . . In the end, though, [*American Nations*] is a smart read that feels particularly timely now, when so many would claim a mythically unified 'Founding Fathers' as their political ancestors."
—*The Boston Globe*

"In *American Nations*, [Colin Woodard] persuasively reshapes our understanding of how the American political entity came to be. . . . [A] fascinating new take on history."
—*The Christian Science Monitor*

"Provocative."
—*Publishers Weekly*

"*American Nations* by journalist-historian Colin Woodard is a superb book. Woodard makes a compelling argument that the United Sates was founded by contradictory regional convictions that continue to influence current attitudes and policy on a national level. . . . *American Nations* smashes the idea of political borders. . . . There is much to grapple with in this well-written book."
—*Portland Press Herald*

"Colin Woodard debunks the simplistic notion of Left Coast, red state, blue state, and other broad-brush efforts to peg America's differences. . . . *American Nations* pulls off the unlikely feat of both offering the tools for just such a broader, deeper understanding—and demonstrates why, in a larger sense, that effort is doomed. . . . The key to the book's effectiveness is Woodard's skill—and irreverence—in delving into history with no qualms about being both brisk and contrarian. . . . In offering us a way to better understand the forces at play in the rumpus room of current American politics, Colin Woodard has scored a true triumph. I am going to order copies for my father and sister immediately—and I hope Woodard gets a wide hearing for his fascinating study." —*The Daily Beast*

"If you want to better understand U.S. politics, history, and culture *American Nations* is to be required reading. . . . By revealing this continent of rivals, *American Nations* will revolutionize the way Americans think about their past, their country, and themselves and is sure to spark controversy." —*The Herald Gazette*

"Well-researched analysis with appeal to both casual and scholarly readers."
—*Library Journal*

"For people interested in American history and sociology, *American Nations* demands reading. . . . *American Nations* is important reading."
—*St. Louis Post-Dispatch*

"Insightful." —*The Portland Daily Dispatch*

"Fascinating." —*Christensen*

"Colin Woodard offers up an illuminating history of North America that explodes the red state–blue state myth. . . . Woodard's *American Nations* is a revolutionary and revelatory take on America's myriad identities, and how the conflicts between them have shaped our country's past and mold its future."
—MaineBusiness.com

"Woodard persuasively argues that since the founding of the United States, eleven distinct geographical 'nations' have formed within the Union, each with its own identity and set of values." —*Military History Quarterly*

For my father,
James Strohn Woodard,
who taught me to read and write

CONTENTS

PART THREE

Wars for the West: 1816 to 1877

PART FOUR

Culture Wars: 1878 to 2010

AMERICAN NATIONS

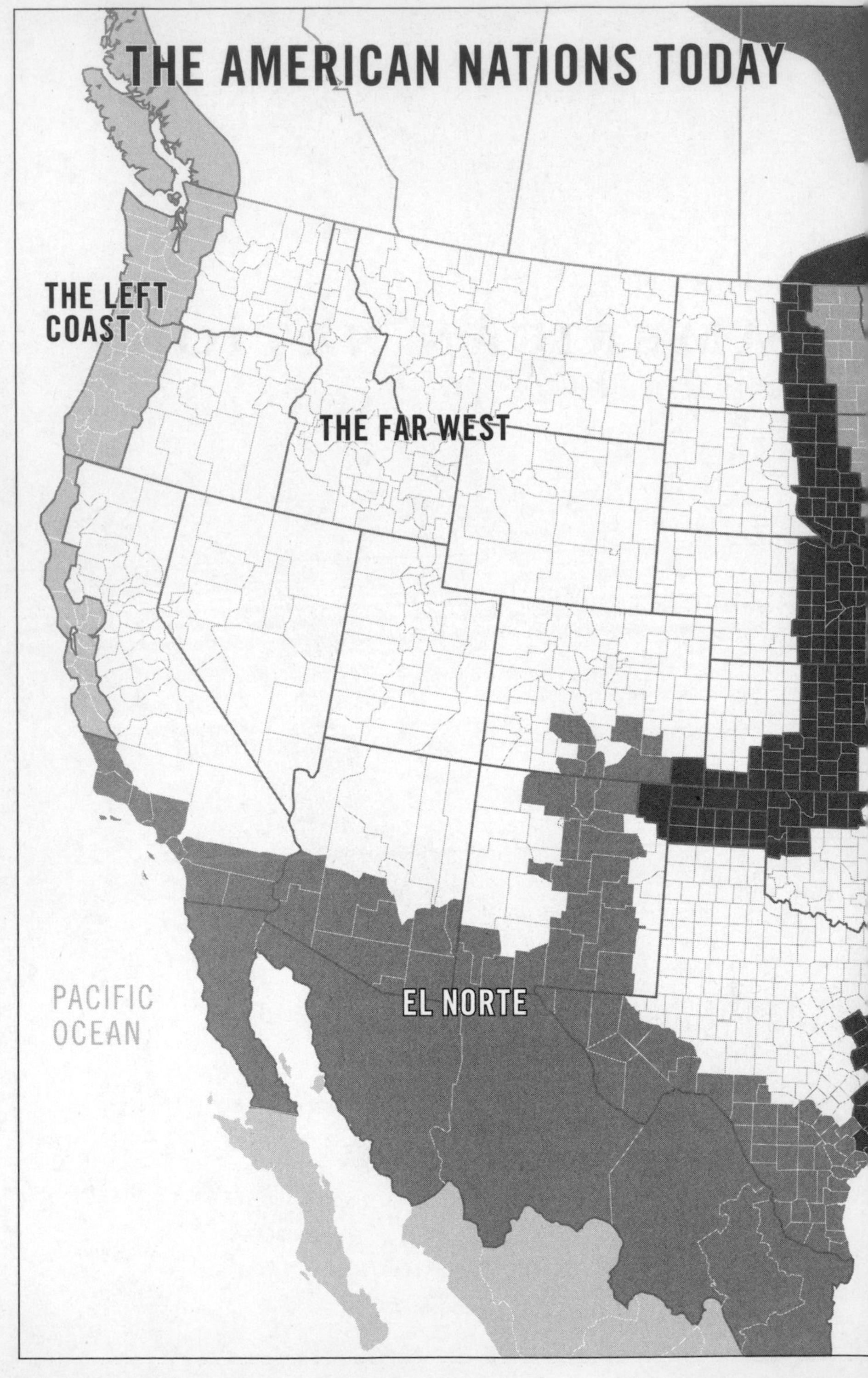

THE AMERICAN NATIONS TODAY
THE LEFT COAST
THE FAR WEST
EL NORTE
PACIFIC OCEAN

FIRST NATION
THE MIDLANDS
NEW
FRANCE
YANKEEDOM
YANKEEDOM
NEW
NETHERLAND
THE MIDLANDS
TIDEWATER
GREATER APPALACHIA
DEEP SOUTH
ATLANTIC
OCEAN
NEW FRANCE
PART OF THE
SPANISH
CARIBBEAN

Introduction

On a hot late-August day in 2010, television personality Glenn Beck held a rally on the steps of the Lincoln Memorial on the forty-seventh anniversary of Martin Luther King Jr.'s "I Have a Dream" speech. Mr. Beck stood where Rev. King had stood and addressed the white, mostly middle-aged crowd encircling the National Mall's Reflecting Pool. "We are a nation, quite honestly, that is in about as good a shape as I am, and this is not very good," he joked. "We are dividing ourselves," he said, "but our values and our principles can unite us. We must discover them again."

It's a theme heard again and again in times of crisis: Americans have become divided on account of having strayed from the core principles on which their country was founded—a "firm reliance on divine providence" and "the idea that man can rule himself," in Mr. Beck's analysis—and must return to those shared values if unity is to be restored. When society was turned upside down by mass immigration at the turn of both the twentieth and the twenty-first centuries, intellectuals counseled that America was in danger of losing the "Anglo-Protestant" culture and associated "American creed" that had supposedly kept the nation unified. In the aftermath of the tumultuous 1960s, conservatives like Irving Kristol denounced liberal intellectuals, philanthropists, and social workers for abandoning America's traditional capitalist values in favor of utopian social engineering; the liberals fervently defended these projects as promoting shared national principles of equality, justice, and freedom from oppression. With the United States allegedly divided between red states and blue ones in 2008, presidential candidate Barack Obama promised to "beat back the politics of fear, doubt, and cynicism" in favor of hope, a sentiment that had allegedly rallied Americans to rebel against Britain, fight and defeat Nazism, and face down segregation in the South. "We are choosing hope over fear," he said before the Iowa caucus. "We're choosing unity over division."[1]

Such calls for unity overlook a glaring historical fact: Americans have been deeply divided since the days of Jamestown and Plymouth. The original North American colonies were settled by people from distinct regions of the British Islands, and from France, the Netherlands, and Spain, each with their own religious, political, and ethnographic characteristics. Throughout the colonial period, they regarded one another as competitors—for land, settlers, and capital—and occasionally as enemies, as was the case during the English Civil War, when Royalist Virginia stood against Puritan Massachusetts, or when New Netherland and New France were invaded and occupied by English-speaking soldiers, statesmen, and merchants. Only when London began treating its colonies as a single unit—and enacted policies threatening to nearly all—did some of these distinct societies briefly come together to win a revolution and create a joint government. Nearly all of them would seriously consider leaving the Union in the eighty-year period after Yorktown; several went to war to do so in the 1860s. All of these centuries-old cultures are still with us today, and have spread their people, ideas, and influence across mutually exclusive bands of the continent. There isn't and never has been one America, but rather several Americas.

Any effort to "restore" fundamental American values runs into an even greater obstacle: Each of our founding cultures had its own set of cherished principles, and they often contradicted one another. By the middle of the eighteenth century, eight discrete Euro-American cultures had been established on the southern and eastern rims of North America. For generations these distinct cultural hearths developed in remarkable isolation from one another, consolidating characteristic values, practices, dialects, and ideals. Some championed individualism, others utopian social reform. Some believed themselves guided by divine purpose, others championed freedom of conscience and inquiry. Some embraced an Anglo-Saxon Protestant identity, others ethnic and religious pluralism. Some valued equality and democratic participation, others deference to a traditional aristocratic order. All of them continue to champion some version of their founding ideals in the present day. The United States had Founding Fathers, to be sure, but they were the grandfathers, great-grandfathers, or great-great-grandfathers of the men who met to sign the Declaration of Independence and to draft our first two constitutions. Our true Founders didn't have an "original intent" we can refer back to in challenging times; they had original *intents*.

America's most essential and abiding divisions are not between red states and blue states, conservatives and liberals, capital and labor, blacks and whites, the faithful and the secular. Rather, our divisions stem from this fact: the United States is a federation comprised of the whole or part of eleven regional nations, some of which truly do not see eye to eye with one another. These nations respect neither state nor international boundaries, bleeding over the U.S. frontiers with Canada and Mexico as readily as they divide California, Texas, Illinois, or Pennsylvania. Six joined together to liberate themselves from British rule. Four were conquered but not vanquished by English-speaking rivals. Two more were founded in the West by a mix of American frontiersmen in the second half of the nineteenth century. Some are defined by cultural pluralism, others by their French, Spanish, or "Anglo-Saxon" heritage. Few have shown any indication that they are melting into some sort of unified American culture. On the contrary, since 1960 the fault lines between these nations have been growing wider, fueling culture wars, constitutional struggles, and ever more frequent pleas for unity.

I have very consciously used the term *nations* to describe these regional cultures, for by the time they agreed to share a federated state, each had long exhibited the characteristics of nationhood. Americans—because of this particular historical circumstance—often confuse the terms *state* and *nation*, and are among the only people in the world who use *statehood* and *nationhood* interchangeably. A *state* is a sovereign political entity like the United Kingdom, Kenya, Panama, or New Zealand, eligible for membership in the United Nations and inclusion on the maps produced by Rand McNally or the National Geographic Society. A *nation* is a group of people who share—or believe they share—a common culture, ethnic origin, language, historical experience, artifacts, and symbols. Some nations are presently stateless—the Kurdish, Palestinian, or Québécois nations, for instance. Some control and dominate their own *nation-state*, which they typically name for themselves, as in France, Germany, Japan, or Turkey. Conversely, there are plenty of states—some of them federated—that aren't dominated by a single nation, like Belgium, Switzerland, Malaysia, Canada and, indeed, the United States. North America's eleven nations are all stateless, though at least two currently aspire to change that, and most of the others have tried to at one time or another.

This is the story of the eleven nations, and it explains much about who we North Americans are, where we've come from, and where we might be going.

American Nations reveals the history of North America's nations from the moment of their respective foundations to their present positions within the continent's three federations: Canada, Mexico, and the United States. It shows how their conflicting agendas shaped the scope and nature of the American Revolution, the Articles of Confederation, the Constitution, and a chain of violent citizen uprisings against the early American Republic. While every American knows about the great intraregional conflict that was the Civil War, it was in fact neither unprecedented (both Appalachia and New England entertained secession in the decades after the revolution) nor strictly two-sided. (The war actually involved a complicated six-nation diplomatic minuet over the future of the West.) Northern Mexicans—including those who built the culture of what is now the extreme southwest of the United States—have for centuries seen themselves as separate from their purported countrymen in central and southern Mexico; they rallied behind numerous secession schemes, including the Texas Revolution of 1836. English-speaking Canadians endlessly ponder the weakness of their identity, and it's no wonder: their federation is comprised of very strong Québécois and far northern aboriginal entities and the northward extensions of four English-speaking regional nations whose cultural cores now lie in the United States.

Disregard the conventional map of North America, with its depiction of a continent neatly divided into three federations, thirteen Canadian provinces and territories, thirty-one Mexican states, and fifty American ones. For the most part, those boundaries are as arbitrary as those chosen by European colonial powers to divide up the African continent. The lines on the map slash through cohesive cultures, creating massive cultural fissures in states like Maryland, Oregon, or New York, whose residents have often found they have more in common with their neighbors in other states than they do with one another. Banish the meaningless "regions" with which we try to analyze national politics—"the Northeast," "the

West," "the Midwest," or "the South"—whose boundaries are marked by those of their constituent states in complete disregard for the continent's actual settlement history and sectional rivalries. The continent's states, provinces, and federations do matter, of course, as they are the official forums through which political power is exercised and expressed. But on carefully examining events of the past four centuries, one realizes these jurisdictions are illusions that mask the real forces that have always driven the affairs of our sprawling continent: the eleven stateless nations of North America.

So what are these nations? What are their defining characteristics? What parts of the continent does each control? Where did they come from? Let me briefly introduce each of them, their spheres of dominance, and the names I have chosen for each.

Yankeedom was founded on the shores of Massachusetts Bay by radical Calvinists as a new Zion, a religious utopia in the New England wilderness. From the outset it was a culture that put great emphasis on education, local political control, and the pursuit of the "greater good" of the community, even if it required individual self-denial. Yankees have the greatest faith in the potential of government to improve people's lives, tending to see it as an extension of the citizenry, and a vital bulwark against the schemes of grasping aristocrats, corporations, or outside powers. For more than four centuries, Yankees have sought to build a more perfect society here on Earth through social engineering, relatively extensive citizen involvement in the political process, and the aggressive assimilation of foreigners. Settled by stable, educated families, Yankeedom has always had a middle-class ethos and considerable respect for intellectual achievement. Its religious zeal has waned over time, but not its underlying drive to improve the world and the set of moral and social values that scholars have sometimes described as "secular Puritanism."

From its New England core, Yankee culture spread with its settlers across upper New York State; the northern strips of Pennsylvania, Ohio, Indiana, Illinois, and Iowa; parts of the eastern Dakotas; and on up into Michigan, Wisconsin, Minnesota, and the Canadian Maritimes. It has been locked in nearly perpetual combat with the Deep South for control of the federal government since the moment such a thing existed.

While short-lived, the seventeenth-century Dutch colony of **New Netherland** had a lasting impact on the continent's development by laying down the cultural DNA for what is now Greater New York City. Modeled on its Dutch namesake, New Amsterdam was from the start a global commercial trading society: multi-ethnic, multi-religious, speculative, materialistic, mercantile, and free trading, a raucous, not entirely democratic city-state where no one ethnic or religious group has ever truly been in charge. New Netherland also nurtured two Dutch innovations considered subversive by most other European states at the time: a profound tolerance of diversity and an unflinching commitment to the freedom of inquiry. Forced on the other nations at the Constitutional Convention, these ideals have been passed down to us as the Bill of Rights.

Despite the defeat of the Dutch by the English in 1664, New Netherland has retained its fundamental values and societal model, having long ago replaced Amsterdam as the leading world center of Western commerce, finance, and publishing. Its territory has shrunk over the centuries, its southern reaches (Delaware and southern New Jersey) absorbed by the Midlands, its northern ones (Albany and the upper Hudson Valley) by Yankeedom. Today it comprises the five boroughs of New York City, the lower Hudson Valley, northern New Jersey, western Long Island, and southwestern Connecticut (where Red Sox fans are outnumbered by Yankee fans). As a center of global commerce, New Netherland has long been the front door for immigrants, who've made it the most densely populated part of North America. Its population—19 million at this writing—is greater than that of many European nations, and its influence over this continent's media, publishing, fashion and intellectual and economic life is hard to overstate.

Arguably the most "American" of the nations, **the Midlands** was founded by English Quakers, who welcomed people of many nations and creeds to their utopian colonies on the shores of Delaware Bay. Pluralistic and organized around the middle class, the Midlands spawned the culture of Middle America and the Heartland, where ethnic and ideological purity have never been a priority, government has been seen as an unwelcome intrusion, and political opinion has been moderate, even apathetic. The only part of British North America to have a non-British majority in 1775, the Midlands has long been an ethnic mosaic, with people of

German descent—not "Anglo-Saxons"—comprising the largest group since the late 1600s. Like Yankees, the Midlanders believe society should be organized to benefit ordinary people, but they are extremely skeptical of top-down governmental intervention, as many of their ancestors fled from European tyrannies. The Midlands is home to a dialect long considered "standard American," a bellwether for national political attitudes, and the key "swing vote" in every national debate from the abolition of slavery to the 2008 presidential contest.

From its cultural hearth in southeastern Pennsylvania, southern New Jersey, and northern Delaware and Maryland, Midland culture spread through much of the Heartland: central Ohio, Indiana, and Illinois; northern Missouri; most of Iowa; and the less-arid eastern halves of South Dakota, Nebraska, and Kansas. It shares the key "border cities" of Chicago (with the Yankees) and St. Louis (with Greater Appalachia). It also has an important extension in southern Ontario, where many Midlanders emigrated after the American Revolution, forming the central core of English-speaking Canada. While less cognizant of its national identity, the Midlands is nonetheless an enormously influential moderating force in continental politics, as it agrees with only part of each of its neighbors' strident agendas.

Tidewater, the most powerful nation during the colonial period and the Early Republic, has always been a fundamentally conservative region, with a high value placed on respect for authority and tradition and very little on equality or public participation in politics. Such attitudes are not surprising, given that it was founded by the younger sons of southern English gentry, who aimed to reproduce the semifeudal manorial society of the English countryside, where economic, political, and social affairs were run by and for landed aristocrats. These self-identified "Cavaliers" largely succeeded in their aims, turning the lowlands of Virginia, Maryland, southern Delaware, and northeastern North Carolina into a country gentleman's paradise, with indentured servants and, later, slaves taking the part of the peasants.

Tidewater elites played a central role in the foundation of the United States and were responsible for many of the aristocratic inflections in the Constitution, including the Electoral College and Senate, whose members were to be appointed by legislators, not chosen by the electorate. But the region's power waned in the 1830s and 1840s, its elite generally following the lead of the planters of the ascendant Deep South in matters of national political importance. Today it is a nation in decline, rapidly losing its influence, cultural cohesion, and territory to its Midland neighbors. Its undoing was a matter of geography: it was blocked by rivals from expanding over the Appalachian Mountains.

Greater Appalachia was founded in the early eighteenth century by wave upon wave of rough, bellicose settlers from the war-ravaged borderlands of Northern Ireland, northern England, and the Scottish lowlands. Lampooned by writers, journalists, filmmakers, and television producers as "rednecks," "hillbillies," "crackers," and "white trash," these clannish Scots-Irish, Scots, and north English frontiersmen spread across the highland South and on into the southern tiers of Ohio, Indiana, and Illinois; the Arkansas and Missouri Ozarks; the eastern two-thirds of Oklahoma; and the Hill Country of Texas, clashing with Indians, Mexicans, and Yankees as they migrated.

In the British Isles, this culture had formed in a state of near-constant war and upheaval, fostering a warrior ethic and a deep commitment to individual liberty and personal sovereignty. Intensely suspicious of aristocrats and social reformers alike, these American Borderlanders despised Yankee teachers, Tidewater lords, and Deep Southern aristocrats. In the Civil War much of the region fought for the Union, with secession movements in western Virginia (creating West Virginia), eastern Tennessee, and northern Alabama. During Reconstruction the region resisted the Yankee effort to liberate African slaves, driving it into a lasting alliance with its former enemies: the overlords of the Tidewater and Deep Southern lowlands of Dixie. The Borderlander's combative culture has provided a large proportion of the nation's military, from officers like Andrew Jackson, Davy Crockett, and Douglas MacArthur to the enlisted men fighting in Afghanistan and Iraq. They also gave the continent bluegrass and country music, stock car racing, and Evangelical fundamentalism. Greater Appalachia's people have long had a poor awareness of their cultural origins. One scholar of the Scots-Irish has called them "the people with no name." When U.S. census takers ask Appalachian people what their nationality or ethnicity is, they almost always answer "American" or even "Native American."[2]

The Deep South was founded by Barbados slave lords as a West Indies–style slave society, a system so cruel and despotic that it shocked even its seventeenth-century English contemporaries. For most of American history, the region has been the bastion of white supremacy, aristocratic privilege, and a version of classical Republicanism modeled on the slave states of the ancient world, where democracy was a privilege of the few and enslavement the natural lot of the many. It remains the least democratic of the nations, a one-party entity where race remains the primary determinant of one's political affiliations.

Beginning from its Charleston beachhead, the Deep South spread apartheid and authoritarianism across the Southern lowlands, eventually encompassing most of South Carolina, Georgia, Alabama, Mississippi, Florida, and Louisiana; western Tennessee; and the southeastern parts of North Carolina, Arkansas, and Texas. Its territorial ambitions in Latin America frustrated, in the 1860s it dragged the federation into a horrific war in an attempt to form its own nation-state, backed by reluctant allies in Tidewater and some corners of Appalachia. After successfully resisting a Yankee-led occupation, it became the center of the states' rights movement, racial segregation, and labor and environmental deregulation. It's also the wellspring of African American culture, and four decades after it was forced to allow blacks to vote, it remains politically polarized on racial grounds. Having forged an uneasy "Dixie" coalition with Appalachia and Tidewater in the 1870s, the Deep South is locked in an epic battle with Yankeedom and its Left Coast and New Netherland allies for the future of the federation.

New France is the most overtly nationalistic of the nations, possessing a nation-state-in-waiting in the form of the Province of Québec. Founded in the early 1600s, New French culture blends the folkways of ancien régime northern French peasantry with the traditions and values of the aboriginal people they encountered in northeastern North America. Down-to-earth, egalitarian, and consensus-driven, the New French have recently been demonstrated by pollsters to be far and away the most liberal people on the continent. Long oppressed by their British overlords, the New French have, since the mid-twentieth century, imparted many of their attitudes to the Canadian federation, where multiculturalism and negotiated consensus are treasured. They are indirectly responsible for the reemergence of First Nation, which is either the oldest or newest of the nations, depending on how you look at it.[3]

Today New France includes the lower third of Québec, northern and northeastern New Brunswick, and the Acadian (or "Cajun") enclaves of southern Louisiana. (New Orleans is a border city, mixing New French and Deep Southern elements.) It is the nation most likely to secure an independent state, although it would first have to negotiate a partition of Québec with the inhabitants of First Nation.

El Norte is the oldest of the Euro-American nations, dating back to the late sixteenth century, when the Spanish empire founded Monterrey, Saltillo, and other northern outposts. Today, this resurgent nation spreads from the United States–Mexico border for a hundred miles or more in either direction. It encompasses south and west Texas, southern California and the Imperial Valley, southern Arizona, most of New Mexico, and parts of Colorado, as well as the Mexican states of Tamaulipas, Nuevo León, Coahuila, Chihuahua, Sonora, and Baja California. Overwhelmingly Hispanic, it has long been a hybrid between Anglo- and Spanish America, with an economy oriented toward the United States rather than Mexico City.

Most Americans are well aware that the United States' southern borderlands are a place apart, where Hispanic language, culture, and societal norms dominate. Fewer realize that among Mexicans, the people of Mexico's northern border states are seen as overly Americanized. *Norteños* ("northerners") have a well-earned reputation for being more independent, self-sufficient, adaptable, and work-centered than Mexicans from the more densely populated hierarchical society of the Mexican core. Long a hotbed of democratic reform and revolutionary sentiment, the northern Mexican states have more in common with the Hispanic borderlands of the southwestern United States—historically, culturally, economically, and gastronomically—than they do with the rest of Mexico. The borderlands on both sides of the United States–Mexico boundary are really part of a single *norteño* culture.[4]

Split by an increasingly militarized border, El Norte in some ways resembles Germany during the Cold War: two peoples with a common culture separated from one another by a large wall. Despite the wishes of their political masters in Washington, D.C., and Mexico City, many *norteños* would prefer to federate to form a third national state of their own. Charles Truxillo, a professor of Chicano studies at the University of New Mexico, has predicted this sovereign state will be a reality by the end of the twenty-first century. He's even given it a name: La República del Norte. But regardless of any future nation-state aspirations, El Norte is going to be an increasingly influential force within the United States. The Pew Research Center predicts that by 2050 the proportion of the U.S. population that self-identifies as Hispanic will reach 29 percent, more than double the figure in 2005. Much of that growth will take place in El Norte, where Hispanics already constitute a majority, increasing the region's relative influence in state and national politics. Mexican writer Carlos Fuentes has predicted the borderlands will become an amalgamated, interdependent culture in the twenty-first century, so long as tolerance prevails. "I have always said it is a scar, not a border," he remarked. "But we don't want the scar to bleed again. We want the scar to heal."[5]

A Chile-shaped nation pinned between the Pacific and the Cascade and Coast mountain ranges, **the Left Coast** extends in a strip from Monterey, California, to Juneau, Alaska, including four decidedly progressive metropolises: San Francisco, Portland, Seattle, and Vancouver. A wet region of staggering natural beauty, it was originally colonized by two groups: merchants, missionaries, and woodsmen from New England (who arrived by sea and controlled the towns) and farmers, prospectors, and fur traders from Greater Appalachia (who arrived by wagon and dominated the countryside). Originally slated by Yankees to become a "New England on the Pacific"—and the target of a dedicated Yankee missionary effort—the Left Coast retained a strong strain of New England intellectualism and idealism even as it embraced a culture of individual fulfillment.

Today it combines the Yankee faith in good government and social reform with a commitment to individual self-exploration and discovery, a combination that has proven to be fecund. The Left Coast has been the birthplace of the modern environmental movement and the global information revolution (it is home to Microsoft, Google, Amazon, Apple, Twitter, and Silicon Valley), and the cofounder (along with New Netherland) of the gay rights movement, the peace movement, and the cultural revolution of the 1960s. Ernest Callenbach's 1975 sci-fi novel *Ecotopia* imagined the U.S. portion of the region as having broken off into a separate, environmentally stable nation at odds with the rest of the continent. The modern secessionist movement seeks to create the sovereign state of Cascadia by adding in British Columbia and southern Alaska as well, creating a "bioregional cooperative commonwealth." The closest ally of Yankeedom, it battles constantly against the libertarian-corporate agenda of its neighbor, the Far West.

Climate and geography have shaped all of the nations to some extent, but **the Far West** is the only one where environmental factors truly trumped ethnic ones. High, dry, and remote, the interior west presented conditions so severe that they effectively destroyed those who tried to apply the farming and lifestyle techniques used in Greater Appalachia, the Midlands, or other nations. With minor exceptions this vast region couldn't be effectively colonized without the deployment of vast industrial resources: railroads, heavy mining equipment, ore smelters, dams, and irrigation systems. As a result, the colonization of much of the region was facilitated and directed by large corporations headquartered in distant New York, Boston, Chicago, or San Francisco, or by the federal government itself, which controlled much of the land. Even if they didn't work for one of the companies, settlers were dependent on the railroads for transportation of goods, people, and products to and from far-off markets and manufacturing centers. Unfortunately for the settlers, their region was treated as an internal colony, exploited and despoiled for the benefit of the seaboard nations. Despite significant industrialization during World War II and the Cold War, the region remains in a state of semidependency. Its political class tends to revile the federal government for interfering in its affairs—a stance that often aligns it with the Deep South—while demanding it continue to receive federal largesse. It rarely challenges its corporate masters, however, who retain near–Gilded Age levels of influence over Far Western affairs. Today, the nation encompasses all of the interior west of the 100th meridian from the northern boundary of El Norte through to the southern frontier of First Nation, including northern Arizona; the interiors of California, Washington, and Oregon; much of British Columbia, Alberta, Saskatchewan, Manitoba, and Alaska; portions of Yukon and the Northwest Territories; the arid western halves of the Dakotas, Nebraska, and Kansas; and all or nearly all of Idaho, Montana, Colorado, Utah, and Nevada.

Like the Far West, **First Nation** encompasses a vast region with a hostile climate: the boreal forests, tundra, and glaciers of the far north. The difference, however, is that its indigenous inhabitants still occupy the area in force—most of them having never given up their land by treaty—and still retain cultural practices and knowledge that allow them to survive in the region on its own terms. Native Americans have recently begun reclaiming their sovereignty and have won both considerable autonomy in Alaska and Nunavut and a self-governing nation-state in Greenland, which stands on the threshold of full independence from Denmark. As inhabitants of a new—and very old—nation, First Nation's people have a chance to put native North America back on the map culturally, politically, and environmentally.

First Nation is rapidly taking control of vast portions of what were previously the northern fringes of the Far West, including much of Yukon, the Northwest Territories, and Labrador; the entirety of Nunavut and Greenland; the northern tier of Ontario, Manitoba, Saskatchewan, and Alberta; much of northwestern British Columbia; and the northern two-thirds of Québec.

These eleven nations have been hiding in plain sight throughout our history. You see them outlined on linguists' dialect maps, cultural anthropologists' maps of material culture regions, cultural geographers' maps of religious regions, campaign strategists' maps of political geography, and historians' maps of the pattern of settlement across the continent. California is split into three nations, and the divide is visible, plain as day, on a map of which counties voted for or against same-sex marriage in 2008. The Yankee-settled portion of Ohio is evident on the county maps of the 2000 and 2004 elections: a strip of blue across the top of a largely red state. Greater Appalachia is rendered almost perfectly in the Census Bureau's map of the largest reported ancestry group by county: its citizens inhabit virtually the only counties in the country where a majority answered "American." In 2008 Gallup asked more than 350,000 Americans if religion was an important part of their daily lives. The top ten states to answer affirmatively were all controlled by Borderlanders and/or Deep Southerners, while eight of the bottom ten were all states dominated by Yankees, with Massachusetts and the three northern New England states ranking the least religious of all. Mississippians were more than twice as likely to answer yes to Gallup's question as Vermonters. In 2007 the most highly educated state (in terms of the percentage of people with advanced degrees) was Yankee Massachusetts (16.0), the least, Deep Southern Mississippi (6.4). The top of the list included Yankee-controlled Connecticut (no. 3), Vermont (no. 6), and Rhode Island (no. 9), as well as New York (no. 5); the bottom included Appalachian-controlled Arkansas (no. 48) and West Virginia (no. 46). Which states first joined together in a carbon-trading compact to reduce greenhouse gas emissions? The ones controlled by Yankees and Left Coasters. Which ones have laws banning labor-union shop contracts? All the ones controlled by Deep Southerners, and most of those in Appalachia. Which counties vote Republican in the Pacific northwest and northern California? Those in the Far West. Which vote Democratic? Those in the Left Coast. Which parts of Texas and New Mexico vote overwhelmingly for Democrats? Those belonging to El Norte. National affinities consistently trump state ones, and they've done so for centuries.[6]

I'm not the first person to have recognized the importance of these regional cultures to North American history, politics, and governance. Kevin Phillips, a Republican Party campaign strategist, identified the distinct boundaries and values of several of these nations in 1969, and used them to accurately prophesy the Reagan Revolution in his *Emerging Republican Majority*, a politico cult classic. In 1981 *Washington Post* editor Joel Garreau wrote *The Nine Nations of North America*, a best seller that observed that the continent was divided into rival power blocs that corresponded to few national, state, or provincial boundaries. His regional paradigm argued the future would be shaped by the competing, conflicting aspirations of these North American nations. But because his book was ahistorical—a snapshot in time, not an exploration of the past—Garreau couldn't accurately identify the nations, how they formed, or what their respective aspirations were.

Brandeis University historian David Hackett Fischer detailed the origins and early evolution of four of these nations—the ones I call Yankeedom, the Midlands, Tidewater, and Greater Appalachia—in his 1989 classic *Albion's Seed*, and added New France in *Champlain's Dream*, published twenty years later. Russell Shorto described the salient characteristics of

New Netherland in *The Island at the Center of the World* in 2004. Virginia senator Jim Webb's *Born Fighting* (2005) is, in effect, a plea to his fellow Borderlanders for a national self-awakening, while Michael Lind of the New America Foundation has called on his fellow Texans to unseat autocratic Deep Southern rule in favor of the progressive Appalachian strain of the Hill Country. Awareness of these American nations has been slowly gestating for the past several decades. This book aims to see them finally delivered into the popular consciousness.

Any argument that claims to identify a series of discrete nations on the North American continent must address the obvious objection: can nations founded centuries ago really have maintained their distinct identities to the present day? We're a continent of immigrants and internal migrants, after all, and those tens of millions of newcomers representing every possible culture, race, and creed surely must have diluted and dissipated those old cultures. Is it not the height of fancy to suggest New York City's distinctive culture is a heritage of having been founded by the Dutch, given that people of Dutch ancestry now account for just 0.2 percent of its population? In Massachusetts and Connecticut—those most Yankee of states—the largest ethnic groups are the Irish and Italians respectively. One might naturally assume that the continent's nations must have long since melted into one another, creating a rich, pluralistic stew. But, as we will see, the expected course of events isn't what actually happened. North American life has been immeasurably enriched by the myriad cultures and peoples who settled there. I personally celebrate our continent's diversity, but I also know that my great-grandfather's people in western Iowa—Lutheran farmers from the island of Funen in Denmark—assimilated into the dominant culture of the Midland Midwest, even as they contributed to its evolution. My Irish Catholic great-grandparents worked the iron and copper mines of the interior West, but their children grew up to be Far Westerners. My great-great-great-grandmother's family fled from the same part of Ireland as their future cousins-in-law, but the mines they found work in happened to be in Québec, so their descendants grew up speaking French and traveling on aboriginal snowshoes. All of them undoubtedly altered the places to which they emigrated—for the better, I hope—but over the generations they assimilated into the culture around them, not the other way around. They may have embraced or rejected the dominant culture, but they didn't replace it. And it wasn't an "American" or "Canadian" culture they confronted and negotiated with or against; it was one of the respective "national" cultures identified earlier.[7]

Cultural geographers came to similar conclusions decades ago. Wilbur Zelinsky of Pennsylvania State University formulated the key theory in 1973, which he called the Doctrine of First Effective Settlement. "Whenever an empty territory undergoes settlement, or an earlier population is dislodged by invaders, the specific characteristics of the first group able to effect a viable, self-perpetuating society are of crucial significance for the later social and cultural geography of the area, no matter how tiny the initial band of settlers may have been," Zelinsky wrote. "Thus, in terms of lasting impact, the activities of a few hundred, or even a few score, initial colonizers can mean much more for the cultural geography of a place than the contributions of tens of thousands of new immigrants a few generations later." The colonial Atlantic seaboard, he noted, was a prime example. The Dutch may be all but extinct in the lower Hudson Valley—and landed aristocracy may have lost control of the Chesapeake country—but their influence carries on all the same.[8]

Our continent's famed mobility—and the transportation and communications technology that foster it—has been reinforcing, not dissolving, the differences between the nations. As journalist Bill Bishop and sociologist Robert Cushing demonstrated in *The Big Sort* (2008), since 1976 Americans have been relocating to communities where people share their values and worldview. As a result, the proportion of voters living in counties that give landslide support to one party or another (defined as more than a 20 percent margin of victory) increased from 26.8 percent in 1976 to 48.3 percent in 2004. The flows of people are significant, with a net 13 million people moving from Democratic to Republican landslide counties between 1990 and 2006 alone. Immigrants, by contrast, avoided the deep red counties, with only 5 percent living in them in 2004, compared with 21 percent in deep blue counties. What Bishop and Cushing didn't realize is that virtually every one of their Democratic landslide counties is located in either Yankeedom, the Left Coast, or El Norte, while the Republican ones dominate Greater Appalachia and Tidewater and virtually monopolize the Far West and Deep South. (The only exceptions to this pattern are the African American majority counties of the Deep South and Tidewater, which are overwhelmingly Democratic.) As Americans sort themselves into like-minded communities, they're also sorting themselves into like-minded nations.[9]

Of course, examining this book's national maps, readers might take issue with a particular county or city belonging to one nation or another. Cultural boundaries aren't usually as clear-cut as political ones, after all, and a particular region can be under the influence of two or more cultures simultaneously. Examples abound: Alsace-Lorraine on the Franco-German border; Istanbul, straddling the borders of Orthodox Byzantium and Turkic Islam; Fairfield County, Connecticut, torn between the discordant gravitational fields of New England and the Big Apple. Cultural geographers recognize this factor as well and map cultural influences by zones: a *core* or nucleus from which its power springs, a *domain* of lesser intensity, and a wider *sphere* of mild but noticeable influence. All of these zones can shift over time and, indeed, there are plenty of examples of cultures losing dominance over even their core and effectively ceasing to exist as a nation, like the Byzantines or the Cherokee. The map immediately preceding this Introduction has boundaries based on the core and domain of each nation circa 2010. If we added each nation's sphere, there would be a great deal of overlap, with multiple nations projecting influence over southern Louisiana, central Texas, western Québec, or greater Baltimore. These boundaries are not set in stone: they've shifted before and they'll undoubtedly shift again as each nation's influence waxes and wanes. Culture is always on the move.[10]

Delve deeply into almost any particular locality and you'll likely find plenty of minority enclaves or even micronations embedded within the major ones I've outlined here. One could argue that the Mormons have created a separate nation in the heart of the Far West, or that Milwaukee is a Midlander city stranded in the midst of the Yankee Midwest. You might argue for the Kentucky Bluegrass Country being a Tidewater enclave embedded in Greater Appalachia, or that the Navajo have developed a nation-state in the Far West. There's a distinct Highland Scots culture on Nova Scotia's Cape Breton Island and on North Carolina's Cape Fear peninsula. One could write an entire book about the acute cultural and historical differences between "Yankee core" Maine and Massachusetts—indeed, this is a subject I treated in *The Lobster Coast* (2004). Digging into regional cultures can be like peeling an onion. I've stopped where I have because I believe the values, attitudes, and political preferences of my eleven nations truly dominate the territories they've been assigned, trumping the implications of finer-grain analysis.

I've also intentionally chosen not to discuss several other nations that influence the continent but whose core territories lie outside what is now the United States and Canada. Cuban-dominated South Florida is the financial and transportation hub of the Spanish-speaking Caribbean. Hawaii is part of the greater Polynesian cultural nation and was once a nation-state of its own. Central Mexico and Central America are, of course, part of the North American continent and include perhaps a half-dozen distinct nations—Hispano-Aztec, Greater Mayan, Anglo-Creole, and so on. There are even scholars who make persuasive arguments that African American culture constitutes the periphery of a larger Creole nation with its core in Haiti and a domain extending over much of the Caribbean basin and on to Brazil. These regional cultures are certainly worthy of exploration, but as a practical matter, a line needed to be drawn somewhere. Washington, D.C., is also an anomaly: a gigantic political arena for the staging of intranational blood-sport competitions, where one team prefers to park their cars in the Tidewater suburbs, the other in the Midland ones.

Finally, I'd like to underscore the fact that becoming a member of a nation usually has nothing to do with genetics and everything to do with culture.* One doesn't *inherit* a national identity the way one gets hair, skin, or eye color; one *acquires* it in childhood or, with great effort, through voluntary assimilation later in life. Even the "blood" nations of Europe support this assertion. A member of the (very nationalistic) Hungarian nation might be descended from Austrian Germans, Russian Jews, Serbs, Croats, Slovaks, or any combination thereof, but if he speaks

*Some national groups would deny membership to racial or religious minorities. At this writing, Germans are still coming to grips with whether a German-speaking Muslim Turk born in Germany can really be a "German," whereas a French-born person of West African heritage can claim French identity with relative ease.

Hungarian and embraces Hungarian-ness, he's regarded as being just as Hungarian as any "pure-blooded" Magyar descendant of King Árpád. In a similar vein, nobody would deny French president Nicolas Sarkozy's Frenchness, even though his father was a Hungarian noble and his maternal grandfather a Greek-born Sephardic Jew.* The same is true of the North American nations: if you talk like a Midlander, act like a Midlander, and think like a Midlander, you're probably a Midlander, regardless of whether your parents or grandparents came from the Deep South, Italy, or Eritrea.[11]

The remainder of the book is divided into four parts organized more or less chronologically. The first covers the critical colonial period, with chapters on the creation and founding characteristics of the first eight Euro-American nations. The second exposes how intranational struggles shaped the American Revolution, the federal Constitution, and critical events in the Early Republic. The third shows how the nations expanded their influence across mutually exclusive sections of the continent, and how the related intranational struggle to control and define the federal government triggered the Civil War. The final part covers events of the late nineteenth, twentieth, and early twenty-first centuries, including the formation of the "new" nations and the intensification of intranational differences over immigration and the "American" identity, religion and social reform, foreign policy and war, and, of course, continental politics. The epilogue offers some thoughts on the road ahead.

Let the journey begin.

*When a woman of North African descent questioned him on his roots on the campaign trail, Sarkozy's response made his attitude toward national identity clear: "You are not Algerian, but French. And I am not Hungarian."

PART ONE

ORIGINS

1590 to 1769

CHAPTER 1

Founding El Norte

Americans have been taught to think of the European settlement of the continent as having progressed from east to west, expanding from the English beachheads of Massachusetts and Virginia to the shores of the Pacific. Six generations of hearty frontiersmen pushed their Anglo-Saxon bloodlines into the wilderness, wrestling nature and her savage children into submission to achieve their destiny as God's chosen people: a unified republic stretching from sea to sea inhabited by a virtuous, freedom-loving people. Or so our nineteenth-century Yankee historians would have us believe.

The truth of the matter is that European culture first arrived from the south, borne by the soldiers and missionaries of Spain's expanding New World empire.

The Americas, from a European's point of view, had been discovered by a Spanish expedition in 1492, and by the time the first Englishmen stepped off the boat at Jamestown a little over a century later, Spanish explorers had already trekked through the plains of Kansas, beheld the Great Smoky Mountains of Tennessee, and stood at the rim of the Grand Canyon. They had mapped the coast of Oregon and the Canadian Maritimes—not to mention Latin America and the Caribbean—and given names to everything from the Bay of Fundy (*Bahia Profunda*) to the Tierra del Fuego. In the early 1500s Spaniards had established short-lived colonies on the shores of Georgia and Virginia. In 1565, they founded St. Augustine, Florida, now the oldest European city in the United States.* By the end of the sixteenth century, Spaniards had been living in the deserts of Sonora and Chihuahua for decades, and their colony of New Mexico was marking its fifth birthday.

*In cultural terms, however, St. Augustine was absorbed by the Deep South centuries ago.

Indeed, the oldest European subculture in the United States isn't to be found on the Atlantic shores of Cape Cod or the Lower Chesapeake, but in the arid hills of northern New Mexico and southern Colorado. Spanish Americans have been living in this part of El Norte since 1595 and remain fiercely protective of their heritage, taking umbrage at being lumped in with Mexican Americans, who appeared in the region only in the nineteenth and twentieth centuries. Their leaders have a passion for genealogy that rivals that of the *Mayflower* descendants, and share the same sense of bearing a torch of culture that must be passed down from generation to generation. In 1610 they built Santa Fe's Palace of the Governors, now the oldest public building in the United States. They retained the traditions, technology, and religious pageantry of seventeenth-century Spain straight into the twentieth century, working fields with wooden plows, hauling wool in crude medieval carts, and carrying on the medieval Spanish practice of *literally* crucifying one of their own for Lent. Today, modern technology has arrived—and the crucifixions are done with rope, rather than nails—but the imprint of old Spain survives.[1]

Spain had the head start on its sixteenth-century rivals because it was then the world's superpower, so rich and powerful that the English looked upon it as a mortal threat to Protestants everywhere. Indeed, Pope Alexander VI considered Spain "the most Catholic" of Europe's many monarchies and in 1493 granted it ownership of almost the entire Western Hemisphere, even though the American mainland had yet to be discovered. It was a gift of staggering size: 16 million square miles—an area eighty times greater than Spain itself, spread across two continents and populated by perhaps 100 million people, some of whom had already built complex empires. Spain, with a population of less than seven million, had received the largest bequest in human history, with just one requirement attached: Pope Alexander ordered it to convert all the hemisphere's inhabitants to Catholicism and "train them in good morals." This overarching mission would inform Spanish policy in the New World, profoundly influencing the political and social institutions of the southern two-thirds of the Americas, including El Norte. It would also plunge Europe into perhaps the most apocalyptic of its many wars and, in the Americas, trigger what demographers now believe was the largest destruction of human lives in history.[2]

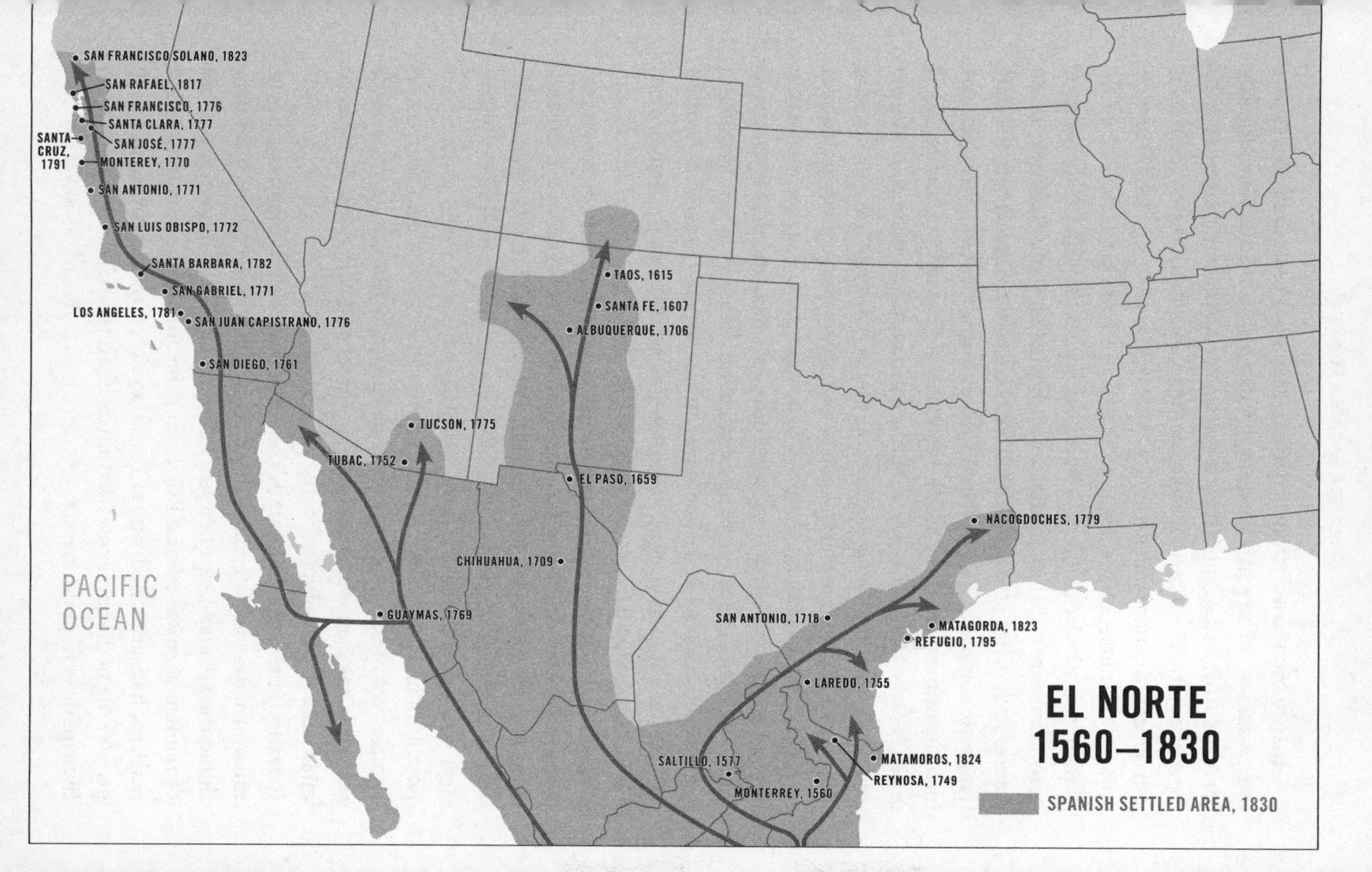
EL NORTE
1560–1830
SPANISH SETTLED AREA, 1830
SAN FRANCISCO SOLANO, 1823
SAN RAFAEL, 1817
SAN FRANCISCO, 1776
SANTA CLARA, 1777
SAN JOSÉ, 1777
SANTA CRUZ, 1791
MONTEREY, 1770
SAN ANTONIO, 1771
SAN LUIS OBISPO, 1772
SANTA BARBARA, 1782
SAN GABRIEL, 1771
LOS ANGELES, 1781
SAN JUAN CAPISTRANO, 1776
SAN DIEGO, 1761
TUCSON, 1775
TUBAC, 1752
TAOS, 1615
SANTA FE, 1607
ALBUQUERQUE, 1706
EL PASO, 1659
CHIHUAHUA, 1709
GUAYMAS, 1769
PACIFIC OCEAN
NACOGDOCHES, 1779
SAN ANTONIO, 1718
MATAGORDA, 1823
REFUGIO, 1795
LAREDO, 1755
SALTILLO, 1577
MONTERREY, 1560
MATAMOROS, 1824
REYNOSA, 1749

History has tended to portray the native peoples of the Americas as mere extras or scenery in a Western drama dominated by actors of European and African descent. Because this book is primarily concerned with the ethnocultural nations that have come to dominate North America, it will reluctantly adopt that paradigm. But there are a few factors to bear in mind at the outset about the New World's indigenous cultures. Before contact, many had a standard of living far higher than that of their European counterparts; they tended to be healthier, better fed, and more secure, with better sanitation, health care, and nutrition. Their civilizations were complex: most practiced agriculture, virtually all were plugged into a continent-spanning trade network, and some built sophisticated urban centers. The Pueblo people the Spanish encountered in New Mexico weren't Stone Age hunter-gatherers; they lived in five-story adobe housing blocks with basements and balconies surrounding spacious market plazas. The Aztecs' capital in Central Mexico, Tenochtitlan, was one of the largest in the world, with a population of 200,000, a public water supply fed by stone aqueducts, and palaces and temples that dwarfed anything in Spain. The Americas were then home to more than a fifth of the world's people. Central Mexico, with 25 million inhabitants, had the highest population density on Earth at the time.[3]

But by 1630 the population of the Americas had crashed by 80 to 90 percent as epidemics and warfare spread from points of European contact. From the forests of Maine to the jungles of Peru, Indian settlements were strewn with corpses, as there were not enough survivors to bury them. Most Europeans viewed the plagues as a divine endorsement of their conquest. The reaction of the Spanish soldier Bernal Díaz del Castillo was typical: "When the Christians were exhausted from war," recalled this veteran of the campaigns against the Aztecs and Maya, "God saw fit to send the Indians smallpox."[4]

Indeed, the swift conquest of the Aztec and Mayan empires and the subsequent discovery of gold mines and an entire mountain of silver convinced the Spanish kings that not only had God smiled upon them, but He wanted them to press on to create the "universal monarchy" that prophets had predicted would bring about Judgment Day. Philip II, Spain's king in the late sixteenth century, used the riches pouring in from the Americas to build massive armies and an enormous naval armada with which to conquer Protestant Europe. When he unleashed them, Europe was plunged into a series of religious wars that lasted for the better part of a century, undermined the solvency of the Spanish state, and left millions dead. During this campaign, his son, Philip III, was advised that the end of time was fast approaching, and that he must conquer the Turks and press on to "Africa, Asia, Calcutta, China, Japan and all the islands adjacent, subduing all 'ere they come."[5] It turned out to be poor advice. By the end of the Thirty Years' War in 1648, the Protestant powers were stronger than ever, and Spain was a weak, deeply indebted, and slowly decomposing influence.

So, how does all this relate to El Norte?

First, by spearheading the effort to snuff out the Protestant Reformation, the Spanish had earned the lasting hatred of the English, Scots, and Dutch, who regarded them as the decadent, unthinking tools of the Vatican's conspiracy to enslave the world. This virulent anti-Spanish feeling became deeply ingrained in the cultures of Yankeedom, Appalachia, Tidewater, and the Deep South. It would be visited upon the people of El Norte in a heightened form in the nineteenth century, buttressed by Victorian notions about racial mixing that inform anti-Mexican racism to this day.

Second, the effort to stamp out Europe's Protestants consumed so much of the Spanish Empire's focus, energy, and resources that it was left incapable of properly supporting the northward expansion of its American empire. As a result, Spain's colonies in El Norte—especially Nuevo México, Texas, Alta California, and northern Sonora—were undermanned, poorly supplied, and staggeringly poor, even by Spanish colonial standards. Many otherwise devout Catholic couples lived in sin because they couldn't afford to pay priests to marry them. Few people could read or write because there were no schools. As late as 1778, San Antonio, one of El Norte's most prominent settlements, was still a poor village where the governor was forced to live in the jailhouse for lack of better alternatives. Colonial El Norte was the neglected, far-flung borderland of a distant, collapsing empire and would remain such for a quarter of a millennium. Isolated from regular contact with other European cultures, it would develop its own unique cultural characteristics, many of them very different from those of Central Mexico.[6]

Third, by the time the Spanish reached El Norte, the empire's religious mission had become the key element of its colonial policy. The plan was to assimilate the Native Americans into Spanish culture by converting them to Catholicism and supervising their faith, work, dress, and conduct in special settlements governed by priests. It was, compared with that of the English, an enlightened Indian policy, at least in theory. Native Americans were considered inferior, not because of any inherent racial characteristics but because of their cultural practices. The Spanish called them *gente sin razón* ("people without reason") but felt they could be educated and disciplined into becoming *gente de razón* over the course of a decade or so. During this training period Native apprentices would be called "neophytes," and every aspect of their lives would be monitored and controlled. It would take a phenomenal effort, to be sure. Missions would have to be built all over the frontier, each a self-sufficient compound with a church; a comfortable residence for the missionaries; a well-manned military post to enforce discipline; tanneries, workshops, kilns, and mills where neophytes would learn their trades; male and female dormitories; and stables, barns, and outbuildings to house horses, mules, and livestock. The friars would protect the neophytes from rapacious settlers or hostile Indians—and lock any females over the age of seven in the barracks at sunset to prevent their rape by the resident soldiers. When the neophytes were considered to have successfully internalized the Catholic faith, Spanish work habits, and the Castilian language, the mission would become their village and the missionaries would move on to oversee new missions on the expanding frontier. Or so the plan went.[7]

This relatively inclusive attitude toward the Indians reflected the particular racial demography of Spain's New World colonies. The empire had never had many female colonists, so Spanish soldiers and officials took Aztec wives or otherwise begat mixed Indian-Spanish children, or *mestizos*. By the early 1700s, mestizos constituted a majority of the population of what is now Mexico and El Norte.[8] The Spanish world had a caste system—pure whites dominated the highest offices—but it broke down over time in the New World, especially on the empire's northern frontier, where almost everyone had at least one nonwhite ancestor. Being part Indian themselves, colonial authorities weren't inclined to denigrate Indians on racial grounds.

Had this social reengineering project succeeded, El Norte might have spread its mestizo society across what is now the western United States, perhaps achieving sufficient strength to maintain its hegemony in the region against political rivals. But the project did not go well, limiting *norteño* cultural influence to a comparatively narrow strip adjacent to more thickly settled parts of New Spain, the Spanish domain that stretched from California to the Isthmus of Panama.

It wasn't for lack of trying. Between 1598 and 1794 the Spanish established at least eighteen missions in what is now the state of New Mexico, twenty-six in what is now Texas, eight in Arizona, and twenty-one in Alta California—in the process founding what have since become the cities of Tucson, San Antonio, San Diego, and San Francisco.[9] But the system had several serious flaws. By cloistering neophytes away from mainstream Hispanic life, the friars made it difficult for them to assimilate. In practice, the system was abusive. Neophytes were not allowed to change their minds about assimilation and return to Native life, and those who escaped were hunted down and then flogged in the public square. The missionaries also used whips to drive neophytes to church services, to compel them to kneel at the right times, and to maintain work discipline in the fields, workshops, and tanneries. French visitors to California's Mission San Carlos (in what is now Carmel) said, "Everything reminded us of a . . . West Indian [slave] colony . . . We mention it with pain [because] the resemblance is so perfect that we saw men and women loaded with irons, others in the stocks, and at length the noise of the strokes of a whip struck our ears."[10] Because neophytes weren't paid for their labor, it was relatively easy for the priests to turn a profit, and they therefore had little incentive to ever declare the neophytes to be civilized and turn the mission properties over to them. The communities themselves also tended not to grow, as malnutrition, smallpox, and syphilis kept mortality high and childbirths low.[11]

Norteño life wasn't any less autocratic outside the mission walls, making it even harder for the civilization to spread or strengthen itself.

Most Hispanics had come to El Norte because they had been ordered to do so by imperial or church authorities. Almost every outpost of civilization—missions, forts, and towns—had been founded by a government expedition as an isolated and highly restricted community. Soldiers, clergy, farmers, ranchers, craftsmen, servants, and livestock traveled en masse to wherever they were assigned and were expected to follow orders for the rest of their lives. People could not travel from town to town or open new areas to farming or ranching without official permission. Spanish imperial policy forbade them from engaging in most manufacturing activities and required that all imports be conducted via an official monopoly. Texans weren't allowed to import or export goods from their own Gulf Coast; rather, they had to transport them in heavy wooden carts across hundreds of miles of arid plains to and from Veracruz. Excise taxes and transportation costs had by then quadrupled the prices of imports, discouraging economic development and personal initiative. The region would remain an exploited colony of the southern provinces throughout the colonial period.[12]

El Norte had no self-government, no elections, and no possibility for local people to play any significant role in politics. Provincial military commanders usually served as governors and ruled without any democratic niceties like governing councils or legislatures. Even in the region's few towns like Santa Fe, San Antonio, Tucson, and Monterey, the town councils were made up of a self-perpetuating oligarchy of the community's wealthiest citizens. Most of these ceased to function by the late 1700s, leaving municipal affairs in the hands of local military officers.[13]

Ordinary people were expected to give their loyalty to their local *patrón*, an elite figure who undertook patriarchal responsibility for their well-being. The patrón provided employment; looked after widows, orphans, and the infirm; and sponsored religious feasts and church activities. His *peons* showed him obedience and respect. This system—similar to the lord-and-serf relationships of the Middle Ages—was common throughout Latin America and still influences El Norte political and social behavior today.[14] Until the late 1960s, political commentators regularly noted that the votes of El Norte could be, and were, bought and sold like cattle futures; if one bribed a community's patrón, he could usually ensure 90-plus percent voter support for the appropriate candidate. In the 1941 Texas Senate race, Lyndon B. Johnson won 90 percent of the vote in the six El Norte counties by making a single telephone call to local boss George Parr, even though the same six counties had given 95 percent support to his opponent in the governor's race the year before. Johnson returned to the Senate in 1948 by "winning" 99 percent of the vote in Parr's home county, where voter turnout was a preposterous 99.6 percent.[15]

While the region inherited New Spain's political legacy, in other respects it was very different from the viceroyalty's tropical, densely populated, and feudalistic core. Within New Spain—and later, Mexico—the people of El Norte were seen as being more adaptable, self-sufficient, hard-working, aggressive, and intolerant of tyranny. Indeed, *norteños* in Mexico would play a leading role in both the Mexican Revolution and the political rebellion against the corrupt Institutional Revolutionary Party (PRI) in the 1980s and 1990s. In the nineteenth century, New Mexican *norteños* would propose seceding from Mexico to join California and what is now Nevada, Arizona, and Colorado to form a democratic República Mexicana del Norte; Texas *norteños* would back the creation of the independent Republic of Texas in 1836, while their neighbors in Tamaulipas, Nuevo León, and Coahuila declared a separate Republic of the Rio Grande, which was put down by force of arms. No wonder the august Mexican historian Silvio Zavala has dubbed the north "the guardian of liberty" in his country.[16]

All of these characteristics evolved in response to the unusual conditions on the northern frontier. The New Mexico, Texas, and California settlements were staggeringly remote from the centers of Spanish American civilization. Manpower, correspondence, tools, foodstuffs, religious articles, and other provisions came in via official government resupply missions, which then carried away any commodities the missions and villages had produced. In the case of New Mexico, resupply caravans of ox-drawn wooden carts arrived only once every three or four years, having taken more than six months just to make the torturous 1,500-mile journey from Mexico City. California's overland connections with the rest of the empire were cut off by hostile Indians, and so the province relied entirely on a handful of government ships sailing the 1,000-plus miles to and from Guaymas on Sonora's Pacific coast; all goods, passengers, and letters then had to continue overland to Mexico City. All the northern provinces were forbidden from conducting trade with foreigners and could ship goods and passengers to Spain only via Veracruz, not through much closer alternatives such as San Francisco or Matagorda, Texas. When Spain briefly experimented with an imperial legislature in the early nineteenth century, New Mexico's delegate spent most of his three-year term just trying to get to Spain, while Texas couldn't afford to send one at all.[17] Nor could the provinces of El Norte help one another, as throughout the colonial period there were no roads connecting them. And as if the isolation wasn't bad enough, El Norte's settlements were under constant threat from (justifiably) hostile Indians and, later, other European powers.

Their remoteness did, however, give *norteños* a greater degree of day-to-day freedom than their counterparts had in the central provinces near Mexico City, shaping the region's character. Hispanics who wanted to escape the oppressive scrutiny of friars and military officers simply made their homes in isolated places and even among the Indians. Record keeping was lax enough that a mestizo, mulatto, or assimilated Indian could often become officially white through a verbal declaration, circumventing the empire's caste system. "Practically all those who wish to be considered Spaniards are of mixed blood," a mid-eighteenth-century Jesuit missionary reported from Sonora. Laborers had more options in the north as well. Farmworkers could choose to become sharecroppers, giving them autonomy from large landowners. On ranches and mission lands, cattle hands spent long periods in remote areas far from the surveillance of superiors, and non-neophytes could move from ranch to ranch in search of the best conditions; indeed, it was these independent, self-sufficient, mobile ranch hands who developed the legendary cowboy culture of the American West.[18]

A little-known fact is that that most American of icons, the open-range cattle industry, originated in El Norte and was based on Spanish precedents. A mix of arid plains, high deserts, and Mediterranean coastline, Spain bears a physical resemblance to El Norte. In southern Spain, the Spanish developed the techniques they would later deploy in their American colonies, such as the use of mounted *vaqueros* (cowboys) to round up, herd, brand, and drive large numbers of cattle on vast, unfenced ranges. The Spanish introduced horses, cattle, sheep, and goats to the New World, along with the clothes, tools, and skills to ranch them, building the common foundations of all subsequent cowboy cultures from the *huasos* of Chile to the cowboys of the American West. Large ranching estates spread northwards from Mexico's central Gulf Coast, and by the time they reached Texas in the 1720s, had developed the lasso (*lazo*), lariat (*la reata*), chaps (short for *chaparreras*), and the wide-brimmed *sombrero*, from which the Texas ten-gallon hat is derived. English-speaking cowboys would later adopt other Spanish vocabulary, including *rodeo*, *bronco*, buckaroo (from *vaquero*), mustang (from *mesteño*), bandoleer (*bandolera*), stampede (from *estampida*), and ranch (*rancho*).[19]

Oddly enough, it was the Franciscans who introduced this cowboy culture to what is now Texas and California, as tallow and hides were among the only products the missions could profitably ship to the rest of Mexico. Short on labor, the friars trained their neophytes to be their vaqueros, flouting Spanish laws against allowing Indians to ride horses. When the governor of California complained about this practice, a friar responded, "How else can the vaquero's work of the missions be done?" The first American cowboys were, in fact, Indians.[20]

But while Spanish ranching techniques were becoming ascendant at the end of the eighteenth century, the *norteños* found themselves facing threats spreading from the north and east. El Norte had new Euro-American neighbors, rival cultures with advantages in manpower and resources. The first such challenger was New France, ensconced in New Orleans at the end of the Mississippi Valley and scattered over a vast province named for its king, Louis XIV. Beyond Louisiana to the northeast lay an uneasy confederation of nations that had recently won its independence from Great Britain—a schizophrenic and populous entity that had just started calling itself the United States.

CHAPTER 2

Founding New France

In the fall of 1604—sixteen years before the *Mayflower*'s voyage—a group of Frenchmen were about to become the first Europeans to confront a New England winter.

By the standards of the day, theirs was an elaborate undertaking. Seventy-nine men had crossed the Atlantic in two ships filled with the prefabricated parts needed to assemble a chapel, forge, mill, barracks, and two coastal survey vessels. They carefully reconnoitered the coasts of what would one day become Nova Scotia, New Brunswick, and eastern Maine, looking for an ideal location for France's first American outpost. They chose to build their fortified settlement on a small island on what is now the easternmost fringe of Maine, in the middle of a river they named the St. Croix. The site appeared to perfectly suit their needs: the island was easy to defend from European rivals, and the mainland shore had ample wood, water, and farmable plots. Most important, there were plenty of Indians in the area, as the river was a major highway for their commerce. Good relations with the Indians, their leaders had decided, would be key to the French project in North America.[1]

The expedition was led by an unlikely pair. Pierre Dugua, the sieur de Mons, was a French noble who had been raised in a walled château and had served as a personal advisor to King Henri IV. His thirty-four-year-old deputy, Samuel de Champlain, was supposedly the common-born son of a small-town merchant but was somehow able to gain personal and immediate access to the king anytime he wished and, inexplicably, had been receiving a royal pension and special favors from him. (Many scholars now believe he was one of Henri IV's many illegitimate sons.) In France, Champlain and de Mons had been neighbors, raised a few miles apart in Saintonge, a coastal province in western France distinguished by its unusually mixed population and tolerance of cultural diversity. Both men had served on the battlefields of France's religious wars, experienced firsthand the atrocities that can result from bigotry, and wished to avoid seeing them again. Their mutual visions of a tolerant, utopian society in the wilds of North America would profoundly shape not only the culture, politics, and legal norms of New France but also those of twenty-first-century Canada as well.[2]

The sieur de Mons envisioned a feudal society like that of rural France, only perfected. It would be based on the same medieval hierarchy with counts, viscounts, and barons ruling over commoners and their servants. Democracy and equality did not enter into the picture. There would be no representative assemblies, no town governments, no freedom of speech or the press; ordinary people would do as they were told by their superiors and their king—as they always had, as they had always been meant to. But there were differences from France as well. While Catholicism would be its official religion, New France would be open to French Protestants, who could freely practice their faith. Commoners would be allowed to hunt and fish—rights unheard of in France, where game belonged exclusively to the nobility. They would be able to lease farmland and, potentially, rise to a higher station in life. It would be a conservative and decidedly monarchical society, but one more tolerant and with greater opportunities for advancement than France itself. It was a plan that would meet unexpected resistance from rank-and-file colonists.

Champlain's vision for New France was more radical and enduring than de Mons's. While he shared de Mons's commitment to creating a monarchical, feudal society in North America, he believed it should coexist in a friendly, respectful alliance with the Native American nations in whose territories it would be embedded. Instead of conquering and enslaving the Indians (as the Spanish had), or driving them away (as the English would), the New French would embrace them. They would intentionally settle near the Indians, learn their customs, and establish alliances and trade based on honesty, fair dealing, and mutual respect. Champlain hoped to bring Christianity and other aspects of French civilization to the Native populations, but he wished to accomplish this by persuasion and example. He regarded the Indians as every bit as intelligent and human as his own countrymen, and thought cross-cultural marriage between the two peoples was not only tolerable but desirable. It was an extraordinary idea, and one that would succeed beyond anyone's expectations. Historian David Hackett Fischer has fittingly dubbed it "Champlain's Dream."[3]

The two Frenchmen's ideal society got off to a poor start, largely because they had underestimated the severity of the New England winter. The first snows came to St. Croix Island in early October. When the river froze in December, the powerful tides from the Bay of Fundy smashed and shattered the ice, turning the waterway into an impassable field of jagged ice floes. Trapped on their tiny island, the settlers quickly ran short of firewood, meat, fish, and drinking water. The depth of the cold was something none of them was prepared for. "During this winter all our liquors froze, except the Spanish wine," Champlain recalled. "Cider was dispensed by the pound . . . [and] we were obliged to use very bad water and drink melted snow." Subsisting entirely on salted meats, the settlers soon began dying from scurvy, their tissues decomposing for lack of vitamin C. They all might have perished had the colonists not already established a friendly rapport with the Passamaquoddy tribe, who delivered an emergency supply of fresh meat during a break in the ice. Even so, nearly half the colonists died that winter, filling the colony's cemetery with disease-ravaged bodies. (In the nineteenth century, when the cemetery area began to erode into the river, locals would begin referring to the site as Bone Island.)[4]

The French learned from their tragic mistake. In the spring de Mons moved the colony to a spacious harbor on the opposite side of the Bay of Fundy in what is now Annapolis Royal, Nova Scotia. Their new settlement, Port Royal, would become the model for the future settlements in New France. It resembled a village in northwestern France, from where almost all the settlers had come. Peasants cleared large fields and planted wheat and fruit orchards. Skilled laborers constructed a water-powered grain mill and a comfortable lodge for the gentlemen, who staged plays, wrote poetry, and journeyed into the fields only for picnics. Although their community was tiny—fewer than 100 men all told, once reinforcements had arrived from France—the gentlemen took little notice of their underlings; in their voluminous written accounts of their experiences, they almost never mention any of them by name. In winter they formed a dining club called the Order of Good Cheer and competed with one another to produce the finest gastronomy from local game and seafood.

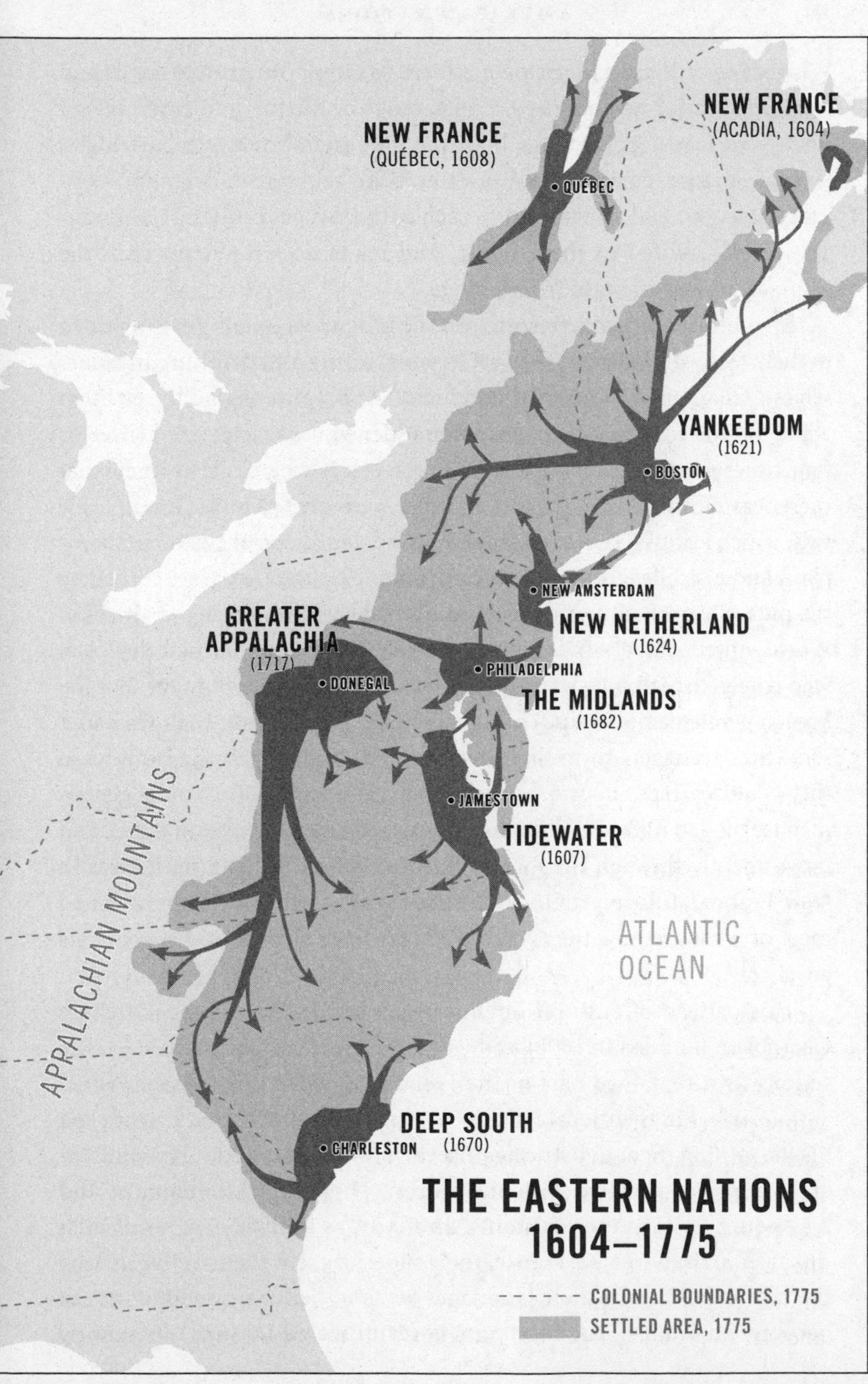
NEW FRANCE
(QUÉBEC, 1608)
QUÉBEC
NEW FRANCE
(ACADIA, 1604)
YANKEEDOM
(1621)
BOSTON
NEW AMSTERDAM
NEW NETHERLAND
(1624)
GREATER
APPALACHIA
(1717)
DONEGAL
PHILADELPHIA
THE MIDLANDS
(1682)
JAMESTOWN
TIDEWATER
(1607)
APPALACHIAN MOUNTAINS
ATLANTIC
OCEAN
DEEP SOUTH
(1670)
CHARLESTON
THE EASTERN NATIONS
1604–1775
COLONIAL BOUNDARIES, 1775
SETTLED AREA, 1775

While early settlers in Jamestown refused to sample unfamiliar foods and resorted to eating neighbors who'd starved to death, the gentlemen at Port Royal were feasting on "ducks, bustards, grey and white geese, partridges, larks . . . moose, caribou, beaver, otter, bear, rabbits, wildcats (or leopards), raccoons and other animals such as the savages caught." Commoners weren't invited to these feasts, and made do with wine and "the ordinary rations brought from France."[5]

By contrast, the gentlemen treated the Indians as equals, inviting them to their feasts and plays. "They sat at table, eating and drinking like ourselves," Champlain wrote of their chiefs. "And we were glad to see them while, on the contrary, their absence saddened us, as happened three or four times when they all went away to the places wherein they knew that there was hunting." The French, in turn, were invited to Mi'kmaq festivals, which featured speeches, smoking, and dance, social customs Champlain and his colleagues were quick to adopt. At first they were helped by the presence of the interpreter de Mons had seen fit to bring to the New World, an educated African servant or slave named Mathieu deCosta, who'd been to Mi'kmaq territory before and knew their language. But the French gentlemen also studied the Mi'kmaq language on their own and sent three teenagers from their own families to live with the Indians so they could learn their customs, technology, and speech. The young gentlemen learned to make birch-bark canoes, track moose on snowshoes, and move silently through the forests. All would become leading figures in New France's future province of Acadia, which theoretically spanned most of what are now the Canadian Maritimes. Two would serve as its governor.[6]

This pattern of cultural openness was repeated in Québec (which Champlain founded in 1608) and would be practiced across New France so long as it remained part of the French kingdom. Champlain visited various tribes in their local villages, sat in their councils, and even risked his life joining them in battle against the powerful Iroquois. He sent several young men to live with the Huron, Nipissing, Montagnais, and Algonquin to learn their customs. Similarly, as soon as new Jesuit missionaries arrived in New France, their superiors sent them to live among the natives and learn their languages so as to better persuade them to become Christians. The Montagnais reciprocated in 1628, entrusting three teenage girls to live in the future Québec City so that they could be "instructed and treated like those of [the French] nation" and perhaps married into it as well. Champlain championed the notion of racial intermarriage, telling the Montagnais chiefs: "Our young men will marry your daughters, and henceforth we shall be one people." Following his example, French settlers in Québec tolerated unusual Indian habits, such as entering homes and buildings "without saying a word, or without any greeting."[7] Other Frenchmen went further, moving into the forest to live with the Indians, a move encouraged by the critical shortage of women in Québec for much of the seventeenth century. All adopted Indian technologies—canoes, snowshoes, corn production—which were more suited to life in New France than heavy boats, horses, and wheat.

In Acadia sixty French peasant families lived happily at the head of the Bay of Fundy for generations, intermarrying with local Mi'kmaqs to such a degree that a Jesuit missionary would predict the two groups would become "so mixed . . . that it will be impossible to tell them apart." Like other Indian tribes with whom the Jesuits worked, the Mi'kmaqs adopted Christianity but continued to practice their own religion, not believing the two to be mutually exclusive. Jesuit priests were seen as having one form of medicine, traditional shamans another. This hybrid belief system was not that dissimilar to the earthy Catholicism practiced by the Acadian peasants, infused with pre-Christian traditions that survive to this day among their Cajun descendants in Louisiana. In Acadia, where official authority and oversight was weak, French and Mi'kmaq cultures blended into one another.

While the French had hoped to peaceably assimilate the Indians into their culture, religion, and feudal way of life, ultimately they themselves became acculturated into the lifestyle, technology, and values of the Mi'kmaqs, Passamaquoddies, and Montagnais. Indeed, New France became as much an aboriginal society as a French one and would eventually help pass this quality on to Canada itself.

The Indians' influence would also be the undoing of the French effort to transplant feudalism to North America. Starting in 1663, Louis XIV's minions tried to bend New France's increasingly aboriginal society to his will. The Sun King wanted a society in which most of the land was divided among nobles with ordinary people bound to it, toiling in the fields and obeying their superiors' commands. A government bureaucracy would attempt to control every aspect of their lives, including how they addressed one another, what clothing and weapons a given class of people could wear, whom they could marry, what they could read, and which types of economic activities they could undertake. There were rules forbidding bachelors from hunting, fishing, or even entering the forests (to prevent them from "going native") and penalizing fathers whose daughters remained unmarried at age sixteen or sons at twenty (to spur the colony's growth). In the St. Lawrence Valley almost all arable land not reserved for the Church was divided among well-born gentlemen to enable them to become landed aristocrats, or *seigniors*. Protestants were no longer welcome because, as Bishop François Xavier de Laval put it, "to multiply the number of Protestants in Canada would be to give occasion for the outbreak of revolutions."[8]

Louis XIV also sent thousands of settlers to New France at the crown's expense, including 774 *filles de roi*, impoverished young women who agreed to wed colonists in Quebec in exchange for a small dowry.[9] Officials at Versailles hired recruiters to round up indentured servants, who would be sold at bargain rates into three years of bondage to aspiring seigniors. Most of those sent to Canada in the seventeenth century came from Normandy (20 percent), the adjacent Channel provinces (6 percent), or the environs of Paris (13 percent), although a full 30 percent came from Saintonge and three adjacent provinces on the central Bay of Biscay. The legacy of these regional origins can still be seen in the Norman-style fieldstone houses around Québec City and heard in the Québécois dialect, which preserves archaic features from the early modern speech of northwestern France. (In Acadia, where the Biscay coast provided the majority of settlers, people have a different dialect that reflects this heritage.) Very few settlers came from eastern or southern France, which were remote from the ports that served North America. During the peak of immigration in the 1660s, most colonists came alone, two-thirds were male, and most were either very young or very old and had little experience with agriculture. The situation became so serious that in 1667 Jean Talon, Québec's senior economic official, begged Versailles not to send children, those over forty, or any "idiot, cripples, chronically ill person or wayward sons under arrest" because "they are a burden to the land."[10]

Regardless of their origins, most colonists found working the seigniors' land to be burdensome. Few accepted their assigned role as docile peasants once their indentures were concluded. Two-thirds of male servants returned to France, despite official discouragement, because of rough conditions, conflict with the Iroquois, and the shortage of French brides. Those who stayed in New France often fled the fields to take up lives in the wilderness, where they traded for furs with the Indians or simply "went native." Many negotiated marriages with the daughters of Native leaders to cement alliances. As John Ralston Saul, one of Canada's most prominent public intellectuals, has characterized it, these Frenchmen were "marrying up." By the end of the seventeenth century, roughly one-third of indentured servants had taken to the forests and increasing numbers of well-bred men were following them. "They . . . spend their lives in the woods, where there are no priests to restrain them, nor fathers, nor governors to control them," Governor Jacques-René de Brisay de Denonville explained to his superior in 1685. "I do not know, Monseigneur, how to describe to you the attraction that all the young men feel for the life of the savage, which is to do nothing, to be utterly free of constraint, to follow all the customs of the savages, and to place oneself beyond the possibility of correction."[11]

In contemporary terms, these woodsmen—or *coureurs de bois*—were first-generation immigrants to aboriginal societies whose cultures and values they partially assimilated. Their numerous children were as much Mi'kmaq, Montagnais, or Huron as they were French; indeed, they formed a new ethnoracial group, the *métis*, who, unlike New Spain's mestizos, tended to be just as comfortable living in an aboriginal setting as in the European settlements. The coureurs de bois were proud of their independence and of the relative freedom of their seminomadic, hunter-gatherer lifestyle. "We were Caesars, [there] being nobody to contradict us," explained one of the most famous, Pierre-Esprit Radisson, in 1664. Among these new Caesars was Jean Vincent d'Abbadie de Saint-Castin, a French baron who had served at Fort Pentagoet (now Castine, Maine), the Acadian administrative capital. Dutch pirates destroyed the fort in 1674, but Saint-Castin didn't bother to rebuild it when he returned to the site three years later. Instead he set up a trading post in the middle of a Penobscot Indian village, married the daughter of Penobscot chief

Madockawando, and raised a métis family in the Penobscot manner. His sons, Joseph and Bernard, would both lead Penobscots in raids against the English in the bloody imperial wars for control of the continent, becoming among the most feared men in New England.[12]

With much of their labor force deserting to Indian ways, the seigniors found themselves sinking into poverty. At least one was forced to work his own grain mill after his miller was drafted. Another donated his land to a nunnery, having become too old to work his own fields. Even leading families like the Saint-Ours and Verchères were forced to beg Louis XIV for pensions, salary-paying appointments, and fur trading licenses. "It is necessary to help them by giving them a means of . . . livelihood," Governor Denonville wrote the crown, "for, in truth, without it there is a great fear that the children of our nobility . . . will become bandits because of having nothing by which to live."[13]

At the same time, commoners displayed an unusual degree of independence and contempt for hierarchy. On the island of Montréal, settlers hunted and fished on the seigniors' reserves, damaged their fences, and threatened their overseers. The obstinacy of the Acadian farmers infuriated an eighteenth-century colonial official. "I really think the Acadians are mad. Do they imagine we wish to make *seigniors* of them?" he asked. "They seem offended by the fact that we wish to treat them like our peasants." Throughout New France, rough equality and self-reliance prevailed over Old World feudal patterns. The French had intended to assimilate the Indians, but inadvertently created a métis society, as much Native American in its core values and cultural priorities as it was French.[14]

By the middle of the eighteenth century, New France had also become almost entirely dependent on Native Americans to protect their shared society from invaders. Even a century and a half after the foundation of Port Royal, there were only 62,000 French people living in Québec and Acadia, and only a few thousand in the vast Louisiana Territory, which encompassed much of the continental interior. To the south, however, France's longtime enemies were gaining strength at an astonishing rate, for in the Chesapeake Tidewater and New England, two aggressive, vibrant, and avowedly Protestant societies had taken root, cultures with very different attitudes about race, religion, and the place of "savages."

Together they numbered over 750,000, and another 300,000 inhabited the other English-controlled colonies of the Atlantic seaboard.[15]

The leaders of Québec and Acadia could only hope that New England and Tidewater would remain what they had been from the outset: avowed enemies of one another with little in common beyond having come from the same European island.

CHAPTER 3

Founding Tidewater

In the traditional account of the Jamestown story, the dashing Captain John Smith leads a can-do party of adventurers as they hunt for gold, fight with savages, and seduce Indian princesses. They construct a fort, tough out the winters, and build the foundations of "real" American society: bold, scrappy, and individualistic. They came seeking a better life and created the New World's first representative assembly, harbinger of the great democracy to follow.

In reality, the first lasting English colony in the New World was a hellhole of epic proportions, successful only in the sense that it survived at all. Founded by private investors, it was poorly planned, badly led, and foolishly located. With much of the American seaboard at their disposal, the leaders of the Virginia Company chose to build on a low-lying island surrounded by malarial swamps on the James River, a sluggish body of water that failed to carry away the garbage and human waste the colonists dumped into it, creating a large disease incubator. To make matters worse, almost none of the settlers knew anything about farming. Half were haughty gentlemen-adventurers, the rest beggars and vagrants rounded up on the streets of London and sent to the New World by force. "A more damned crew hell never vomited," the Virginia Company president later said of them.

Of the 104 settlers who arrived in April 1607, only 38 were alive nine months later. That spring John Smith arrived with a fresh company of settlers and within weeks became the colony's leader after typhoid carried off his predecessor. Smith would last only two years, largely because he forced the colonists to work for six hours a day in the fields, which they found intolerable. ("Most of them would rather starve than work," Smith later recalled.) Instead of growing food to survive the following winter, the colonists spent their time digging up great piles of mica and, believing it to be gold, convinced the resupply ship to delay its departure by three months until fully loaded with the worthless mineral. During that time, the ship's crew ate a large proportion of the provisions they'd brought for the colony. As a result, in the winter of 1609–1610 food ran out again, and the settlers were forced to eat rats, cats, snakes, and even their boots and horses. They dug up the bodies of those who'd died and ate those. One man killed, salted, and ate his pregnant wife. Only 60 of 220 colonists survived to the spring, at which point they loaded all their possessions on a ship and abandoned the colony. Unfortunately, at the mouth of the James River they were cut off by supply ships carrying 300 fresh colonists and a humorless new governor, who forced them back to the island, which was pockmarked with shallow graves into which corpses had been dumped face-first into the mud. Despite these sobering experiences, the colonists continued to refuse to tend crops, preferring to bowl in the streets instead.[1]

These first Virginians proved to be such incompetent settlers because they hadn't come to the New World to farm and build a new society, but rather to conquer and rule, much as the Spanish had. The Virginia Company's founders expected their hirelings to act like the *conquistadors*, seizing control of awestruck Indian kingdoms and putting their new subjects to work mining gold and silver or slaving in the fields to feed their new masters. After all, the English had been following much the same program in Ireland, where Gaelic-speaking "savages" toiled on English-owned plantations. Jamestown wasn't meant to feed itself, which is why it lacked farmers. It was, in essence, a corporate-owned military base, complete with fortifications, martial law, a small elite of officers, and a large contingent of rank-and-file soldiers.[2]

But the Virginia Company's plan was based on the faulty assumption that the Indians would be intimidated by English technology, believe their employers were gods, and submit, Aztec-like, to their rule. The Indians, in fact, did none of these things. The local chief, Powhatan, saw the English outpost for what it was: weak and vulnerable but a potential source of useful European technology such as metal tools and weapons. Powhatan ruled a confederation that spanned the lower Chesapeake, comprising 30 tribes and 24,000 people. He lived in a large lodge on the York River, attended by forty bodyguards, a hundred wives, and a small army of servants, all supported by tributes paid by subordinate chiefs. In his sixties when Jamestown was founded, Powhatan had built his confederation piece by piece, defeating rival chiefs and taking them as sons in ritual adoption ceremonies. His plan was to isolate the English and make them into vassals, securing tools and firearms in tribute. The ensuing struggle would turn Tidewater into a war zone.[3]

While the gentlemen of New France were inviting Mi'kmaq chiefs to their gastronomic competitions, hungry Virginians resorted to extorting corn from Powhatan's Indians by force, triggering a cycle of violence. The Indians ambushed one raiding party, killed all seventeen soldiers, stuffed their mouths with corn, and left the corpses for the English to find. John Smith led another party to try to capture Powhatan but instead stumbled into another ambush. Brought before the chief, Smith was subjected to the Indians' adoption ritual—a mock execution (interrupted by the chief's eleven-year-old daughter, Pocahontas) and theatrical ceremony which, from the Indians' point of view, made Smith and his people into Powhatan's vassals. Smith interpreted the situation differently: the child, overwhelmed by his charm, had begged that he be spared. Smith returned to Jamestown and carried on as if nothing had changed, flabbergasting the Indians. Skirmishes eventually led to massacres, and in 1610 the English wiped out an entire Indian village, throwing its children into a river and shooting them for sport. (Pocahontas herself was captured in 1613, married off to a colonist, and sent to back to England, where she died of illness a few years later.) The Indians gained revenge in 1622, launching a surprise attack on the expanding colony that left 347 English dead—a third of Virginia's entire population. The English offered peace the following spring but poisoned the drinks they served at the treaty ceremony and slaughtered all 250 attendees. Warfare would continue, off and on, for decades.[4]

Despite the incompetence of Jamestown's leaders, the Indians were on the losing side of a war of attrition. The Virginia Company continued to send wave after wave of colonists to the Chesapeake, particularly after it was discovered that tobacco grew marvelously there. Between 1607 and 1624, 7,200 colonists arrived; although only 1,200 survived, for every Virginian who died, two more came to take his or her place. Indian losses—from warfare, disease, and war-induced hunger—could not be replaced so easily. By 1669 Tidewater's Indian population had been reduced to 2,000,

8 percent of its original level, while the English population had grown to 40,000, spreading across Tidewater, clearing Indian lands to grow tobacco.[5]

Two events changed the trajectory of Tidewater society, setting cultural patterns that persist to this day. The first came in 1617, when Pocahontas's husband, John Rolfe, successfully transplanted West Indian strains of tobacco to Chesapeake soil, transforming Virginia from a corporate military base to a booming export-oriented plantation society almost overnight. The second was the English Civil War in the 1640s, the results of which prompted a mass exodus of the families who would form Tidewater's aristocracy.

While tobacco was a lucrative crop and one that could be shipped back to England, cultivating it was quite labor-intensive, involving unskilled work but a great deal of it. Seedbeds had to be prepared, raked, and tended until the young plants were ready to be relocated to the main field. Knee-high hills were dug for each one and picked clean of weeds and pests every week. Plants had to be pruned, harvested, dried, and packed for shipment by hand. Tobacco was also quick to wear out the soil and grew best on newly cleared fields.

Tidewater's leaders recruited their workforce from the masses of desperate, malnourished laborers who'd been crowding London and other English cities. They offered prospective laborers transportation to Virginia or Maryland and a fifty-acre plot of land free of charge, in exchange for three years' service as a "white slave" or indentured servant. Most of those who responded were single men aged fifteen to twenty-four. They quickly came to represent the majority of Tidewater's European population. Scholars estimate indentured servants comprised between 80 and 90 percent of the 150,000 Europeans who emigrated to Tidewater in the seventeenth century. Few survived their period of servitude: the mortality rate was as high as 30 percent a year. Those who did had a reasonable chance of becoming independent farmers, and a few became very rich.

From the outset this was a society of a few haves and a great many have-nots. At the top a small cadre of increasingly wealthy plantation owners quickly came to dominate the economic and political affairs of the colony. At the bottom was an army of bound laborers who were effectively without political rights; they were expected to do as they were told and could be subjected to corporal punishment if they did not. It was a pattern that would carry on well into the twentieth century.

Life was harsh at the bottom. Indentured servants—some of whom had been kidnapped in England—were bought, sold, and treated like livestock. Wealthier colonists had a great incentive to buy the passage (and work contracts) of as many individuals as possible: the Virginia Company gave them twenty-five acres of land for every servant they transported. If, in building oneself a land empire, one wound up with surplus labor, their indentures could be sold, traded, or auctioned. As the frontier pushed farther inland in the eighteenth century, servants were bought in large groups by notorious distributors called "soul drivers" who would shackle them and "drive them through the country like a parcel of sheep," under armed guard, to remote courthouses, where they were sold at a markup to local planters. Purchasers had an incentive to work their servants as hard as possible in order to maximize the return on their investment. Masters were allowed to beat their workers; William Byrd, gentleman of Virginia, whipped a young houseboy repeatedly and, when the boy began wetting his bed, forced him to drink pints of piss—facts Byrd matter-of-factly recorded in his diary. If a servant resisted, disobeyed, or attempted to run away, masters could add years to their terms of service. If they felt wronged or abused, they had little chance of finding redress in Tidewater's courts, which were run by their masters' peers.[6]

Most servants in the seventeenth-century Tidewater were from the hinterlands of London, Bristol, and Liverpool, but a handful were of African descent, starting with twenty bought from Dutch traders in 1619. Unlike the Deep South, however, Tidewater appears to have treated its African servants much as it did their white counterparts through the 1660s. White and black settlers were not segregated, and at least some blacks enjoyed the few civil rights available to commoners. Some even became masters themselves, like Anthony Johnson, who in the 1650s owned several African servants and 250 acres of land on Virginia's Eastern Shore. Tidewater was inequitable, but it was not yet a racially based slave society.[7]

Life as a servant was harsh, brutal, and demeaning, but it did not last a lifetime, and it wasn't an inherited condition. Those who survived their indenture received land, tools, and freedom. Like Anthony Johnson, many of them were able to become landowners, a status they could never have achieved in England. For the few immigrants who could pay their own way to Tidewater, obtaining land was even easier: as soon as they stepped off the boat in Virginia, they were entitled to 50 acres, plus 50 more for every relative or servant they brought with them. With land and servants, the aspiring planter could make a great deal of money growing tobacco for export. Profits could be reinvested in more land and servants, ultimately building considerable estates. After 1634, new arrivals could get an even better deal in the new colony of Maryland—100 acres per person—an offer that prompted many ambitious planters to move up the bay. With good health, perseverance, and a little luck, some built up substantial birthrights to pass down to their children, who were beginning in many respects to resemble the landed gentry back home.

Maryland was an oligarchy from the outset, the vast feudal preserve of Cecilius Calvert, second Lord Baltimore, whose coat of arms still graces the Maryland flag today. Calvert was given this 12-million-acre domain by a fellow Catholic, King Charles I, who liked the nobleman's proposal to create a nominally Catholic colony where all religions would be tolerated. The initial settlement was a mixed outpost of English Catholics and Protestants at St. Mary's City, eighty miles up the bay from Jamestown. As it attracted settlers from across the bay, Maryland would quickly come to resemble Tidewater Virginia: a Protestant-dominated tobacco colony, where indentured servants worked the land and the emergent aristocracy commanded most of the profits.[8]

Indeed, as we will see, Tidewater and Yankee New England stood at the opposite poles of the mid-seventeenth-century English-speaking world, with diametrically opposed values, politics, and social priorities. And when civil war came to England in the 1640s, they backed opposing sides, inaugurating centuries of struggle between them over the future of America.

England had been careening toward civil war for much of the century, torn between those faithful to the medieval traditions of the past and those who had embraced more modern ideas about power, trade, and religious governance. On one side was Parliament—dominated by Puritans and lawyers from London and the east of England—which was resisting the monarchy's efforts to consolidate power, repress religious dissent, and head off what we would now call "free market reforms." Opposing Parliament were the conservative allies of King Charles I, or "Cavaliers": country gentlemen from the partly feudal north and west of England, the majority of England's nobles, and the rural poor under their influence. When fighting broke out in 1642, Puritan New England backed Parliament while Tidewater remained loyal to the king.

Virginia's governor at the time, Sir William Berkeley, was not only a Royalist but also a close acquaintance of the king, having served as one of his personal advisers in the last years of peace. One of England's oldest noble families—the Berkeleys had arrived with William the Conqueror in 1066 and are still living in their eleventh-century family castle today—the Berkeleys were steadfast in their support of the monarchy. One of Berkeley's brothers led a royal army while another served as the king's wartime adviser. Berkeley himself returned to England briefly in 1644, where he fought for his king in the West Country before returning to Tidewater with a cache of weapons. In Virginia he deported the colony's Puritan minority who, led by their Massachusetts-trained preachers, resettled across the bay to Maryland.* After the king's defeat and execution, Berkeley declared his loyalty to the king's exiled son, Charles II, from whom he took his orders. The gentlemen who comprised Virginia's General Assembly endorsed this view, passing a law that made questioning Charles II's authority punishable by death.[9]

Berkeley strove to make his colony into a Royalist stronghold from which high-born allies of the king could continue their fight against the Puritans and their allies. Through his brothers and other supporters, Berkeley invited hundreds of these "distressed Cavaliers" to Virginia and granted them large estates and high offices on their arrival. These hardcore Royalists—many of them the younger sons or grandsons of landed aristocrats—were the founders of the vast majority of Tidewater's leading

* Berkeley correctly identified the Puritans as a threat to Royalists: once in Maryland, they skirmished with Lord Baltimore's Royalist forces, briefly seized the colony's capital, and in 1655 won a decisive naval battle that drove the Calverts out of power for nearly a decade.

families. Among them were Richard Lee (grandson of a Shropshire manor owner and great-great-great-grandfather to Robert E. Lee), John Washington (grandson of a Yorkshire manor owner and great-great-grandfather of George Washington), and George Mason (Royalist member of Parliament and great-great-grandfather of the namesake founding father).[10]

For these new elites in both Chesapeake colonies, the overriding goal wasn't to build a religious utopia (as in early Yankeedom or the Midlands) or a complex network of Indian alliances (as in New France). Whether highborn or self-made, the great planters had an extremely conservative vision for the future of their new country: they wished to re-create the genteel manor life of rural England in the New World. By a quirk of history, they succeeded beyond their imaginations.

In the seventeenth century the English country gentlemen were, in effect, the kings of their domains. From their genteel manor houses they directed the lives and labors of the tenant farmers and day laborers who lived in the villages associated with their manors. As justices of the peace, they presided over the local courts while their sons, nephews, and younger brothers often served as the parsons of the village churches, which belonged, of course, to the official Church of England (the "Anglican" church, rebranded "Episcopal" in America after the Revolution). One of their peers represented the area in Parliament. The gentlemen were expected to show benevolence to their inferiors, host wedding parties for their servants, sponsor funerals for the poor, and display hospitality to their neighbors. They alone had the right to hunt, which was often one of their favorite pastimes. Their estates were largely self-sufficient, producing their own food, drink, livestock feed, leather, and handicrafts. (Surpluses were sold to England's towns and cities.) On the lord's death, virtually everything passed to his firstborn son, who had been groomed to rule; daughters were married off to the best prospects; younger sons were given a small sum of money and dispatched to make their own way as soldiers, priests, or merchants. One gentleman said children were treated like a litter of puppies: "Take one, lay it in the lap, feed it with every good bit, and drown [the other] five!"[11]

Tidewater's successful tobacco planters and Royalist émigrés strove to duplicate this world. They built graceful brick manors and housed their indentured tenants in cottages modeled on those at home, clustered in village-like residential areas. They bought servants with the skills to build and operate mills, breweries, smokehouses, and bakeries so that their plantations could meet all of their needs. Together with their neighbors they oversaw the construction of tidy Anglican churches and stately courthouses at convenient crossroads—institutions they controlled through their monopolization of the church vestry (which hired and fired priests) and the office of the justice of the peace (which presided over the courts). In Virginia they set up an analog to the English Parliament called the House of Burgesses, which required that all members be wealthy. (Maryland's General Assembly had similar stipulations.) They, too, were expected to assume the role of benign patriarch toward ordinary residents, and they also sent their surpluses to England's cities. But in one key respect they deviated from English practice: they did not disinherit their younger sons, with whom Tidewater gentlemen often felt a special bond; most had come to America precisely because they were themselves the disinherited younger sons of country gentlemen.[12]

Tidewater's aspiring gentry created a thoroughly rural society without towns or even villages. It had no need for commercial ports and thus for cities, because the land was riven with navigable fingers of the Chesapeake, allowing each of the great planters to build his own dock. On clearing customs, oceangoing ships could sail directly to a plantation, unload the latest books, fashions, and furniture from London, and load barrels of tobacco. (Later, slaves would also arrive in this way.) "Anything may be delivered to a gentleman [in Virginia] from London, Bristol and etc., with less trouble and cost than to one living five miles in the country in England," one English observer remarked. Few local manufacturers could compete with cheaply sourced English goods, discouraging craftsmen and industry.[13]

There were no towns at all until the end of the seventeenth century, apart from Jamestown and St. Mary's City, and even these twin capitals remained little more than villages with a few hundred inhabitants each. Gentlemen would travel to them occasionally to convene their assembly or perhaps make a rare call on the governor but otherwise had little to do with them. Both capitals were crude and appeared abandoned when the provincial assembly was out of session, with many houses uninhabited and the taverns empty. New capitals would eventually be built in

Williamsburg and Annapolis, but they, too, were government campuses, not urban communities.[14] In sharp contrast to New England, there were no public schools (gentlemen's children had live-in tutors) or town governments (the county courthouse sufficed).

By the early 1700s the Cavaliers and their descendants had turned Tidewater into a country gentlemen's utopia, their manors lining the creeks and tributaries of the Chesapeake. Plantations were also taking shape on Albemarle and Pamlico sounds in the new colony of North Carolina and on the Atlantic shores of southern Delaware and the lower Delmarva peninsula.

Power in Tidewater had become hereditary. The leading families intermarried in both America and England, creating a close-linked cousinage that dominated Tidewater generally and Virginia in particular. The Virginia Royal Council served as that colony's senate, supreme court, and executive cabinet, and it controlled the distribution of land. By 1724 every single council member was related by blood or marriage. Two generations later, on the eve of the American Revolution, every member was descended from a councilor who had served in 1660. In the interceding century they rewarded one another with the majority of the public lands under the colony's control and appointments to the (very lucrative) post of collector of customs. At the county level, gentlemen controlled the distribution of justice and charity in their roles as justices of the peace and could hire and fire pastors at will from their seats on the church vestry. One newcomer recalled a gentleman's warning him "against disobliging or offending any person of note in the Colony [because] either by blood or marriage we are almost all related and so connected in our interests that whoever of a stranger presumes to offend any one of us will infallibly find an enemy of the whole."[15]

Running afoul of Tidewater gentlemen was a dangerous proposition. Late seventeenth- and early eighteenth-century visitors constantly remarked on their haughty sense of personal honor and their furious reaction to the slightest insult. While the Yankee elite generally settled their disputes through the instrument of written laws, Tidewater gentry were more likely to resort to a duel. Commoners were equally prideful: arguments in the tavern commonly led to nasty fights in which it was acceptable to kick, bite, strangle, gouge out eyes, and dismember genitals of one's opponent. Lower-status people almost never challenged their betters for fear of savage retribution, as gentlemen could have lesser persons whipped for minor offenses. When one commoner spoke out against a governor, a court ordered that he be brutally beaten by forty men, be fined £200 (a decade's income for a peasant), have a hole bored through his tongue, and then be forever banished from Virginia. Indeed, cases that came to court were resolved by gentlemen judges who believed that issues should be decided by their own sense of justice rather than by precedents written in law books, even in matters of life and death. Court records show a clear pattern: leniency for masters and males, harsh sentences for servants and women. Even before the spread of full-fledged slavery, Tidewater's hierarchy was maintained by the threat of violence.[16]

One might ask how such a tyrannical society could have produced some of the greatest champions of republicanism, such as Thomas Jefferson, George Washington, and James Madison. The answer is that Tidewater's gentry embraced *classical* republicanism, meaning a republic modeled after those of ancient Greece and Rome. They emulated the learned, slaveholding elite of ancient Athens, basing their enlightened political philosophies around the ancient Latin concept of *libertas*, or liberty. This was a fundamentally different notion from the Germanic concept of *Freiheit*, or freedom, which informed the political thought of Yankeedom and the Midlands. Understanding the distinction is essential to comprehending the fundamental disagreements that still plague relations between Tidewater, the Deep South, and New Spain on one hand and Yankeedom and the Midlands on the other.

For the Norse, Anglo-Saxons, Dutch, and other Germanic tribes of northern Europe, "freedom" was a birthright of free peoples, which they considered themselves to be. Individuals might have differences in status and wealth, but all were literally "born free." All were equal before the law, and all had come into the world possessing "rights" that had to be mutually respected on threat of banishment. Tribes had the right to rule themselves through assemblies like Iceland's Althingi, recognized as the world's oldest parliament. Until the Norman invasion of 1066, the Anglo-Saxon tribes of England had ruled themselves in this manner. After the invasion, the lords of Normandy imposed manorial feudalism on England, but they never fully did away with the "free" institutions of the Anglo-Saxons and

(Gaelo-Norse) Scots, which survived in village councils, English common law, and the House of Commons. It was this tradition that the Puritans carried to Yankeedom.

The Greek and Roman political philosophy embraced by Tidewater gentry assumed the opposite: most humans were born into bondage. Liberty was something that was granted and was thus a privilege, not a right. Some people were permitted many liberties, others had very few, and many had none at all. The Roman republic was one in which only a handful of people had the full privileges of speech (senators, magistrates), a minority had the right to vote on what their superiors had decided (citizens), and most people had no say at all (slaves). Liberties were valuable because most people did not have them and were thought meaningless without the presence of a hierarchy. For the Greeks and Romans there was no contradiction between republicanism and slavery, liberty and bondage. This was the political philosophy embraced and jealously guarded by Tidewater's leaders, whose highborn families saw themselves as descendants not of the "common" Anglo-Saxons, but rather of their aristocratic Norman conquerors. It was a philosophical divide with racial overtones and one that would later drive America's nations into all-out war with one another.[17]

Tidewater's leaders imposed *libertas* on their society in countless ways. They referred to themselves as "heads" of their respective manors, dictating duties to their "hands" and other subservient appendages. Finding Jamestown and St. Mary's City too crude, they built new government campuses in Williamsburg and Annapolis from central plans inspired by Rome; Williamsburg featured a sumptuous formal "palace" for the governor (surrounded by Versailles-like formal gardens) and the elegant Capitol (not "state house") decorated with a relief of Jupiter, the god whose temple stood at the center of Roman civic life. They named counties, cities, and colonies after their superiors: English royals (Prince George, Prince William, Princess Anne, Jamestown, Williamsburg, Annapolis, Georgetown, Virginia, Maryland) or high nobles (Albemarle, Baltimore, Beaufort, Calvert, Cecil, Cumberland, Caroline, Anne Arundel, Delaware). While they were passionate in defending their liberties, it would never have occurred to them that those liberties might be shared with their subjects. "I am an aristocrat," Virginian John Randolph would explain decades after the American Revolution. "I love liberty; I hate equality."[18]

While the gentry enjoyed ever-greater liberties—including leisure (liberty from work) and independence (liberty from the control of others)—those at the bottom of the hierarchy had progressively fewer. Tidewater's semifeudal model required a vast and permanent underclass to play the role of serfs, on whose toil the entire system depended. But from the 1670s onward, the gentry had an increasingly difficult time finding enough poor Englishmen willing to take on this role. Those who completed their indentures often could not support themselves in an agricultural export economy increasingly dominated by great plantations, and ex-servants led or joined rebellions in 1663, 1675, and 1683.

Slave traders offered a solution to this shortage, one developed on the English islands of the Caribbean and recently introduced in the settlements they'd created in the Deep South: the purchase of people of African descent who would become the *permanent* property of their masters, as would their children and grandchildren. This slave caste grew from a tenth of Tidewater's population in 1700 to a quarter in 1720 and 40 percent in 1760. As one scholar would later put it: "The South was not founded to create slavery; slavery was recruited to perpetuate the South." As we will see, this statement does not hold true for "the South" as a whole but rather for the distinct cultural nation of Tidewater.[19] It was a strategy that would set Tidewater on a path to destruction.

CHAPTER 4

Founding Yankeedom

By a twist of history, the dominant colonies of New England were founded by men who stood in total opposition to nearly every value that Tidewater gentry held dear. Hostile to landed aristocracy, noble privilege, the Anglican Church, and the Royalist cause, the Pilgrims of Cape Cod and the Puritans of Massachusetts Bay had an entirely different vision for their new society. A moralistic nation of churches and schoolhouses, where each community functioned as its own self-governing republic, Yankeedom would leave an indelible mark on a vast swath of the continent.

The Pilgrims and, to a greater extent, the Puritans came to the New World not to re-create rural English life but rather to build a completely new society: an applied religious utopia, a Protestant theocracy based on the teachings of John Calvin. They would found a new Zion in the New England wilderness, a "city on a hill" to serve as a model for the rest of the world in those troubled times. They believed they would succeed because they were God's chosen people, bound to Him in an Old Testament–style covenant. If they all did his will, they would be rewarded. If any member did not, they might all be punished. In early Massachusetts, there was no such thing as minding one's own business: the salvation of the entire community depended on everyone doing their part.

According to a central myth of American history, the founders of Yankeedom were champions of religious freedom fleeing persecution at home. While there is some truth to this in regard to the Pilgrims—a few hundred English Calvinists who settled Cape Cod in 1620—it is entirely false in regard to the Puritans of Massachusetts Bay, who would soon bring Plymouth and the other colonies of New England under their control. The Puritans left England en masse in the 1630s—25,000 in just twelve short years—because of their unwillingness to compromise on matters of religious policy. While other colonies welcomed all comers, the Puritans forbade anyone to settle in their colony who failed to pass a test of religious conformity. Dissenters were banished. Quakers were disfigured for easy identification, their nostrils slit, their ears cut off, or their faces branded with the letter H for "heretic." Puritans doled out death sentences for infractions such as adultery, blasphemy, idolatry, sodomy, and even teenage rebellion. They fined farmers who tended their cows, raked hay, or hunted birds on the Sabbath. Boston magistrates put Captain Thomas Kemble in the stocks in 1656 because, having returned from a three-year absence, he kissed his wife at his doorstep—"lewd and unseemly behavior" in the eyes of the court. Early Yankeedom was less tolerant of moral or religious deviance than the England its settlers had left behind.[1]

But in other respects, the Puritans created a genuinely revolutionary society. Having secured, through deception, a royal charter for their colony, they were not beholden to feudal nobles (as were early Maryland and New France) or distant corporations (as were Virginia and, later, the Carolinas). New Englanders intended to rule themselves.

Nearly half of Yankeedom's early settlers came from East Anglia, the most economically sophisticated part of the British Isles. Its seven easternmost counties were the most densely settled, urbanized, and educated part of England, with a burgeoning middle class and a long history of rebellion against arbitrary rule. It was a region profoundly influenced by the Netherlands, the most commercially and politically advanced nation in Europe, which lay just across the English Channel. Dutch Calvinism, republicanism, agriculture, architecture, art, and commerce had left their mark on the region, which had tulip gardens, gabled houses, and a highly literate population of artisans, craftsmen, and yeoman farmers. Champions of the Germanic notions of freedom, East Anglians participated in town meetings and chose selectmen to run local affairs. Not surprisingly, the region would strongly support Parliament against the king in the English Civil War. Many of these East Anglian characteristics were transplanted to New England.

The Puritan exodus had a demographic character entirely unlike that of Tidewater, New France, and El Norte. The Yankee settlers came as families and were generally middle class, well-educated, and roughly equal in material wealth. While Tidewater was settled largely by young, unskilled male servants, New England's colonists were skilled craftsmen, lawyers, doctors, and yeoman farmers; none of them was an indentured servant. Rather than having fled poverty in search of better lives, the early Yankees had traded a comfortable existence at home for the uncertainties of the wilderness. Seventy percent came as part of an established family, giving early Yankeedom far more typical gender and age ratios than those of the other nations. This demographic advantage—and the fact that New England had relatively few epidemic diseases—enabled the population to expand rapidly from its initial settlement base. Although few immigrants entered the region for a century after 1640, colonial New England's European population doubled every generation. By 1660 it had reached 60,000, more than twice the population of Tidewater, which had a generation's head start. The largest population center north of the Rio Grande, Yankeedom was already the most cohesive, given that nearly everyone had arrived at the same time and for much the same reasons.[2]

The Puritan emigrants were led not by highborn nobles or gentlemen—virtually none ever came to Yankeedom—but by an elite distinguished by education. "These men possessed, in proportion to their number, a greater mass of intelligence than is to be found in any European nation of our own time," the French aristocrat Alexis de Tocqueville wrote of early New England in 1835. "All, perhaps without exception, had received a good education and many of them were well known in Europe for their talents and achievements."[3]

The Puritans had been hostile to royal and aristocratic prerogative at home and continued to be so in America. From the beginning Yankeedom was opposed to the creation of a landed aristocracy and suspicious of inherited privilege and the conspicuous display of wealth. Unique among the colonies, its leaders didn't hand out massive swaths of land to friends, family, and allies so the latter could become rich by retailing lots out to others. Instead the Puritans gave town charters to approved groups of settlers, who in turn elected a committee of their peers to select the location of the public road, church, schoolhouse, and town green and to divvy up family lots. While larger or wealthier families might have been granted larger lots, the division was surprisingly egalitarian. The townspeople often named settlements for the eastern English towns they'd left behind: Haverhill, Ipswich, and Groton (all in Suffolk), Springfield, Malden, and Braintree (in Essex), Lynn, Hingham, and Newton (in Norfolk), and the southern Lincolnshire port of Boston. Townspeople were supposed to work together toward the common good of their community. Squabbling over land and other material things was thought a distraction from their true calling before God.[4]

The New England settlement model differed from Tidewater not merely in the presence of towns but in the power vested in them. Puritans believed every community of the chosen should govern itself without interference from bishops, archbishops, or kings; every congregation was to be completely self-governing. Worldly matters were to be dealt with in exactly the same way. Every town was to be a little republic unto itself, with total control over the enforcement of laws, the administration of schools and real estate, the collection and (for the most part) spending of taxes, and the organization of militias for self-defense. While counties had almost no powers at all, every town had its own government: a group of selectmen elected by the adult male members of the church. The selectmen acted as a plural executive, while the town's eligible voters gathered for town meetings and functioned as a miniature parliament. Although New England was an intolerant and in many ways authoritarian place to live, it was, by the standards of the age, shockingly democratic: 60 to 70 percent of adult males (or 30 to 35 percent of the total adult population) had the right to vote, and the rich and wellborn were given no special privileges either in politics or before the law. This tradition of self-government, local control, and direct democracy has remained central to Yankee culture. To this day, rural communities across New England still control most local affairs through an annual town meeting at which every expenditure is debated and voted on not by an elected representative but by the inhabitants themselves.

Indeed, Yankees would come to have faith in government to a degree incomprehensible to people of the other American nations. Government, New Englanders believed from the beginning, could defend the public good from the selfish machinations of moneyed interests. It could enforce morals through the prohibition or regulation of undesirable activities. It could create a better society through public spending on infrastructure and schools. More than any other group in America, Yankees conceive of government as being run by and for themselves. Everyone is supposed to participate, and there is no greater outrage than to manipulate the political process for private gain. Yankee idealism never died.

The Puritan belief that each individual had to encounter divine revelation through reading the scriptures had far-reaching implications. If everyone was expected to read the Bible, everyone had to be literate. Public schoolhouses, therefore, were built and staffed by salaried teachers as soon as a new town was established. While the other American nations had no school systems of any kind in the mid–seventeenth century—education was a privilege of the rich—New England required all children to be sent to school under penalty of law. While few Englishmen could read or write in 1660, two-thirds of Massachusetts men and more than a third of women could sign their own names. And while basic education was universal, those with higher education were accorded the sort of respect and deference other societies reserved for the highborn. Early New England had an elite, a group of leading families who intermarried and came to dominate political and religious affairs, but it was an elite based not on wealth but education. Of the original 15,000 settlers who came to Massachusetts Bay, at least 129 were graduates of Oxford or Cambridge, a shockingly high figure for the age; virtually all of them assumed leadership roles. None of the men who served as governors in early Massachusetts or Connecticut was a noble, but many had graduated from the English universities or Harvard, a homegrown alternative founded just six years after the first Puritans had arrived. (It was instituted, according to a 1645 brochure, "to advance Learning and perpetuate it to Posterity; dreading to leave an illiterate Ministry to the Churches.") Boston today is said to be the intellectual capital of the continent; indeed, it has been so since its very foundation.[5]

If the Puritans had kept to themselves, their neighbors might have taken little notice of them. But what would cause Yankeedom eventually to be so loathed by the other nations was its desire—indeed, its *mission*—to impose its ways on everyone else. For the Puritans didn't merely believe they were God's chosen people, they believed God had charged each and every one of them to propagate his will on a corrupt and sinful world. All Yankee Calvinists were thought to have a "calling," a vocation through which they would, priestlike, further God's work. They had to be constantly vigilant in the performance of their calling, be it as a missionary, a merchant, or a cobbler. Idleness was ungodly. Personal wealth was expected to be reinvested in one's good works—professional or philanthropic—to bring the world in closer accord with the divine plan. Other societies and cultures would presumably see the "light on the hill" and wish to conform; woe be to those who did not.

The Puritans tended to be affronted by and fearful of otherness, which could make them rather dangerous to have as one's neighbors. They especially feared the wilderness, a disorderly, impulsive place at the edge of their fields where Satan lurked, ready to tempt those who wandered too far from the watchful eyes of the community. The people of the forest, the Native Americans of New England, had clearly fallen under devilish influence, what with their unrestrained manners, open sexuality, skimpy clothing, belief in spirits, and disrespect for the Sabbath. Unlike the settlers in New France, the Puritans regarded the Indians as "savages" to whom normal moral obligations—respect of treaties, fair dealing, forgoing the slaughter of innocents—did not apply. When a group of dissatisfied Puritan settlers marched into the wilderness to found a squatter's colony called Connecticut in 1636, Massachusetts authorities engineered a genocidal war against the Pequot Indians so as to have a pretext to seize the region from under the squatters by conquest. In one notorious incident they surrounded a poorly defended Pequot village and butchered virtually every man, woman, and child they found there, mostly by burning them alive. The slaughter was shocking to the Puritans' temporary Indian allies, the Narragansetts, who called it "too furious." Plymouth governor William Bradford conceded that it had been "a fearful sight to see them thus frying in the fire and the streams of blood quenching the same" but concluded that "the victory seemed a sweet sacrifice" which God "had wrought so wonderfully for them." Full-scale conflicts with the Indians continued throughout the colonial period, many of them made worse by the Puritan practice of attacking a neutral or friendly tribe while at war with another. Captured Indian children were killed or sold to slaveholders in the English Caribbean. Puritan preacher William Hubbard endorsed this practice, seeing the seizure of so many "young serpents of the same brood" as another sign of "Divine Favour to the English."[6]

The Puritans' program of conquest was not limited to Indian peoples. During and immediately after the English Civil War, Massachusetts soldiers and preachers attempted Yankee coups in Maryland and the

Bahamas, annexed the Royalist colony of Maine, and reduced Connecticut, Plymouth, and New Hampshire to mere satellites of their Bible Commonwealth. For four decades, Boston ruled the region as the capital of the United Colonies of New England, a confederation that incorporated all the Yankee settlements save those in Rhode Island. Puritan courts enforced Calvinist morality on hard-living Maine fishermen and drove Anglican priests from New Hampshire.[7]

Here were the kernels of the twin political ideologies of America's imperial age: American Exceptionalism and Manifest Destiny. The first held that Americans were God's chosen people, the second that He wished Americans to rule the continent from sea to sea. Both ideas had their origins in Yankee Puritan thought and would be developed and championed by the sons of New England. The concepts would remain popular in Yankeedom until the early nineteenth century, when it became clear that their own culture would not dominate the United States as it had New England. To Yankee frustration, the other nations would actively resist their hegemony.

From the outset, the Yankees were opposed to the very values cherished by the aristocratic society taking shape in Tidewater, including their "Norman" cultural identity. When the English Civil War broke out, hundreds of Puritans returned home to fight in Oliver Cromwell's New Model Army, a military force founded on the radical notion that promotions should be based on proficiency rather than social status. As they clashed with Royalist armies, they grew to believe they were fighting to liberate their Anglo-Saxon lands from the Norman invaders six hundred years after the latter had arrived with William the Conqueror. "What were the lords of England," a group of common soldiers declared to a wartime visitor to their encampment, "but William the Conqueror's colonels?" King Charles, they decreed, was "the last successor of William the Conqueror" who had to be cast out if the people were to "have recovered ourselves from under the Norman yoke." The soldiers drew up a lofty document called the Agreement of the People, which asserted their natural freedom, called for every parish to select its own clergy, and demanded an end to aristocratic privileges before the law. "Our very laws were made by our conquerors," one New Model Army veteran asserted. "We are now engaged for our freedom."[8]

Tensions with Tidewater did not end with the English Civil War. The New Model Army's victory (and the military dictatorship that followed) sparked the "Cavalier Exodus" to Virginia while freeing the Puritans of Massachusetts to annex their neighbors. For Tidewater gentry, New England—complicit in a treasonous rebellion and the execution of the king—was a seditious land populated by radicals committed to destroying the foundations on which society stood. For Yankees, Tidewater was a bastion of reactionary forces, its lords committed to perpetuating the enslavement of the English people begun by their Norman ancestors. Their fears were given new urgency after Cromwell's death in 1658 when, in short order, the monarchy was restored and a "Cavalier Parliament" of Royalist sympathizers convened in Westminster. The gentlemen of Virginia and the Calverts of Maryland once again had the backing of London, and the Puritans faced a mortal threat to their young nation.

America's English colonies were rushing toward their first revolution. But first, there were some foreigners to contend with.

CHAPTER 5

Founding New Netherland

Most Americans know the Dutch founded what is now Greater New York City. Few realize that their influence is largely the reason New York is New York, the most vibrant and powerful city on the continent, and one with a culture and identity unlike that of anyplace else in the United States. Incredibly, its salient features developed when Manhattan was still largely a wilderness and the greatest city on Earth was but a tiny village clinging to the island's southern tip.

New Netherland was founded in 1624, just four years after the *Mayflower* voyage and six years ahead of the Puritans' arrival in Massachusetts Bay. Its capital and principal settlement, New Amsterdam, was clustered around the wooden Fort Amsterdam, which stood where the Museum of the American Indian is now located, next to Battery Park and Bowling Green, where the Dutch had their cattle market. When New Amsterdam was conquered by the English in 1664, the city extended only as far as Wall Street (where, in fact, the Dutch had built a wall). The main road, Breede weg (Broadway), passed through a gate in the wall and continued on past farms, fields, and forests to the village of Haarlem, on the north end of the island. Ferrymen rowed goods and people across the East River to Lange Eylandt and the villages of Breukelen (Brooklyn), Vlissingen (Flushing), Vlacke Bos (Flatbush) and New Utrecht (now a Brooklyn neighborhood) or across the harbor to Hoboken and Staaten Eylandt. The area had but 1,500 inhabitants.[1]

But this small village was already unlike anywhere else in North America. Established as a fur-trading post, it was an unabashedly commercial settlement with little concern for either social cohesion or the creation of a model society. A global corporation, the Dutch West India Company, dominated the city's affairs and formally governed New Netherland for the first few decades. Standing between Yankeedom and Tidewater, the city had emerged as a trading entrepôt for both, its markets, ships, and warehouses filled with Virginia tobacco, New England salt cod, Indian-caught beaver pelts, linens, dishes, and other manufactured goods from the mother country, and produce from the farms of Harlem and Brooklyn. Its population was equally diverse, including French-speaking Walloons; Lutherans from Poland, Finland, and Sweden; Catholics from Ireland and Portugal; and Anglicans, Puritans, and Quakers from New England. Jews were banned from setting foot in New France, Yankeedom, and Tidewater, but dozens of Ashkenazim and Spanish-speaking Sephardim settled in New Amsterdam in the 1650s, forming the nucleus of what would eventually become the largest Jewish community in the world. Indians roamed the streets, and Africans—slave, free, and half-free—already formed a fifth of the population. A Muslim from Morocco had been farming outside the walls for three decades. Visitors were shocked by the village's religious, ethnic, and linguistic diversity. In 1643 Father Isaac Jogues, a Jesuit working in New France, estimated New Amsterdam's population at 500 and the number of its languages at 18, an "arrogance of Babel" that "has done much harm to all men."[2] The different ethnic and national groups often kept to themselves and squabbled with one another for power, with not even the Dutch forming a majority within the settlement. The local elite was comprised almost entirely of self-made men who'd risen from humble origins in the worlds of commerce and real estate speculation. The government, desirous above all to promote trade, embraced diversity even as it eschewed democracy. The village was, to put it simply, New York, and many of its characteristics have endured to the present day.

These characteristics—diversity, tolerance, upward mobility, and an overwhelming emphasis on private enterprise—have come to be identified with the United States, but they were really the legacy of the United Provinces of the Netherlands. Indeed, many of the historic achievements of the American Revolution were accomplished by the Dutch nearly two centuries before the Battle of Lexington: a successful war of independence against an enormous monarchical empire (the kingdom of Spain), the declaration of an inborn human right to rebel against an oppressive government (the 1581 Act of Abjuration), and the creation of a kingless republic.

In the early 1600s, the Netherlands was the most modern and sophisticated country on Earth, producing art, laws, business practices, and institutions that became the standards for the rest of the Western world. They invented modern banking, creating at the Bank of Amsterdam the first clearinghouse for the disparate coins and currencies of the world, all exchangeable for Dutch florins, which became the preferred medium of international exchange. In 1602, they invented the global corporation with the establishment of the Dutch East India Company, which soon had hundreds of ships, thousands of employees, and extensive operations in Indonesia, Japan, India, and southern Africa. Shareholders were drawn from all levels of society—wealthy merchants to maidservants and day laborers—fostering broad social support for the company's enterprises. Dutch oceangoing ships—10,000 of them in 1600—were of advanced design and dominated the shipping of northern Europe. By the time the Dutch West India Company founded New Amsterdam, the Netherlands had assumed a role in the world economy equivalent to that of the United States in the late twentieth century, setting the standards for international business, finance, and law.[3]

Uniquely among the people of seventeenth-century Europe, the Dutch were committed to free inquiry. Their universities were second to none, attracting thinkers from countries where the use of reason was curtailed. Among the émigré intellectuals living in Holland was René Descartes, the French philosopher who believed inquiry should be based on "good sense" rather than the authority of the Bible or the philosophers of antiquity. His ideas would form the basis of modern science, and they were first published in the Netherlands—as was Galileo's *Discourses and Mathematical Demonstrations Concerning Two New Sciences* (1638), a book that would never have been approved by the Pope's censors back in Italy and that effectively founded modern physics. Baruch Spinoza, an Amsterdam-born Sephardic Jew who had been excommunicated by his rabbi, published philosophical texts that have been credited with inspiring everything from biblical criticism to deep ecology. While in exile in Amsterdam, John Locke composed his *A Letter Concerning Toleration* (1689), which argued for a separation of church and state. Dutch scientists invented the telescope and microscope and used them to discover everything from the rings of Saturn to the existence of sperm cells. They were able to share their discoveries and ideas with the world because Dutch officials accepted the freedom of the press. Modern scholars have estimated that Dutch printers were responsible for half of all the books published in the seventeenth century. The Netherlands' tiny oasis of intellectual freedom squeezed between the North Sea and the Catholic Inquisition was the incubator for the modern world.[4]

The Dutch Republic had also become a haven for persecuted people across Europe. While heretics were being burned at the stake in Spain, the 1579 treaty that created the Netherlands stated that "everyone shall remain free in religion and . . . no one may be persecuted or investigated because of religion." While Jews were barred from entering France or England, thousands of Sephardic refugees from Spain and Portugal lived in Amsterdam, worshipped in the world's largest synagogue, and invested in the trading companies that founded New Netherland and the Dutch East Indies. Catholics, Mennonites, and Lutherans lived peaceably alongside the Calvinist majority. In 1607, the Englishman William Bradford and his band of Pilgrims arrived in Holland, where they were welcomed so long as they promised to "behave themselves honestly and submit to all the laws." From Leiden—a university city where foreign refugees comprised a third of the population—the Pilgrims published pamphlets denouncing King Charles, an activity local officials refused to suppress, even after being requested to do so by the English monarch. But the Netherlands' religious pluralism wasn't for everyone, including the Pilgrims. "Many of their children," Bradford explained, "were drawn away by evil examples," by "manifold temptations" and "the great licentiousness of the youth of that country" and "into extravagant and dangerous courses" that got "the reins off their necks." The Netherlands was too free; the Pilgrims would eventually flee to the American wilderness where they could exert stronger control over their children's upbringing.[5]

Relatively few people, however, wanted to leave the Netherlands for an uncertain life across the Atlantic. There were no armies of desperate paupers willing to be sold off as temporary slaves, no oppressed religious sects seeking a more tolerant environment to nurse their faith. New Netherland, like New France, would be challenged by a shortage of colonists. Those who did come tended to be either adventurers seeking their fortunes or foreigners with weak ties to the Netherlands who perhaps shared the Pilgrims' desire for a simpler, more controllable environment. In 1655, thirty-one years after its foundation, the colony still had only 2,000 residents. There were only 9,000 when the British took control in 1664, a quarter as many as were living in the younger colonies of New England.[6]

New Netherland's growth was also hindered by its decidedly corporate character. The Dutch founded the colony as a means to prevent the English from dominating the American continent, but they tried to run it as cheaply as possible. Already engaged in Asia, Africa, Brazil, and the Caribbean, the government didn't wish to invest many resources in North America, a relatively low-priority project lacking the obvious economic returns of the spice, sugar, and tea trades. Instead, the republic's authorities outsourced the project to the private sector, turning governance of its North American colony over to the West India Company. The people of New Netherland would enjoy religious tolerance and considerable economic freedom, but they would not have a republican government. To the contrary, the West India Company would appoint its own governor and advisory council who would rule the colony without interference from any sort of elected body. All trade with the mother country had to be carried out on the company's ships, and it had a monopoly over the most profitable commodity, beaver furs. Even so, the company found it difficult to bear the costs of expanding the colony beyond the Manhattan area. To help, it offered wealthy investors the opportunity to create their own aristocratic estates on the manorial model farther up the Hudson Valley in exchange for transporting settlers to New Netherland. The would-be manor lords, or "patroons," were granted county-sized parcels of land where they would serve as judge and jury over all civil and criminal proceedings, including capital crimes, literally giving them the power of life and death over their tenants. Most of these patroonships failed because few settlers were willing to become tenant farmers when there was free land for the taking elsewhere (the great Van Rensselaer estate near Albany being the one exception). The patroons themselves often became exceedingly wealthy, but usually through trade; with only a few exceptions, a landed aristocracy did not develop in New Netherland.[7]

The result was a colony as tolerant and diverse as the mother country. In 1654, a boatload of penniless Jewish war refugees from the Dutch colony of Brazil was met with hostility from the anti-Semitic governor, Peter Stuyvesant, who called them a "deceitful race" and tried to cast them from the colony. His superiors in Amsterdam overruled him, calling his plans "unreasonable and unfair" and pointing out that Jewish shareholders had invested a "large amount of capital" in their company. When Stuyvesant tried to limit Quaker immigration ("this new unheard of, abominable heresy"), the people of Flushing protested, writing that "the law of love, peace and liberty in the states extends to Jews, Turks [i.e., Muslims] and Egyptians [Gypsies], which is the glory of the outward state of Holland." Company officials warned the bigoted governor to "not force people's consciences but allow every one to have his own belief, as long as he behaves quietly and legally, gives no offense to his neighbors, and does not oppose the government." Tolerance, they noted, had served the mother country well and was vital to the success of its colonies. Today, it lies at the heart of what makes New York City possible.[8]

While relations with the Indians were generally fair and cordial, this was more the result of Dutch self-interest than of enlightened thinking. Unlike their European rivals on the eastern seaboard, the New Netherlanders remained outnumbered by the Indians throughout the period of Dutch rule. Offending the five tribes of the Iroquois nation would have been not only suicidal but also bad for business, as they were the source of most of New Amsterdam's fur supply. The weaker Algonquin-speaking tribes of the lower Hudson were another matter. Occupying prime farmland and, after 1640, possessed of few beaver, the Algonquins were an obstacle to the colony's expansion. Tensions over land provoked a series of bloody wars in the 1640s, 1650s, and 1660s, with terrible bloodshed on both sides. New Netherlanders didn't regard the Indians as servants of the devil—intermarriage was perfectly legal—but did not particularly value their presence beyond what it meant for the bottom line.[9]

The Dutch trait of tolerance was just that. They didn't celebrate diversity but *tolerated* it, because they knew the alternative was far worse. The Dutch people, much like those of Champlain's native Saintonge, had internalized the lessons of Europe's horrific (and ongoing) religious wars, in which many of their countrymen had perished. Insistence on conformity—cultural, religious, or otherwise—was self-defeating, causing strife and undermining trade and business. This begrudging acceptance of difference remains a hallmark of Greater New York City today, where it seems all the cultures, religions, and classes of the world are thrown together onto the same street, wrestling with one another for advantage in the markets of commerce, politics, and ideas.

The elite families that came to dominate the region in the late seventeenth century were founded by a very Dutch type, the self-made man. The founder of the Van Cortlandt dynasty arrived in New Amsterdam as a soldier, became a carpenter, trader, alderman, and, ultimately, the city's mayor. Frederick Philipse was a butcher when he arrived, worked as a pawnbroker and fur trader, and was able to attract the hand of a wealthy widow, Margaret de Vries, who managed the activities of her own merchant vessel; by 1679 he was the wealthiest man in New York, with a plantation in Barbados and a manor house in Yonkers. Jan Aertsen Van der Bilt arrived as an indentured servant in 1650; his third great-grandson, Cornelius—born on Staten Island—would make the "Vanderbilt" family one of the wealthiest in history. The first Van Burens were tenant farmers on the Rensselaers' manor; their sons became independent farmers, and their fifth great-grandson was president of the United States.[10]

New Netherland was primarily a commercial society in which much of the governing elite was associated with the Dutch West India Company. This company was no more moral than its English counterparts: if a commodity was profitable, it was pursued, including trade in captive humans. Indeed, full-on slavery was introduced to what is now the United States not by the gentlemen planters of Virginia or South Carolina but by the merchants of Manhattan. In 1626, while Africans in Tidewater were still being treated as indentured servants, the company imported eleven slaves to address its shortage of laborers. By 1639 there was a slave camp five miles north of the city, presumably providing workers to man the company's farms and docks. In 1655, the company slave ship *Witte Paert* arrived in New Amsterdam from West Africa with 300 slaves who were sold at public auction, increasing the city's population by 10 percent. In the last decade before the English conquest, New Amsterdam was rapidly evolving into North America's greatest slave market. Even though most slaves were transported to Tidewater, an estimated 20 percent of the city's population was of African origin by 1670. Not all were enslaved, however. Some were granted their freedom by their owners, and many company slaves eventually earned "half freedom," which allowed them to marry, travel, and own property while paying a fixed lease on themselves. By the time New Amsterdam became New York, the city already had a multiracial character and multigenerational legacy of slavery; the latter institution would continue to be present in Greater New York right into the 1860s.[11]

Bolstered by the slave trade, New Netherland was beginning to flourish when a hostile English fleet arrived in August 1664. New Amsterdam was taken by surprise—the two countries were not then at war—and grossly outgunned, not only by the ships in the harbor but by Yankee rebels from eastern Long Island who marched to Brooklyn, ready to loot the city. During a tense standoff, the Dutch negotiated an unusual surrender agreement to ensure the survival of Dutch norms and values. New Netherlanders would keep their business and inheritance laws, property, churches, language, and even their local officials. They could continue to trade with the Netherlands, making New Amsterdam the only city in the world with simultaneous ties to both major trading empires. Most important, religious toleration was ensured. New Netherland would be renamed New York, but its culture carried on.[12]

Unfortunately, the new regime also retained New Netherland's autocratic government. The new colony of New York was to be the personal preserve of King Charles's brother and heir, James, Duke of York. Indeed, James himself had organized the surprise attack against the Dutch, the king having already granted him the land. James, a military man with an eye to creating an authoritarian empire, placed all executive and legislative power in the hands of his governor. There would be no elected assemblies in "the Duke's province." As for the Yankee settlements of eastern Long Island (which pledged allegiance to Connecticut), they would be part of New York whether they liked it or not. While ignoring the Yankees' protests, James gave two of his war colleagues title to the sparsely populated lands between the Hudson and Delaware rivers, creating the new colony of New Jersey. After a brief 1673–74 episode in which the Dutch briefly recaptured New Netherland in 1673, James released all Dutchmen from the administration, banned the use of the Dutch language in the courts, and garrisoned undisciplined imperial troops throughout the province.

The duke had carte blanche. When he became king a few years later, his autocratic plans for North America would provoke the first American revolution.[13]

CHAPTER 6

The Colonies' First Revolt

While everyone knows that the English-controlled colonies rebelled against the tyrannical rule of their distant king, few realize they first did so not in the 1770s, but in the 1680s. And they did so not as a united force of Americans eager to create a new nation, but in a series of separate rebellions, each seeking to preserve a distinct regional culture, political system, and religious tradition threatened by the distant seat of empire.

These threats came in the form of the new king, James II, who ascended the throne in 1685. James was intent on imposing discipline and political conformity on his unruly American colonies. Inspired by the absolutist monarchy of France's Louis XIV, King James planned to merge the colonies, dissolve their representative assemblies, impose crippling taxes, and install military authorities in the governors' chairs to ensure that his will was obeyed. Had he succeeded, the nascent American nations might have lost much of their individual distinctiveness, converging over time into a more homogeneous and docile colonial society, resembling that of New Zealand.

But even at this early stage of their development—only two to three generations after their creation—the American nations were willing to take up arms and commit treason to protect their unique cultures.

James wasted little time executing his plans. He ordered the New England colonies, New York, and New Jersey to be merged into a single authoritarian megacolony called the Dominion of New England. The Dominion replaced representative assemblies and regular town meetings with an all-powerful royal governor backed by imperial troops. Across Yankeedom, Puritan property titles were declared null and void, forcing landowners to buy new ones from the crown and to pay feudal rents to the king in perpetuity. The Dominion governor seized portions of the town commons in Cambridge, Lynn, and other Massachusetts towns and gave the valuable plots to his friends. The king also imposed exorbitant duties on Tidewater tobacco and the sugar produced around the recently formed settlement of Charleston. All of this was done without the consent of the governed, in violation of the rights granted all Englishmen under the Magna Carta. When a Puritan minister protested, he was tossed in jail by a newly appointed Dominion judge, who told him that his people now had "no more privileges left . . . [other] than not to be sold for slaves." Under James the rights of Englishmen stopped at the shores of England itself. In the colonies the king would do whatever he wished.[1]

Whatever their grievances, the colonies probably would not have dared revolt against the king had there not also been serious resistance to his rule back in England. At a time when Europe's religious wars were still in living memory, James had horrified many of his countrymen by converting to Catholicism, appointing numerous Catholics to public office, and allowing Catholics and followers of other faiths to worship freely. England's Protestant majority feared a papal plot, and between 1685 and 1688 three domestic rebellions erupted against James's rule. The first two were put down by royal armies, but the third succeeded through a strategic innovation; instead of taking up arms themselves, the plotters invited the military leader of the Netherlands to do so for them. Invading from the sea, William of Orange was welcomed by a number of high officials and even James's own daughter, Princess Anne. (Supporting a foreign invader against one's own father may seem a bit odd, but William, in fact, was James's nephew and was married to his daughter Mary.) Outmaneuvered by friends and family alike, James fled into exile in France in December 1688. William and Mary were crowned king and queen, ending a bloodless coup Englishmen dubbed the "Glorious Revolution."

Because it took months for news of the coup to reach the colonies, rumors of a planned Dutch invasion continued to swirl there throughout the winter and early spring of 1689, confronting the colonials with a difficult choice. The prudent course would have been to wait patiently for confirmation of how events in England had played out. A bolder alternative was to defend their societies by rising up against their oppressors in the hopes that William actually had invaded England, that he would be successful, and, if so, that he would look kindly on their actions. Each of the American nations made its own choice, for its own reasons. In the end, the only ones not to opt for rebellion were the young colonies around Philadelphia and Charleston, which, with just a few hundred settlers each, were in no position to engage in geopolitics even if they wanted to. But many people in Yankeedom, Tidewater, and New Netherland were ready and willing to risk everything for their respective ways of life.

Not surprisingly, Yankeedom led the way.

With their deep commitment to self-government, local control, and Puritan religious values, New Englanders had the most to lose from King James's policies. The Dominion governor, Sir Edmund Andros, lived in Boston and was particularly eager to bring New England to heel. Within hours of stepping off the boat in Massachusetts, the governor had issued a decree that struck at the heart of New England identity: he ordered Puritan meetinghouses opened for Anglican services and took away the New Englanders' charters of government—which the people of Boston described as "the hedge which kept us from the wild beasts of the field." Anglicans and suspected Catholics were appointed to top government and militia positions, backed by uncouth royal troops who witnesses said "began to teach New England to drab, drink, blasphemy, curse, and damn." Towns were forbidden to use taxpayer funds to support their Puritan ministers. In court, Puritans faced Anglican juries and were forced to kiss the Bible when swearing their oaths (an "idolatrous" Anglican practice) instead of raising their right hand, as was Puritan custom. Liberty of conscience was to be tolerated, Andros ordered, even as he built a new Anglican chapel in what had been Boston's public burial ground. A people who believed they had a special covenant with God were losing the instruments with which they had executed his will.[2]

The Dominion's policies, the inhabitants of Boston concluded, had to be part of a "Popish plot." Their "country," they would later explain, was "New England," a place "so remarkable for the true profession and pure exercise of the Protestant religion" that it had attracted the attention of "the great Scarlet Whore" who sought "to crush and break" it, exposing its people "to the miseries of utter exploitation." God's chosen people could not allow this to happen.[3]

In December 1686 a farmer in Topsfield, Massachusetts, incited his neighbors into what was later described as a "riotous muster" of the town militia, in which they pledged allegiance to New England's old government. Neighboring towns, meanwhile, refused to appoint tax collectors. Governor Andros had the agitators arrested and fined. The Massachusetts elite defied Andros's authority by secretly dispatching theologian Increase Mather across the Atlantic to make a personal appeal to King James. In London, Mather warned the monarch that "if a foreign prince or state should . . . send a frigate to New England and promise to protect [us] as under [our] former government, it would be an unconquerable temptation." Mather's threat to abandon the empire did not move James to change his policies. Yankeedom, Mather reported after his royal audience, was to be left in "a bleeding state."[4]

When rumors of William's invasion of England reached New England in February 1689, Dominion authorities did their best to stop them from spreading, arresting travelers for "bringing traitorous and treasonable libels" into the land. This only fueled Yankee paranoia about a Popish plot, now imagined to include an invasion by New France and its Indian allies. "It is high time we should be better guarded," the Massachusetts elite reasoned, "than we are like to be while the government remains in the hands by which it hath been held of late."[5]

The Yankee response was swift, surprising, and backed by nearly everyone. On the morning of April 18, 1689, conspirators raised a flag atop the tall mast on Boston's Beacon Hill, signaling that the revolt was to begin. Townspeople ambushed Captain John George, commander of HMS *Rose*, the Royal Navy frigate assigned to guard the city, and took him into custody. A company of fifty armed militiamen escorted a delegation of pre-Dominion officials up the city's main street and seized control of the State House. Hundreds of other militiamen seized Dominion officials and functionaries, placing them in the town jail. By midafternoon, some 2,000 militiamen had poured into the city from the surrounding towns, encircling the fort where Governor Andros was stationed with his royal troops. The first officer of the twenty-eight-gun *Rose* sent a boatload of sailors to rescue the governor, but they, too, were overpowered as soon as they stepped ashore. "Surrender and deliver up the government and the fortifications," the coup leaders warned Andros, or he would face "the taking of the fortification by storm." The governor surrendered the following day and joined his subordinates in the town jail. Faced with the guns of the now rebel-held fort, the acting captain of the *Rose* effectively surrendered as well, turning his vessel's sails over to the Yankees. In a single day the Dominion government had been overturned.[6]

News of the Yankee rebellion reached New Amsterdam within days, electrifying many of the town's Dutch inhabitants. Here was an opportunity to put an end not only to an authoritarian government but possibly to the English occupation of their country as well. New York might become New Netherland once again, liberating the Dutch, Walloons, Jews, and Huguenots from the stress of living under a nation that could not be relied upon to tolerate religious diversity and freedom of expression. The colony's Dominion lieutenant governor, Francis Nicholson, made their choice easier when he declared New Yorkers to be "a conquered people" who "could not expect the same rights as English people."[7]

Defiant New Netherlanders placed their hopes in William of Orange, who, after all, was the military leader of their mother country and might therefore be persuaded to liberate the Dutch colony from English rule. As the members of the Dutch congregation in New York City would later explain, William's "forefathers had liberated our ancestors from the Spanish yoke" and "had now come again to deliver the kingdom of England from Popery and Tyranny." Indeed, the majority of those who took up arms against the government that spring were Dutch, and they were led by a German-born Dutch Calvinist, Jacob Leisler. Opponents would later denounce their rebellion as simply a "Dutch plot."[8]

But the first disturbances came, not surprisingly, from the Yankee settlements of eastern Long Island, whose people had never wanted to be a part of New York. Longing to join Connecticut and fearful of a French Catholic invasion, they overthrew and replaced local Dominion officials. Hundreds of armed Yankee militiamen then marched on New York City and Albany, intending to take control of their forts and seize the tax money Dominion officials had extorted from them. "We, having like them at Boston, groaned under arbitrary power," they explained, "think it our bounden duty to . . . secure those persons who have extorted from us" an action "nothing less than what is our duty to God." The Long Islanders got within fourteen miles of Manhattan before Lieutenant Governor Nicholson organized a meeting with their leaders. He offered the successful gambit of a large cash payment to the assembled soldiers, ostensibly representing back wages and tax credits. The Yankees stopped their advance, but the damage to Dominion authority had been done.[9]

Emboldened by the Yankee Long Islanders, dissatisfied members of the city's own militia took up arms. Merchants stopped paying customs. "The people could not be restrained," a group of the city's Dutch inhabitants reported. "They cried out that the magistrates here ought also to declare themselves for the Prince of Orange." Lieutenant governor Nicholson withdrew to the fort and ordered its guns trained on the city. "There are so many rogues in this town that I am almost afraid to walk in the streets," he fumed to a Dutch lieutenant, adding, fatefully, that if the uprising continued he would "set fire to the town."[10]

Word of Nicholson's threat spread through the city, and within hours the lieutenant governor could hear the beating of drums calling the rebellious militia to muster. The armed townspeople marched on the fort, where the Dutch lieutenant opened the gates and let them in. "In half an hour's time the fort was full of armed and enraged men crying out that they were betrayed and that it was time to look to themselves," one witness recalled. The city secured, the Dutch and their sympathizers anxiously waited to see if their countryman would bring New Netherland back from the grave.[11]

On the face of it, Tidewater seemed an unlikely region to revolt. After all, Virginia was an avowedly conservative area, Royalist in politics and Anglican in religion. Maryland was even more so, with the Lords Baltimore ruling their portion of the Chesapeake like medieval kings of yore; their Catholicism only made them all the more attractive to James II. The king might wish to make his American colonies more uniform, but the Tidewater gentry had reason to believe their own aristocratic societies might serve as a model for his project.

As the establishment back in England began to turn on James, many in Tidewater followed their lead, and for many of the same reasons. Domestically the king was undercutting the Anglican Church, appointing Catholics to high office and usurping powers from the landed aristocracy, fraying the fabric of the English life the Chesapeake elite held so dear. In America, James sought to deny the Tidewater aristocracy their representative assemblies and threatened the prosperity of all planters with exorbitant new tobacco duties. As fears grew that the king was complicit in a Popish plot, the public became convinced that the Catholic Calverts were probably involved as well. On both shores of the Chesapeake, Protestants feared their way of existence was under siege, with those in Maryland convinced their very lives were in danger.

As reports on the crisis in England grew dire in the winter of 1688–1689, Anglican and Puritan settlers across Chesapeake country became alarmed that Maryland's Catholic leadership was secretly negotiating with the Seneca Indians to massacre Protestants. Residents of Stafford County, Virginia—just across the Potomac from Maryland—deployed armed units to fend off the suspected assault and, according to one Virginia official, were "ready to fly in the face of government." In Maryland, the governing council reported, "the whole country was in an uproar." Word of William and Mary's coronation arrived before the anti-Catholic hysteria got out of hand in Virginia, but it was not sufficient to quell growing unrest in Maryland.[12]

In Maryland, the Calverts' handpicked, Catholic-dominated governing council refused to proclaim its allegiance to the new sovereigns. In July, more than two months after official word of the coronations had reached Tidewater, the colony's Protestant majority decided they could wait no longer. The Protestants—almost all of whom had emigrated from Virginia—decided to topple the Calverts' regime and replace it with one that better conformed to Tidewater's dominant culture.

The insurgents organized themselves in a ragtag army called, appropriately enough, the Protestant Associators. Led by a former Anglican minister, they marched by the hundreds on St. Mary's City. The colonial militia dispersed before them, ignoring orders to defend the State House. Lord Baltimore's officers tried to organize a counterattack, but none of their enlisted men reported for duty. Within days the Associators were at the gates of Lord Baltimore's mansion, supported by cannon seized from an English ship they'd captured in the capital. The governing councilors hiding inside had no choice but to surrender, forever ending the Calvert family's rule. The Associators issued a manifesto denouncing Lord Baltimore for treason, discriminating against Anglicans, and colluding with French Jesuits and Indians against William and Mary's rule. The surrender terms banned Catholics from public office and the military, effectively turning power over to the Anglican, mostly Virginia-born elite.[13]

The insurgents had succeeded in remaking Maryland along the lines of their native Virginia, consolidating Tidewater culture across the Chesapeake country.

While the American "revolutionaries" of 1689 were able to topple regimes that had threatened them, not all of them achieved everything they had hoped for. The leaders of all three insurgencies sought King William's blessing for what they had accomplished. But while the new king endorsed the actions and honored the requests of Tidewater rebels, he did not roll back all of James's reforms in either New England or New Netherland. William's empire might have been more flexible than James's had been, but it was not willing to cede to the colonials on every point.

The New Netherland Dutch were the most disappointed. William, not wishing to alienate his new English subjects, declined to return New York to the Netherlands. Meanwhile the insurgency itself collapsed into political infighting, with various ethnic and economic interests struggling for control of the colony. The rebels' interim leader, Jacob Leisler, was unable to consolidate power but made plenty of enemies trying to do so. On the arrival of a new royal governor two years later, Leisler's foes managed to get him hanged for treason, deepening divisions in the city. As one governor would later observe: "Neither party will be satisfied with less than the necks of their adversaries." Instead of returning to Dutch rule, New Netherlanders found themselves living in a fractious royal colony, at odds with themselves and the Yankees of eastern Long Island, the upper Hudson Valley, and New England.[14]

More than anything, the Yankees had wanted their various governing charters reactivated, restoring each of the New England colonies to their previous status as self-governing republics. ("The charter of Massachusetts is . . . our Magna Carta," a resident of that colony explained. "Without it, we are wholly without law, the laws of England being made for England only.") William, however, ordered that Massachusetts and the Plymouth colony remain merged under a royal governor with power to veto legislation. The Yankees would be given back their elected assemblies, land titles, and unfettered town governments, but they had to allow all

Protestant property owners to vote, not just the ones who had been given membership in the Puritan churches. Connecticut and Rhode Island could continue to govern themselves as they had previously, but the mighty Bay Colony would be kept on a tighter leash. If God's chosen people wished to carry on building their utopia, they would have to fight another revolution.[15]

CHAPTER 7

Founding the Deep South

The founding fathers of the Deep South arrived by sea, their ships dropping anchor off what is now Charleston in 1670 and 1671. Unlike their counterparts in Tidewater, Yankeedom, New Netherland, and New France, they had not come directly from Europe. Rather, they were the sons and grandsons of the founders of an older English colony: Barbados, the richest and most horrifying society in the English-speaking world.

The society they founded in Charleston did not seek to replicate rural English manor life or to create a religious utopia in the American wilderness. Instead, it was a near–carbon copy of the West Indian slave state these Barbadians had left behind, a place notorious even then for its inhumanity. Enormously profitable to those who controlled it, this unadulterated slave society would spread rapidly across the lowlands of what is now South Carolina, overwhelming the utopian colony of Georgia and spawning the dominant culture of Mississippi, lowland Alabama, the Louisiana Delta country, eastern Texas and Arkansas, western Tennessee, north Florida, and the southeastern portion of North Carolina. From the outset, Deep Southern culture was based on radical disparities in wealth and power, with a tiny elite commanding total obedience and enforcing it with state-sponsored terror. Its expansionist ambitions would put it on a collision course with its Yankee rivals, triggering military, social, and political conflicts that continue to plague the United States to this day.

In the late seventeenth century, Barbados was the oldest, richest, and most densely populated colony in British America. Wealth and power were concentrated in the hands of an oligarchy of acquisitive, ostentatious plantation owners. These great planters had earned a reputation throughout the British Empire for immorality, arrogance, and excessive displays of wealth. Founding Father John Dickinson later dismissed them as "cruel people . . . a few lords vested with despotic power over myriad vassals and supported in pomp by their slavery." Another visitor declared, "For sumptuous houses, clothes, and liberal entertainment, they cannot be exceeded by their Mother Kingdom itself." Said a third, "The gentry here doth live far better than do ours in England." They bought knighthoods and English estates for themselves, sent their children to English boarding schools, and filled their homes with the latest and most expensive furnishings, fashions, and luxury goods. By imposing onerous property requirements for the right to vote, the great planters monopolized the island's elected assembly, governing council, and judiciary. With so many planters returning to newly purchased estates in England to rule in absentia, the Barbadians also had the most effective colonial lobbying force at the English Parliament, ensuring the imperial tax burden was shifted to others. "The Barbadians," the philosopher John Locke warned, "endeavor to rule all."[1]

The Barbadian planters' wealth was built on a slave system whose brutality shocked contemporaries. Like their Tidewater counterparts, they had first manned their plantations with indentured servants but had treated them so hellishly that the English poor began actively avoiding the place. The planters then resorted to shipping in hundreds of Scottish and Irish soldiers who'd been taken prisoner during Oliver Cromwell's conquest. When that supply ran out, they took to kidnapping children, so many that a new term was coined: "barbadosed" meant the same thing in the late seventeenth century as "shanghaied" would in the twentieth. The treatment of servants inevitably attracted the scrutiny of English officials, particularly after an island-wide servants revolt in 1647 that nearly put an end to the planters' regime. A new source of cheap, docile labor had to be found, particularly once the Barbadians perfected the cultivation of immensely valuable sugarcane.[2]

The planters' solution was to import shipload after shipload of enslaved Africans, whom they treated as fixed possessions, like their tools or cattle, thereby introducing chattel slavery to the English world. Barbadians adopted another novelty from South America: the gang labor system, wherein slaves were worked to death in the sugar fields and workhouses. On Barbados the rate of slave mortality was double that of Virginia. While the Tidewater gentry's slave supply replenished itself through natural increase, Barbados's planters had to import huge numbers every year just to replace the dead. Sugar was so profitable, however, that the planters could afford to simply feed more bodies to the cane fields. But by 1670 the planters had run out of land on the tiny island, leaving their younger sons with no hope of securing estates of their own. Barbadian society needed to expand—to the other English islands in the Leeward chain, to Jamaica, and, most significantly, to the subtropical lowlands of the east coast of North America.[3]

This was the culture that spawned Charleston and, by extension, the Deep South. Unlike the other European colonies of the North American mainland, South Carolina was a slave society from the outset. Established by a group of Barbadian planters, "Carolina in ye West Indies" was, by its very founding charter, a preserve of the West Indian slave lords. Written by John Locke, the charter provided that a planter would be given 150 acres for every servant or slave he brought to the colony; soon a handful of Barbadians owned much of the land in lowland South Carolina, creating an oligarchy worthy of the slave states of ancient Greece. The leading planters brought in enormous numbers of slaves, so many that they almost immediately formed a quarter of the colony's population. The slaves were put to work cultivating rice and indigo for export to England, a trade that made the large planters richer than anyone in the colonial empire save their counterparts in the West Indies. By the eve of the American Revolution, per capita wealth in the Charleston area would reach a dizzying £2,338, more than quadruple that of Tidewater and almost six times higher than that of either New York or Philadelphia. The vast majority of this wealth was concentrated in the hands of South Carolina's ruling families, who controlled most of the land, trade, and slaves. The wealthy were extraordinarily numerous, comprising a quarter of the white population at the end of the colonial period. "We are a country of gentry," one resident proclaimed in 1773; "we have no such thing as Common People among us." Of course, this statement ignored the lower three-quarters of the white population and the enslaved black majority, who by that time comprised 80 percent of the lowland population. To the great planters, everyone else was of little consequence. Indeed, this elite firmly believed the Deep South's government and people existed solely to support their own needs and aspirations.[4]

Not wishing to idle away their time on their sweltering plantations, the planters built themselves a city where they could enjoy the finer things in life. Charleston—"Charles Town" until the revolution—quickly became the wealthiest town on the eastern seaboard. It resembled Bridgetown, the capital of Barbados, with its fine townhouses painted in pastel colors, adorned with tiled roofs and piazzas and built along streets covered in crushed seashells. Unlike Williamsburg or St. Mary's City, Charleston was a vibrant city, for the planters spent as much time there as possible, leaving the day-to-day management of their estates to hired overseers. They filled their city with distractions: theaters; punch houses; taverns; brothels; cockfighting rings; private clubs for smoking, dining, drinking, and horse racing; and shops stocked with fashionable imports from London. Like the nouveaux riches everywhere, they were fixated on acquiring appropriate status symbols and followed the latest fashions and customs of the English gentry with a dedication that startled visitors. "Their whole lives are one continued race," one resident wrote, "in which everyone is endeavoring to distance all behind them and to overtake and pass by all before him."[5]

Like Tidewater's aristocracy, many of the planters had ancestors who had fought for the king in the English Civil War, and they embraced the trappings and symbolism of the British nobility, if not the social responsibilities that were supposed to attend them. Thrilled by the end of Puritan rule at home, they had named Carolina and Charleston for the restored king, Charles II. The Barbadian-born aristocracy trumpeted their genetic association with English knights and nobles by displaying coats of arms on their imported French porcelain. These often included the heraldic symbol for a younger son: a crescent moon tilted with the horns to the wearer's right. This device was later incorporated into the South Carolinian flag and worn as an emblem on the uniforms of its revolutionary-era military forces, loyalist and rebel alike.[6]

While not particularly religious, the planters embraced the Anglican Church as another symbol of belonging to the establishment. Locke's charter for the colony had guaranteed freedom of religion—Sephardic Jews and French Huguenots emigrated to the region in great numbers—but the elite overturned these provisions in 1700, giving themselves a monopoly on church and state offices. Their Anglican religious orientation also gave the Deep South elite unfettered access to London high society and the great English universities and boarding schools, milieus generally denied to Puritans, Quakers, and other dissenters. Whether English or French in origin, the Deep South's planters would also come to embrace the Tidewater gentry's notion of being descendants of the aristocratic Normans, lording over their colony's crass Anglo-Saxon and Celtic underclass.[7]

The low country's wealth depended entirely on a massive army of enslaved blacks, who outnumbered whites nine to one in some areas. To keep this supermajority under control, the planters imported Barbados's brutal slave code almost word for word. Their 1698 law declared Africans to have "barbarous, wild, savage natures" that made them "naturally prone" to "inhumanity," therefore requiring tight control and draconian punishments. The law's provisions focused on guaranteeing that no slave escaped. Runaways were to be severely whipped (after a first attempt), branded with the letter R on the right cheek (after the second), whipped and have one ear chopped off (after the third), castrated (after the fourth), and then either have an Achilles tendon severed or, simply, be executed (after a fifth attempt). Masters who failed to mete out the required punishments were fined, and anyone—white or black—who helped the runaways was subject to fines, whipping, or even death. The oligarchs reserved far more severe punishments for runaways who attempted "to go off from this province in order to deprive his master of mistress of his service." Such slaves were executed, along with any whites found assisting them. Capital punishment was mandated if a slave "maimed and disabled" a white person. If a white person out of "wantonness or only of bloody mindedness or cruel intention" were to kill a slave, he would be fined a mere £50, about the cost of a good gentleman's wig. But tellingly, if the murderer happened to be a servant, he would be given a far stronger sentence: thirty-nine lashes, three months in prison, and four years indentured servitude to the murdered slave's owner. Slaves were not allowed to leave their plantations without a pass from their masters, and should they have been caught stealing so much as a loaf of bread they were whipped forty times; repeat offenders had their ears cut off, or their nostrils slit, and, on the fourth conviction, were put to death. But the code was not without compassion . . . for the slave owner. If a slave was killed while being apprehended, castrated, or whipped, the master would be compensated from the state treasury. The act also allowed for slaves to be baptized because "the Christian religion which we profess obliges us to wish well to the souls of all men," but it made clear that such an act "may not be made a pretense to alter any man's property" by releasing slaves from bondage. Such provisions would remain on the books until the end of the Civil War, and served as the model for the slave codes of the future governments of the Deep South.[8]

Of course, the Deep South wasn't the only part of North America practicing full-blown slavery after 1670. Every colony tolerated the practice. But most of the other nations were societies with slaves, not slave societies per se. Only in Tidewater and the Deep South did slavery become the central organizing principle of the economy and culture. There were fundamental differences between these two slave nations, however, which illuminate a subtle difference in the values of their respective oligarchies.[9]

We've seen how Tidewater's leaders, in search of serfs, imported indentured servants of both races—men and women who could earn their freedom if they survived their servitude. After 1660, however, the people of African descent who arrived in Virginia and Maryland increasingly were treated as permanent slaves as the gentry adopted the slaveholding practices of the West Indies and Deep South. By the middle of the eighteenth century, black people faced Barbadian-style slave laws everywhere south of the Mason-Dixon line.

Even so, in Tidewater, slaves made up a much smaller proportion of the population (1 to 1.7 whites, rather than 5 to 1), lived longer, and had more stable family lives than their counterparts in the Deep South. Tidewater's slave population naturally increased after 1740, doing away with the need to import slaves from abroad. With few new arrivals to assimilate, Afro-Tidewater culture became relatively homogeneous and strongly influenced by the English culture it was embedded within. Many blacks whose ancestors had come to the Chesapeake region prior to 1670 had grown up in freedom, owning land, keeping servants, even holding office and taking white husbands or wives. Having African blood did not necessarily make one a slave in Tidewater, a fact that made it more difficult to dismiss black people as subhuman. Until the end of the seventeenth century, one's position in Tidewater was defined largely by class, not race.[10]

The Deep South, by contrast, had a black supermajority and an enormous slave mortality rate, meaning thousands of fresh humans had to be imported every year to replace those who had died. Blacks in the Deep South were far more likely to live in concentrated numbers in relative isolation from whites. With newcomers arriving with every slave ship, the slave quarters were cosmopolitan, featuring a wide variety of languages and African cultural practices. Within this melting pot, the slaves forged a new culture, complete with its own languages (Gullah, New Orleans Creole), Afro-Caribbean culinary practices, and musical traditions. From the hell of the slave quarters would come some of the Deep South's great gifts to the continent: blues, jazz, gospel, and rock and roll, as well as the Caribbean-inspired foodways today enshrined in Southern-style barbeque joints from Miami to Anchorage. And because the Deep South's climate, landscape, and ecosystem resembled those of West Africa far more than they did those of England, it was the slaves' technologies and practices that guided the region's agricultural development. "Carolina," a Swiss immigrant remarked in 1737, "looks more like a negro country than like a country settled by white people."[11]

In the Deep South, African Americans formed a parallel culture, one whose separateness was enshrined in the laws and fundamental values of the nation's white minority. Indeed, the Deep South was for at least the three centuries from 1670 to 1970 a caste society. And caste, it should be noted, is quite a different thing from class. People can and do leave the social class they are born into—either through hard work or tragedy—and can marry someone of another class and strive for their children to start life in a better position than they did. A caste is something one is born into and can never leave, and one's children will be irrevocably assigned to it at birth. Marriage outside of one's caste is strictly forbidden. So while the Deep South had rich whites and poor whites and rich and poor blacks, no amount of wealth would allow a black person to join the master caste. The system's fundamental rationale was that blacks were inherently inferior, a lower form of organism incapable of higher thought and emotion and savage in behavior. Although pressed into service as wet nurses, cooks, and nannies, blacks were regarded as "unclean," with Deep Southern whites maintaining a strong aversion to sharing dishes, clothes, and social spaces with them. For at least three hundred years, the greatest taboo in the Deep South was to marry across the caste lines or for black men to have white female lovers, for the caste system could not survive if the races began to mix. Even the remotest suspicion of violating the Great Deep Southern Taboo would result in death for a black male.[12]

However, like so many institutions in the Deep South, the caste system had convenient loopholes for the rich white men who created it. Having sex with your enslaved women and girls was perfectly acceptable, so long as you did it only for "fun." Many Tidewater and Deep Southern oligarchs raped or had affairs with slaves and housemaids—from colonial segregationists such as Virginia's William Byrd (born in 1674) to modern-day ones such as South Carolina senator Strom Thurmond (who died in 2003). "The enjoyment of a Negro or mulatto woman is spoken of as quite a common thing," a Yankee guest of South Carolina planters reported in 1764. "No reluctance, delicacy or shame is made about the matter." Any children that resulted from such liaisons were, by law, assigned to the black caste and were explicitly denied any claim on their father's property, a practice that also continued into the late twentieth century. Many planters did, however, take an interest in their illegitimate children, often assigning them to be household servants and sometimes even paying to send them to school in Yankeedom, where such things were permitted. This helped foster the creation of a privileged mulatto social group that came to dominate the middle and upper classes of the black caste, and their later successes in trade, business, and other fields challenged the underlying justification for the entire apartheid system.[13]

Greatly outnumbered, the planters were haunted by the fear that their slaves would rebel. They organized themselves into mounted militia, training regularly to respond to any uprising and awarding themselves honorary ranks like "colonel" or "major." Their fears were not unfounded. In 1737, a group of Catholic slaves who had probably been warriors for the Christian kingdom of Kongo—a West African kingdom recognized by the Pope—tried to fight their way to freedom in Spanish-controlled Florida. This disciplined force of twenty to thirty men sacked an armory in Stono and marched south with drums beating and banners flying, drawing hundreds of slaves to join their exodus, and slaughtering planters who stood in their way. Most died in pitched battles with militia units, who then decorated the road back to Charleston by impaling a rebel slave's head on each milepost. "On this occasion every breast was filled with concern," South Carolina legislators reported shortly thereafter. "We could not enjoy the benefits of peace like the rest of mankind [because] . . . our own industry should be the means of taking from us all the sweets of life and rendering us liable to the loss of our lives and fortunes."[14]

Deep Southern society was not only militarized, caste-structured, and deferential to authority, it was also aggressively expansionist. From their cultural hearth in the South Carolina low country, the planters expanded to similar terrain both up and down the coast. To the north lay North Carolina, a sparsely settled backwater whose coastal region would soon be split between poor Tidewater farmers (in the northeast, along the shores of Albemarle Sound) and wealthy Deep Southerners in the southeast. But south of the Savannah River in Georgia, the South Carolina planters encountered resistance to the spread of their way of life.

The young colony of Georgia didn't start as part of the Deep South. Founded in 1732, it had been a lofty philanthropic endeavor planned by a group of upper-class British social reformers who sought to address urban poverty by moving the poor to the American south. There the people the philanthropists termed "drones" and "miserable wretches" would be put to work on their own farms, an experience expected to cure them of their alleged laziness. The philanthropists banned slavery from Georgia, as the presence of slaves was thought to discourage poor whites from hard work, and they limited farms to a maximum size of fifty acres in an attempt to prevent plantations from forming. Georgia's benefactors even forbade liquor and lawyers, as they thought both eroded moral character. Once redeemed, Georgia's paupers would continue to serve the empire's geostrategic interests by forming a buffer state against Spanish attack from the south and by helping intercept South Carolina slaves as they tried to make their escape to freedom in Spanish Florida.[15]

The dream was not to be. The planters of South Carolina needed new land for plantations, and the paupers of Georgia were eager to buy slaves to relieve them of the most unpleasant menial tasks. In the 1740s and 1750s, South Carolinians seized control of Georgia's government and ensured that the best land was granted to themselves and their friends. A strict Barbadian-style slave code was adopted; plantations sprung up throughout the coastal lowlands, and Savannah was turned into a little Charleston. Lowland Georgia would become not a yeoman farmers' utopia but rather an extension of the West Indian slaveocracy that got its start in Charleston.[16]

The Deep South was on the move, and, unlike Tidewater, it would face no competing European civilization to block its path to the Mississippi and beyond.

CHAPTER 8

Founding the Midlands

The most prototypically American of the nations was one of the last to be founded. From its inception in the 1680s, the Midlands was a tolerant, multicultural, multilingual civilization populated by families of modest means—many of them religious—who desired mostly that their government and leaders leave them in peace. Over the past three centuries, Midland culture has pushed westward from its hearth in and around Philadelphia, jumped over the Appalachians, and spread across a vast swath of the American heartland, but it has retained these essential qualities. It is Middle America, the most mainstream of the continent's national cultures and, for much of our history, the kingmaker in national political contests.

Ironically, its beginnings were far from ordinary. Like Yankeedom, the Midlands were intended to be a model society, a utopia guided by the tenets of an unorthodox religion. In fact, Pennsylvania was created by perhaps the most controversial religious cult of the era, a group contemporaries accused of undermining "peace and order" and "sowing . . . the seeds of immediate ruin of . . . religion, Church order . . . and . . . the state." Difficult though it may be to understand today, the Quakers were considered a radical and dangerous force, the late-seventeenth-century equivalent of crossing the hippie movement with the Church of Scientology. Quakers spurned the social conventions of the day, refusing to bow or doff their hats to social superiors or to take part in formal religious services of any sort. They rejected the authority of church hierarchies, held women to be spiritually equal to men, and questioned the legitimacy of slavery. Their leaders strode naked on city streets or, daubed with excrement, into Anglican churches in efforts to provide models of humility; one Quaker rode naked on a donkey into England's second-largest city on Palm Sunday in an unpopular reenactment of Christ's entry into Jerusalem. Overcome with rapture, they would fall into violent fits, or "quakes," that frightened nonbelievers. Many embraced martyrdom, repeatedly marching into unfriendly neighborhoods or onto New England town greens to preach or challenge ministers, reveling in the imprisonment, whippings, tongue borings, and executions that followed. "The will of the Lord be done," martyr Mary Dyer told a Yankee governor after he handed down her death sentence. "Yea, joyfully shall I go."[1]

These disruptive behaviors were the expression of deep-held religious convictions. The Quakers believed that each person had an "Inner Light" holding the Holy Spirit within him or her. They didn't study and obey scripture to achieve salvation, but instead found God through personal mystical experience—meaning that priests, bishops, and churches were superfluous. All humans were thought to be essentially good and were to treat one another as they would wish themselves to be treated. All were equal before God, regardless of sect, race, or gender, and all earthly authority was ultimately without legitimacy. Some individuals might be richer or poorer than others, but that didn't give the wealthy any special powers over the lives of their neighbors. And by the 1690s, just a half-century after its creation, Quakerism had developed an intense aversion to violence and war, a commitment to pacifism that was so total it would doom the Quakers' control of the Midlands.[2]

So how did so unpopular a cult ever get permission to found its own colony—especially from Catholic, authority-loving King Charles II?

Like a lot of strange experiments, the founding of Pennsylvania came about because a rich, respectable man had accumulated favors that were later cashed in to benefit a rebellious, unorthodox young man. In this particular case, the gifts were made posthumously. Admiral William Penn was a self-made man who'd trimmed his sails to the political winds, first fighting for Parliament in the English Civil War, then championing the restoration of the monarchy. Cromwell made him rich by giving him confiscated Irish estates, but Admiral Penn later loaned £16,000 to Cavalier King Charles. He groomed his son William to be a respectable gentleman and sent him to study at Oxford. But young William was expelled for criticizing Oxford's Anglican Church services and in 1667, at age twenty-six, he horrified everyone by joining the Quakers. His father tried everything to get his son on the right track—beatings, whippings, banishment, a plum posting at the court of Louis XIV in Versailles, a turn at managing the family estate in Ireland—but nothing seemed to work for very long. William came back from France with "a great deal, if not too much, of the vanity of the French garb and affected manner of speech and gait," according to family friend Samuel Pepys, but still defiantly claimed allegiance to the Quakers, or Friends of God, as they by then called themselves. He published dozens of belligerent pamphlets extolling Quakerism, was arrested four times, and spent a year in prison. He used his father's connections at the royal court to gain the release of Quaker converts and spent his allowance traveling in Germany and the Netherlands as a Quaker missionary. He became close to the sect's founder, George Fox, and helped shape the Friends' practices. On his father's death in 1670, William Penn was one of the most famous Quakers in England and very, very rich.[3]

Penn enjoyed the finer things in life—confiscated manor houses, expensive clothing, fine wines, a staff of servants—but nurturing Quakerism was his first priority. Quakers, he decided, needed their own country, a place where they could conduct a "holy experiment" that would serve as an "example to all nations" that would prompt "all Mankind to go hither." In 1680 he settled King Charles's debt to his late father in exchange for a grant of 45,000 square miles of real estate located between Lord Baltimore's Maryland and the Duke of York's New York. The province (which was as large as England itself) would be named Pennsylvania, after the late admiral. William Penn would have the authority to do pretty much whatever he wished there.[4]

Penn envisioned a country where people of different creeds and ethnic backgrounds could live together in harmony. Since his faith led him to believe in the inherent goodness of humans, his colony would have no armed forces and would exist in peace with local Indians, paying them for their land and respecting their interests. While all the other American colonies severely restricted the political power of ordinary people, Pennsylvania would extend the vote to almost everyone. The Quaker religion would have no special status within the colony's government, the Friends wishing to inspire by example, not by coercion. Government would be limited, unable to levy taxes without the annual approval of the elected assembly. Pennsylvania itself would be centered around a new, centrally planned capital on the Delaware River with a gridiron street pattern, systemized street names, and uniform distances between buildings. (Indeed,

Philadelphia, the City of Brotherly Love, would become the model for later American towns and cities across the Midlands.) But Penn's civilization was to extend well beyond the borders of Pennsylvania to incorporate the Quaker-controlled colony of West Jersey (now southern New Jersey), the scattered Dutch, Swedish, and Finnish settlements along the lower reaches of Delaware Bay (now the state of Delaware), and northwestern Maryland (which Penn believed, erroneously, to be part of his royal grant).[5]

Penn's colonization effort was extremely well organized. Offering political and religious liberty and land on cheap terms, he advertised Pennsylvania aggressively, printing pamphlets not just in England and Ireland but in the Netherlands and wide swaths of what is now Germany. He presold 750,000 acres of farm lots to some 600 investors, raising the money needed to underwrite the initial wave of colonists, establish Philadelphia, and keep the colonial government running for several years without having to collect taxes. In 1682 Penn sent twenty-three ships to Pennsylvania carrying 2,000 colonists with tools, provisions, and livestock. Four years later 8,000 people were living in and around Philadelphia, a population level that took Tidewater twenty-five years to achieve and New France seventy years. Most were skilled artisans and farmers of modest means who had come as families, instantly giving the Midlands a settled and civilized tone. With ample food, good relations with the Indians, and a Quaker majority, the "holy experiment" had gotten off to a highly promising start.[6]

Penn's marketing campaign was so successful that it soon brought an even larger wave of settlers, one that would give the Midlands its pluralistic and decidedly un-British character, with lasting effects on the spirit and identity of the future United States.

This second immigration wave consisted of German-speaking peasants and craftsmen from the Palatinate. They were essentially refugees, fleeing famine, religious persecution, and war, traumatized by generations of horrific imperial and religious conflicts that had made their south German homeland a killing field. They were Protestants almost without exception, and they arrived in large extended family groups, or even as entire transplanted villages, reinforcing the Midlands' existing middle-class ethos. Some were from sects that wished to order their lives in a particular way, like the Amish, the Mennonites, or the Brethren of Christ.

Thousands more were mainstream Lutherans and German Calvinists, wanting nothing more than to build prosperous family farms in a peaceful setting. Penn let them all settle their own communities where they could maintain their ethnic identity and practice whatever Christian religion suited them. This plan proved incredibly successful: Pennsylvania *Deitsch*, a Palatinate dialect of German, continued in everyday use in Germantown and other "Pennsylvania Dutch" settlements well into the twentieth century; the Amish and Mennonites maintain their way of life to the present day. Altogether some 5,000 German speakers emigrated to the Midlands between 1683 and 1726, imprinting their cultural values on the region early on. Between 1727 and 1755 another 57,000 flooded in, making Pennsylvania the only English-founded colony without an English majority.[7]

The Germans easily adapted themselves to Quaker plans for this new society. They were generally content to let the Quakers run things, supporting Quaker candidates in elections and endorsing Quaker policies. The Germans' small-scale farming skills became legendary; they knew how to select farmland with top-quality soil, conserve it through crop rotation, and improve livestock through selective breeding. For the next two centuries, visitors invariably remarked on their tidy and prosperous farms, usually comparing them favorably with those of their non-German neighbors. "It is pretty to behold our back settlements where the barns are large as palaces," a Wales-born surveyor remarked in 1753. "How much we are indebted to the Germans for the economy they have introduced [to this] . . . infant colony." They were also renowned for their skills as craftsmen, having perfected the building of log cabins (a design learned from the Swedes and Finns of the "lower counties" of Delaware) and invented the famed Conestoga wagon, which carried generations of settlers over the Appalachians and beyond. Most of them belonged to disciplined religious sects that prized thrift and sobriety, solidifying their affinity with their Quaker neighbors.[8]

The Germans and Quakers also shared a strong aversion to slavery, a stance that would set the Midlands apart from New Netherland, Tidewater, and the Deep South. As family farmers, the Germans had little need for slaves, but their antipathy seems to have been a function of cultural values, as well. Small groups of Germans also settled in the Deep South (in places like New Bern, North Carolina, and New Braunfels, Texas) but had markedly lower rates of slave ownership than their Anglo- and Franco-American neighbors, who were also small farmers. Indeed, the first formal protest against slavery in North America was articulated by German Quakers in Germantown, Pennsylvania. "We shall do to all men like as we will be done ourselves," the protestors declared in 1712, "making no difference of what generation, descent or color they are." Many wealthy Quakers, Penn included, had come to Pennsylvania with slaves, but within a decade, Friends were advising one another that slaveholding violated the Golden Rule. In 1712, the Quaker-run legislature even imposed a prohibitive duty on the import of slaves, but it was overturned by a royal court. With German support, they tried again to suppress slavery in 1773 but were vetoed by the crown. By then most Quaker slaveholders had freed their slaves, and some also tried to compensate them for their past labor. It was a moral stand that would later lead the Midlands to side with Yankeedom against the ambitions of its neighbors to the south.[9]

Early Pennsylvania was an economic success, but its Quaker-run government was a complete disaster.

The Quakers' ideals proved to be at odds with successful governance. Believing that all people were followers of Christ and innately good, the Quakers assumed citizens could govern themselves through mere self-discipline and the application of the Golden Rule. This turned out not to be the case, as Quakers were also by nature inclined to challenge authority and convention at every juncture. The community's leaders quarreled with one another over doctrinal questions while government fell into disarray, failing to maintain public records or to pass laws essential to the functioning of the court system. The governing council couldn't manage to hold regular meetings, while the colony went through six governors in its first decade. The Dutch, Swedes, and Finns of the "lower counties" became so desperate for proper government that they broke away to form one of their own, founding the tiny colony of Delaware in 1704. "Pray stop those scurvy quarrels that break out to the disgrace of the province," Penn wrote from London. "All good is said of [Pennsylvania] and but little good of [its] people. These bickerings keep back hundreds [of settlers], £10,000 out of my way, and £100,000 out of the country." In desperation Penn finally appointed a succession of outsiders to run the place, including a Yankee Puritan (John Blackwell), a successful Anglican merchant from Boston (Edward Shippen), and an arrogant English gentleman (David Lloyd). None of them succeeded in getting Quaker leaders to assume responsibility for the community they'd created. Philadelphia's Quakers preferred to focus on their respective Inner Lights than to tend to the worldly responsibilities of running a colony.[10]

The Quakers' expectation that immigrants from other cultures would embrace the Friends' worldview also proved unfounded. While the Germans caused few troubles, starting in 1717 a new group of colonists began arriving on Philadelphia's docks, one whose values were in stark opposition to all the Quakers held dear. They were a warrior people from the bloody borderlands of Britain, contemptuous of the Indians, quick to turn to violence to solve problems, and committed to a Calvinist faith that held that humans were inherently wicked. Fleeing their blighted homelands in Scotland and Ulster, these Borderlanders poured into Pennsylvania in staggering numbers: over 100,000 by 1775. The vast majority went straight to the hilly frontier in central Pennsylvania and would soon surge down the spine of the Appalachian Mountains, founding a powerful regional culture of their own. But while they stood apart from the Midlands as a cultural nation, tens of thousands of Borderlanders lived within the borders of the arbitrary rectangle of territory called Pennsylvania. They would prove the undoing of Quaker control of that colony. "It looks as if Ireland is to send all her inhabitants hither," a worried colonial official reported. "The common fear is that if they continue to come, they will make themselves proprietors of the province."[11]

The Borderlanders occupied Indian lands without paying for them, launched preemptive attacks on Indian villages, and pushed generally peaceful tribes into alliances with New France, who provided them guns and ammunition with which to attack their British rivals during the eighteenth century's many imperial wars. The dysfunctional Quaker government, secure behind concentric rings of German and Scots-Irish settlements, made no effort to respond to the mounting crisis except to send the Indians gifts and supplies. Even when French mercenaries sailed into Delaware Bay and began sacking plantations a few miles from Philadelphia, the government refused to consider any defense preparations. Benjamin Franklin, a Boston Yankee who'd relocated to Philadelphia, railed at the Friends for their complacency. "To refuse defending one's self or one's country is so unusual a thing among mankind that . . . [our enemies] may not believe it," he wrote in 1747, "till by experience, they can come higher and higher up our river, seize our vessels and plunder our plantations and villages and retire with their booty unmolested." The Quakers, steadfast in their pacifism, ignored Franklin, leaving him to raise private donations to organize the colony's defense.[12]

Things came to a head in 1755 when the Lenni Lenape Indians launched a full-on assault on the Scots-Irish and German settlements in the western part of the colony, wiping out entire towns and massacring or taking prisoner hundreds of settlers. Thousands of survivors fled eastward, some going all the way to Philadelphia to demonstrate before the impotent assembly. Residents from the previously peaceful German settlements in Lancaster County suddenly found themselves living in a war zone, but without arms or ammunition with which to defend themselves. As refugees choked the capital, Quaker politicians refused to endorse military appropriations. One leading Quaker, Daniel Stanton, wrote in his diary that the fact that few Friends had been killed in the fighting indicated that God approved of their inaction. Few non-Quakers endorsed Stanton's analysis, noting that the Friends' lack of casualties had more to do with the fact that they were clustered in the safest corner of the province. Even London Quakers were appalled. "You owe the people protection and yet withhold them from protecting themselves," an influential Friend there wrote his coreligionists in Philadelphia. "Will not all the blood that is spilt lie at your doors?" Forced to choose between defending their society and upholding their religious principles, key Quaker officials resigned from office. The Friends would never again monopolize political affairs in the Midlands.[13]

The Quakers were replaced by a partisan system of competing interest groups, with Franklin and his allies often dominating the scene. On the eve of the American Revolution, the Midlands was a civilization unsure of itself, its leaders, and the cause of independence. And by then, large swaths of what was to have been part of William Penn's utopia were being incorporated into other nations. Connecticut Yankees were pouring across the north country and were ready to fight a war if need be to keep Pennsylvania's Wyoming Valley under New England rule. And in the west a new power had taken hold and was spreading southward across the highlands. This Borderlander civilization didn't control a single colonial government—indeed, it was barely represented at all in the coastal capitals—but it would radically reshape the future of all the American nations and the strange federation in which they would soon find themselves.

CHAPTER 9

Founding Greater Appalachia

The last of the nations to be founded in the colonial period, Greater Appalachia was the most immediately disruptive. A clan-based warrior culture from the borderlands of the British Empire, it arrived on the backcountry frontier of the Midlands, Tidewater, and Deep South and shattered those nations' monopoly control over colonial governments, the use of force, and relations with the Native Americans. Proud, independent, and disturbingly violent, the Borderlanders of Greater Appalachia have remained a volatile insurgent force within North American society to the present day.

The nations that we have encountered to this point have been largely contained within the jurisdiction of one or more colonial governments, controlled by their own political elite. But Greater Appalachia started as a civilization without a government. The Borderlanders weren't really colonists, brought to the New World to provide some lord or shareholding company with the manpower for a specific colonial project. They were immigrants seeking sanctuary from a devastated homeland, refugees who generally arrived without the encouragement or direction of officials, and often against their wishes. Having no desire to bow to "foreign" rule or to give up their ways, the Borderlanders rushed straight to the isolation of the eighteenth-century frontier to found a society that was, for a time, literally beyond the reach of the law, and modeled on the anarchical world they had left behind.

The founders of Appalachia came from the war-torn borderlands of northern Britain: lowland Scotland, the adjacent Marches of northern England, and the Scots-Irish-controlled north of Ireland. Their ancestors had weathered 800 years of nearly constant warfare, some of them fighting in (or against) the armies of William "Braveheart" Wallace or Robert the Bruce. By the time America was being colonized, the borderlands were in ruins. "The country is so stored with infinite numbers of begging and vagrant poor, who by reason of their extreme want and misery are very bold in their behavior and impudent," an English spy said of Scotland in 1580. The north of England, a foreign diplomat wrote in 1617, "was very poor and uncultivated and exceedingly wretched . . . from the perpetual wars with which these nations have savagely destroyed each other."[1]

Under such conditions, Borderlanders learned to rely only on themselves and their extended families to defend home, hearth, and kin against intruders, be they foreign soldiers, Irish guerrilla fighters, or royal tax collectors. Living amid constant upheaval, many Borderlanders embraced a Calvinist religious tradition—Presbyterianism—that held that they were God's chosen people, members of a biblical nation sanctified in blood and watched over by a wrathful Old Testament deity. Suspicious of outside authority of any kind, the Borderlanders valued individual liberty and personal honor above all else, and were happy to take up arms to defend either. When Queen Elizabeth I and her successors needed tough, warlike people to settle Northern Ireland and crush native resistance, they turned to border Scots who, in Ulster, became the Scots-Irish. A century later, many Americans would value their willingness to hold down frontier lands against restive Native Americans, creating a protective buffer for more docile settlers near the coast.[2]

The Borderlanders arrived in five increasingly massive waves between 1717 and 1776, each a response to a disaster back in the British Isles. The first followed a drought and sheep-killing blight in Ulster, a fall in demand for the region's principal export (linen), and a shocking increase in the rents Ireland's absentee English landlords began exacting from their tenants as their long-term leases expired. "I do not see how Ireland can on the present foot pay greater taxes than it does without starving the inhabitants and leaving them entirely without meat or clothes," one visitor warned the Anglican archbishop of Ireland in 1716. "They have already given their bread, their flesh, their butter, their shoes, their stockings, their beds, their house furniture and houses to pay their landlords and taxes. I cannot see how any more can be got from them, except we take away their potatoes and butter milk, or flay them and sell their skins." Taxes were increased all the same, leaving thousands of tenants with no other option than to sell their tenancy rights and book passage to the New

World. As rents on newly expired leases doubled, cattle prices fell by half, and more crop failures occurred, the initial group of emigrants would be followed by tens of thousands and, later, hundreds of thousands of countrymen.[3]

By the early 1770s the exodus had grown so enormous that London authorities feared that Ireland and the Scottish borderlands would be economically crippled. "They emigrate in swarms to America," one official in Ireland warned. "Something must be done to give the Irish poor a means of getting bread. If the cow is to be milked, she must be fed." A land agent on the Isle of Skye reported that the manor estates were becoming a "wasteland." The bishop of Derry in Northern Ireland told imperial officials that "the rebellious spirit" then brewing in the American backcountry was due to the emigration from Ireland of 33,000 "fanatical and hungry republicans in the course of a very few years." Newspapers and magazines across Britain carried worried predictions of a deserted kingdom. When the American Revolution broke out, British officials were still debating how best to restrict the emigration of the Borderlanders.[4]

While small groups of Borderlanders settled in New England, the Deep South and, later, British Canada, the vast majority arrived in North America via the Midlands: over 100,000 by 1775. The Midland-governed colonies were attractive because official Quaker policy was to welcome immigrants of all nations and let them practice their faith unmolested. Still, Midlanders were alarmed by the newcomers' rough manners and clannish loyalties. Philadelphia newspapers accused them of a litany of misdeeds: counterfeiting of currency, murder, the rape of a six-year-old child, and making "threatening words against authority" should the government dare execute one of their countrymen as punishment for his crimes. Officials did their best to get them out of town and onto the frontier, where they could serve as a buffer against French or Native American attack.[5]

Destitute and land hungry, the vast majority were indeed happy to move straight to the backcountry, where they seized, in the words of a senior colonial official, "any sort of vacant land they can find without asking questions." Some had a little money left from their passage and could have rented land in settled areas closer to Philadelphia but chose not to.

As one explained: "We having been, before we came here, so much oppressed and harassed by under landlords in our own country, from which we with great losses, dangers, and difficulties came [to] . . . this foreign world [to be] freed from such oppression." The Scots-Irish, who came in extended families, traveled for days on narrow Indian paths in search of vacant land in the forested hills of what is now south-central Pennsylvania. Settling on widely dispersed parcels, they built rude cabins, cleared small garden plots, and set about herding their livestock over unfenced country. Rather than trying to produce cash crops for export, the Borderlanders embraced a woodland subsistence economy. They hunted, fished, and practiced slash-and-burn agriculture, moving every few years as the soil became depleted. Life in Britain had taught them not to invest too much time and wealth in fixed property, which was easily destroyed in time of war. Instead, they stored their wealth in a very mobile form: herds of pigs, cattle, and sheep. When they did need cash, they distilled corn into a more portable, storable, and valuable product: whiskey, which would remain the de facto currency of Appalachia for the next two centuries.[6]

This was a lifestyle that allowed for long periods of leisure, an indulgence that visitors from the other nations condemned. "They are very poor owing to their extreme indolence, for they possess the finest country in America and could raise but everything," a Deep Southern minister wrote of the southern Appalachians in 1768. "They delight in their present low, lazy, sluttish, heathenish, hellish life and seem not desirous of changing it." Indeed, the Borderlanders' top priority rarely seemed to be increasing their wealth; rather, it was maximizing their freedom, especially from outside forces.[7]

There weren't any towns to speak of in the early days, but the settlers maintained close communities of kin and neighbors scattered among the hills. Throughout the Appalachians they would often name settlements for places they had left behind: Donegal, Galloway, Londonderry (or Derry), New Scotland, Newcastle, Durham and Cumberland. These communities started in considerable isolation from the outside world, to which they owed no loyalty. With no roads, trade was almost entirely by barter. With the nearest courthouse often several days' journey away, the Borderlanders fell back on their old-country practice of taking the law into their own hands. Justice was meted out not by courts but by the aggrieved individuals and their kin via personal retaliation. "Every man is a sheriff in his own hearth" was a Borderlander creed that informed the Scottish practices of "blackmail" (as protection money), the blood feud (most famously practiced by the Hatfields and McCoys), and "Lynch's law," named for Appalachian Borderlander William Lynch, who advocated vigilante justice in the lawless Virginia backcountry. Between outlaws, outlaw justice, and conflicts with the Indians, Appalachia quickly earned an unsavory reputation. "The conduct of my countrymen from the North of Ireland . . . ," Penn's secretary reported, "their violence and injustice to each other [is something] this province till their arrival was very much stranger to."[8]

While hostile to external restraints on their behavior, the Borderlanders could be uncompromising in enforcing their own internal cultural norms. Dissent or disagreement—whether by neighbors, wives, children, or political opponents—was unacceptable and often crushed savagely. Borderlanders tolerated enormous inequalities within their communities. In many areas, the wealthiest tenth of the population controlled the majority of the land while the bottom half had none at all and survived as tenants or squatters. The lucky tenth were usually the heads of "good families," charismatic figures who commanded loyalty that was more a function of their personalities, character, and horizontal genealogical connections than of any particular policies they supported. They earned social standing from their individual deeds and accomplishments, rather than any sort of inherited station. Borderlanders recognized as "family" individuals out four generations in either direction, effectively creating enormous clans. Intermarriage between first cousins was commonplace, reinforcing the bonds of kinship. At the lower end of the social scale were the families who survived on hunting, foraging, and preying on their neighbors' crops, livestock, valuables, and daughters. Containing the predations of the latter group would become a major political issue as Appalachian civilization took root.[9]

From their initial stronghold in south central Pennsylvania, the Borderlanders spread south down the mountains on an ancient 800-mile-long Indian trail that came to be known as the Great Wagon Road. This crude passage led out of Lancaster and York, through Hagerstown (in what is now the western panhandle of Maryland), down the length of Virginia's Shenandoah Valley, and through the highlands of North Carolina to terminate in what is now Augusta, Georgia. Tens of thousands of Borderlanders and their herds migrated along this trail to new land in the rugged, barely explored Southern upcountry. As Ulster and the Scottish Marches emptied between 1730 and 1750, the population of North Carolina doubled, and then doubled again by 1770. Southwestern Virginia was growing at 9 percent a year, and in the South Carolina backcountry in the 1760s, almost the entire population had come from Pennsylvania or interior Virginia. The Borderlanders may have technically moved into colonies controlled by Tidewater gentry and the great planters of the Deep South, but in cultural terms their Appalachian nation effectively cut Tidewater off from the interior, blocking the West Indian slaveocracy from advancing into the southern uplands. Not until after the revolution would they control any formal governments; places called Tennessee, Kentucky, and West Virginia did not yet exist.[10]

Borderlanders lived among the Native Americans on whose land they were usually trespassing. As in New France, a significant proportion of settlers essentially "went Native," abandoning farming and husbandry for an aboriginal life. They hunted and fished, wore furs and clothing similar to those of the natives in their area, adopted Indian customs, took Indian wives, and had mixed-race children, several of whom grew up to be prominent Native American statesmen. Some learned Indian languages and conducted extended trapping and trading expeditions deep into aboriginal territory. Others became nomadic outlaws, hunting and stealing their way through the backcountry, annoying just about everyone. They were "little more than white Indians," one disgruntled South Carolinian observed, while backcountry Virginians complained of those "who live like savages." The mainstream of Appalachian society, however, regarded the Lenni Lenape, Shawnee, Cherokee, Creek, and other Indians as opponents in a struggle for control of the backcountry. It was an attitude often reciprocated, especially as the Borderlanders increasingly hunted, cleared, and squatted on Indian land. The result was a series of brutal wars that left staggering numbers of dead on both sides.[11]

Indian wars and other violence in Appalachia had profound effects on the other nations, particularly the Midlands. We've already seen how the Lenni Lenape invasion in the 1750s forced Quakers to relinquish much of their control over the region, but this was merely a dress rehearsal for a much more destabilizing series of events during a later conflict. In December 1763, a Scots-Irish band from in and around Paxton, Pennsylvania, attacked and burned a peaceful Christianized Indian settlement on Penn family land, killing six individuals on the spot and butchering fourteen more at the Lancaster jail, where Midlanders had brought them for protection. Among the dead were two three-year-old children who had been scalped and an old man who'd been hacked up with an axe in the jail yard. After the killings, these so-called "Paxton Boys" rallied together an armed force of 1,500 Scots-Irish neighbors and marched on Philadelphia, intending to murder more peaceful Native Americans who had fled there for their safety on the invitation of Governor John Penn, the late founder's grandson.

The result was a tense military showdown between Borderlanders and Midlanders, with control of what was then British North America's premier city hanging in the balance. When the Paxton Boys arrived outside Philadelphia on a rainy day in February 1764, a thousand Midlanders rallied to defend the State House. The city militia deployed a row of artillery pieces on the parade ground of their garrison, each loaded with grapeshot. As the Borderlander army surrounded the city, 200 Quakers actually set aside their principles and took up arms. On the city outskirts the Paxton Boys, dressed in moccasins and blanket coats, "uttered hideous cries in imitation of the [Indian] war whoop, knocked down peaceable citizens, and pretended to scalp them," according to an eyewitness. With German citizens generally remaining neutral and the Scots-Irish underclass in Philadelphia sympathetic with the invaders, the Midlands stood on the brink of occupation.[12]

In the end Benjamin Franklin saved the day, leading a negotiating team that promised to address the Borderlanders' grievances if they agreed to go home. A party of them was allowed to inspect the Indian refugees in the city but was unable to identify a single enemy combatant among them. When they later submitted their demands to Penn, foremost among them was to be given proper representation in the provincial assembly. (At the time, Midlander counties had twice as many representatives per capita as

Borderlander ones.) Philadelphians were horrified, the governor dallied, and the city was "daily threatened with the return of a more formidable force." Quakers turned to London for help, and kept a standing military force posted in the city for the first time in Midlands history. Only the end of hostilities with Indians farther west allowed the situation to normalize. But the Paxton Boys' actions had revealed fault lines across Pennsylvania and other colonies that would break open during the American Revolution.[13]

Other parts of colonial Appalachia were just as turbulent. On the disputed Pennsylvania-Maryland border in the 1730s, Scots-Irish were recruited by both governments to hold down the land; while the first parties were happy to use force to expel ethnic Germans, they proved unwilling to fight one another, leaving the colonial governments at an impasse. National background had again trumped state affiliation.

In the South Carolina backcountry, Borderlanders invaded Cherokee lands in the 1750s, poaching deer and taking human scalps, which they passed off as Shawnee to collect a generous bounty in neighboring Virginia. These unprovoked incursions triggered a bloody war in 1759–61 that left hundreds dead on both sides by the time imperial British troops forced a peace settlement. A few years later, Creek Indians in upland Georgia complained of Borderlander hunters "wandering all over the woods destroying our game." At the end of the hunting season these poachers began stealing cattle, hogs, and horses from their more law-abiding Borderlander neighbors. Some formed organized gangs that robbed backcountry people at gunpoint and forced some to reveal hidden coins and valuables via beatings, brandings, and burning off toes.[14]

This crime wave discouraged settlers from accumulating wealth, reinforcing the old Borderlander pattern. "The person who by his honest labour has earned £50 and lays it up for his future occasions, by this very step endangers his own life and his own family," one South Carolinian observed. "If we buy liquor for to retail or for hospitality they break into our dwellings and consume it," backcountry settlers in that colony reported in 1769. "Should we raise fat cattle or prime horses for market, they are constantly carried off [even when] well guarded." Runaway slaves from Deep South plantations joined the "banditti" in considerable numbers, some of them rising to lead their own gangs. This threatened the expansion of the Deep South as that nation could not survive in a region where bandits offered refuge to runaways. "The lands, though the finest in the province, [are] unoccupied and rich men [are] afraid to set slaves to work to clear them," Anglican minister Charles Woodmason warned, "lest they should become a Prey to the Banditti."[15]

With the highlands of South Carolina and Georgia beginning to resemble the lawless frontiers of Scotland, leading Appalachian families responded in the familiar Borderlander fashion: they formed a vigilante gang to hunt the bandits down. They called themselves the Regulators, and they swept up and down the highlands from Georgia to Virginia, whipping, branding, and lynching suspected outlaws. (Many bandits were woodsmen and poachers, but some leaders turned out to have been Cherokee War veterans from respectable families who'd apparently gotten a taste for plunder.) The Regulators then turned on "rogues and other idle, worthless people" in their communities, adopting a Plan of Regulation under which they whipped and banished anyone they considered lazy or immoral and forced others to farm land "on pain of flagellation." For three years starting in 1768, the Regulators had total control of interior South Carolina, driving off sheriffs and judges sent in from the lowlands. They demanded the Deep Southerners grant them proportional representation in the legislature; at the time the backcountry had three-quarters of the colony's white population but only two of the forty-eight assembly seats. They "treat us," one noted, "as if we were a different species from themselves." No substantive progress was made before attention began turning to a conflict with Britain, one in which the divide between the Deep South and the Borderlanders would prove critical.[16]

The cultural divide was even more disruptive in North Carolina, where Tidewater gentry, who effectively controlled the colony's government, tried to assert jurisdiction over the Borderlanders in the 1760s. The legislature—which gave ten times more representation per capita to the coastal lowlands—imposed a property tax system based on acreage, not property values, effectively shifting the burden from wealthy plantation owners to impoverished Borderlanders. The new royal governor, Sir William Tryon, increased the burden in 1765 in order to build himself a lavish £15,000 palace. Again the backcountry responded with a vigilante movement of

"Regulators" who violently seized control of the Appalachian portion of the colony for three years starting in 1768. Beating lawyers, sacking courthouses, and expelling tax collectors, the Regulators remained in power until their army of 2,000 was defeated in a pitched battle with Tidewater militia at Alamance Creek in 1771. Many Regulator leaders took refuge in the deep backcountry of what would one day be called Tennessee. Here, too, the inter-national tensions between Appalachia and the coast would profoundly shape allegiances when the American Revolution erupted a few years later.[17]

Frustrated by outside rule, some Borderlanders tried to create nation-states of their own, flouting the authority of both the British crown and their Native American neighbors. In north-central Pennsylvania, a group of squatters with a Scots-Irish majority set up its own "fair play system" of government modeled on the democratic principles of the Presbyterian Church and the radical individualism of the Scottish Marches. The forty families of this independent Fair Play territory continued their experiment in frontier self-sovereignty for five years until 1784, when the line of settlement overran the area and they were absorbed, perhaps unwillingly, into the general population.[18]

A larger-scale experiment took place farther south in what is now the eastern part of Tennessee and central Kentucky, where several thousand Borderlanders insituted an improvised government deep inside Indian territory. Their new nation, Transylvania, was created in direct violation of the Royal Proclamation of 1763 (which prohibited settlement west of the Appalachians), the legal jurisdictions of North Carolina and Virginia (which then claimed the territory), and His Majesty's property rights (as the Crown legally controlled all undeeded land on the continent). Without any permission they created their own constitution, government, courts, and land offices. Their leaders, including the lowland Scot immigrant James Hogg, dispatched frontiersman Daniel Boone to hack a 200-mile access trail into what is now central Kentucky, enabling settlers to stream in to found Boonesborough. There, in early 1775, they convened a "House of Delegates" under a massive elm tree in a clearing declared to be "our church, state house, [and] council chamber." When word came that the other colonies were convening a Continental Congress to discuss tensions with Great Britain, Transylvania sent Hogg to Philadelphia with a request to be admitted as the fourteenth member.[19]

As the British-controlled nations careened toward a series of conflicts with the mother country, the Borderlanders of Appalachia would play a decisive role. In some regions they would fight in support of Britain, in others, against, but they all did so for the same reason: to resist the threats to their clansmen's freedom, be it from Midland merchants, Tidewater gentlemen, Deep Southern planters, or the British crown itself. It was a pattern that would define Appalachia to the present day.

PART TWO

UNLIKELY ALLIES

1770 to 1815

CHAPTER 10

A Common Struggle

The event we call the American Revolution wasn't really revolutionary, at least while it was underway. The military struggle of 1775–1782 wasn't fought by an "American people" seeking to create a united, continent-spanning republic where all men were created equal and guaranteed freedom of speech, religion, and the press. On the contrary, it was a profoundly conservative action fought by a loose military alliance of nations, each of which was most concerned with preserving or reasserting control of its respective culture, character, and power structure. The rebelling nations certainly didn't wish to be bonded together into a single republic. They were joined in a temporary partnership against a common threat: the British establishment's ham-fisted attempt to assimilate them into a homogeneous empire centrally controlled from London. Some nations—the Midlands, New Netherland, and New France—didn't rebel at all. Those that did weren't fighting a revolution; they were fighting separate wars of colonial liberation.

As we've already seen, the four nations that did rebel—Yankeedom, Tidewater, Greater Appalachia, and the Deep South—had little in common and strongly distrusted one another. So how did they overcome their differences to fight a war together? The answer is with great difficulty. In fact, they sometimes weren't even fighting on the same side, as Appalachia was engaged in a struggle of liberation not against Britain but against the Midlands, Tidewater, and the Deep South. To complicate matters, the elites of the Deep South were ambivalent about the revolt, with many of them changing sides in the course of it. (Georgia even rejoined the empire during the conflict.) The main reason the Deep Southerners joined the "revolution" at all was because they feared they would otherwise lose control of their slaves. The nations on the whole cooperated with one another only because they saw no other way to overcome an existential threat to their respective cultures. They allied themselves with the enemies of their enemy but had little intention of merging with one another.

The American rebellion was precipitated by the Seven Years' War, a massive global military conflict between Britain and France that lasted from 1756 to 1763. It's remembered in the United States as the French and Indian War, because here the British fought against New France and its aboriginal allies. The war effected a major change in the North American balance of power. In the end, the French were defeated, and all of New France (save the tiny islands of St. Pierre and Miquelon) was handed over to the British Empire. This had two consequences for the people of the continent. First, it removed from the political and military stage the only European society on which Native North Americans could rely. Second, it fostered arrogant triumphalism within the British establishment, which believed it could now remake its North American empire in whatever way it saw fit. These developments played out badly for Indians and British imperialists alike.

When the oldest American nations were founded in the seventeenth century, England was still a minor power grasping at the territorial scraps the Spanish Empire had left behind. Riven by internal disagreements—the English Civil War, Cromwell's dictatorship, the Glorious Revolution—England had outsourced much of the responsibility for creating overseas colonies to private companies, wealthy aristocrats, and religious sects thought safer to observe from afar. This inattention allowed the earliest distinct cultures of Anglo-America to form and develop. By the 1680s, when the Crown tried to impose uniformity and centralization of power, it was already too late to easily do so. Some of the nations were by then several generations old and had traditions, values, and interests of their own.

So what had changed in England to bring about this shift from benignly neglecting the colonies to trying to control them? The answer: the formation of an aggressive new elite.

By the mid-eighteenth century, England had become far more powerful than it had ever been. It had absorbed Scotland, Ireland, and Wales to become the United Kingdom, a truly great Britain with an empire that spanned the globe from the muggy lowlands of India to the frigid wastes of Hudson's Bay. In the decades since the Puritans, Quakers, Cavaliers, and Barbadians first left England, a new social force had taken shape to run this expanding empire: an arrogant ruling class. It even had its own "upper-class" accent, created in the early eighteenth century and regarded (by colonials and the English lower classes alike) as artificial and pretentious. Its members married one another almost exclusively. It founded new elite boarding schools like Eton, Westminster, and Harrow to educate and assimilate its children into its ways. It created powerful new institutions like the Bank of England, the modern Royal Navy, and the East India Company, through which it could control lesser mortals at home and abroad. In the early 1600s England was ruled by aristocrats who had been raised and tutored on their family manors or in their regional shire towns and had provincial identities, accents, and agendas. By 1763 the British ruling class was made up of men who had been educated among their elite peers in centralized patrician boarding schools and who thought of themselves as members of an imperial elite. In the aftermath of the Seven Years' War, they sought to do what King James II had failed to do eighty years earlier: subjugate the American colonies to their will, institutions, bureaucracy, and religion.[1]

Their standardization campaign advanced on many fronts simultaneously. Since the average American colonist's tax burden was just one-twenty-sixth that of his British counterpart, London imposed a vast range of new colonial duties on everything from sugar and tobacco to paper products. Some of the taxes were designed to effect social change; new fees for the issuance of university diplomas and licenses to practice law were higher than those in Great Britain "to keep mean [lowborn] persons out of those institutions in life which they disgrace." This desire to prevent the uncouth from assuming positions of influence also led the London elite to revoke the charter for one of Appalachia's first colleges, the Presbyterian-run Queens College in North Carolina, on the grounds that it would "add encouragement to toleration" of an undesirable religion. In an effort to enhance the strength of the empire's official, tax-sponsored Anglican Church, Presbyterian clergy were banned from solemnizing marriages, Anglican bishops were to be dispatched to America for the first time (horrifying the previously independent Virginia Anglicans), and Anglican missionaries were sent to Boston to convert the "heathen" Puritans there.

Although Britain was deeply in debt from the Seven Years' War, much of the new tax revenue was spent to maintain 10,000 imperial troops in North America whose "main purpose," in the words of a senior British official, was "to secure the dependence of the colonies on Great Britain." This large standing army—unprecedented in America—was charged with enforcing imperial laws, including a 1763 proclamation that banned the colonists from usurping the Indian lands on the other side of the Appalachians. Meanwhile, the Royal Navy stepped up enforcement of trade laws that blocked Yankee merchants from trading with French and Dutch territories in the Caribbean. Smugglers—and there were many—were tried in new military courts that did not provide for jury trials. The East India Company, a favored corporation controlled by the British ruling class, was given special permission to bypass trade laws and colonial merchants to ship and sell tea directly to North America. That these taxes, laws, and occupation forces were imposed on British North America without the consent of each colony's elite or elected representatives made many colonials rightly fear their distinct regional cultures were slated for extinction.[2]

The Native Americans who inhabited what had been New France also feared for their cultural survival. For a century and a half, Indians and New French had enjoyed a mutually satisfactory relationship cemented by gift-exchange ceremonies. But the British military commander, Baron Jeffrey Amherst, canceled all gift-giving and made it clear the savages were to obey or be slaughtered. The result was a massive, coordinated 1763 uprising of a dozen major tribes under the Ottawa tribal leader Pontiac aimed at hurting the British and restoring French control of New France. This war—the one that led the Paxton Boys to march on Philadelphia—resulted in Indians killing or capturing 2,000 colonists in the Appalachian sections of Pennsylvania, Maryland, and Virginia. Baron Amherst, seeking to "Extirpate this Execrable Race," instructed his troops to distribute smallpox-infested blankets to the Indians. Ultimately even biological warfare was unable to bring them to heel, and Amherst was recalled in disgrace.[3] "We tell you now: the French never conquered us, neither did they purchase a foot of our country," Pontiac told Amherst's successor. "If you expect to keep these [Great Lakes region trading] posts, we will expect to have proper returns from you." After making peace, it was all the more important to British imperial officials that the colonists be kept in line and out of the Indians' land beyond the Appalachians.[4]

Once again, Yankeedom was first to rebel.

The nation with the greatest religious and ethnic cohesion, national self-awareness, and commitment to self-governance, Yankees were willing to fight and die to preserve "the New England Way." Some of them saw the struggle as a sequel to the English Civil War and the Glorious Revolution, with good Calvinists fighting the forces of despotism and Popery, this time in the form of a grasping monarch and the "Catholic Lite" Anglican Church with its bishops and idols. From eastern Maine to southern Connecticut, the Puritan churches—now termed Congregationalist—lined up on the patriot side, urging their members to resist. The Puritan notion that self-denial is virtuous was applied in the form of consumer boycotts of British luxury and manufactured goods. As a Rhode Island newspaper put it, citizens must "forsake the use of one of their delights to preserve their liberty." As one Revolutionary War veteran would later explain: "What we meant in going for those Redcoats was this: we always had governed ourselves and we always meant to. They didn't mean that we should."[5]

In December 1773 an organized mob threw £11,000 worth of East India Company tea into Boston Harbor. The British Parliament responded by revoking Massachusetts's governing charter, blockading the port of Boston, and imposing martial law. General Thomas Gage, Amherst's replacement as military commander for North America, was named governor and authorized to house his troops in private homes should he see fit.

This draconian response alarmed the leaders of all the British-controlled nations, prompting them to call a diplomatic meeting among themselves—the First Continental Congress, which convened in September 1774. Meanwhile, each nation reacted in its own way to the developments in New England.

The Yankees' response was culturally revealing: Massachusetts's rebel leaders promptly announced a new representative assembly—the Provincial Congress—and asked all towns to hold elections to fill its seats. By early 1775 the 200 elected delegates had become the de facto government of the colony, collecting taxes and organizing revolutionary militia forces. Even in a time of crisis, Yankees had acted on a community basis, implementing critical decisions at the ballot box and directing their military response through a representative government. New Englanders were so united in their resistance that General Gage's imperial government ceased to function outside of Boston and only existed there because thousands of red-coated British regulars controlled the streets. Impotent and outnumbered, Gage wrote to London asking for 20,000 more soldiers, as many as had been deployed against New France in the Seven Years' War. Open conflict was inevitable.[6]

The aristocratic gentlemen who controlled Tidewater were not nearly as unified and saw no need to gauge public opinion. Like the Yankees, they opposed the new imperial policies, but were divided as to whether to go so far as to contemplate treasonous acts. As usual, the Chesapeake gentry were primarily motivated by the threat the empire posed to their own privileges or "liberties." For generations they had enjoyed near-total control over the politics, courts, and vestries of lowland Virginia, Maryland, and North Carolina, and their influence was spreading in Delaware. They felt themselves to be the equals of the country gentlemen of Britain, to whom many were related, and they were insulted by the idea that English liberties stopped at the shores of England. The arrival of British-appointed bishops intruded on their dominance of parish affairs. The new imperial taxes reduced their plantations' profitability. But in Virginia the Tidewater gentry were divided into two regional camps. Those gentlemen living in the Piedmont—Thomas Jefferson, James Madison, George Mason, and George Washington—had more regular contact with the Appalachian backcountry and a greater awareness of the enormous potential of the lands beyond the mountains, of which Virginia claimed a wide ribbon running all the way to the Pacific. Confident their society could stand on its own, they spearheaded resistance to Britain, applauded the Boston Tea Party, and refused to pay debts to British creditors. But gentlemen from the core Tidewater settlements south of the Rappahannock River were far more cautious, opposing efforts to create a provincial militia and condemning the Tea Party as an attack on private property. They were outvoted in the House of Burgesses, however, as their colony included a large swath of Appalachia, whose representatives were eager to throw off

British restraints on the settlement of what would become Kentucky and Tennessee. But the social cohesion among the gentry was such that even the losers took things in stride; ultimately very few members of the Tidewater elite were willing to fight either for the empire or against their Chesapeake countrymen. As for white commoners in the lowlands, they pretty much did as they were told.[7]

This was not, unsurprisingly, the case in Greater Appalachia. These sprawling borderlands contained the most fervent and committed champions of *both* the patriot and loyalist causes. Each local area chose sides based on whom they saw as the biggest threat to their natural freedoms: the colonial elite on the coast or the British elite across the Atlantic. In Pennsylvania the Borderlanders wanted any excuse to march down to Philadelphia and topple the soft, Madeira-sipping elite there, perhaps putting an end to the Midlands as a separate culture; this made them enthusiastic patriots. In Maryland and Virginia, backcountry folk saw the British as their greatest enemy and threw their lot in with the Piedmont faction of Tidewater aristocrats. Farther south, however, the Borderlanders most hated the great lowland planters and saw the troubles with Britain as an opportunity to throw off their masters and settle old scores. Nowhere was this hatred as great as in North Carolina, where just a few years earlier the Tidewater elite had enthusiastically crushed the Regulator army. The Appalachian people were divided, but whatever side they fought for, their goal was the same: to vanquish their oppressors.[8]

The Midlands wanted nothing to do with a revolution and, in fact, were quite happy with London's centralization effort. Their leaders did their best to stay out of the conflict altogether. Religious pacifism played a key role, particularly among the Amish, Mennonites, and Moravians who'd fled the horrors of war in Germany. Most Germans, wanting to be left alone and content with the status quo, saw no advantage in leaving the empire, which would likely give greater power to their unpleasant Scots-Irish and Tidewater neighbors. Quakers, who still had considerable influence over Midlands affairs, had little complaint with the monarchy, which had granted William Penn the charter that made their colony possible. Tolerant of other religions, they had no qualms about the increased influence of the Anglican Church, which many of their own sons and grandsons were joining. The promise of greater imperial control over the

Midlands would spare them from having to take up arms in its defense, as some had been compelled to do when the Paxton Boys marched on Philadelphia a few years before. It would also protect them from their real enemies, the bigoted Yankees and, especially, the belligerent, expansive Borderlanders, who now formed a majority of Pennsylvania's population. As the revolution approached, Quakers declared their neutrality but carried on their business with the empire. The Midlands—southeastern Pennsylvania, western New Jersey, and the northern parts of Maryland and Delaware—would be passively loyalist throughout the conflict, frustrating transplanted Philadelphians who supported the patriot cause. "The principles of Quakerism," fumed the British-born ex-Quaker Thomas Paine, "have a direct tendency to make a man the quiet and inoffensive subject of any and every government which is set over him."[9]

New Netherland was the loyalists' greatest stronghold on the continent. In the Dutch settlement area—the three counties that now comprise Brooklyn, Queens, and Staten Island plus the Bronx, southern Westchester, and Manhattan—public opinion was overwhelmingly against resisting the empire. Both the Dutch and the British imperial elite who governed the province feared a revolution would cause themselves to be toppled from power and that much of New York would fall under Yankee control. Indeed, large swaths already were. Areas settled by Yankees—eastern Long Island, northern Westchester, rural Albany County, and the seven northeastern counties in the Green Mountains (*Verts monts*, the New French called them)—had followed the rest of Yankeedom into open rebellion. If the colonies revolted, everyone knew the province would descend into civil war and could very well be dismembered.[10]

British officials had grounds to hope the slave lords of the Deep South would also remain loyal. The great planters were mostly Anglican, hostile to democratic ideas, and entirely dependent on the export of sugar and cotton for their livelihoods. Like the Tidewater gentry, they identified themselves as Normans or Cavaliers, with all those terms' Royalist overtones, and ran the lowlands of South Carolina, Georgia, and southernmost North Carolina as they pleased. Unlike their Chesapeake cousins, they were outnumbered by their slaves three to one and greatly feared any disruption that might give their property an opportunity to revolt. There was no talk of rebelling against the crown among their counterparts in the

British West Indies, where British power was the best guarantee of internal and external security. But Deep Southern planters didn't live on an island and therefore had more room to maneuver. While they did express their disapproval of imperial efforts to increase their taxes and limit their authority, their protests were balanced against the need to keep what they called their "domestic enemies" in bondage. Planter Henry Laurens summed up the great planters' position in a letter to a friend in January 1775: they sought only "reasonable liberty" within the empire; "Independence is not [a] view of America . . . a sober sensible man wishes for."[11]

Accordingly, the slave lords acted through their provincial assemblies to support boycotts of British goods and sat back expecting London to relent. "A bloodless self-denying opposition was all that South Carolina designed, and was all the sacrifice which, as she supposed, would be required at her hands," a Charleston physician recalled of the sentiments there in early 1775. While the planters' own goal was extremely conservative—to avoid any change in the status quo—plenty of people in the colonies they controlled felt differently. In the backcountry, Borderlanders were eager to break the planters' monopoly on power and would be happy to take whatever side allowed them to do so. And in the lowlands, planters shuddered as rumors began circulating among their slaves "that the present contest [with Britain] was [about] obliging us to give them liberty." The planters prayed the other nations wouldn't pull the continent into open warfare, for they knew their tyrannical system might not withstand a major shock. The "great part of our weakness," a militia officer reported, "consists in having such a number of slaves among us."[12]

The First Continental Congress, held in Philadelphia in early September 1774, was the first time the leaders of the nations came together to coordinate policy across the colonies. The fifty-six delegates all knew that forging colonial collaboration wasn't going to be easy, not least because of negative stereotypes associated with one another's regional cultures. New Englanders were distrusted by the elites of New Netherland, Tidewater, and the Deep South for their commitment to equality. John Livingston, a delegate from New York City, left John Adams of Massachusetts with the impression that he "dread[ed] New England, the leveling spirit, etc." Quakers had not forgotten how their ancestors had been tortured and executed by the Puritans. Many others feared the Yankees were scheming to seize control of all of British North America. "Boston aims at nothing less than the sovereignty of the whole continent, I know it," a South Carolina planter told Adams's cousin, Josiah Quincy Jr., at a 1773 dinner party. "There is a certain degree of jealousy in the minds of some that we aim at total independency," Sam Adams reported, ". . . and that as we are a hardy and brave people we shall in time rule over them all." Quincy, for his part, found on a visit to the Deep South that the "luxury, dissipation, life, sentiments and manners of the leading people [made] them neglect, despise, and be careless of the true interests of mankind in general."[13]

Adams would famously recall that the subsequent rebellion expressed "principles as various as the thirteen states that went through with it." They "had grown up under [different] constitutions of government," their "manners, and habits had so little resemblance . . . their intercourse had been so rare and their knowledge of each other so imperfect that to unite them in the same principles and the same system of action was certainly a very difficult enterprise." But while the differences Adams described were real, there weren't thirteen varieties represented in the revolution; there were six, and they didn't correspond to colonial borders.[14]

Throughout the proceedings, representatives of the four New England colonies moved in lockstep with one another, backed by the delegates from Yankee-settled Suffolk County, Long Island, and Orange County, New York. Having been the ones to call the conference, they pushed for the other delegations to agree to a full embargo of British goods and an immediate complete ban on exports to Britain as well. The Yankees also wanted the other colonies to refuse to pay British taxes and to establish their own militia forces and provisional governments.[15]

The Yankees' greatest allies were the representatives from the Piedmont section of Tidewater: Richard Henry Lee, Patrick Henry, and George Washington of Virginia and Thomas Johnson of Maryland. Confident in their ability to rule independent states, they aligned with the Yankees and convinced their more moderate "old Tidewater" colleagues to join them.

The Deep South's delegates were far more ambivalent. Georgia had refused to send any delegates at all because, its leaders explained, elite opinion "seemed to fluctuate between liberty and convenience." Four of South Carolina's five representatives to the Congress were fearful of taking steps that might result in a break with the empire. They opposed the proposed ban on exports and generally hoped that the boycott on British imports would convince London to back down.[16]

True to stereotype, the New Netherland delegation was wracked by internal bickering. Of their nine delegates, five were against resisting London. The four revolutionaries were all men opposed to the imperial status quo in New York: two middle-class Dutchmen, a lawyer transplanted from Yankee-settled Orange County, and Philip Livingston, an Albany-born, Yale-educated Presbyterian. The conservatives looked on these men as rustic, uncouth commoners. The New Netherland conservatives—who represented a majority of both the New York and New Jersey delegations—were proper gentlemen who wished to avoid open rebellion and outright independence, as they knew they would be unlikely to win many popular elections on account of heavy Yankee in-migration, especially in upstate New York. As distant commerce was the essential foundation of New Netherland's economic system, they also opposed the proposed boycotts of British trade but would ultimately be outvoted by delegates from the other nations.[17]

Delegates from the Midlands were nearly unanimous in their timidity, regardless of whether they represented Pennsylvania, New Jersey, Delaware, or Maryland. Eleven of the thirteen Midlander delegates were opposed to armed resistance and believed Britain had every right to tax and govern its colonial subjects. The leader of the overall conservative movement at the Congress was Midlander Joseph Galloway of Philadelphia, who argued that intercolonial cooperation was impossible because the colonies were "totally independent of each other" in law, customs, and goals. He put forward an alternative to the Yankee strategy: the colonies would remain in the empire but would demand an "American legislature" which would share lawmaking powers with the British Parliament, with each body able to veto the other. While supported by conservative New Netherlanders, the plan was rejected by the Yankee, Tidewater, and Deep Southern delegates, who refused to transfer further control of what they explicitly termed their "countries" to a central authority.[18]

Most revealing, the sixth nation was not represented at the Congress at all, though it held perhaps a majority of the population of Pennsylvania and both Carolinas. The colonial assemblies refused to allow Appalachia to participate, depriving the enormous region of any voice at the proceedings. The closest thing they had to a delegate was Thomas McKean, a fiery Ulster-Scots patriot from Philadelphia who represented northern Delaware at the meeting and foiled his Midland colleagues at every turn. In North Carolina, where Borderlanders formed a majority, two of three congressional delegates had played key roles in crushing the backcountry Regulators in 1771. Excluded from the proceedings in Philadelphia, Appalachian people reflexively opposed whatever position their respective provincial delegations took. Thus Pennsylvania Borderlanders became ardent patriots (in opposition to the passivity of the Midland elite), while the Carolina and Virginia backcountry became a stronghold of loyalism (in response to the cautious patriotism of the lowland oligarchs).

While the Congress did bring the other five nations together, it was as an alliance of treaty partners, not as a prelude to national unity. When the meeting adjourned in late October 1774, the diplomats had agreed to a joint boycott of British goods and to impose an export moratorium if London failed to back down by mid-1775. They endorsed a petition to the king in which they acknowledged his authority and begged him for redress of their grievances. The delegates returned home, waiting anxiously for the British response. "We wait to know," a South Carolinian planter wrote that winter. "God knows we have little power to resist by arms."[19]

But the British ruling class had no intention of backing down to the colonials. By the time the export ban went into effect, the cemeteries of New England were already filling up with the bodies of Yankee and British war dead. The American wars of liberation had begun.

CHAPTER 11

Six Wars of Liberation

In *Albion's Seed* (1989), historian David Hackett Fischer makes the case for there having been not one American War of Independence but four: a popular insurrection in New England, a professional "gentleman's war" in the South, a savage civil war in the backcountry, and a "non-violent economic and diplomatic struggle" spearheaded by the elites of what I call the Midlands. The four wars, he argues, were fought sequentially and waged in different ways and for different goals.

What we call the American Revolution did indeed play out very differently in the various nations of the Atlantic seaboard. But there weren't four neat struggles, one unfolding as the previous one concluded; rather, there were six very different liberation wars, one for each affected nation. Some occurred simultaneously and two involved invasions by one American nation into another. Despite the presence of a nominally continental army, most of the fighting was done by militia forces and guerrilla bands with local loyalties, and many bloody battles occurred in the complete absence of British forces. Wars of colonial liberation are often ugly, combining resistance to imperial forces with a civil war between rival factions hoping to seize control. Ethnic minorities and indigenous elites often side with the colonial power for fear of what might happen to them in the new order. The American wars of liberation were no exception.

Recognizing what each nation was fighting for—and how it did so—is essential to understanding what the "revolution" was all about and the limits it placed on the strange confederation to which it gave birth.

The first of the wars broke out in Yankeedom, where it took the form of a mass uprising against the British effort to dismantle the region's self-governance and key cultural institutions. Nowhere in British America was rebellion more universally supported than in New England and the parts of New York and Pennsylvania settled by New Englanders. By 1775

Yankees had already organized a clandestine intelligence and communication systems, a shadow government of "public safety committees," and a network of community-based military units ready to turn out at a minute's notice. Yankees fought not for the universal rights of man, freedom of religion, or the liberties of their ruling class, but in defense of the way they'd always lived their lives and regulated their affairs. They were defending local control by elected representatives (where local usually meant town governments, not provincial ones), the primacy of the Congregational (i.e., Puritan) Church, and their Anglo-Saxon birthright of freedom from tyranny. God's "chosen people" would not give up their divinely ordained ways easily.

In true Yankee fashion, the war was largely fought by citizen militias organized at the local level and led by elected officers. In founding the new units, townspeople literally drew up their own "covenants" spelling out how each would function. Fiercely independent, the Yankee minutemen regarded their commanders as public servants rather than superiors, and in the early stages of the war often challenged their decisions; since Yankees were fighting to not be given orders, they were hardly going to passively accept them on the battlefield.

This egalitarian streak frustrated and alarmed Continental Army officers from other regions. When General Washington arrived to take command of the Yankee forces besieging occupied Boston in the summer of 1775, he was amazed at their ragtag appearance, insubordinate attitude, and insistence on serving in units made up of and led by their own neighbors. Only when outside commanders learned to explain their reasons for giving a particular order did they begin to earn the trust of their Yankee subordinates. Washington denounced them as "nasty people" in his private letters, even as he publicly pleaded "that all distinctions of colonies will be laid aside" among "troops of the United Provinces of North America." When a few companies of Tidewater sharpshooters joined the siege a few weeks later, Virginians expressed horror that ex-slaves were serving alongside whites in the New England militia.[1]

Open warfare broke out on April 19, 1775, when a column of British soldiers was sent out from Boston to seize gunpowder stockpiled in Concord, Massachusetts. Fighting erupted when citizen militia confronted them on the town green of Lexington, and again at Concord Bridge, where local militiamen forced a British retreat. Imperial troops suffered heavy casualties during their withdrawal as militia from surrounding towns attacked them from the roadsides. Narrowly escaping across the water to Boston, the British found themselves besieged by thousands of Yankee minutemen. Meanwhile, word of the fighting spread to the other colonies with explosive effect.

Ultimately, the British were unable to break the siege of Boston, retreating eleven months later to Nova Scotia, itself threatened by seaborne raids organized by Yankees in eastern Maine. In effect, Yankeedom had won its independence in March 1776. From that point forward, New England would serve as the primary stronghold for liberation forces in the other nations, providing the lion's share of food, supplies, money, and troops to Washington's Continental Army. Coastal settlements would face occasional British raids, and for more than a year Yankees had reason to fear a British attack from the west, but by 1778, George III had given up hope of forcing New England back into the empire. Overall, American independence was still very much in doubt, but the Yankee war of liberation was complete.

If Yankeedom was the stronghold of the rebellion, New Netherland was its antithesis: the capital of loyalist North America and the nexus of British military power on the continent. It was to here that loyalist refugees from the other nations fled, and from here that the Royal Navy and British Army organized in their campaigns of reconquest. Under the uninterrupted control of British forces from September 1776 onward, Greater New York City became a thriving, self-sufficient city-state with a near-monopoly on imperial trade.

New Netherlanders were generally suspicious of the rebel cause for three reasons. Unlike the nations around them, they didn't feel the need to defend their sovereignty because they never truly had it, given that the Dutch West India Company, the Duke of York, and crown governors had all ruled the place without reference to local opinion. The Dutch, who still comprised about a fifth of the population, were by no means certain that their tradition of cultural and religious tolerance would be safe in an independent province of New York, which would likely be dominated by Yankees (who already controlled much of the province's interior). For New

Netherland elites of all ethnicities, liberation could not be expected to bring either freedom or independence. When the Second Continental Congress convened in early 1775, the provincial assembly voted two to one against sending delegates, and even those appointed by a rebel committee were not given the authority to vote on independence.

Nonetheless, when news of Lexington reached Manhattan, a rebel minority seized power by forming gangs that terrorized the authorities and their supporters. The royal governor fled to the *Duchess of Gordon*, a Royal Navy frigate stationed in the harbor, where he lived for months, holding council meetings and issuing impotent decrees. Other prominent residents departed for England, while many of those who stayed behind were beaten, taunted, jailed, or "carried and hauled" through the city by angry mobs. In February 1776 Washington's Yankee-dominated army occupied the city, but it was not universally welcomed. "Hundreds in this colony are active against us," a New York City patriot wrote John Adams. "Tories openly express their sentiments in favor of the enemy and live unpunished."[2]

New Netherland's patriot uprising met with sudden and complete defeat in the summer of 1776 following the arrival of a British armada of 30 warships, 400 transports, and 24,000 soldiers. This invasion force scattered General Washington's army, retook the city, and by the end of September occupied an area conforming almost exactly to the boundaries of the New Netherland nation. The rebels dispersed and ecstatic townspeople carried British soldiers around on their shoulders. "A Universal joy," a German-born minister reported, "spread over all countenances." Loyalist refugees came to the city in droves, first from hiding places in the surrounding countryside, then from Boston, the Midlands, Norfolk, Charleston, and Savannah. Secure behind British lines, New York City's population swelled from 22,000 to 33,000 during the course of the war, the newcomers joining loyalist military units or rebuilding transatlantic commerce. Civil government was restored; theaters, taverns, and coffeehouses prospered; and propagandist John Rivington returned from exile to edit the most influential loyalist newspaper on the continent, the *Royal Gazette*. Thousands of loyalists joined militias and provincial forces in the New Netherland zone and regularly foraged in Connecticut and New Jersey, skirmishing with Yankee counterparts throughout the war.[3]

As the headquarters of both Admiral Richard Howe's fleet and his brother General William Howe's North American military command, New Netherland was the primary staging area for both the ultimately disastrous counteroffensive against Yankeedom and the initially successful occupation of the neutral Midlands. Both strategies were based on the Howes' recognition of regional cultural differences in British North America. The first campaign correctly identified Yankeedom as the source of the rebellion and sought to quarantine the region by a two-pronged invasion of the Hudson River Valley; once the Yankee-settled interior of New York was pacified, New England proper could be simultaneously invaded from three sides. The Midlands strategy correctly assumed that most people in that region wished to settle imperial differences without resorting to open warfare. The Howe brothers realized that victory in the Midlands depended on winning hearts and minds, not on unleashing total military power upon its inhabitants. They accordingly moved gingerly against Washington's army after it withdrew to upper Manhattan, herding it out of New Netherland with obvious flanking maneuvers in an effort to avoid civilian casualties while still demonstrating the invincibility of British forces. They even hosted a dinner for rebel leaders aboard a warship in the harbor in an unsuccessful effort to convince them to stand down peaceably.[4]

Unfortunately for the Howes, the first part of their strategy collapsed with the defeat and surrender of their northern army at Saratoga, New York, in October 1777 to an essentially Yankee army from New Hampshire, Massachusetts, and upstate New York. The victory was a decisive turning point in the war, not only because it preserved Yankeedom's independence but because it convinced France to join the conflict, radically altering the balance of power. The fate of the Howes' second strategy will be described momentarily, but neither it nor subsequent British efforts would save Britain's North American empire.

Even after the ultimate British surrender at Yorktown in 1782, many New Netherlanders held out hope that the crown would keep control of the region as a condition of the peace treaty they were negotiating with a weak new confederation calling itself "the United States." When news came in 1783 that no part of the thirteen colonies would be retained, some 30,000 civilians—perhaps half the area's wartime population—fled

Greater New York City for Britain, Nova Scotia, and New Brunswick. New Netherland had fought a war *against* liberation and had lost badly.[5]

The pacifist Midlands did its best to remain neutral in a conflict which most of its inhabitants had wanted no part in. Even after Lexington and Concord, leading figures such as James Wilson and John Dickinson opposed independence, and their political allies were the big winners in the Pennsylvania assembly elections of May 1776. The region wouldn't have rebelled at all if a majority of the states attending the Second Continental Congress hadn't voted to "totally suppress" Pennsylvania's government. In effect, representatives of Yankeedom, Tidewater, and the Deep South intervened in Midlands affairs, sanctioning a coup d'état against their legitimate, but cautious, government.

The result, in mid-1776, was the assumption of power in Pennsylvania by a vocal patriot minority backed by the Appalachian half of the colony and entirely dependent on the Congress for validity. With little local support, this patriot government and its Delaware counterpart arrested anyone who opposed the war and searched the homes of any who hadn't "manifested their attachment to the American cause." Pennsylvania Quaker leaders were rounded up in 1777, denied habeas corpus, and deported to the Appalachian section of Virginia for imprisonment, further alienating the sect's followers. New Jersey simply fell into anarchy. "The state is totally deranged [and] without government," a Continental Army general observed before the British moved in. "Many [officials] have gone to the enemy for protection, others are out of the state, and the few that remain are mostly indecisive in their conduct."[6]

Shortly after occupying New York, General Howe sent troops into the Midlands to bring the region under British control and encourage its inhabitants to stand with the empire. After skirmishing with Washington's weakening army in the winter of 1776–1777, British forces invaded the Midlands sections of Maryland, Delaware, and Pennsylvania by sea. Encountering little resistance, they captured Philadelphia in September 1777, sending the Continental Congress into exile in the Appalachian backcountry. Greeted enthusiastically by the city's inhabitants, Howe's army swatted back a counterstrike by Washington's Yankee-and-Borderlander-dominated army at Germantown and settled into warm and comfortable urban quarters for the winter. Washington's forces bivouacked in Valley Forge, twenty miles to the north, and soon discovered that Midlands farmers preferred to supply the British because they paid in hard currency. Some German pacifists offered support to the rebel army in the form of medical care or humanitarian supplies but shunned direct participation in the war on either side. Meanwhile, former congressional delegate Joseph Galloway assumed leadership of the civil administration and organized a corps of loyalist troops in Philadelphia that raided rebel supply lines to Valley Forge. Galloway did his best to make Philadelphia a showplace for the merits of benevolent royal administration in the hopes of negotiating a peace based on his previous plan for an "American Assembly." But while the city's social life bloomed with balls, concerts, and theater performances, the British defeat at Saratoga doomed Galloway's scheme. Fearing a French naval attack, the British abandoned the Midlands in the summer of 1778, transferring their forces to New York and the West Indies.[7]

With the British withdrawal, the Midlands were subjected to a Continental Army occupation spearheaded by Pennsylvania's Appalachian residents. Pennsylvania's rebel assembly, which had operated in exile in Lancaster, enforced laws that made it illegal to speak or write in opposition to any of its decisions. Ordinary citizens were given the power to jail without trial anyone they considered to be an "enemy to the American cause." The executive organ of the revolutionary government, the revolutionary Supreme Executive Council, was controlled by Borderlanders from the backcountry who were by design grossly overrepresented in the body; they had the power to have anyone accused of disloyalty stripped of his possessions or simply executed. The law was used against opponents and pacifists alike, with a number of Mennonite farmers being left destitute after all their property was taken from them for refusing, on religious grounds, to take an oath of loyalty. For the duration of the war, the tolerance and pluralism of the Midlands was suppressed by occupation forces from neighboring nations.[8]

Until the Battle of Lexington, the Deep South's all-powerful ruling class was ambivalent about fighting a war of liberation. This was not surprising, given that the region's identity was based on hierarchy, deference, inherited privilege, and aristocratic rule—all in perfect accord with the aims of the British ruling classes. There was no pressure from below to take up arms against Britain, as members of the white underclass weren't allowed to participate in politics and were dependent on planters as landlords, buyers of their products, and judges of their legal disputes. The planters regarded their slaves as an excellent argument for not doing anything that might create instability and provoke another uprising. Ironically, they would soon conclude that the only way to protect their status quo was to free themselves from British rule.

The news of Lexington horrified the Deep Southern slave lords, changing their attitudes almost overnight. The white inhabitants, congressional delegate Henry Laurens wrote, were swept into "a delirium" of "Fear & Zeal." They had supported the Continental Congress's boycotts, fully expecting Britain to back down. Their bluff called, the planters saw their world turned upside down, and many began imagining conspiracies everywhere. Rumors circulated that the British were smuggling arms to the slaves in preparation for a mass uprising. The region's newspaper published reports that ships had been sent from England carrying 78,000 bayonet-equipped guns to distribute to blacks, "Roman Catholics, the Indians, and Canadians" to "subdue" the colonies. "His Majesty's ministers and other servants," the surgeon to the royal garrison in Charleston reported, were imagined to be organizing "slaves to rebel against their masters and to cut their throats." Residents were advised to bring arms and ammunition with them to Sunday church services, in case there was a rebellion. Slaves were rounded up on the slightest suspicion and executed in public in slow, horrible ways. The royal governor, Archibald Campbell, tried to pardon one obviously innocent slave but was warned that if he did so, vigilantes would hang the condemned man at the governor's door and then "raise a flame [that] all the water in the Cooper River could not extinguish." The frightened governor backed down and would soon go into hiding himself.[9]

In this most reactionary of rebellions, the Deep Southern leadership didn't try to overthrow a royal government it distrusted but simply isolated and ignored it. As soon as the slave conspiracy rumors reached the planters, they organized military resistance through their Provincial Congress and a newly formed Council of Safety, which in June 1775 raised militia troops to meet the threat. In effect, they seized power without contemplation, debate, or combat. Governor Campbell's presence was tolerated so long as he posed no threat, but when he began making contact with the planters' opponents in Greater Appalachia, the planters considered arresting him. Campbell, seeing the game was up, fled to the sloop-of-war HMS *Tamar* in September. In February 1776 he was forced from the harbor when South Carolina militia seized a strategic island. Even then the colony's planters stopped short of declaring independence, announcing their government to be in force only during "the present dispute between Great Britain and the colonies." Their provisional constitution was a near-carbon copy of the colonial one. Planter William Henry Drayton, not one for introspection, would later claim that the British had left them with a stark choice: "Slavery or Independence." In reality, the planters had been forced into independence in order to preserve slavery.[10]

The situation in lowland Georgia was much the same, except that the planters there were even more reluctant to sever ties with Britain. Loyalist sentiment was so strong that, after refusing to participate in the First Continental Congress, the colony sent only one delegate to the Second Congress: a Yankee transplant living in a Congregationalist enclave. Another Georgian "founding father," James Wood, became so frustrated with the planters' early failure to support the war that he returned to his native Pennsylvania and joined the militia there. A later delegate to the Continental Congress, John Zubly, expressed the Deep Southern point of view to that body in no uncertain terms: "A republican government is little better than a government of devils." Rumors of a British-backed slave rebellion played a part in changing prevailing attitudes, with royal governor James Wright himself predicting they would have "an exceeding bad effect." But in the end, the governor later concluded, the planters of Georgia had simply followed "the voice and opinions of men of overheated ideas" in South Carolina.[11]

The British easily recaptured the Deep South at the end of 1778 when they executed their "Southern Strategy." Having accepted the loss of Yankeedom, London focused on reclaiming Georgia and the Carolinas, rightly judging the Deep Southerners to be tepid revolutionaries. If things went well, Virginia might be squeezed from both sides, creating a rump British North America stretching from Greater New York to Florida (a sparsely populated territory then under British control).[12] In January 1779 a small invasion force of 3,500 recaptured Savannah without firing a shot and in a few weeks had complete control of lowland Georgia. (Docile Georgia would be the only rebel colony to be formally reabsorbed into the empire, where it would remain for the rest of the war.) Charleston successfully resisted an initial 1779 siege but surrendered to a second one in early 1780. Leading "patriots" like Henry Middleton pledged loyalty to the crown to avoid having their property seized, while others were shot and killed by their numerous loyalist neighbors. The Deep South was pacified. Had the British not also had to deal with the Appalachian sections of Georgia and the Carolinas, their Southern strategy would almost certainly have succeeded.[13]

If so much of British North America was ambivalent toward or hostile to independence, how is it that the non-Yankee colonies managed to liberate themselves from the empire? There are two reasons: the firm commitment of the Tidewater gentry to their personal independence, and the presence of an Appalachian majority in Pennsylvania, the Carolinas, and Georgia, a people willing to fight anyone who tried to lord it over them.

Greater Appalachia—poor, isolated, and not in control of a single colonial government—had the most complicated involvement in the wars of liberation. The Borderlanders seized on the pretext of the "revolution" to assert their independence from outside control, but, as previously mentioned, this took different forms in each region, sometimes in each community.

In Pennsylvania the Borderlanders were the shock troops of the revolution, which provided them an opportunity to usurp power in the province from the Midlander elite in Philadelphia. Here the Scots-Irish so dominated the rebel armies that one British officer called them the "line of Ireland." In London King George III referred to the entire conflict as "a Presbyterian War," while Horace Walpole told Parliament: "Cousin America has run off with a Presbyterian parson!" The army that famously shivered at Valley Forge was made up almost entirely of Yankees and Borderlanders, and it was the Scots-Irish backcountry leadership that drafted Pennsylvania's 1776 Constitution, granting the Appalachian districts effective control over the colony. By war's end they had liberated themselves from the Midlanders and British alike.[14]

In the Tidewater-controlled colonies of Maryland and Virginia, the Scots-Irish-led Borderlanders saw the British as the greatest threat to their freedom. Eager to expand over the mountains, they found common cause with the Tidewater gentry who had given them reasonably fair government representation. What loyalist forces there were tended to be from German communities—Midlander cultural enclaves lost in a forest of patriots.

By contrast, most Borderlanders in North Carolina identified the Tidewater elite as their primary oppressors and took up arms against them to avenge the suppression of the Regulator movement a few years before. The colony's backcountry settlers, John Adams would later observe, had "such a hatred toward the rest of other fellow citizens that in 1775, when the war broke out, they would not join them." Backed by a sympathetic royal governor, they fought an unsuccessful campaign against the gentry-led rebel army in 1776. Meanwhile, other backcountry communities were fighting the British, carrying the banner of Scotland into battle, to which some Borderlanders added the Scottish motto: *Nemo me impune lacessit*, loosely translated as "Don't Tread on Me." When the British Army under Cornwallis arrived in the area in 1780, the Borderlanders turned on one another, plunging the colony into a civil war with horrors worthy of the conflicts their ancestors had fought on the British borderlands. Loyalist forces raped young girls in front of their parents, while patriots whipped and tortured suspected enemy collaborators. Many armed gangs had no loyalties whatsoever and simply preyed on whomever they wished, kidnapping children for ransom, looting homes, and assassinating rivals.[15]

The South Carolina and Georgia backcountry also descended into civil war, albeit for different reasons. Here the Deep Southern oligarchs who controlled the colonial governments were especially resistant to sharing power with the rabble. In South Carolina the backcountry made up three-quarters of the colony's white population but had only two of forty-eight seats in the provincial assembly; this arrangement led one agitator to denounce the planters for keeping "half their subjects in a state of slavery," by whom he meant not blacks but Borderlanders like himself. Here few "loyalists" cared about Britain, but they aligned themselves with the king simply because he was fighting their lowland enemies. In some communities,

Borderlanders regarded the British as their greatest oppressors, creating the ingredients for a backcountry civil war in addition to the struggle with the lowlanders. Once it started, the fighting became exceedingly ugly, a guerrilla war marked by ambushes, the execution of prisoners, and the torture, rape, and plunder of noncombatants. One British officer said the Carolina backcountymen were "more savage than the Indians," while a Continental Army officer, Robert E. Lee's father, Henry, observed that those in Georgia "exceeded the Goths and Vandals in their schemes of plunder, murder, and iniquity."[16]

The situation became even worse during the British reconquest of the Deep South when Lord Cornwallis made the unwise decision to send zealous subordinates to "pacify" the backcountry. Leading mixed legions of British troops, Hessian mercenaries, New Netherlander volunteers, and backcountry militiamen, these commanders adopted the Borderlanders' tactics, hacking prisoners to death with swords and burning homes. Patriot Borderlanders returned in kind, unleashing an orgy of barbarism that laid waste the countryside. By exacerbating a bloody civil war, loyalist sympathizer Francis Kinloch told a former royal governor, the British had lost the war for hearts and minds in South Carolina. "The lower sort of people, who were in many parts . . . originally attached to the British government, have suffered so severely and been so frequently deceived, that Great Britain has now a hundred enemies where it had one before."[17]

By the end of the war, South Carolina was completely devastated. "Every field, every plantation showed marks of ruin and devastation [and] not a person was to be met with in the roads," a traveler in the lowlands reported. "Not the vestiges of horses, cattle, hogs, or deer, &c. was to be found [and] the squirrels and birds of every kind were totally destroyed," another said of the backcountry. "No living creature was to be seen, except now and then a few [vultures] picking the bones of some unfortunate fellows who had been shot or cut down and left in the woods above ground."[18]

Dispersed over a thousand miles of difficult terrain and without a government of their own, Appalachia's people did not act in political unison, but their conduct was similar. Faced with external threats to their freedom, individual neighborhood communities did not hesitate to take up arms and fight using any means at their disposal. Those in the northern parts of the region quickly vanquished their enemies and captured political power, not only in Pennsylvania, but in what would become Kentucky and West Virginia. But in the less-developed southern half of the region, victory was elusive, reducing the area to a condition much resembling the British borderlands from which their parents had fled. Here, a war of liberation had been fought and lost.

Tidewater was largely spared from the fighting until the final phases of the war, but it committed large numbers of officers and troops to fight on other fronts. The gentry, accustomed to giving orders and having them followed, assumed they would dominate the Continental Army's officer class, especially as Yankeedom and Appalachia had so few well-bred people. But while the commander in chief, George Washington, was a Tidewater gentleman, most of the Continental Army's generals were Yankees—including a number of very successful common-born men such as Henry Knox, John Stark, and William Heath—reflecting the fact that most of its enlisted men also came from New England. The Tidewater gentry did organize some of their subjects into units like the Virginia Sharpshooters and led them in campaigns from Boston to Georgia, but in general, Chesapeake Country contributed few enlisted men to the conflict. In battle the Tidewater officer class usually adhered to the gentlemanly codes of eighteenth-century warfare, with honor and decorum paramount.

Tidewater liberated itself very early on and with relatively little bloodshed. In Virginia, royal governor John Murray did himself few favors by threatening to arm slaves to defend royal authority. Driven from Williamsburg in June 1775, he, too, found himself hiding on a Royal Navy frigate in the Chesapeake. A few months later he called on loyalists everywhere to rally to him there and issued a proclamation offering slaves their freedom if they took up arms for the king, a proposition that turned Tidewater against him. Hundreds of slaves rallied to Governor Murray and some would die fighting the Tidewater militia at the Battle of Great Bridge, near Norfolk, where Murray was defeated and forced to abandon the Chesapeake, taking some of his "black loyalists" with him.[19]

When the British returned to the Virginia Tidewater in 1780, some 10,000 slaves fled their masters to join them, forming the region's largest loyalist force. "Slaves flock to them from every quarter," one planter lamented. Unfortunately for the slaves, Cornwallis's forces became pinned down between a French fleet and the Continental Army in the little tobacco port of Yorktown and surrendered in October 1781. The event ended the war, confirmed Tidewater's liberation, and ended any hope of freedom for its quarter-million slaves.[20]

Though confronted by a common threat, the nations had not been united in the conflict. Each fought its own war of liberation, but most in New Netherland, the Midlands, and southern Appalachia fought on the losing side and were vanquished in 1781. The victors—Yankeedom, Tidewater, the Deep South, and northern Appalachia—would fight over the spoils, including the terms under which they would try to cement their wartime alliance.

CHAPTER 12

Independence or Revolution?

By the end of the American wars of liberation, the six nations of the eastern seaboard had forged closer connections to one another than they had ever had before. Forced into a military alliance, the dominant nations had successfully fought off threats to their identities and practices and vanquished pacifist Midlanders and loyalist-minded New Netherlanders. But the effort to preserve their separate cultures had produced two unexpected side effects: a loose political alliance with some characteristics of statehood, and a popular movement demanding "democracy," a prospect the national leaders found quite alarming. In the immediate postwar period, the nations confronted both developments and each had its own take on how to deal with them. The compromises they negotiated or imposed profoundly shaped the American experience.

When the wars began, the only structure the colonies shared was a diplomatic body, the Continental Congress. The Congress was essentially an international treaty group whose member states passed resolutions by a majority vote. If one party didn't stand by its obligations, there wasn't much the other members could do to address the problem, short of imposing their will by military force. To have the ability to achieve the latter, and to better fight off the British threat, the treaty parties created a joint military command, much as the North Atlantic Treaty Organization did a century and a half later. They called this the Continental Army and, with much inter-national bickering, it was placed under a supreme commander, George Washington.

During the wars it became clear that the treaty group needed more powers if it was to provide for the alliance's military needs and, more important, maintain peaceful relations among the member states. In July 1776 John Dickinson of (Midland) Pennsylvania feared New England would part ways with the other colonies, causing a collapse in the alliance. Such a breakdown, he once warned, would unleash "a multitude of commonwealths, crimes, and calamities—centuries of mutual jealousies, hatreds, wars, and devastations, until at last the exhausted provinces shall sink into slavery under the yoke of some fortunate conqueror." "Disunion among ourselves [is] the greatest danger we have," John Witherspoon of (New Netherland) northern New Jersey, warned his congressional colleagues that same month. Richard Henry Lee of (Tidewater) Virginia argued a formal union was vital for ensuring "internal peace." If the colonies remained separate after the war, Witherspoon added, there would be "a more lasting war, more bloody and more hopeless war, among the colonies themselves."[1]

The response to these fears was the first United States constitution, the Articles of Confederation, drafted in the midst of the war and not ratified until 1781. Due to the distrust between the nations, this document did not create a nation-state, or even a unified federation, but rather a political entity much like the early twenty-first-century European Union—a voluntary alliance of sovereign states that had agreed to delegate certain powers to a common administration. Reflecting the conservative nature of the American leaders, the powers designated were essentially those that had previously been the duty of the British crown: foreign relations and the making and waging of war. The member states themselves could continue to govern themselves as they always had, without taking on new responsibilities. The Continental Congress would take over the role of the British Parliament (or today's European Parliament), passing alliance-level legislation connected with diplomacy and war and leaving most powers with the individual states. Each state could reject any congressional measure with which it disagreed, and each retained "its sovereignty, freedom, and independence." As in the European Union, Confederation institutions didn't derive from or serve "the people," but rather the member states, as represented by their own sovereign legislatures.[2]

Even after drafting and endorsing this first constitution, Congress remained starkly divided along regional lines. Between August 1777 and May 1787, Yankee New England faced off against the four Southern states represented by delegates from Tidewater and the Deep South. Over this decade-long time period, not a single delegate from either of these blocs ever voted consistently with a colleague from the other. Delegates from "the middle states" served as the kingmakers, allying with one bloc or the other; traditional scholars have described these middle delegates as acting like swing voters, but a closer examination shows that delegates from New Netherland, the Midlands, and Appalachia tended to stick with their own. In New Jersey, for instance, voting habits in both Congress and the new state assembly were split into a northern New Netherlander bloc and a southern Midlander bloc, each of which had more in common with its cultural kin in New York City or southwestern Pennsylvania than with its "fellow" New Jerseyians. Similarly, even during the war, two parties struggled for control in Pennsylvania, one (the Constitutionalists) supported by the Scots-Irish of Appalachia, the other (the Republicans) by the Quakers and Anglicans in and around Philadelphia; the Appalachian bloc sided without exception with the Yankees, while the Midlands bloc often sided with the Southerners.[3]

On many issues, economic considerations drove the voting decisions of each region's delegates, but others were related to fundamental values. Take the 1778 vote on whether to raise taxes on the public at large in order to give half-pay for life to officers of the Continental Army but *not* to enlisted men (who had been paid their regular salaries with worthless paper currency). Yankee delegates voted en masse against the measure, because they found it immoral to tax the poor to give a special entitlement to the (generally wealthy) officer class. The aristocrats of Tidewater, the Deep South, and New Netherland enthusiastically supported the proposal, which was in perfect accord with their worldview that society existed to support the privileged. Those from the Midlands and (Pennsylvanian) Appalachia took a practical approach: granting pensions to the officers was a small price to pay to ensure their commitment to defeating the British. (The rest of Appalachia remained essentially unrepresented for the duration of the war, increasing their resentment of the coastal nations.) In 1782 the split was renewed when rumors began swirling that the Continental Army might mutiny against the cash-strapped Congress if debts to military contractors weren't honored immediately and in full; Yankees rejected the demands of wealthy contractors and officers for preferential treatment, but were overruled by a coalition of Southerners, Midlanders, and New Netherlanders.[4]

Regional divisions were so profound that in 1778 British secret agent Paul Wentworth reported there appeared to be not one American republic but three: an "eastern republic of Independents in church and state" (i.e., Yankeedom), a "middle republic of toleration in church and state" (New Netherland and the Midlands), and a "southern . . . mixed government copied nearly from Great Britain" (Tidewater and the Deep South); the differences among them, he argued, were greater than those among the nations of Europe. Even after the war, London papers were reporting "that the States consider themselves thirteen independent provinces, subject to no other control than their own assemblies. The authority of Congress, to which they submitted but from necessity during the war they have now almost generally thrown off," a development the British considered worrying because they would be easy pickings for Spain. A postwar British spy, Edward Bancroft, predicted the American confederation would surely splinter, leaving only the "question whether [to] have thirteen separate states in alliance or whether New England, the middle, and the southern states will form three new Confederations."[5]

But the leaders of America's nations had another major challenge to contend with outside the halls of Congress: an unexpected wartime upsurge in popular support for a novel idea called "democracy." It proved a great enough threat to their authority to push them toward closer collaboration and stronger central control.

Outside of Yankeedom, most people had never really participated in the political process, having been legally excluded from voting due to lack of wealth. (Nowhere were women or blacks allowed to vote or hold office.) Even in New England, where property requirements were low enough to allow 80 percent of adult males to qualify, voters tended to defer to the region's intellectual and commercial elite, who held a near-total lock on statewide offices. The same families appeared in the colonial assemblies and senior positions generation after generation, particularly in Tidewater and the Deep South, where they openly called themselves aristocrats. In any case, in almost every colony people got to vote only for legislators in the lower house. Governors, councilors, and other high officials were selected by the legislators or the king, to ensure the rabble didn't put the "wrong sort" into office.[6]

Early in the imperial crisis, however, American leaders started becoming concerned about unusual turbulence from below. "God gave mankind freedom by nature," a New Hampshire Yankee had loudly declared. "Let it not be said in future generations that money was made by the founders of the American states an essential qualification in the rulers of a free people." Such thinking seemed particularly virulent in Appalachian sections. In early 1776 Virginia Tidewater lord Landon Carter warned Washington of the "ambition" that had "seized on so much ignorance all over the colony." Among the ignorant masses, he reported, independence "was expected to be a form of government that, by being independent of rich men, every man would then be able to do as he pleased." In upland Mecklenburg County, North Carolina, Borderlanders instructed their delegates to the state's constitutional convention to fight for a "simple democracy, or as near as possible," and to "oppose everything that leans to aristocracy or power in the hands of the rich men and chief men [and used for] the oppression of the poor." Members of volunteer militia units from the Appalachian sections of Pennsylvania informed legislators "that all persons . . . who expose their lives in defense of a country should be admitted to the enjoyment of all the rights and privileges of a citizen of that country." Everywhere the demands were similar: the creation of democratic state governments, in which all legislative officials were directly elected, and most white male adults could vote.[7]

In mobilizing for war, colonial leaders had framed the struggle in terms of fighting tyranny and oppression. They had encouraged common people to organize militia, to participate in mass meetings where they would boisterously approve the resolutions presented to them by their leaders, and to form mobs to enforce those resolutions with clubs, hot tar, and feathers. But the process had led many commoners to realize that they could actually participate in politics and some began reading and writing about democracy. The publication of Thomas Paine's *Common Sense* and the Declaration of Independence in 1776 inflamed these sentiments. Throughout the colonies the wars of liberation were instigating calls for genuinely revolutionary change. Commoners in Boston rioted in 1776 when they learned that the rich could buy their way out of the draft, chanting, "Tyranny is tyranny!" Soldiers from the Scots-Irish backcountry of Pennsylvania deposed their officers and marched on Philadelphia to demand their long-overdue pay in 1781; Washington hastened to meet their demands before their cannon could be trained on the Congress hall.

Poor white agitators in Tidewater Virginia were telling fellow militiamen that they were fighting in "a war produced by the wantonness of the gentlemen" that was of little interest to ordinary people. Free blacks began asserting their citizenship rights from Boston to Charleston, with those in Norfolk pressing to be allowed to testify in court, and a group of seven in Massachusetts petitioning the legislature for voting rights. Such popular pressures forced elites to make uncomfortable wartime concessions. Property requirements were lowered in many colonies and eliminated entirely by Pennsylvania's Appalachia-controlled revolutionary government. Maryland's assembly shifted the tax burden to fall more heavily on slave-holding planters. Disgruntled tenant farmers in New Netherland's lower Hudson Valley were promised their own farms, as were Yankee, Appalachian, and Midland soldiers who agreed to reenlist in the Continental Army. Women were (briefly) allowed to vote in New Jersey, and Tidewater rulers were under pressure to allow free blacks to vote and (in Maryland) to hold office. Meanwhile, impoverished war veterans in western Massachusetts staged an armed rebellion against authorities' efforts to foreclose on the homes of farmers who'd never really been paid for their wartime service; the insurrectionists seized the federal arsenal in Springfield and ultimately had to be put down by federal forces.[8]

Concerned that the "lower orders" were getting out of hand, many of the national leaders came to believe that their safety and hold on power required a stronger union with plenty of checks on the popular will and the independence of the various states. John Adams was shocked by *Common Sense*'s call for directly elected single-chamber legislatures because they were "so democratical" and so devoid of "any restraint or even an attempt at any equilibrium or counter-poise [by wealthy interests] that it must produce confusion and every evil work." Alexander Hamilton of New York City called the confederation a "shadow of a federal government" and predicted that if left in place, there would soon be a "War between the States" over territorial and economic differences. "I predict the worst consequences from a half-starved, limping government, always moving upon crutches at every step," Washington wrote in 1786. "I do not conceive we can long exist as a nation without having lodged somewhere a power which will pervade the whole union in as energetic a manner as the authority of the state governments extends over the several states."[9]

After the rebellion in western Massachusetts, these and other wealthy American leaders urged Congress to call a special meeting of the states to reform the system of government. At this Constitutional Convention, held in 1789 in Philadelphia, the elite delegates from Yankeedom, Tidewater, and the Deep South gravitated around the so-called "Virginia Plan," a scheme modeled on Tidewater and featuring a strong central government with an appointed president and senate. (Alexander Hamilton of New York City carried things even further, calling for a powerful monarch who would rule for life and keep politics out of reach of the great unwashed and local interests.) Their opponents—delegates from the Midlands and New Netherland—coalesced around the "New Jersey Plan," which envisioned only minor reforms to the existing E.U.-like alliance. The Virginia Plan won the day, seven states to five, with Maryland's delegation evenly split between Midland and Tidewater delegates.

Thereafter, the critical debate concerned representation in the two legislative houses, with the final compromise (seats in the House based on population, those in the Senate divided evenly among the states) passed five states to four. The split, oddly enough, was not between large states and small ones, but rather between Yankees and the Deep South. New Netherland backed the Yankees. Tidewater and the Midlands were split between states with and without territorial claims in the west (as those with such claims were expected to become more populous than those that did not). As usual, Appalachia was all but closed out of the discussion, with only one representative at the convention (James Wilson of Pennsylvania); that region's exclusion from the proceedings would prove a curse to the young United States.[10]

Agreeing to a new constitution was one thing, getting each of the states to ratify it was quite another. Between 1787 and 1790 every state convened its own ratification convention to vote on the measure, while propagandists for and against the Constitution churned out speeches, pamphlets, and newspaper articles, some with outrageous claims. (Opponents warned the wording of the document made it possible for the Pope to be elected president and for the capital of the country to be relocated to China.) New Netherlanders refused to vote on it at all until Congress agreed to add amendments modeled on the civil liberties enumerated in the Articles of Capitulation on the Reduction of New

Netherland, which the Dutch had brokered before turning the colony over to England in 1664. The people of New Netherland had lived under the arbitrary rule of distant powers for a very long time and wanted assurances their tolerant approach to religion and freedom of inquiry would not be trampled on by a new empire. Had the Congress not agreed to these demands by passing the Bill of Rights, the United States would probably not have lived to see its tenth birthday.[11]

A close examination of the geographical distribution of the voting results at the various state ratifying conventions reveals a split along national lines. Delegates from Yankee areas, including those in the northern part of Pennsylvania and on eastern Long Island, generally supported the constitutional changes. They were joined by delegates representing New Netherlanders, Midlanders, Deep Southerners, and Tidewaterites. Opposing them were the people of Appalachia (whose delegates rejected the Constitution everywhere save Virginia) along with Scots-Irish enclaves in New Hampshire, the farmers whose rebellion had been crushed in western Massachusetts, and disgruntled Yankee and Scots-Irish farmers in upstate New York. The vote in New York State was a cliff-hanger, prompting New Netherlanders to threaten to secede and join the new union on their own if delegates from the Yankee interior counties did not ratify the new constitution. The effects on "the islands of [Manhattan], Long Island, and Staten Island will be almost ruinous," one editorialist warned. "If Staten Island were to associate herself with New Jersey and the islands of New York and Long Island with Connecticut, these two respectable states and the new union would be bound to defend them." In the end the threats likely won the day. On July 26, 1788, New York accepted the new constitution by a vote of 30 delegates to 27, ensuring the practical existence of the new union.[12]

In the end, the U.S. Constitution was the product of a messy compromise among the rival nations. From the gentry of Tidewater and the Deep South, we received a strong president to be selected by an "electoral college" rather than elected by ordinary people. From New Netherland we received the Bill of Rights, a set of very Dutch guarantees that individuals would have freedom of conscience, speech, religion, and assembly. To the Midlands we owe the fact that we do not have a strong unitary state under a British-style national Parliament; they insisted on state sovereignty as insurance against Southern despots and Yankee meddling. The Yankees ensured that small states would have an equal say in the Senate, with even the very populous state of Massachusetts frustrating Tidewater and the Deep South's desire for proportional representation in that chamber; Yankees also forced a compromise whereby slave lords would be able to count only three-fifths of their slave population when tabulating how many congressmen they would receive. People who aren't allowed to vote, went the very Yankee reasoning, were not really being represented, and that fact ought to be reflected in the apportionment of congressional delegates.[13]

The uneasy alliance this new federation represented could not help but be a volatile one, and it would soon face two powerful secession movements that threatened to tear it apart, first from Appalachia, then from Yankeedom.

CHAPTER 13

Nations in the North

If you're an American, have you ever really asked yourself why Canada exists? When the American Revolution came about, why did only thirteen rather than eighteen North American colonies wind up revolting? Why would the young colony of Nova Scotia be any more committed to the British Empire than the young colony of Georgia? And why would the people of New France, recently conquered by the British, not be eager to throw off their occupiers and become a sovereign state or states? As with their neighbors to the south, the answer has everything to do with the respective parties' cultures and what they thought was the best way to ensure their survival.

Some people in what we now call the Canadian Maritimes did in fact revolt, and virtually all who did so were newcomers from New England who viewed the region as an extension of Yankeedom. In 1775 half of the 23,000 European Americans living in what is now Nova Scotia and New Brunswick were Yankees, who re-created the New England communities they'd left behind, with strong town governments and equitably distributed farmland. The Yankee fishermen of Cape Sable, at the far western end of Nova Scotia, were completely oriented toward Boston across the Gulf of Maine and barely acknowledged the jurisdiction of British authorities based in the new village of Halifax. In the words of Nova Scotia historian John Bartlet Brebner, the Yankees "laid the abiding foundations of Nova Scotian life," by influencing "the Loyalists and other subsequent immigrants to produce an amalgam far more similar to New Hampshire and Maine than to the other Loyalist refuge," Ontario. When the revolution broke out, Yankee settlers refused to fight their brethren and successfully petitioned the Nova Scotia Assembly to be excused from militia service. The settlers of eastern Passamaquoddy Bay (in today's New Brunswick) asked the Continental Congress to admit them into the revolutionary alliance, while those in the St. John Valley petitioned Massachusetts to annex and protect them. The representatives of Yankee settlements on the Nova Scotia peninsula stopped showing up at meetings of their provincial legislature, while British officers warned their superiors that much of the populace would support a rebel invasion. Yankees in both Maine and the Maritimes petitioned George Washington to endorse a 1775 invasion plan, but the general declined to divert scant resources from his siege of Boston. Any hope of an uprising ended with the arrival of massive British reinforcements in Halifax in April 1776. But, as we will see, the dominant culture of the Maritimes has remained Yankee to the present.[1]

New France presented a surprisingly similar picture. The province of Acadia couldn't participate in any rebellion because the British had wiped it clean off the map and cleansed most of its Francophone population at the start of the Seven Years' War. (Thousands of these displaced people wound up in the swamps of southern Louisiana, which was still controlled by France at the time; to this day, these Cajuns retain key cultural characteristics of New France.) Québec, however, was simply too populous for ethnic cleansing, and at a 1763 peace conference, Britain guaranteed its 70,000 people the freedom to speak French and practice Catholicism. Thus the core of New France survived the British takeover—and, indeed, the centuries since—with its culture essentially intact. As the American Revolution got under way, nobody was entirely certain where Québécois loyalties would lie.[2]

Québec, unlike Nova Scotia, was considered strategically vital by General Washington's staff. After the British abandoned Boston, Yankee-dominated units of the Continental Army invaded the sprawling colony from two fronts in the winter of 1775–1776. The New French made no effort to defend the British-controlled colony and thousands greeted the New Englanders as liberators. "Our yoke is broke," a group of Montrealers proclaimed as American forces entered the city. "A glorious liberty, long wished for, has now arrived and which we will now enjoy, assuring our sister colonies . . . of our real and unfeigned satisfaction at our happy union." Hundreds of Québécois joined the rebel army, forming two Canadian regiments, one of which fought through the entire war, even in campaigns far to the south. A foundry at Trois Rivières churned out mortars and ordnance to help the invading army lay siege to Québec City. Unfortunately, perhaps, for the Québécois, the siege did not succeed, and in May

1776 Yankee forces beat a retreat in the face of British reinforcements. They made few friends along the way, stealing supplies from *habitants* at bayonet point or paying for them in near-worthless paper currency. By the time the last New Englanders left Québec, few were sad to see them go.

Two centuries would pass before New France would again have independence within its grasp.[3]

From the time of Canada's creation and right up into the 1970s, generations of Canadians were brought up on the "Loyalist Myth," the assertion that their country's identity sprang from the politics, attitudes, and values of the 28,000 refugees who fled there at the end of the American Revolution. The loyalists were cast as heroic and honorable British subjects who'd been driven from their homes by violent, uncouth American mobs simply because they'd refused to commit treason against king and country. Arriving after much suffering, they founded a more civilized society on the firm foundations of hierarchy, order, and deference to authority. Proud of their Britishness and their place in the empire, the loyalists built the North America that should have been, a pleasant and law-abiding land, whose people were committed to a higher communal purpose than simply letting the most rugged individual take all. The Loyalist Myth defined Canada and Canadians as fundamentally British and proudly un-American. The first assertion was almost entirely false and the second not entirely true.

The truth is that the loyalist refugees did not succeed in laying down the cultural DNA of English-speaking Canada and completely failed to displace that of New France. Their efforts to create a British imperial utopia in the Canadian Maritimes failed to supplant the Yankee and New French precedents in the region, particularly as the area continued to be profoundly influenced by neighboring New England and Québec. Their project in Ontario faltered on account of the fact that the vast majority of "loyalists" who migrated there weren't British at all but rather Germans, Quakers, and Dutch from the Midlands, and New Netherland. While imperial officials kept a firm hand on Anglo-Canada's political development, its dominant cultural inheritance was Yankee to the east of Québec, and Midlander to the west.

The loyalist effort came closest to succeeding in the Maritimes, where an entirely new colony was carved out of Nova Scotia as a haven for the massive wave of civilian refugees and vanquished militia forces fleeing the rebel colonies. New Brunswick, named in honor of King George III (of the House of Brunswick), came into being precisely because refugee leaders regarded Nova Scotia as being under Yankee and republican influences. "They have experienced every possible injury from the old inhabitants of Nova Scotia, who are even more disaffected towards the British Government than any of the new States ever were," Baron Thomas Dundas reported to his superiors from Saint John in 1786, adding that the "old inhabitants" of the new territory were "a despicable race." The loyalists had reason to hope they would overwhelm the Yankees by force of numbers; in 1783, 13,500 emigrated to what is now Nova Scotia, almost doubling the population there, while 14,500 moved to what would become New Brunswick, where they outnumbered the despicable old settlers five to one. But the Yankees had something the loyalists did not: a unified and cohesive culture buttressed by easy access to Maine and Massachusetts just across the St. Croix River and the Gulf of Maine. The same could be said of the 1,600 or so remnant French Acadians in the north and east of New Brunswick who benefited from immediate access to Québec.[4]

The loyalists, by contrast, lacked any sort of cultural cohesion. The vast majority arrived as part of a single massive wave as the British abandoned their stronghold of New Netherland in late 1783. At that time Greater New York City had become the final American refuge for opponents of independence, attracting families and militia units from all over the colonies. Almost 70 percent of the emigrants to New Brunswick came from New Netherland or the Midlands, an eclectic group including Philadelphia Quakers, Anglican merchants from Manhattan, farmers and tradesmen from New Jersey, and German-speaking pacifists from the Pennsylvania "Dutch" country. Seven percent were from the Chesapeake and Deep Southern lowlands, and many brought household slaves with them. Another 22 percent were New Englanders who, politics aside, had more in common with the "old settlers" than with their fellow refugees; the only cohesive loyalist settlements were those on the peninsulas and islands of Passamaquoddy Bay, settled by Yankees from Maine. The loyalist mix in Nova Scotia was similar, but with the addition of 3,000 African Americans, most of them slaves who'd responded to the British offer to fight for the king in return for their freedom. Bereft of leadership and lacking natural cohesion, the loyalists splintered into rival religious, professional, class, and ethnic factions. Far from absorbing the Yankees in their midst, they were themselves largely assimilated into an expansive Yankee culture, their trade and cultural life oriented more toward nearby Boston than faraway London. Indeed, when Britain and the young United States clashed in the War of 1812, the people of southwestern New Brunswick not only refused to fight their neighbors, cousins, and friends in eastern Maine, they loaned them gunpowder to ensure the popular July 4th fireworks display wasn't canceled.[5]

The loyalist project had better initial prospects in the Great Lakes region, where a new colony was created for their benefit. Upper Canada was hacked off from British-controlled Québec to give loyalist refugees exactly what they lacked in the Maritimes: a clean slate on which to create a new society, free from Euro-American competitors. The colony would later be known by a different name, Ontario, and host the seat of the government of the Canadian federation, with its Westminster-style Parliament and the British crown emblazoned on its automobile license plates. Its landscape would become dotted with place-names worthy of the British Empire: Kingston, London, Windsor, and York. But loyalist it was not. For despite getting there ahead of their North American rivals, these "loyalists" also discovered they had little in common, not even politics.

Ontario's initial wave of "true" loyalists in 1783–1784 was small: about 6,000 Yankee farmers from upstate New York, along with British and Hessian soldiers whose units had been disbanded. But they were soon joined by 10,000 "late loyalists" who arrived in a steady stream between 1792 and 1812. British authorities and latter-day mythmakers liked to imagine that these latecomers were also good, monarchy-loving British subjects who'd happened to take an extra decade or two to flee the abhorrent American republic. In reality they were poor, opportunity-seeking immigrants attracted by British offers of dirt-cheap land and extremely low taxes. Traveling overland from their old homes in the middle states, three-quarters of the "late loyalists" were farmers, less than a fifth were craftsmen, and almost all the rest were impoverished laborers or sailors; only 1 in 250 was a gentleman. "In Canada, the settlers are more humble in their views," a visitor to upstate New York and Ontario reported in 1798.

"They are mostly poor people, who are chiefly concerned to manage, in the best manner, the farms which have been given them by the government." But unlike the real loyalists, these settlers actually did have a shared culture. They were Midlanders, and their tolerant, pluralistic cultural heritage would take hold on the northern shores of the Great Lakes.[6]

British records from the period indicate that nearly 90 percent of these immigrants came from the "middle states" of New Jersey, New York, and Pennsylvania, and contemporary accounts indicate that vast numbers were from the pacifist sects of the Delaware Valley. Persecuted for their refusal to choose sides or take up arms in the wars of liberation, thousands of English-speaking Quakers and German-speaking Mennonites and Dunkers (Church of the Brethren) decided to find a place where they would be left alone and in peace. Many of their countrymen would later move westward into the Ohio Valley, exporting Midlands society across the American Heartland. But in the 1790s, the Indians of the Iroquois Confederacy were violently resisting incursions onto their land. Ontario, by contrast, was peaceful because the British had learned a diplomatic lesson in the thirty years they'd occupied New France, and had come to treat the Indians as valued strategic partners. Imperial officials also offered to grant the Midlanders entire townships and a promise not to interfere in their day-to-day affairs. Thousands relocated before the War of 1812 interrupted immigration, settling in ethnically distinct towns alongside smaller numbers of New Netherland Dutch, New England Yankees, and Scots highlanders. Early Midland emigrants wrote their friends at home that in Ontario "they will find a second edition of Pennsylvania, as it was before the American War." Tolerant, diverse, and apathetic about the wider world, Ontario's founding settlers were happy to let imperial officials bother with the politics and messy affairs of state. By the 1820s, when large numbers of Irish, English, and Ulster Scots began moving to the province from the British Isles, Ontario's cultural norms were already in place. The densely populated southern tier of this vast province remains essentially Midlander to this day.[7]

One caveat in this account: unlike their American countrymen, neither the Yankee sections of the Maritimes nor the Midlander swaths of Ontario had much say in the development of their political institutions. In the late eighteenth century and throughout the nineteenth, officials in

London dictated how and by whom the king's provinces would be governed. Stung by the American revolt, British officials took measures to ensure that these colonies would not develop distinctive political institutions, values, and practices. Government followed the Tidewater model, only with imperial appointees standing in for the local gentry. Voting rights were extremely limited, and the press was tightly controlled. The actions of the elected legislative assemblies had to be approved by councils of crown-appointed grandees who served for life as well as by the crown-appointed governor and the imperial administration in London. The governor—always a Briton, never a colonial subject—could dissolve the local legislatures at any time, and his budget was not subject to their review. It was a system that, in the words of Ontario's first governor, aimed "ultimately to destroy or to disarm the spirit of democratic subversion."[8]

Ontario, Québec, and the Maritimes were culturally distinct from one another, but they shared the experience of being controlled by a distant power. Another century would pass before any of them would reclaim control of their destiny.

CHAPTER 14

First Secessionists

We've been taught to think of the ratification of the 1789 Constitution as the crowning achievement of the American Revolution. Most people living in the United States at the time, however, didn't see it in quite those terms.

Outside Tidewater and the Deep South, many were alarmed by a document they regarded as counterrevolutionary, intentionally designed to suppress democracy and to keep power in the hands of regional elites and an emerging class of bankers, financial speculators, and land barons who had little or no allegiance to the continent's ethnocultural nations. Indeed, the much-celebrated Founding Fathers had made no secret of this having been one of their goals. They praised the unelected Senate because it would "check the impudence of democracy" (Alexander Hamilton), and stop the "turbulence and follies of democracy" (Edmund Randolph), and applauded the enormous federal electoral districts because they would "divide the community," providing "defense against the inconveniences of democracy" (James Madison).[1]

Many in Yankeedom were not enthusiasts of the new United States. During the war the Yankee settlers of northeastern New York had seceded to form an independent republic called Vermont, governed by a constitution that banned slavery and property requirements for voting. Disgusted by the machinations of New York land speculators and new confederal policies that taxed poor people to bail out already wealthy war bond speculators, Vermont's leaders had refused to join the confederation. After the war they even tried to negotiate an alliance with Great Britain to safeguard their residents from the federal elite. Farmers in western Massachusetts and northwestern Connecticut, in turn, lobbied to have their territories annexed by the little mountain republic. Only after Alexander Hamilton pressured the New York land barons to settle their claims judiciously did Vermonters reluctantly agree to join the United States.

It was in Greater Appalachia that resistance to the constitutional changes was most intense. The new constitution trespassed on the Borderlanders' belief in natural liberty and overturned the radical 1776 constitution they'd forced on Pennsylvania. Effectively unrepresented at either the Continental Congress or the Constitutional Convention, Appalachian people regarded both bodies with considerable suspicion. Their representatives in Pennsylvania—the only state where Borderlanders had any real political power at the time—opposed ratification, and stormed out of the assembly when they learned Midlanders intended to force a statewide vote on the measure before copies of the proposed constitution had even reached the western counties. These delegates were later dragged out of their beds by a posse of "volunteer gentlemen," taken to the assembly hall, and literally dumped into their seats to create the necessary quorum. Ratification passed in Pennsylvania only after Midlander postal authorities destroyed all anti-Constitutional newspapers, pamphlets, and letters they found in the mails; in the end, only 18 percent of eligible voters cast a ballot, most of them in the Midlands. In other states, Appalachian sections had few polling places, ensuring the turnout would be lower than in the elite-controlled Tidewater or Deep Southern sections. In 1789 Appalachian people were dead set against the creation of a strong, elite-controlled federal government. Many of them feel the same way today.[2]

The Borderlanders' uprisings were long dismissed as the thuggish behavior of backcountry louts too ignorant to understand the merits of taxation or the need to settle their debts. In reality, the Borderlanders weren't against taxation or creditworthy behavior but were resisting a scheme so corrupt, avaricious, and shameless it ranks with those of Wall Street in the first decade of the twenty-first century.

In the dark hours of the wars of liberation, the Continental Congress had no money to pay salaries to their soldiers or to compensate farmers for requisitioned food and livestock. Instead Congress gave all these people government IOUs. This practice continued for years until, under the financial administration of the notoriously unethical banker Robert Morris, the state of Pennsylvania announced it would no longer accept the congressional IOUs as payment for taxes. With no other form of money in circulation in much of the countryside, many poor families had no choice but to sell the notes for whatever they could get, and wealthy speculators purchased them for one-sixth to one-fortieth of their face value. Soon just over 400 individuals held over 96 percent of Pennsylvania's war debt, and nearly half was controlled by just twenty-eight men, most of whom were Robert Morris's friends and business partners. Shortly thereafter, Morris and his protégé Alexander Hamilton took control of federal financial policy, rigging it so as to literally turn their friends' worthless paper into silver and gold. Under Morris and Hamilton, the federal government would buy back the bonds for face value, plus 6 percent interest, paid in precious metals raised by assessing new federal excise taxes designed to fall most heavily on the poor people who'd been forced to take the worthless congressional scrip in the first place.

But, wait—there's more. Most people in Appalachia hadn't seen hard cash in years. The closest thing to cash that Borderlander farmers could create was whiskey, which was nonperishable, marketable, and easy to transport. Knowing this, Morris and Hamilton cynically imposed a sharp tax on this all-important Appalachian product, even as they discouraged their underlings from collecting taxes owed by merchants on the coast. Meanwhile, they used their influence to give themselves and their private banker friends effective control over the new nation's currency supply—much of it printed by Morris's private Bank of North America—but with federal taxpayers on the hook to clean up their mess if things went wrong. It's also worth noting that Morris and Hamilton were both immigrants without ethnoregional allegiances; English-born Morris and West Indies-born Hamilton both saw North America as the British had: as a cow to be milked for all it was worth.[3]

But unlike in 1929 or 2008, the victims of this scheme were well aware of what was going on, and it was the people of Appalachia who resisted the federal elite's machinations most strongly. The greatest uprising that followed would come to be known, derisively, as the Whiskey Rebellion. But what it was really about was the fact that enlisted war veterans had gone unpaid and had been forced to sell the government's IOUs to pay government taxes, only to then be taxed again to allow vultures to make a 5,000 percent profit on their misery. Those taxes had to be paid in gold and silver, which nobody in the countryside had seen in years. When they couldn't pay, their farms and possessions would be seized and liquidated to further enrich Morris, Hamilton, and their speculator friends from the coastal nations.[4]

The Borderlanders didn't give up their farms or their individual God-given sovereignty without a fight. When confederal and federal authorities started trying to collect taxes and seize property, the Borderlanders took up arms and tried to leave the union they now thoroughly disapproved of. This Appalachian resistance movement raged for more than a decade and encompassed the highlands from the cultural heartland of Pennsylvania through the Appalachian sections of Maryland, Virginia, North Carolina, and the future states of West Virginia, Kentucky, and Tennessee. It began in 1784, when people in the western territories of North Carolina (now eastern Tennessee) became disgusted with Tidewater control. Their solution was pure Borderlander: they created their own sovereign State of Franklin on nobody's permission but their own. They drafted a constitution that prohibited lawyers, clergy, and doctors from running for office, set up a government in the village of Greeneville, and passed laws making apple brandy, animal skins, and tobacco legal tender. They even applied for membership in the Continental Congress and were supported by seven states; opposition from Tidewater and the Deep South delegates denied them the necessary two-thirds majority. Tidewater-controlled North Carolina forces invaded Franklin shortly thereafter, setting up a rival government and defeating local militia in a skirmish in what is now Johnson City, Tennessee, in 1788. The State of Franklin's leadership established communications with foreign officials in the Spanish-controlled lower Mississippi Valley, hoping to negotiate an alliance. But war soon broke out again with the Cherokee, driving the Borderlanders back under North Carolina's protection and ending their experiment in self-government.[5]

While the State of Franklin was being dismantled, Borderlanders throughout western Pennsylvania had cut their region off from the outside world. For nearly a decade, settlers had kept tax collectors, sheriffs, and federal officials out of their communities, cutting off the roads by various means: digging ditches, chopping down trees, diverting streams, provoking winter avalanches, and, in one case, creating a four-foot wall of manure. Government offices were burned in an effort to destroy records of debts. Citizen gangs attacked sheriffs, tax collectors, and judges; repossessed livestock, furniture, and tools taken by creditors; and freed neighbors from debtors' prisons. Many rebel communities created their own militia units and, in at least one case, signed a pledge to "oppose the establishment of the new constitution at the risk of our lives and our fortunes."[6]

As Hamilton's 1790 whiskey tax began to force backcountry settlers into foreclosure, the Midlander-controlled state government passed a law prohibiting county officials from foreclosing on large land speculators' holdings. Borderlanders reacted to this latest outrage much as their Scots and Scots-Irish ancestors would have: they surrounded tax collectors and demanded they turn over their ledgers and any funds or valuables they had collected. If the collector refused, he would be beaten, tortured, or stripped naked, covered in searing hot tar, and rolled in feathers. The same fate befell law enforcement officers who tried to investigate.

By 1792 such tactics had been widely adopted by Borderlanders in Kentucky, Virginia, Georgia, and the Carolinas. As excise tax collection and property foreclosures in the region ground to a halt, emboldened Appalachian leaders started talking of bringing down the entire federal financial system. Finally Pennsylvanian Borderlanders proposed creating "a cordial union of the people west of the Allegheny Mountains" that would link them with their countrymen in western Maryland and what is now West Virginia and Kentucky.[7]

Convinced that state and federal officials were betraying the revolution, the Borderlanders initiated an outright rebellion. In August 1794 Appalachian Pennsylvanians formed an army of 9,000 men and marched on the Midlander city of Pittsburgh, threatening to burn it to the ground. Pittsburgh officials promptly surrendered and spared their town from destruction by ordering their militia to join the insurgency. A week later Borderlanders staged a regional independence congress in an open field nearby, with 226 delegates from western Pennsylvania and Virginia in attendance. The delegates raised a new flag with six alternating red and white stripes representing the four western counties of Pennsylvania and two in western Virginia. They discussed reaching out to Spain and Britain for protection. The northern Borderlands, it seemed, were on the verge of nationhood.

In the midst of the independence conference, the delegates learned that President Washington was on his way to crush them, riding at the head of an army of 10,000 well-armed troops recruited from the poorest strata of the Midlands and Tidewater. Faced with the likely prospect of military defeat, the regional congress voted to submit to federal authority. Washington's army received a cold reception as it passed through the towns of central and western Pennsylvania, where people erected liberty poles—tall wooden flagstaffs that had been the symbol of Patriot allegiance during the Revolution—as signs of defiance. Still, no shots were fired, and by summer's end, the Borderlander insurgency had petered out.[8]

In Yankeedom, by contrast, resistance died down quickly. For all their concerns about federal corruption, turn-of-the-century New Englanders had made a pleasant discovery: their nation had come to dominate the federal government.

With the retirement of Washington in 1796, the Electoral College of the United States chose John Adams to be the country's second president by an extremely close vote. Only half of the sixteen states then in existence chose their electors by popular vote, while the rest let their legislators appoint them. In both cases, however, electors followed regional trends. Adams, the quintessential Yankee, won every Yankee and New Netherland electoral vote and the vast majority of those of the Midlands. His rival, the gentleman planter Thomas Jefferson, swept the Deep South and Appalachia and the vast majority of Tidewater. In the end, Adams won 71 to 68.

Adams's presidency proved to be extremely controversial because, as historian David Hackett Fischer has observed, he attempted to force Yankee cultural and political values on the other nations. New Englanders believed that freedom belonged primarily not to the individual but to the community. Unfettered individual pursuit of absolute freedom and property accumulation, they feared, would destroy community ties, create an aristocracy, and enslave the masses, resulting in a tyranny along the lines of the British or the Deep South. To a civilization founded by people who believed they were God's chosen, protecting the common good meant maintaining internal conformity and cultural unity. Foreigners—whether Virginians, Irish, or African slaves—were considered a threat because they didn't share Yankee values, so immigration, religious diversity, and the importation of slaves were all actively discouraged in New England. "The grand cause of all our present difficulties," Adams's nephew and personal secretary explained in 1798, was due to "so many hordes of foreigners immigrating to America."[9]

While this belief system worked fairly well domestically, its policy implications were enormously threatening to the value systems of the other nations, leaving Adams to face a difficult presidency, which began in the midst of a geostrategic crisis. In 1789 the people of France had risen up in revolution, captured and beheaded their king, and declared themselves a republic. But their revolution had descended into chaos and terror, with state-enforced atheism, arbitrary arrests and executions, and, finally, a military coup by Napoleon Bonaparte. As Napoleon's armies spread across Europe, North Americans were caught up in fear and hysteria. Yankee newspapers reported that France was preparing a reconquest of its North American territories and that a 10,000-man invasion force was already assembling. Some 25,000 French refugees poured into the United States—most fleeing a successful slave rebellion in Haiti—triggering fears that they might be plotting with Napoleon.[10]

Amid the fear and xenophobia, Adams pushed through a package of legislation to crush dissent, enforce conformity, strengthen the courts, and drive out foreigners. Congress passed the infamous Alien and Sedition Acts of 1798 by the slimmest of margins, with Yankees and Deep Southerners in favor, and Appalachian representatives deeply opposed. The acts granted the president the right to expel any foreigner or unnaturalized immigrant or to arrest anyone born in a hostile country at will. The acts also increased the number of years of residency required for citizenship from four to fifteen. Meanwhile, anyone who spoke, wrote, or published anything against the government, Congress, or the president that might bring them "into contempt or disrepute" or that might be considered "scandalous and malicious" would be subject to up to five years in prison and a $5,000 fine. Two dozen people were arrested for sedition, including Philadelphia Quaker James Logan (for undertaking a peace mission to Paris), a number of critical newspaper writers and editors (for accusing Adams of overstretching his authority), and Vermont congressman Matthew Lyon (who subsequently relocated to Kentucky, where Borderlanders elected him to Congress four times).[11]

Yankees defended the acts, which were in accord with their concept of communal liberty. All citizens had the right to elect their own representatives, the thinking went, but once they did, they owed them their absolute deference—not just to the laws they passed but to everything they said or did while in office. If they disapproved, they were to keep quiet until the next election, when they could vote in another candidate. "The government ought, especially in great measures, to be [sure] of the harmonious and cheerful cooperation of the citizens," Yale president Timothy Dwight explained in a 1798 sermon. "By putting power into the hands of their rulers, [the people] put it out of their own," another New England minister proclaimed. The Adams presidency, the Massachusetts legislature would later declare, "was the golden age of America."[12]

In the "War Fever of '98," many North Americans gave their support to their commander in chief and his draconian laws. Adams's party, the Federalists, even made electoral gains in Appalachia, whose people have supported every war the United States has ever fought once the fighting began, regardless of cause, opponent, or consequences. Deep Southern planters had no qualms about authoritarianism, and one of them, Robert Harper of South Carolina, even sponsored the sedition bill, deeming it necessary to stamp out subversives. Opponents were concentrated among the Tidewater gentry (who believed their own liberties were threatened by federal power) and the multiethnic, pacifistic Midlands. Thomas Jefferson and James Madison drafted resolutions against the acts that were passed by the Virginia and Kentucky legislatures; these denounced "the principle of unlimited submission" to the federal government and insisted that the states "are in duty bound" to prevent the United States from usurping their powers. The resolution's sponsor in the Virginia House, John Taylor of Tidewater's Caroline County, even advocated secession. Meanwhile, German-speaking farmers in southwestern Pennsylvania rebelled in 1799, accosting federal tax assessors attempting to collect a special war tax on property. The Midlanders broke colleagues out of jail, denounced Adams for seeking to "be a King of the Country," and hoisted signs declaring "No Gag Laws—Liberty or Death." Adams deployed federal troops to put down the protestors, whom he later dismissed as "miserable Germans, as ignorant of our language as they were of our laws."[13]

But Adams soon realized that suppressing dissent wasn't serving to strengthen the republic; rather, it had opened the door to the very aristocratic tyranny the New England Way had been engineered to prevent. The threat emerged within Adams's own administration, where Hamilton was consolidating military power as the effective head of the federal army. His officers were interfering in elections, beating up civilians and even a federal congressman who didn't share their political opinions. Jefferson feared this "military enclave" might attack Virginia at any time, triggering a civil war. The threat of a federal military coup persuaded Adams to make a complete about-face in foreign policy, making peace with France and ending the war hysteria. He purged Hamilton and his associates from his cabinet, replacing them with New Englanders.[14]

With the threat of war removed, Appalachia promptly abandoned Adams, whose policies were otherwise completely at odds with their own values. Deep Southerners were furious at Adams, with South Carolina congressman Robert Harper privately hoping he would break his neck on the trip home to Massachusetts. Jefferson was relieved, although he remained upset that Adams had established diplomatic and commercial relations with the "rebellion Negroes" of Haiti. Even with the opposition operating under the shadow of the Sedition Acts, Adams was routed in the election of 1800, retaining only the support of Yankee electors. New England had lost control of the twelve-year-old federal government, and in only a few years' time, it would be trying to leave it altogether.[15]

For the next quarter century, the United States was dominated by the unstable coalition that brought down New England rule: Appalachia, the Midlands, New Netherland, Tidewater, and the Deep South put aside their differences to reject the New England ideal of "communal freedom" and internal conformity. These nations did their best to wipe away Adams's presidency by overturning his entire legislative agenda, including the Alien and Sedition Acts, the Bankruptcy Act of 1800, the Judiciary Act of 1801, and all of his new tax measures.

Under President Jefferson the federation embraced France, turned its back on Britain, and expanded westward, all of which contributed to alienating Yankeedom. Allying with Bonaparte's atheistic, imperialistic regime was amoral, Yankees argued. Severing ties with Britain would only harm New England's commercial shipping fleet, undermining the region's economy. The rapid move west, they warned, was a dire threat to the republic.

The United States had already taken a great leap into the interior of the continent. During Washington's administration, the federal government had taken possession of the former Indian territories comprising what is now Ohio, Indiana, Illinois, Wisconsin, and Michigan. The creation of this so-called "Northwest Territory" had been accepted by New Englanders largely because they correctly recognized it would be largely settled by Yankees. Ownership of the first part to be colonized—the northern portions of the future state of Ohio—was split between the State of Connecticut (its so-called Western Reserve) and the Yankee-controlled Marietta Company. While some feared an exodus that would depopulate New England itself, most took pride in the opportunity to extend the Yankee nation, increasing its relative power over its competitors.

But President Jefferson's purchase of the 828,000-square-mile Louisiana Territory from France* in 1803 was another matter altogether. The United States had suddenly acquired 50,000 Louisiana Creoles; a tropical enclave of New France where French and Spanish blended with blacks, Indians, and one another in the port of New Orleans; and French-speaking Acadians who practiced an idiosyncratic form of Catholicism in the swamps of the Mississippi's delta. Future congressman and Harvard College president Josiah Quincy warned that the transaction had "introduced a population alien to [U.S. constitutional principles] in every element of character, previous education, and political tendency" and unleashed "the opportunity and power of multiplying slave states, for which their climate was adapted." This would lead, Quincy warned, to the "ultimate predominancy of slave power in the Union." These fears over an expansion of the Deep South deepened with Jefferson's annexation of the Spanish territories of west Florida (now the Florida Panhandle and the Gulf coasts of Alabama and Mississippi) in 1810, leaving the slaveocracy free to expand all the way to the frontiers of Spanish Texas. In fact, Jefferson encouraged Deep Southerners to do so to ensure that lower Louisiana would be admitted as "an American, rather than a French state." Yankees like Boston merchant Stephen Higginson saw this all as confirmation of a Southern conspiracy "to govern and depress New England" and "secure the influence and safety of the south."[16]

*Spain controlled the region from 1762 to 1800, when it was ceded to Napoleon's France.

Yankee influence over national affairs was increasingly compromised. As other states attracted immigrants or imported slaves, Massachusetts' share of the Union's tangible resources had sunk from second to fourth place between 1790 and 1813; by 1820 its population had fallen from second to fifth, behind even the new state of Ohio. The region wouldn't field a serious presidential candidate for a quarter century after Adams's defeat. With Yankeedom in decline, New Englanders began to look on the election of 1800 as a "moral revolution proceeding from the vices and passions of men" and even a symbol of "God's displeasure." "God does not send a wicked ruler to a good people," one minister said in reference to Jefferson. "It demonstrates the wickedness of the nation." A hopeful alliance of "free republics," Congressman Samuel Thatcher warned, had been replaced by "a consolidated empire" and "the deep abyss of a frightful despotism." Saving the young republic, some prominent figures began muttering, might compel New England to leave the Union and create a free Northern Confederacy.[17]

The issue of Yankee secessionism moved to the mainstream after Congress passed an oppressive series of embargo acts in 1807 and 1808, which prohibited trade with foreign possessions. Yankees, who controlled most trade with Britain, the Maritimes, and the West Indies, saw it as a reprise of King George's Boston Port Bill and "the utmost streak of despotism." They compared Jefferson and his allies in Tidewater and the Deep South with Napoleon, whose empire the embargo benefited. They saw the people of Appalachia and the Midlands as democratic rabble poised to bring the French Revolution's terror to American shores. Shortly thereafter, British agents in New England reported talk of "an armed truce along the [Canadian] borders and even a Union with Great Britain." One recounted from Boston, "In a few months more of suffering and privation of all the benefits of commerce, the people of the New England States will be ready to withdraw from the confederacy [and] establish a separate government." Indeed, Massachusetts Senate president Harrison Gray Otis soon called for a regionwide convention to be held to find "some mode of relief that may not be inconsistent with the union of these [New England] states." (Recognizing the Yankee dominance of large swaths of New York, Otis considered inviting that state as well.) The *Boston Gazette* concurred: "It is better to suffer the amputation of a limb, than to loose the whole body.

We must prepare for the operation." Other newspapers carried reports that New England's political leaders were preparing "to form a northern confederacy, separate from the United States, in alliance with Great Britain, and eventually connected with Nova Scotia, New Brunswick and the Canadas."[18]

President James Madison's declaration of war against Great Britain in the spring of 1812 finally pushed Yankeedom over the edge. Having effectively allied the federation with Napoleon, the Southerners had, in New England's view, completed their betrayal of the revolution and revealed their devotion to tyrannical empires. Massachusetts governor Caleb Strong immediately proclaimed a day of public fasting to atone for a war "against the nation from which we are descended, and which for many generations has been the bulwark of our religion." Strong and his counterparts in Connecticut, Rhode Island, and Vermont all declined the president's requests to requisition state militia units, dismissing them as orders from the "little man in the Palace." Boston bankers refused to issue loans to the federal government. "We ought never to volunteer our services in a cause which we believe to be morally wrong," George Cabot declared. Lavish festivities were held in Boston to celebrate Russian and British victories over Napoleon's armies in Europe, and mobs tried to liberate captured British sailors when American privateers arrived in New England ports. The people of Newburyport, Massachusetts, began flying a modified American flag with only five stars and five stripes, one for each New England state.[19]

New Englanders also refused to fight their Canadian counterparts, particularly those in the Yankee-dominated Maritime provinces. When the federal government invaded Canada with the intention of forcing it into the Union, Yankees roundly condemned the action as an immoral war of imperial conquest. "We will give you millions for defense," said Congressman Morris Miller of (Yankee) Oneida County, New York. "But not a cent for the conquest of Canada—not a ninety-ninth part of a cent for the extermination of its inhabitants." New Englanders not only chose not to attack their Maritime neighbors, they declined to defend or attempt to liberate eastern Maine after British forces invaded in 1814. (New Brunswick and Nova Scotia militia, for their part, had refused to participate in the British action.) Governor Strong even sent an envoy to meet with his counterpart in Nova Scotia to determine if Great Britain would give New Englanders military assistance if they attempted to secede from the United States. The answer from London, which arrived too late to affect events, was yes; the governor of Nova Scotia was authorized to sign a separate armistice with the Yankees and offer them "arms, accoutrements, ammunition, clothing, and naval cooperation."[20]

Yankee frustration culminated with a convention of New England leaders held in Hartford in December 1814. In the run-up to the meeting, John Lowell, scion of one of the region's most powerful families, called for delegates to draft a new federal constitution and offer membership only to the original thirteen states. The Revolutionary Era alliance would be restored on Yankee terms, and the uncouth Borderlander-settled territories beyond the mountains would be allowed to join Great Britain. Lowell's plan was extremely popular, and was backed by nearly all New England's newspapers. "We must no longer suffer our liberties to be made the sport of theorists . . . neither allow the region of the West, which was a wilderness when New England wrought the Independence of America, to wrest from us those blessings which we permitted them to share," the influential *Columbian Centinel* declared. "When we have once entered on the high road of honor and independence, let no difficulties stay our course, nor dangers drive us back." Even opposition papers admitted that a majority of Massachusetts' citizens supported secession. Proposals poured in to delegates calling for the seizure of federal customs houses and an end to conscription and the war.[21]

Standing on the brink, the conventioneers themselves pulled back. After a series of secret meetings, they emerged with a list of proposed constitutional amendments to initiate negotiations with the federal government. The South would no longer be able to count three-fifths of its enslaved population when determining its representation in Congress—a measure that would have gutted Tidewater and Deep Southern political power, guaranteeing Yankee preeminence in the United States. The president would be limited to a single term and could not be succeeded by an individual from his own state, ending Virginia's near-lock on the office. Wars, trade embargos, and the admission of new states would hereafter require a two-thirds majority in Congress, effectively giving Yankeedom veto power.

Massachusetts subsequently dispatched three commissioners to Washington to negotiate these terms.[22] But shortly after their arrival at the languid capital—where the White House and Capitol building had been burned by British troops—astonishing news broke that changed everything.

The British had signed a peace treaty and U.S. forces had defeated an invading British army in New Orleans. With the nation victorious, the Yankees' demands appeared preposterous and the Hartford conventioneers treasonous. The Yankees quietly dropped their demands while the rest of the country celebrated the gallant new war hero who'd saved the day at New Orleans. He was an Appalachian country lawyer from the old State of Franklin; fiery, bellicose, and profoundly un-Yankee, he was about to lead his long-neglected nation into the very heart of American power. His name was Andrew Jackson.

PART THREE

WARS FOR THE WEST

1816 to 1877

CHAPTER 15

Yankeedom Spreads West

After the revolution, four of the American nations hurdled the Appalachians and began spreading west across the Ohio and Mississippi valleys. There was very little mixing in their settlement streams, as politics, religion, ethnic prejudice, geography, and agricultural practices kept colonists almost entirely apart in four distinct tiers. Their respective cultural imprints can be seen to this day on maps created by linguists to trace American dialects, by anthropologists codifying material culture, and by political scientists tracking voting behaviors from the early nineteenth century straight through to the early twenty-first. With the exception of the New French enclave in southern Louisiana, the middle third of the continent was divided up among these four rival cultures.

New Englanders rushed due west to dominate upstate New York; the northern parts of Pennsylvania, Ohio, Illinois, and Iowa; and the future states of Michigan and Wisconsin. Midlanders poured over the mountains to spread through much of the American Heartland, characteristically mixing German, English, Scots-Irish, and other ethnicities in an ethnonational checkerboard. Appalachian people rafted down the Ohio River, dominating its southern shore, and conquered the uplands of Tennessee, northwestern Arkansas, southern Missouri, eastern Oklahoma, and, eventually, the Hill Country of Texas. Deep Southern slave lords set up new plantations in the lowlands of the future states of Florida, Alabama, and Mississippi; on the floodplains of the Big Muddy from northern Louisiana to the future city of Memphis; and, later, on the coastal plains of eastern Texas. Cut off from the west by their rivals, Tidewater and New Netherland remained trapped against the sea as the others raced across the continent, vying to define its future.

New England pushed west because of the shortcomings of its land. By the end of the eighteenth century, farmers were finding that the thin, rocky soils of much of Vermont, New Hampshire, and Maine were played out. In one of the continent's most densely populated regions, the best farmland was already spoken for, and farmers' younger children had to settle for ever-worsening prospects on the glacially scoured frontiers of eastern Maine. Even before the revolution, thousands had moved over the New York border and into northern Pennsylvania; afterward they flooded western New York in incredible numbers and drowned Dutch Albany and the upper Hudson Valley in a Yankee sea.

Their early efforts were supported by their political leaders, whose states laid claim to great swaths of New York, Pennsylvania, and what would become Ohio. Connecticut asserted its jurisdiction over the northern third of Pennsylvania, and its people even fought a now-forgotten war with Scots-Irish guerrillas for control of the area in the 1760s and 1770s. Connecticut settlers won the opening matches with the help of Scots-Irish mercenaries and a favorable ruling from King George I, and founded Wilkes-Barre and Westmoreland; after the revolution, the Continental Congress gave the region back to Pennsylvania, which tried to evict the Yankees by force. Connecticut and Vermont sent soldiers to help the settlers repel the attack, resulting in a final "Yankee-Pennamite War" in 1782. In the end Pennsylvania kept jurisdiction, but the settlers retained their land titles.

Similarly, Massachusetts laid claim to all of present-day New York west of Seneca Lake—six million acres in all—an area larger than Massachusetts itself. Based on contradictory royal grants, the claim was strong enough to compel New York to agree to a major compromise in 1786: the region would be part of the state of New York, but Massachusetts would own the property and could sell it at a profit. The result: settlement of much of the region was directed by Boston-based land speculators, and virtually all of its settlers came from New England. Traveling in the region in the early nineteenth century, Yale president (and Congregational minister) Timothy Dwight remarked on how much its towns looked like those in his native Connecticut and prophesied the Empire State would soon become "a colony from New England." The towns of Yankee-settled areas such as Oneida and Onondaga counties in the west or Essex, Clinton, and Franklin in the north still look and vote much like their New England counterparts.[1]

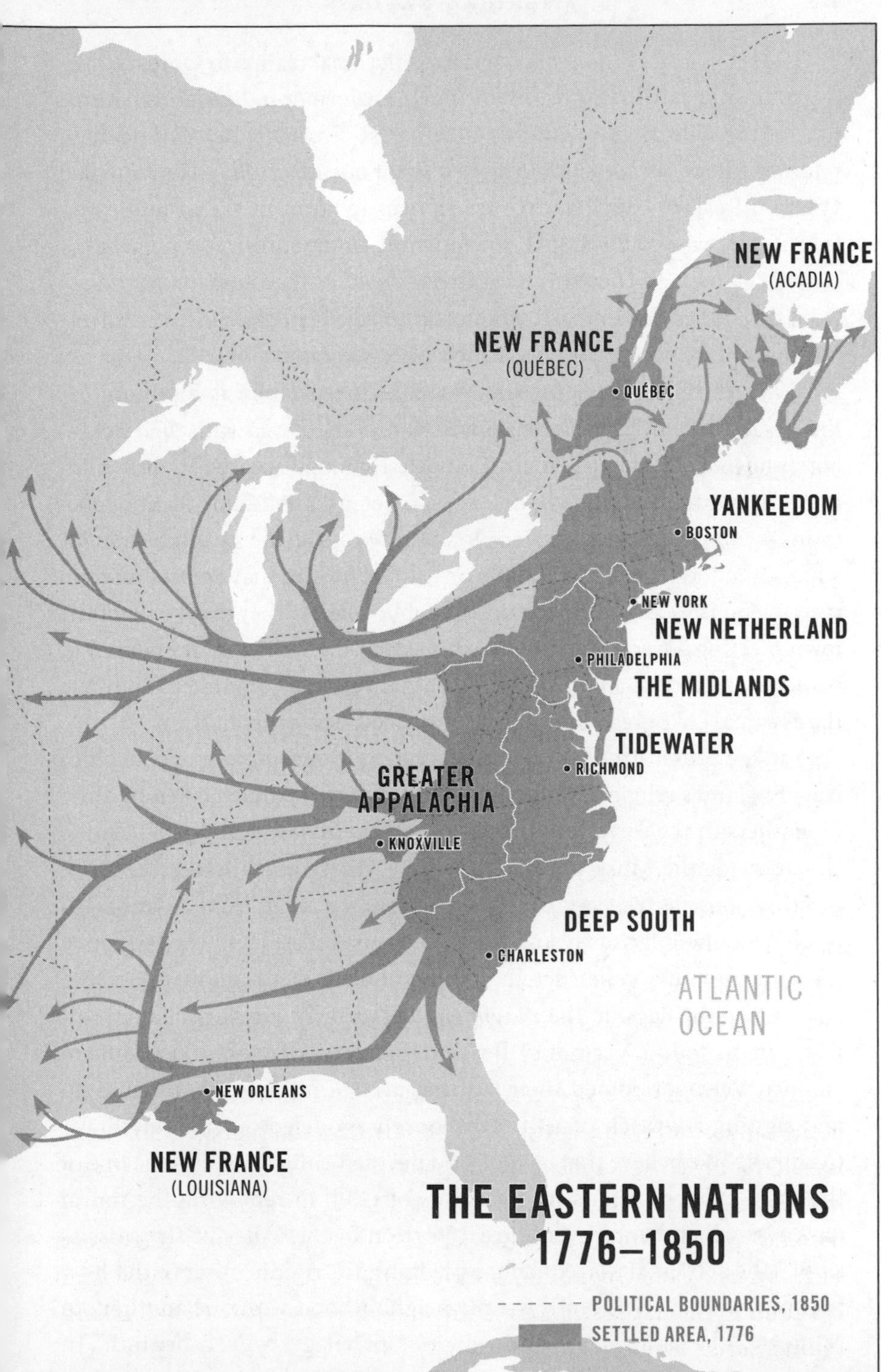

NEW FRANCE
(ACADIA)
NEW FRANCE
(QUÉBEC)
QUÉBEC
YANKEEDOM
BOSTON
NEW YORK
NEW NETHERLAND
PHILADELPHIA
THE MIDLANDS
TIDEWATER
RICHMOND
GREATER
APPALACHIA
KNOXVILLE
DEEP SOUTH
CHARLESTON
ATLANTIC
OCEAN
NEW ORLEANS
NEW FRANCE
(LOUISIANA)
THE EASTERN NATIONS
1776–1850
POLITICAL BOUNDARIES, 1850
SETTLED AREA, 1776

The states had relinquished any jurisdictional claims to Ohio and the rest of the upper Midwest in 1786, when these former Indian lands became part of the federal government's Northwest Territory. But Connecticut retained title to a three-million-acre strip of northern Ohio—its so-called Western Reserve—which was turned over to some of the same Boston speculators who had retailed out much of western New York. Another New England land company obtained a swath of the Muskingum Valley from the federal government. Both parcels were settled almost exclusively by Yankees.

True to form, the New Englanders tended to move west as communities. Entire families would pack their possessions, rendezvous with their neighbors, and journey en masse to their new destination, often led by their minister. On arrival they planted a new town—not just a collection of individual farms—complete with a master plot plan with specific sites set aside for streets, the town green and commons, a Congregational or Presbyterian meeting house, and the all-important public school. They also brought the town meeting government model with them. In a culture that believed in communal freedom and local self-governance, a well-regulated town was the essential civic organism and the very definition of civilization.

Yankee settler groups often viewed their journey as an extension of New England's religious mission, a parallel to those undertaken by their forefathers in the early 1600s. The first group to depart Ipswich, Massachusetts, for the Muskingum Valley in 1787 paraded before the town meeting house to receive a farewell message from their minister modeled on the one the Pilgrims heard before leaving Holland. On the last leg of their journey, they constructed a flotilla of boats to float down the Ohio and named the flagship the *Mayflower of the West*. Similarly, before setting out to found Vermontville, Michigan, ten families in Addison County, Vermont, joined their Congregational minister in drawing up and signing a written constitution loosely modeled on the Mayflower Compact. "We believe that a pious and devoted emigration is to be one of the most efficient means in the hands of God, in removing the moral darkness which hangs over a great portion of the valley of the Mississippi," the settlers declared before pledging to "rigidly observe the holy Sabbath" and to settle "in the same neighborhood with one another" to re-create "the same social and religious privileges we left behind." In

Granville, Massachusetts, settlers drew up a similar compact before undertaking the journey to create Granville, Ohio.[2]

These New England outposts quickly dotted the map of the Western Reserve, their names revealing the origins of their Connecticut founders: Bristol, Danbury, Fairfield, Greenwich, Guilford, Hartford, Litchfield, New Haven, New London, Norwalk, Saybrook, and many more. Not surprisingly, people quickly started calling the region New Connecticut.

The Yankees consciously sought to extend New England culture across the upper Midwest. The emigrants aboard the *Mayflower of the West* were typical. On arrival in eastern Ohio, they founded the town of Marietta, and happily imposed taxes on themselves to fund the construction and operation of a school, church, and library. Nine years after their arrival, they founded the first of the Yankee Midwest's many New England–style colleges. Marietta College was headed by New England–born Calvinist ministers and dedicated to "assiduously inculcating" the "essential doctrines and duties of the Christian religion." Also, "No sectarian peculiarities of belief will be taught," the founding trustees decreed. Similar colleges popped up wherever the Yankees spread, each a powerful outpost of cultural production: Oberlin and Case Western Reserve (in Ohio), Olivet (in Michigan), Beloit, Ripon, and Madison (in Wisconsin), Carleton (Minnesota), Grinnell (Iowa), and Illinois College.[3]

In this way, the Yankees laid down the cultural infrastructure of a large part of Ohio, portions of Iowa and Illinois, and almost the entirety of Michigan, Wisconsin, and Minnesota. They had near-total control over politics in the latter three states for much of the nineteenth century. Five of the first six governors of Michigan were Yankees, and four had been born in New England. In Wisconsin, nine of the first twelve governors were Yankees, and all the rest were either New Netherlanders or foreign-born. (By contrast, in Illinois—where Midlands and Appalachian cultures were in the majority—not one of the first six governors was of Yankee descent; all had been born south of the Mason-Dixon line.) A third of Minnesota's first territorial legislature was New England–born, and a great many of the rest were from upstate New York and the Yankee Midwest. In all three upper Great Lakes states, Yankees dominated discussions in the constitutional conventions and transplanted their legal, political, and religious norms. Across the Yankee Midwest, later settlers—be they immigrants or transplants from the other American nations—confronted a dominant culture rooted in New England.[4]

Nineteenth-century visitors often remarked on the difference between the areas north and south of the old National Road, an early highway that bisected Ohio and which is now called U.S. 40. North of the road, houses were said to be substantial and well maintained, with well-fed livestock outside and literate, well-schooled inhabitants within. Village greens, white church steeples, town hall belfries, and green-shuttered houses were the norm. South of the road, farm buildings were unpainted, the people were poorer and less educated, and the better homes were built with brick in Greco-Roman style. "As you travel north across Ohio," Ohio State University dean Harlan Hatcher wrote in 1945, "you feel that you have been transported from Virginia into Connecticut." There were exceptions (Yankees skipped over the marshlands of Indiana and northeastern Ohio en route to Michigan and Illinois), and between Appalachian "Virginia" and Yankee "Connecticut" one passed through a Midland transition zone. But the general observation holds true: the place we call "the Midwest" is actually divided into east-west cultural bands running all the way out to the Mississippi River and beyond.[5]

Foreign immigrants to the Midwest often chose where to settle based on their degree of affinity or hostility to the dominant culture, and vice versa. The first major wave was German, and, not surprisingly, many of them joined their countrymen in the Midlands. Those who did not faced a choice between the Yankees and the Appalachian folk; few opted to settle in areas controlled by the latter.

Swedes and other Scandinavians, for their part, were comfortable with the Yankees, with whom they shared a commitment to frugality, sobriety, and civic responsibility; a hostility to slavery; and an acceptance of a state-run church. "The Scandinavians are the 'New Englanders' of the Old World," a Congregational missionary in the Midwest informed his colleagues. "We can as confidently rely upon them to help American Christians rightly [make] . . . 'America for Christ' as we can rely upon the good *old* stock of Massachusetts."[6]

Other groups who fundamentally disagreed with New England values avoided the region on account of the Yankees' reputation for minding other people's business and pressuring newcomers to conform to their cultural norms. Catholics—whether Irish, south German, or Italian—did not appreciate the Yankee educational system, correctly recognizing that the schools were designed to assimilate their children into Yankee culture. In areas where Catholic immigrants cohabitated with Yankees, the newcomers created their own parallel system of parochial schools precisely to protect their children from the Yankee mold. Yankees often reacted with hostility, denouncing Catholic immigrants as unwitting tools of a Vatican-directed conspiracy to bring down the republic. Whenever possible, Catholic immigrants chose to live in the more tolerant, multicultural Midlands or in individualistic Appalachia, where moral crusaders were looked upon as self-righteous and irritating. Even German Protestants found themselves at odds with their Yankee neighbors, who would try to pressure them into giving up their brewing traditions and beer gardens in favor of a solemn, austere observance of the Sabbath. Multiculturalism wouldn't become a Yankee hallmark until much later, after Puritan values ceased to be seen as essential to promoting the common good.[7]

Political scientists investigating voting patterns have probed electoral records dating back to the early nineteenth century, matching polling-place returns with demographic information about each precinct. The results have been startling. Previous assumptions about class or occupation being the key factors influencing voter choices have turned out to be completely wrong, with the nineteenth-century Midwest providing some of the most intriguing evidence that ethnographic origins trumped all other considerations from 1850 onward. Poor white German Catholic miners in northern Wisconsin tended to vote entirely differently from poor white English Methodist miners in the same area. English Congregationalists tended to vote alike regardless of whether they lived in cities or on farms. Scandinavian immigrants voted with native-born Yankees in opposition to candidates and policies preferred by immigrant Irish Catholics or native-born Southern Baptists of Appalachian origin.[8]

As the nation careened toward civil war in the 1850s, areas first settled by Yankees gravitated to the new Republican Party. Counties dominated by immigrants from New England or Scandinavia were the strongest Republican supporters, generally backed by German Protestants. This made Michigan, Wisconsin, and Minnesota reliably Republican straight through the mid-twentieth century; the other states split along national lines. Later, when the Republicans became champions in the fight against civil rights, Yankee-dominated states and counties in the Midwest flipped en masse to the Democrats, just as their colleagues in New England did. The outlines of the Western Reserve are still visible on a county-by-county map of the 2000, 2004, or 2008 presidential elections.

While much of the upper Midwest is indeed part of Greater Yankeedom, its greatest city is not. Chicago, founded by Yankees around Fort Dearborn in the 1830s, quickly took on the role of a border city, a grand trading entrepôt and transportation hub on the boundary of the Yankee and Midland Wests. New Englanders were influential early on, establishing institutions such as the Field Museum (named for Marshall Field of Conway, Massachusetts), the Newberry Library (for Walter Newberry of Connecticut), the *Chicago Democrat* and *Inter Ocean* newspapers, and the Chicago Theological Institute. But New Englanders were soon overwhelmed by new arrivals from Europe, the Midlands, Appalachia, and beyond. Purists fled north to found the very Yankee suburb of Evanston. Other Yankees looked disapprovingly upon the brash, unruly, multiethnic metropolis. By the 1870 census, New England natives comprised just one-thirtieth of the city's population.[9]

However assiduously New Englanders had set out to transform the frontier, they themselves were also transformed by it. Yankee culture may have maintained its underlying zeal to improve the world, setting it on the path toward the secular Puritanism of the present day, but it was stripped of its commitment to religious orthodoxy.

On the frontier, many Yankees would remain true to the Congregational faith or its near-cousin Presbyterianism, but others experienced a religious conversion. An essentially theocratic society, New England produced an unusual number of intense religious personalities—people, in the words of the late historian Frederick Merk, "eager to get into direct touch with God, to see God in person, to hear His voice from on high." In the tightly controlled Yankee homeland, mystics and self-declared prophets generally were kept in check, but out on the frontier, the enforcement of orthodoxy was laxer. The result was an explosion of new religions, starting in western New York, where religious fervor was so incendiary that people started calling it the "Burnt-over District."[10]

Many religions came into being, but nearly all of them sought to restore the primitive simplicity of the early Christian faith before it accreted elaborate institutions, a written canon, and a bevy of clerical authorities. If Lutherans, Calvinists, or Methodists had sought to bring people closer to God by eliminating the upper levels of ecclesiastical hierarchy (archbishops, cardinals, and the Vatican), these new evangelicals took things several steps further, removing the middle ranks almost entirely. People were to contact God directly and personally, and would become born again when they did so. They were to seek their own path to the divine, guided by one or more trailblazers who allegedly enjoyed unusually good communication with their maker. Like the prophets, these charismatic leaders believed they had been personally contacted by God and shown the true path to salvation.

On the Yankee frontier, God apparently handed out conflicting instructions. William Miller, a farmer born in Massachusetts and raised on the Vermont frontier, announced that Christ was to return, cleanse, and purify the Earth in 1843. When this failed to occur, he recalculated the date to October 22, 1844, setting his tens of thousands of followers up for an event known as the Great Disappointment. The movement's adherents still await the second coming, worshipping on Saturdays and emphasizing a diet featuring cold grains and cereals. (They're now known as the Seventh-Day Adventists and number over a million members.) John Humphrey Noyes, a Yale-educated Vermonter, decided the second coming had already occurred and, having declared himself "perfect and free of sin," led his followers to create a utopian society in upstate New York; intended as a model for Christ's millennial kingdom, Noyes's Oneida Community featured communal manufacturing, property ownership, and sexual relations, with older men and postmenopausal women encouraged to deflower the virgins. Vermont farmer Joseph Smith and his son were among hundreds of "divining men" who claimed special abilities to find buried treasures and dispel the charms protecting them, services they were paid in advance to perform. After being arrested for defrauding his clients, Joseph Smith Jr. found a set of golden plates in a hillside in Manchester, New York (others were not allowed to see them), which revealed to him (in a language only he could read) that Jesus would return to Independence, Missouri. Tens of thousands were drawn to his polygamous millennial kingdom in Nauvoo, Illinois, which tried to secede from the state to become a separate U.S. territory. After Smith's assassination, his followers moved to Utah and, as the Church of Jesus Christ of Latter-day Saints, now number over 5 million. These and kindred utopian movements on the Yankee frontier had a dramatic effect on future developments on the continent.[11]

Across Yankeedom the official Congregational and Presbyterian churches were also losing adherents to rival denominations, shattering religious homogeneity. Some New England congregations embraced Unitarianism (the belief in a unitary God as opposed to a holy trinity), and some of those later moved on to Unitarian Universalism, which holds that each individual is free to search for his own answers to the great religious and existential questions. Far more Yankees shifted to Methodism, an eighteenth-century splinter from the Anglican Church with an emphasis on effecting social change, or, following in the footsteps of Rhode Island's founders, became Baptists, who believed in salvation through faith alone. This amounted to a major shift in Yankee religious heritage, and was deplored by Congregational authorities. Lyman Beecher, perhaps the most influential mid-nineteenth-century Yankee theologian, decried Baptists and Methodists as "worse than nothing" and Unitarians as "enemies of the truth."[12]

While religious orthodoxy in New England was undermined during the nineteenth century, the deep-seated Yankee belief that it was possible to make earthly society resemble God's kingdom above remained intact. Lyman Beecher and other members of the orthodox elite would fight a ferocious rearguard action against the insurgents, but the effort was ultimately futile. The Yankee moral project was by no means over, however. Its greatest battles lay just ahead and would be waged against its rival nations to the south.

CHAPTER 16

The Midlands Spread West

As New Englanders headed west across the northern tier of the Northwest Territory, land-hungry settlers from the Midlands were pouring into the central Midwest. The Midlanders—a great many of them German speaking—carried their pluralistic culture into the Heartland, a place long since identified with neighborliness, family-centered progress, practical politics, and a distrust of big government. Spanning the north-central portions of Ohio, Indiana, and Illinois, the Greater Midlands spread through central and southern Iowa, northern Missouri, eastern Nebraska and Kansas, and even northernmost Texas—an area many times greater than its original hearth on the shores of the Delaware Bay. Its settlements—a collection of mutually tolerant ethnic enclaves—served as a buffer between the intolerant, communitarian morality of Greater Yankeedom and the individualistic hedonism of Greater Appalachia, just as they had earlier on the eastern seaboard. New Englanders and Appalachian people often settled among them, but neither group's values took hold. The Midland Midwest would develop as a center of moderation and tolerance, where people of many faiths and ethnicities lived side by side, largely minding their own business. Few Midwestern Midlanders were Quakers, but they unconsciously carried aspects of William Penn's vision to fruition.

Most Midlanders reached the region on the National Road, which guided their settlement to the Mississippi and beyond. Pennsylvania Germans did their best to replicate the towns they'd left behind. New Philadelphia, Ohio, was founded by a congregation of Moravians and soon attracted German-speaking Mennonites. In Ohio, Pennsylvania Dutch dominated a fifty-mile-wide belt of farms south of the Yankee Western Reserve in settlements called Berlin, Hanover, Dresden, Frankfort, Potsdam, Strasburg, or Winesburg. Amish and Dunkers founded Nazareth, Canaan, and Bethlehem. Pennsylvania Dutch barns and United Brethren churches sprang up amid tidy farmhouses and fields of wheat. From the 1830s this familiar cultural environment attracted huge numbers of immigrants directly from Germany who congregated in Cincinnati.[1]

In Indiana the Midlander belt of settlement was narrower due to their discomfort with the Appalachian dominance over the territory's affairs. Indiana's Borderlanders called themselves Hoosiers, came from the backcountry of Kentucky and western Virginia, and were ambivalent about slavery. But to Yankees and Midlanders they might as well have come from the Deep South. "Avoid settling in those states where negro slavery prevails," a Philadelphia newspaper advised would-be emigrants to the west. "Your children will be corrupted by their vices and the slave lords will never treat you like Christians or fellow citizens." To settle in Yankee-dominated Michigan or Wisconsin, meanwhile, meant putting up with the New Englanders' irritating desire to make everyone into a Yankee. Many Midlanders did ultimately put down roots there (Milwaukee would declare itself the "German capital of America"), but they had to expend time and energy resisting Yankee attempts to close their beer gardens on the Sabbath, to force English-only public schools on their children, and to stamp out their Germanness. In the Midland zone, foreigners, Catholics, and others found a society untroubled by diversity but skeptical of slave labor, warfare, and the cult of the individual.[2]

Midlanders settled a swath of the north-central area of Illinois, anchored by the border cities of Chicago and St. Louis. Northern Missouri became a Midland stronghold as well, with St. Louis supporting two German-language daily newspapers by 1845. Bavarian immigrant George Schneider founded the Bavarian Brewery there in 1852, selling it to Eberhard Anheuser and Adolphus Busch a few years later. Continued immigration from Germany enabled Midland civilization to dominate the American Heartland despite competition from aggressive Yankees and Borderlanders. By midcentury, German immigrants were arriving by riverboat in St. Louis and from there fanning out across northern Missouri and the eastern prairies. Railroads followed, carrying immigrants from Europe and the coastal Midlands alike.[3]

Germans had many reasons to abandon central Europe, where forty independent German states were squabbling over the great issues raised by the French Revolution: the legitimacy of feudalism, monarchies, and an economic system in which most people lived in dire poverty. Efforts to unify the region into a single state under a representative government failed in 1848, and many Germans looked to escape the military autocracy that followed. Even before the collapse of the so-called '48 Revolution, liberals had wished for a place where they could build a New Germany, a model for the democratic, egalitarian society they had hoped their own splintered nation could become. "The foundations of a new and free Germany in the great north American republic can be laid by us," the leader of one German colonization expedition to the American Midwest told his followers in 1833. "We may in at least one of the American territories create a state that is German from its foundations up, in which all those to whom the future here at home may seem . . . intolerable, can find refuge." This and other expeditions were drawn to northern Missouri by the writings of Prussian-born resident Gottfried Duden, who extolled the region as a ready-made utopia. They were further encouraged by the new German Society of Philadelphia, which sought to found "a New Germany" in the west as "a secure refuge for ourselves, our children, and our descendants." As the United States headed to the brink of civil war in the late 1850s, two leading German political analysts predicted the union would break into a number of independent states, some "under German rule." These ideas are probably not what ultimately motivated the hundreds of thousands of ordinary Germans who actually made the move to the American Midlands, but they did provide the means for many of them to get there, in the form of useful information, organized emigration societies, and political assistance. No state would ever come close to being dominated by the German-born—Wisconsin stalled at 16 percent in 1860—but the 1830–1860 exodus from the Fatherland ensured that the diverse and tolerant Midlander civilization would come to dominate the American Heartland.[4]

The flow of Quaker migrants was much smaller, but they were drawn to the Midland Midwest for similar reasons. In the early nineteenth century, Friends still sought to separate themselves from the world, and many found it harder and harder to do so on the densely populated eastern seaboard. During the course of the century, a number of Quaker enclaves outside of the Midlands relocated to Ohio and Central Indiana. Disgusted by slavery, century-old Quaker communities abandoned Tidewater and the Deep South. Indiana eclipsed Philadelphia as the center of North American Quakers in the 1850s. To this day, Richmond, Indiana, is second only to the City of Brotherly Love in total Quaker population. Nestled among communities of Germans, Scots-Irish, English Methodists, Moravians, Amish, and others, the Quakers had found a cultural landscape almost identical to that of southeastern Pennsylvania.[5]

Like the Yankee Midwest, the Greater Midlands was settled by groups of families who had been neighbors on the eastern seaboard or in Europe. Unlike Yankees, they generally weren't interested in assimilating people in neighboring communities, let alone in entire states. As in the Delaware Valley, individual towns were often dominated by a particular ethnic group, but counties tended to be pluralistic. Midwestern towns took their gridiron street plans from Pennsylvania precedents. The Germans set the tone, generally buying land with the intent to build lasting family homesteads rather than as speculative investments. They sought a permanent, organic connection to their land, taking unusual care to ensure its long-term productivity through soil and forest conservation measures first perfected on the tiny farm plots of central Europe. Whether arriving from Europe or Pennsylvania, they built their homes from stone whenever possible, as it was more durable than the wood used by the Yankees or Appalachian people.[6]

Scholars have observed that the Germans insisted on entering the American melting pot collectively, on their own terms, and bearing ingredients they felt the country was lacking. Germans arriving from Europe usually had a higher standard of education, craftsmanship, and farming knowledge than most of their American neighbors, whom they found grasping and uncultured. "Americans are in their regard for art half-barbarian," immigrant Gustave Koerner remarked in 1834, "and their taste is not much better than that of the Indian aborigines, who stick metal rings through their noses." The Germans avoided assimilating, using their language in schools and newspapers and almost exclusively marrying other Germans as late as the 1880s. In a country rushing madly toward the frontier, the Germans distinguished themselves by their emphasis on stable, permanent, rooted communities, where families would work the same piece of land for generations. This rootedness would be perhaps their most lasting contribution to the culture of the Midlands and, by extension, the American Midwest.[7]

The people of the Midland Midwest had political values that distinguished the region from both the Yankee upper Midwest and the Appalachian lower Midwest. Midland areas resisted Yankee cultural imperialism and thus voted against the new Yankee-controlled political vehicle that emerged in the 1850s: the Republican Party. Midlanders did not wish to create a homogeneous nation: Quakers championed religious freedom, at least for Christians; new British immigrants were coming for economic opportunity, not to create an ideal Calvinist republic; Germans were accustomed to living among people of different religions. While these and other groups settling in the Midlands zone may have disliked and disagreed with one another, none sought to rule or assimilate the others beyond the town or neighborhood level. All rejected the Yankee efforts to do so.

As a result, throughout the 1850s a majority of Midlanders supported the anti-Yankee Democratic Party, which, at the time, was the party of the Deep South, Tidewater, and immigrants, especially Catholics. Democrats in this era rejected the notion that governments had a moral mission to better society, either through assimilating minorities or eliminating slavery. People—whether Deep Southern slave lords or the impoverished Irish Catholic immigrants of Boston—should be left to go about their business as they wished.

But at the end of the 1850s this allegiance to the Democrats began to change as tensions built over the extension of slavery to Missouri, Kansas, and other new states and territories. Midland opinion began to splinter along doctrinal lines. Religious groups whose beliefs emphasized the need to redeem the world through good works, moral reforms, or utopian experiments found common ground with the Yankees, first on slavery, and later on efforts to curb alcoholism, blasphemous speech, and antisocial behaviors; this led Dutch Calvinists, German Sectarians, Swedish Lutherans, Northern Methodists, Free Will Baptists, and General Synod German Lutherans to embrace the Republican Party. People whose religious beliefs did not emphasize—or actively discouraged—efforts to make the present world holy stuck with the laissez-faire Democrats: Confessional German Lutherans, Roman Catholics, Southern Baptists, and

Southern Methodists. Groups occupying the middle ground on these issues (Anglicans, the Disciples of Christ) were split.[8]

The end result was characteristically Midland: a large region of swing voters whose support could make or break nearly every future federal coalition around any given issue. On the eve of the Civil War, slavery would push a narrow majority of Midlanders into the Republican camp. Careful forensic analysis of the 1860 presidential vote by late twentieth-century political scientists has shown that this shift in Midlander opinion—particularly among Germans—tipped Illinois, Ohio, and Indiana into Abraham Lincoln's column, giving him control of the White House. Defeated on the federal stage by the defection of the Midland Midwest, the Deep South would move to secede almost immediately.[9]

CHAPTER 17

Appalachia Spreads West

It is little wonder that historians have long identified the Appalachian people with the frontier. Borderlanders were the first to move across the Appalachians, forcing their way into Native American territory in the immediate aftermath of the American Revolution. They were founding renegade governments like Transylvania and the State of Franklin long before the Continental Congress got around to creating the Northwest Territory or conquering the Indians that lived within it. Yankees and Midlanders generally waited until federal military forces had defeated Indian peoples before moving into their lands; Borderlanders often carried out the conquest themselves. While New Englanders were still colonizing upstate New York, Appalachian folk were rafting down the Ohio River to stake out claims in southern Indiana and Illinois. By the time Midlanders reached Ohio, Borderlanders were skirmishing with Cherokees in central Tennessee. They were very often on the cutting edge of Euro-American expansion because of their willingness—even desire—to live beyond the effective reach of government.

Greater Appalachian culture spread faster and wider than that of the other nations. Attracted by better soils, cheap and properly surveyed land, and easier access to markets (via the Ohio and Mississippi rivers), hundreds of thousands fled Virginia in the first half of the nineteenth century, causing the Old Dominion to cease to be the most populous state in the Union. This mass movement out of Virginia and other eastern states came to be known as the Great Migration, and it was in large part an Appalachian movement. By 1800 Borderlanders had colonized much of what is now Kentucky, north-central Tennessee, and southwestern Illinois. Thirty years later—at a time when Yankeees had yet to reach Illinois or Wisconsin—Borderlanders had seized control of northern Alabama, much of the rest of Tennessee, the Ozarks of Arkansas, and the Mississippi Valley of southern Illinois and Missouri. In 1850 they were spreading across north Texas, carrying the speech patterns of Ulster and the English Marches to their homes on the range. The culture's turbulent, highly mobile people were deflected only by the power of the Deep Southern planters and stopped short only upon reaching the treeless, arid prairies they encountered at the edge of the Far West. The culture they laid down—allegedly that of "real Americans"—was very different from that of its neighbors, many of whom found its disorderliness distasteful.

But during the second quarter of the nineteenth century, Borderlanders became so numerous and widespread that their leaders were able to seize control of national affairs, occupying the White House and branding an epoch of American history with their values.

Greater Appalachia was a decidedly rural nation. Borderlanders expanded across Kentucky and the southern Midwest not as transplanted communities but as individuals or in small groups. Scattering themselves through the forests and hollows, they formed towns almost as an afterthought, spurning investments in communal resources. Across Greater Appalachia local taxes were low, schools and libraries rare, and municipal governments few and far between. The proportion of Kentuckians enrolled in public schools in 1850 was about one-sixth that of Maine, the poorest and most frontier-like New England state, while its libraries had fewer than half as many books per capita.[1]

Appalachian illiteracy has complicated historians' efforts to trace its people's progress. Most accounts of Midwestern Borderlanders come from the voluminous writings of Yankee neighbors and visitors to the region, who were generally shocked by their poverty. Philadelphia physician Richard Lee Mason crossed southern Indiana in the winter of 1819 and described coming upon "one of the most miserable huts ever seen," a pile of slabs laid against a pigsty containing a woman and "two shivering and almost starving children," all of them bareheaded and barefoot; the father was "absent in search of bread." One farmer reported, "Southern Illinois has been a city of refuge for the poor people of the Slave States. I saw children here . . . last year, eat dirt, they were so hungry." Midwestern Yankees took to calling the Borderlanders "butternuts"—a reference to the color of their crude homespun clothes. "Hoosier"—a Southern slang term for a frontier hick—was adopted as a badge of honor by the Appalachian people of Indiana.[2]

Appalachia's farming was an improvised and destructive affair. Borderlanders, who were primarily a society of herdsmen, sought forested land, where they burned the trees or killed them by girdling. Corn was planted between the stumps and, when ripened, fed to hogs and cattle or made into corn bread, cornmeal mush, or whiskey. Families often stayed in a particular location for only a few years before moving on, sometimes because they had been squatting and the real owners appeared, but more often because the area had started to get too thickly settled. As one scholar explained, "When neighbors got as close as five miles, they felt crowded." Scholars have since found that 60 to 80 percent of frontiersmen moved within a decade of arrival, with the poorest people relocating most often.[3]

Outsiders blamed the settlers themselves for their poverty. Dr. Mason said the people of southern Indiana were "imprudent and lazy beyond example." "Yankee energy and enterprise do not enter into the composition of their character," an Ohio-based journalist agreed. "The resources of southern Illinois are limited only because its inhabitants have not been adequate to develop its resources," Yankee-born state senator Jason Strevell told his colleagues on the floor of that state's capitol. "Sloth and independence are prominent traits in their character," a Massachusetts pastor said of West Virginians, alleging these were "their principal enjoyment" and "chief ambition," respectively. Another described the Butternut as a "long, lank, lean, ignorant animal . . . little in advance of the savage state [and] content to squat in a log-cabin with a large family of ill-fed and ill-clothed, idle, ignorant children." One Illinois newspaper deplored "the intellectual, moral, and political darkness which covers the land" in Appalachian-settled areas.[4]

Outsiders also remarked on the unsettled nature of the region's people. Indiana—a state dominated by Appalachian people—was reported to be populated by those with a "prevailing thirst for immigration," a "floating, unsettled class waiting [for] an opportunity to sell out and move further." A correspondent for the *New England Farmer* worried such individuals would never "settle down into anything like the moral and religious society of New England." A Massachusetts farmer predicted in 1839 that "a long period" would have to elapse before the region's inhabitants became "assimilated and melted down into one homogenous mass."[5]

Yankeedom sent missionaries to Appalachian areas in an effort to encourage assimilation, but religious and cultural differences frustrated their work. College-trained New Englanders soberly read from carefully prepared written sermons to listeners accustomed to the fiery, improvised oratory of itinerant preachers. "They are not generally a reading people, but a thinking and talking people," one missionary reported from southern Illinois. "They are accustomed to catch the glance of the living eye and to be instructed and animated by the counsels and persuasions of a living voice." Others complained of the Borderlanders' overly casual manners: men didn't take their hats off when entering church, toddlers were allowed to run about the pews at will, and adults came and went as they pleased. More troubling was the Borderlanders' refusal to provide Yankee ministers with full financial support, as they were accustomed to having preachers with honest day jobs as farmers or craftsmen. Others were distrusted simply because they were from New England, and, as one Borderlander put it, "no good can come from hence."[6]

Yankees also had difficulty understanding Appalachian dialects and vocabulary. In Indiana one noted the difference in how the members of the two cultures would describe a runaway team of horses. "It run into the bush and run astride astraddle, and broke the neap, reach, and evener," a Yankee would say. His Hoosier neighbor would interpret these remarks thus: "The horses got skeert and run astraddle of a sapling and broke the tongue, double-tree, and couplin pole." Yankees were perplexed when young Borderlanders called their spouses "old woman" or "old man" and amused by their use of "yon" for "that," "reckon" for "guess," "heap" for "a lot of" and "powerful" where a New Englander would say "very."[7]

There were other differences, as well. Yankee Midwesterners placed their homes on the road, ate potatoes as their starch, planted fruit orchards, built barns and straight board fences, harnessed their horses to carts for a race, negotiated written contracts, and buried their dead in town graveyards. Appalachian Midwesterners built their homes near the center of their plots (for privacy), preferred corn as their starch, spurned orchards, built open sheds if they sheltered their livestock at all, enclosed pastures with split-rail fences, rode their horses when racing, negotiated verbal, honor-bound agreements, and put their relatives to rest in family plots or isolated graves.[8]

The Borderlanders had resented the arrogance of their Tidewater and

Deep Southern overlords, and they resented Yankee condescension, as well. Orlando Ficklin, a Kentucky-born Illinoisan, was thankful "that God made the world before He made the Yankees, for they would have interfered with His business and destroyed the beautiful world in which we live." Kentuckians reportedly regarded a Yankee "as a sort of Jesuit" because of his religious zeal, while in Illinois the term *yankeed* was synonymous with *cheated*.[9]

Not surprisingly, Borderlanders also had very different political preferences from those of their Yankee neighbors. They generally championed the "honest farmer and mechanic" in their struggle against educated professionals, the wealthy, aristocratic planters, or lowland slave lords. One Hoosier editorialist urged his countrymen to vote for "men who know what it is to eat their bread in the sweat of the face" because "they will know how to represent your interest." Otherwise, "the produce of our labor shall be filched from us to support an aristocracy that in the end will overturn our liberties." Appalachian people everywhere distrusted political parties, seeing them as cartels of powerful interests, and voted for whichever one appeared to advocate for ordinary individuals.[10]

For Appalachian Midwesterners it was the meddlesome Yankees who represented the greatest threat to their ideas of individual freedom. As a result, Borderlander-dominated regions solidly supported the Deep Southern–led Democratic Party throughout the nineteenth century and right up into the civil rights era. As Kevin Phillips has observed, "Butternut Democrats did not care much about slavery, but they could not stand the Yankees." Their political representatives railed against Yankee efforts to use the federal government to impose their morals on the other nations. "The Puritan Roundhead of New England and the Cavalier of Virginia—the slavery-hating, though sometimes slave-trading, saint of Boston and the slaveholding sinner of Savannah . . . all joined hands in holy brotherhood to ordain a Constitution which, silent about temperance, forbade religious tests and establishments, and provided for the extradition of fugitive slaves," Ohio congressman Clement Vallandigham noted, before blaming Yankees for endangering the Union by opposing the expansion of slavery. "You are a peculiar people," he said of New Englanders, "for you have dethroned Jehovah, and set up a new and anti-slavery god of your own." On a national level the Democrats capitalized on this libertarian zeal by emphasizing the need to protect personal freedom—including the freedom to own slaves—from government interference. Borderlander-settled counties generally supported Jefferson over Adams in 1800, Andrew Jackson over John Quincy Adams in 1828 and 1832, and Douglas over Lincoln in 1860, while sending Democrats to represent them on Capitol Hill.[11]

Farther south, migrating Borderlanders contended not with Yankees but with a powerful nation that was in the midst of adopting European ways. In the 1740s the Cherokee Indian nation controlled the core of what we now think of as Appalachia: most of what is now Kentucky and Tennessee, a third of South Carolina, Georgia, Alabama, and West Virginia, and the westernmost swaths of Virginia and North Carolina. For centuries the Cherokees had defended their farming villages and hunting turf from incursions by Iroquois, Creeks, and Shawnee. When Borderlanders began invading their land in the 1750s, they fought back. During the American Revolution they sided with the British on the accurate assumption that imperial power was the only thing keeping land-hungry backcountry squatters in check. "The great God of Nature has placed us in different situations," Cherokee elder Corn Tassel told negotiators at a Revolutionary-era peace conference. "It is true he has endowed you with many superior advantages; but he has not created us to be your slaves. We are a separate people."[12]

Separate, yes, but despite their conflicts with the Borderlanders, considerable cultural and genetic exchange continued to occur. Some Appalachian people "went Native," marrying into Cherokee villages; many more carried on dalliances with Cherokee women. By the end of the eighteenth century, a mixed-blood Cherokee upper class had formed whose members spoke English, converted to Christianity, and could act as cultural interlocutors. As president, Thomas Jefferson had urged the Cherokee "to go on learning to cultivate the Earth," promising that "in time, you will be as we are." Their mixed-race elite took this advice to heart, encouraging their people to emulate the Tidewater ways of Jefferson's Virginia. Corn Tassel's métis nephew, Sequoyah, developed a written Cherokee script that was quickly adopted by his people. The Bible was translated into Cherokee, and, in 1828, the *Cherokee Phoenix* newspaper began rolling off the press at their capital, New Echota. Cherokee leaders passed a written constitution modeled on that of the United States, while healers, herbalists, and conjurers recorded their ancient practices and knowledge for the first time. Farms and villages grew into plantations and towns. Leading families first hired whites to help maintain their growing business enterprises, then began purchasing large numbers of African slaves to do the most difficult work. By 1825 the elite owned 1,277 slaves, accounting for 10 percent of their nation's population. Meanwhile, they made it clear that they would surrender no more of their land, by then limited to the northern third of Georgia and Alabama, and adjacent sections of North Carolina and Tennessee—not "one foot more," a delegation to Washington announced.[13]

Unfortunately for the Cherokee, the growing population and influence of Appalachia launched a Borderlander warrior into the White House in 1829, one with little patience for the rule of law or tolerance for people of other races.

Andrew Jackson, our first Appalachian president, was born to Scots-Irish immigrants on the border between the two Carolinas. In keeping with the Borderlanders' warrior ethic, he fought in the American Revolution, led the Tennessee militia against the Creeks in the War of 1812, and emerged as a national hero after defeating the British at the Battle of New Orleans. A resident of the short-lived State of Franklin and, later, Tennessee, Jackson was a slaveholder, country lawyer, U.S. senator, and irrepressible Indian fighter. On his own initiative he invaded Spanish Florida in 1818 to punish the Seminole Indians for sheltering runaway slaves. By the time he won the presidency, he had personally overseen the expropriation of tens of millions of acres of Native American land, facilitating the expansion of the Deep South to Florida, Alabama, and Mississippi. Indians, he would later tell Congress, "have neither the intelligence, the industry, the moral habits, nor the desire of improvement which are essential to any favorable change in their condition. Established in the midst of another and a superior race, and without appreciating the causes of their inferiority or seeking to control them, they must necessarily yield to the force of circumstances and ere long disappear."[14]

Jackson won the presidency with the overwhelming support of Appalachia, Tidewater, and the Deep South, claiming every electoral vote west of the Appalachians and south of the Mason-Dixon line. His principles—minimal government, maximum freedom for individuals, aggressive military expansion, white supremacy, and the right of each American nation to uphold its customs without the interference of others—earned him few friends in the Midlands and Yankeedom. The tone for his two-term administration was set on Inauguration Day, when thousands of his supporters mobbed the White House, destroying furniture and breaking thousands of dollars' worth of china and glassware in their haste "to get the refreshments, punch and other articles" inside. "The noisy and disorderly rabble in the President's House brought to my mind descriptions I had read, of the mobs in the Tuileries and at Versailles," one witness wrote. "I fear [if such people] get the Power in their hands, that of all tyrants, they [would be] the most ferocious, cruel and despotic." Jackson, for his part, handed out government jobs to his friends with abandon, initiating what one of his allies called "the rule that to the victors belong the spoils of the enemy." Regarding the Cherokee, he would soon demonstrate contempt for the Constitution he had just sworn to uphold.[15]

Ridding Appalachia of the Cherokee was Jackson's top priority. Previous presidents had supported the tribe against the treachery of Georgia's political elite, who wished to steal by force the lands of all "barbarous and savage tribes." Jackson let the Georgians do as they pleased. He remained silent as their legislature passed a bill unilaterally applying all of Georgia's racially discriminatory laws to the Cherokee nation; like other "inferior races" in the Deep South, they would not be allowed to vote, own property, testify against a white person, obtain a loan, or sue in court. When gold was discovered in the Cherokee lands a few months later, Jackson ordered the federal troops assigned to protect the Indians to leave the area, replacing them with predatory Georgia militiamen. He then drafted and put forward the obscene Indian Removal Bill, a measure to ethnically cleanse the Cherokee and neighboring nations and to relocate them a thousand miles to the west in the arid plains of Oklahoma. The measure passed the House by only five votes, with Yankeedom and the Midlands opposed and the Deep South enthusiastically supportive. Meanwhile, the

Supreme Court ruled Georgia's annexation of Cherokee territory unconstitutional, as it violated the tribe's treaty with the federal government. Georgia and the Jackson administration simply ignored the decision. The Cherokees' Georgia lands were raffled off to white people; the Cherokee themselves were rounded up into detention camps by the U.S. Army, then force-marched to Oklahoma under conditions so abominable that 4,000 of them died. The Creek and Chicksaw followed the Cherokees' Trail of Tears a few years later, when Alabama and Mississippi annexed their territories.[16]

Appalachia, the immediate beneficiary, was actually split on the annexations, with Tennessee's famous Davy Crockett denouncing on the House floor the Indian Removal Act as "oppression with a vengeance." But while the region may not have been entirely supportive of its president's actions, the southernmost Appalachians were now open for Borderlander expansion.

Historians traditionally speak of the culture of the "Upland South" as if the presence of slavery alone created a culture distinct from places north of the Ohio River also settled by Borderlanders. The people of Greater Appalachia in fact shared consistent cultural values and characteristics whether they lived in slaveless Indiana or slavery-friendly Tennessee and Arkansas. However, southern Borderlanders confronted a far more dangerous, uncertain, and precarious existence than their prairie kin. Life on the mountain frontier was more lawless, isolated, and combative, with Indian conflicts, banditry, blood feuds, and vigilantism all commonplace occurrences. Early-nineteenth-century visitors were shocked by the violence and debauchery they witnessed on the southern frontier, where men engaged in "rough and tumble" public brawls over minor slights or disagreements in which they gouged out one another's eyes, bit off lips and ears, and tore off noses. Violence that would be considered disreputable in Yankeedom or the Midlands earned one honor and respect in Greater Appalachia, where men were judged based on their toughness and ferocity rather than hard work, righteousness, or material achievements. Leading brawlers grew out their fingernails, hardened them in candle flames, and slicked them with oil to more easily remove their opponent's eyeballs. Victors were celebrated in the region's rich, boastful oral folklore, which celebrated their bloodiness. As one fighter put it: "I can out-run, out-jump, out-shoot, out-brag, out-drink, an' out-fight, rough-an'-tumble, no holds barred, any man on both sides of the [Mississippi] river from Pittsburgh to New Orleans an' back ag'in to St. Louiee. Come on you . . . milk white mechanics an' see how tough I am to chaw. I ain't had a fight for two days an' I'm spilein' for exercise. Cock-a-doodle-doo!"[17]

Like Yankees, Borderlanders experienced a wave of intense religious conversion and experimentation in the aftermath of the American Revolution, particularly in the southern region, where frontier conditions undermined the influence and authority of the Presbyterian Church. But while Yankee frontiersmen joined or invented faiths that emphasized good works, utopian communities, and righteous behavior, Borderlanders were drawn to those that stressed individual salvation, a bilateral relationship with God, and the rewards of the next world.

The Borderlander religious heritage was also far more emotional and spontaneous than that of Yankee Puritans or Anglicans of south English origins. Their ancestors in Scotland and Ulster had participated in Presbyterian "holy fairs," huge outdoor events where thousands of worshippers cried, swooned, and otherwise interacted with the divine. After the revolution such gatherings became commonplace in Appalachia. Some 20,000 worshippers from Tennessee, Kentucky, western Virginia, and southern Ohio gathered in Cane Ridge, Kentucky, in August 1801, for a massive Christian revival. "Hundreds fell prostrate under the mighty power of God, as men slain in battle," a witness to the outdoor gathering recalled. "At times more than one thousand persons broke into loud shouting all at once, and that the shouts could be heard for miles around." By the 1830s, specifically Southern Baptist and Methodist churches had formed, distinguished from their northern brethren by their praise of slavery. Both denominations spread rapidly in Greater Appalachia due to their emphasis on personal spiritual rebirth and on each person's being able to connect directly with God without the mediation of books, reverends, or church hierarchies. Impoverished preachers promised to help their followers open personal conduits to the divine, and even encouraged each of them to preach, pray, or share their emotions if the feeling came upon them. In harmony with Borderland conditions and culture, these evangelical faiths dominated Greater Appalachia by 1850, attracting adherents at the expense of the more learned and literary Presbyterian and Anglican churches. In the process, they widened the cultural divide between Appalachia and Yankeedom, and partially closed the one with their increasingly powerful neighbors to the south.[18]

CHAPTER 18

The Deep South Spreads West

It's often argued that prior to the 1830s, "the South" looked upon slavery as an embarrassment, an anachronistic institution that should be allowed to fade away. But after 1830 "Southerners" increasingly celebrated the practice, championing its expansion across the continent and even casting it as a virtuous institution endorsed by the Bible.

But while these developments did in fact take place, the process that drove them has largely gone unexplained. The sanctification of slavery in the emerging Confederacy was the result of a major shift in the relative power of the continent's two principal slave cultures, Tidewater and the Deep South. The third, Appalachia, wouldn't truly join the coalition we call Dixie until *after* the Civil War.

Prior to 1820 Tidewater had dominated the southeastern part of the continent. During the colonial period and the Early Republic, Virginia had been the most populous of the British colonies and American states. By depriving Appalachian districts of proper representation, the Tidewater gentry had maintained an outsized influence over regional and national politics, providing the intellectual foundation for the Declaration of Independence and 1789 Constitution as well as four of the first five U.S. presidents. Larger, wealthier, and more sophisticated than its Deep Southern neighbor, Tidewater had spoken for "the South" on the national stage. Coming from a society that idealized the enlightened rural English gentry, the Tidewater elite expressed regret at the existence of slavery and looked forward to its gradual disappearance.[1]

But during the 1820s and 1830s, Tidewater lost most of its power and influence to the rapidly expanding Deep South. Hemmed in by Borderlanders, Tidewater was unable to meaningfully expand its influence westward during the great migrations of the early nineteenth century. Meanwhile, the people of Appalachia and the Deep South rapidly extended the area under their respective cultures' control. Greater Appalachia more than doubled in geographical size between 1789 and 1840, gaining effective control over the governments of four new states. The Deep South grew nearly tenfold in territory in this period, expanding the number of statehouses under its dominion from two to six. With this expansion, the voices of slaveholding America were no longer those of Virginian gentlemen in the mold of Washington, Jefferson, and Madison, but rather of South Carolinian firebrands like John C. Calhoun, Louis Wigfall, and Robert Rhett.

Unlike Tidewater, the Deep South was able to plow aside the Borderlanders through its masterful control of a lucrative resource. The market for tobacco, the traditional mainstay of Tidewater plantations, was in decline, but cotton, which grew only in the subtropical climes of the Deep South, was booming, with a seemingly insatiable demand from the textile mills of both Old and New England. The marketability of cotton allowed the Deep Southern plantation system to break out of the coastal lowlands, as the plants grew well on higher and drier ground. Since it was a labor-intensive crop, slaveholding planters could easily outcompete the small family cotton farmers. As demand grew, so did the value of land suitable for cotton production, encouraging its transfer to those with greater capital. Appalachian herdsmen, hunters, and small farmers tended to sell out and move on when land prices rose. They found ready buyers, particularly after 1791, when Connecticut Yankee Eli Whitney invented the cotton gin, which made cotton processing more efficient and profitable. In this way the Deep South wrested control of much of the South Carolina and Georgia backcountry from Borderlanders in the opening years of the nineteenth century, then expanded across much of Georgia, Alabama, Mississippi, northern Florida, and Louisiana, and on to western Tennessee, eastern Arkansas, and Texas. As it did so, it expanded its share of world cotton production from 9 percent in 1801 to 68 percent in 1850, even as global production tripled.[2]

The cotton boom produced a simultaneous explosion in the demand for slaves. Since the United States had banned their importation in 1808, planters in the new Gulf states and territories began purchasing them from counterparts in Tidewater and Appalachia. Tidewater alone exported 124,000 slaves between 1810 and 1820. Slave traders marched their "goods" through the countryside, chained to one another; most were young men who would never see their families again, a traumatic event the historian Ira Berlin has called the "Second Middle Passage." Most found harder working conditions than they'd left behind, as the climate was harsher and the labor more difficult than in the mountains and the Chesapeake region. The least fortunate wound up on the sugar plantations of southern Louisiana and Mississippi, where it was sometimes profitable to work one's slaves to death. Being "sold down the river" originally referred to slaves being sold by Appalachian people in Kentucky and Tennessee to downriver plantation owners in the Deep South.[3]

Deep Southerners still had an abiding fear of slave uprisings, and not without cause. In 1822 a charismatic freed slave named Denmark Vesey organized thousands of slaves to rise up, slay their masters, seize Charleston, and escape by ship to the free black state of Haiti. The plot was thwarted when Vesey was betrayed by slave informants, and he and thirty-four colleagues were hanged. In response, Charlestonians established a military school called The Citadel, charged with training their youth to suppress future slave insurrections.

As the Deep South spread, it developed a social and political philosophy that went beyond defending slavery to actually celebrating it. What others regarded as an authoritarian society built on an immoral institution that concentrated wealth and power in the hands of a small elite, Deep Southern oligarchs viewed as the pinnacle of human achievement. Theirs was a democracy modeled on the slave states of ancient Greece and Rome, whose elites had been free to pursue the finer things in life after delegating all drudgery to slaves and a disenfranchised underclass. The Southern gentry were superior to northerners because they had a "nobility to cultivate some of the higher and more ennobling traits of humanity," according to one Deep Southern political boss. Yankees, this boss added, were a "nation of shop keepers" while Deep Southerners were a "race of statesmen, orators, military leaders and gentlemen equal and probably superior to any now existing on this or any other continent." They were also spared the "ignorance, bigotry, and envy resulting from an oppressed and starving laboring class" by the presence of slaves. Following the philosophy of *libertas*, theorists such as South Carolina chancellor William Harper declared that humans are "born to subjection," and that it was in "the order of nature and of God that the beings of superior faculties and knowledge, and superior power, should control and dispose of those who are inferior." On the eve of the Civil War, Alexander Stephens of Georgia gave a speech condemning the Founding Fathers for "the assumption of the equality of races," an idea that was "fundamentally wrong." The Confederacy, he asserted, "rests upon the great truth that the negro is not equal to the white man; that slavery subordination to the superior race is his natural and normal condition." This statement represented mainstream opinion in the Deep South: Stephens was the Confederacy's vice president.[4]

Southern Baptist and Methodist preachers broke with their northern counterparts to endorse slavery on the grounds that Africans were descendants of Ham, who was condemned in the Bible to be a "hewer of wood and drawer of water" for his white masters. Slave lords welcomed the proselytizing of such ideas among the black population. They found allies among Appalachian Presbyterians like the influential northern Alabama minister, the Reverend Fred A. Ross. "Man south of the Equator—in Asia, Australia, Oceanica, America, especially Africa—is inferior to his Northern brother," Ross wrote in his 1857 opus, *Slavery Ordained of God*. "Slavery is of God, and [should] continue for the good of the slave, the good of the master, the good of the whole American family."[5]

As tensions over slavery increased, Deep Southerners began asserting their racial superiority over Yankees as well. The region's thinkers reaffirmed the thesis that they belonged to a master Norman race, separate from and superior to the Yankee Anglo-Saxons. "The Cavaliers, Jacobites, and Huguenots who settled the South naturally hate, contemn [sic] and despise the Puritans who settled the North," the Deep South's leading journal, *DeBow's Review*, declared. "The former are master races—the latter a slave race, the descendants of Saxon serfs . . . [who] came from the cold and marshy regions of the North, where man is little more than a cold-blooded amphibious biped." "We are the most aristocratic people in the world," *DeBow's* continued. "Pride of caste and color and privilege makes every white man an aristocrat in feeling. Aristocracy is the only safe guard of liberty, the only power watchful and strong enough to exclude monarchical despotism." Another paper proclaimed, "The Norman cavalier cannot brook into the vulgar familiarity of the Saxon

Yankee, while the latter is continually devising some plan to bring down his aristocratic neighbor to his own detested level."[6]

As this "master race" expanded westward, its members were offended by other cultures with which they came in contact. Ironically, this included a more genuinely Norman society than their own.

In southern Louisiana, which was ceded to the United States in 1803, they confronted an enclave of New France consisting of the descendants of Acadian refugees living in the bayous, as well as merchants and sugar planters from the French West Indies. The former people—still hunters and trappers with a reputation for enjoying life—were dismissed as peasants. One might think Deep Southerners would be predisposed to getting along with the planters of New Orleans and the river parishes, given their shared Caribbean economic models and alleged Norman racial affinities. On the contrary, Deep Southerners were disgusted with New Orleans, where a more lenient French and Spanish form of slavery and race relations had produced a far less rigid slave society. Since the Spanish had given all slaves the right to buy their freedom, 45 percent of the city's black population was free. Whites and blacks were not allowed to marry one another, but liaisons, affairs, and unsanctioned marriages were carried out in the open, in violation of Deep Southern mores. Many free blacks ranked higher up on the social scale than most of the Irish and other white immigrants who were crowded into the city's poorer quarters. Free blacks even had their own militia regiments and had the confidence to protest when they were excluded from voting in the first U.S. congressional election there in 1812.[7]

Tension between the white Franco-Spanish residents of New Orleans—the "Creoles"—and the "new population" continued throughout the first half of the nineteenth century. Americans arrived from all sections of the continent, but most came from the Deep South, which had a similar geography and climate. Regardless of their origin, the new settlers looked on the Creoles with suspicion given their Roman Catholicism and their unusual ways. Creole women wore rouge, which was unheard of in the other nations. Creole leaders organized bizarre Mardi Gras celebrations and parades and kept to themselves socially. Even in the 1860s intermarriage between the old and new populations was rare. Politics remained split between the "French" and "American" factions, with Francophones fighting to retain French legal and parish-based administrative norms. Sixty years after being absorbed into the United States, and surrounded by the Deep South and Appalachia, New Orleans and the sugar-planting parishes of the lower Mississippi still retained their own identity; they voted Republican and opposed Southern secession. A New French enclave in the heart of the Deep South, southern Louisiana resisted assimilation, remaining a land apart right into the twenty-first century.[8]

By midcentury, the Deep South's rapid expansion had come to a halt. In a little over forty years, it had absorbed the subtropical lowlands surrounding the Gulf of Mexico and pushed plantation agriculture as far north as southern Missouri and south to the edge of the arid ranges of Texas. In 1850, however, there was nowhere else in the United States for it to go. Limited by climate, ecology, and its northerly rivals, the Deep South was hemmed in. Its leaders could see that their culture could not hope to take hold in the Far West, where slave crops could not flourish. They could envision a future unfolding in which Yankees, Midlanders, and Borderlanders would continue to expand across the continent, gaining relative strength in population, economics, and congressional representation. If the Yankees gained control of the federal government, slavery—the basis of Deep Southern society—might be criminalized. The Deep South and Tidewater aristocracies would be laid low, their countries turned into "nations of shopkeepers," their underlings meddling in politics to undermine their genteel, deferential society. They feared that if the Deep South stopped growing, there would be no future for it within the federation.[9]

But what if they could expand outside the United States?

In the 1850s, Deep Southerners became fixated on annexing their tropical neighbors. Spain's New World empire had come apart in the early 1820s, when its various colonies rose up in a series of independence wars. By the 1850s, the empire had splintered into two dozen smaller, weaker, and less stable states. Several of those closest to the United States—including Mexico and Nicaragua—had outlawed slavery, a development disturbing to the slave lords of the American South. The possibility that Spain might grant Cuba and its black majority independence was particularly frightening, as the island was just ninety miles off Florida and would be an easy refuge for runaway slaves. Cuba, one Texan declared, would soon be "writhing and dying in the dust, suffocated by a million negro hands!" Rumors began circulating that Spanish officials were arming blacks and encouraging interracial marriages. Mississippi senator John Quitman urged a U.S. invasion to prevent the emergence of "a negro or mongrel empire" that could only encourage slave rebellions across the Deep South. The Deep Southern majority in the Louisiana assembly passed a resolution in 1854 condemning Spain's "abolition of slavery in [Cuba] and the sacrifice of the white race."[10]

The solution was to conquer and absorb Cuba, and Deep Southerners set out to do so with zeal. Private mercenaries tried to invade the island, backed by the sitting governor of Mississippi and one of that state's former senators. Several more expeditions failed before U.S. president Franklin Pierce, a New Hampshire Yankee, made it clear he would prosecute participants in any sequels. Pierce tried to buy Cuba from Spain in 1854–55, but when negotiations failed, he was roundly attacked by Deep Southerners for caving to "antislavery elements." President James Buchanan, a Scots-Irish Borderlander, also tried to purchase Cuba as a way of rallying Deep Southern support; his 1858 effort was stymied by an unlikely alliance of Yankee and Midland congressmen on one hand (who opposed acquiring a new slave state) and Deep Southern representatives on the other (who tried to amend the necessary funding bill to force the president to invade the island). Newspapers across the Deep South, Tidewater, and Appalachia continued to call for Cuba's annexation up until the outbreak of the Civil War. What Deep Southern opposition there was centered around fears the annexations would prompt a mass export of slaves from their own nations. The *Richmond Enquirer* warned that the drain would change the "political status of Maryland, of Virginia, of the Carolinas, of Tennessee, Kentucky, Missouri, Arkansas—even of the Gulf states themselves." One of Tidewater's few abolitionists, Matthew Maury of Virginia, supported tropical annexations because they would "relieve our blessed Virginia of the curse" and "the horrors of that war of the races [that is] almost upon us."[11]

There were also schemes to annex Nicaragua. When an Appalachian mercenary named William Walker seized control of the tiny Central American republic in 1856, his first act as "president" was to reestablish slavery, hoping to win Deep Southern support. His plan worked. Accolades poured in from Deep Southern newspapers. The New Orleans *Daily Delta* proclaimed Nicaragua a "home for Southern men." The *Selma Sentinel* proclaimed Walker's actions to be more vital to the South than any other "movement on Earth."[12]

Walker's movement was crushed a few months later by cholera and an insurgency, but he returned to a hero's welcome in New Orleans and plotted another invasion. "The white man took the Negro from his native wastes and teaching him the arts of life, bestowed on him the ineffable blessings of a true religion," he announced in a book published in Mobile, from which his second invasion force departed. Slavery was a "positive good," Walker argued, and should be extended in a slaveholding empire. Walker had intended to extend his slave empire northward from Nicaragua to encompass much of Central America and Mexico. But his second expedition ended in his arrest by a U.S. naval officer. Deep Southern congressmen tried to have the officer punished but were opposed even by their Appalachian colleagues on this matter of military honor.[13]

In the aftermath of his arrest, Deep Southerners rallied around a secretive group called the Knights of the Golden Circle, which sought to create an even larger slave empire than Walker had. The "Golden Circle" was centered on Cuba, and its curve took in the Deep South, Mexico, Central America, part of South America, and the entire West Indies. The Knights' founder, a Tidewater-born, Kentucky-based magazine editor named George Bickley, estimated Mexico alone would yield twenty-five new slave states with fifty senators and sixty representatives. It would guarantee Deep Southern hegemony over the federal government (if the Union survived) or "every element of national wealth and power" for a "Southern Confederacy" (if it did not). With the core of its support in east Texas and Georgia, the Knights plotted to conquer all of Mexico.[14]

But by this time, a great deal of Mexican territory had already been annexed to the United States. The conquest of El Norte was well under way.

CHAPTER 19

Conquering El Norte

By the time the slave lords' eyes turned its way, El Norte was in an extremely vulnerable position. Mexico was born into bankruptcy and chaos in 1821, its economy destroyed in a bloody war for independence that had killed a tenth of its people. Gross national product fell by half and would not recover its 1805 level until the 1870s. Governments in far-off Mexico City fell with alarming frequency—the presidency changed hands thirty-six times between 1833 and 1855—leaving the provinces largely on their own.[1]

What little support El Norte had received from central authorities broke down in the aftermath of independence. Soldiers and missionaries stopped receiving their pay. The money supply disappeared. Caravans no longer arrived to resupply the region's outposts and to carry away the hides and tallow it produced. Soldiers began sacking mission complexes in search of provisions. Franciscan missionaries were banned from entering Mexico, and El Norte officials received orders to expel the rest. (California's governor refused, noting that if he did so,"the rest of the inhabitants and troops would perish.") What little assistance the central government did provide was counterproductive. A shipment of convicts was sent to California to bolster the local population, but without supplies; they spent their time raiding gardens and orchards and causing trouble for the governor. Newly promulgated Mexican laws, like the requirement of an annual income of 1,500 pesos to be a congressman and 2,000 pesos to be a governor, alienated *norteños*. "No one in California has the capital to become a governor, senator, or deputy," one observer noted.[2]

Cut off from central Mexico, El Norte's leaders looked to the United States for trade, supplies, and settlers. *Tejanos* flouted Mexico's ban on foreign trade by driving their horses to markets in Louisiana, while Franciscan *Californios* sold cowhides and sea otter skins to smugglers. Government officials made no attempt to stop the trade, with one noting that "necessity makes licit what is not licit by law." California governor Mariano Chico noted that without smuggling, "the Californias would not exist."

El Norte's border had become porous to more than goods, however. In the 1820s Mexican authorities were helpless to defend their frontier from waves of illegal immigrants pouring across from the north and east in search of economic opportunity. Texas bore the brunt of this flood of immigration due to its long borders with increasingly populated Louisiana and Arkansas. Under Mexican law, Anglo-Americans were unwelcome, but Texas officials were desperate enough for settlers to look the other way. "I cannot help seeing advantages which . . . would result if we admitted honest, hard working people, regardless of what country they come from . . . even Hell itself," said San Antonio politico Francisco Ruiz.[3]

By 1823, some 3,000 Anglo-Americans (mostly Deep Southern or Appalachian in origin) were living in Texas illegally, roughly equal to the official population of the territory. Several hundred more had followed Moses and Stephen Austin, a father-and-son team who'd convinced Spanish authorities to give them a large land grant on the eve of Mexican independence. Proponents of immigration reform were encouraged by the Austins' behavior: Stephen, who took over after his father's death, learned Spanish, took Mexican citizenship, and acted as an arbiter between immigrants and local authorities. (Southern California's few early immigrants behaved similarly, generally assimilating into and respecting the local culture.) Reformers won the day in 1824–25, when federal authorities and those in what was then the territory of Coahuila y Texas legalized immigration. Most of Texas north of Corpus Christi would practically be given away to colonization agents like Austin, who then retailed it to settlers in 4,400-acre grants. Authorities hoped the newcomers would adapt to El Norte's ways; to encourage this, they banned slavery and required settlers to convert to Roman Catholicism.[4]

The immigration experiment, however, quickly got out of hand. Settlers—many of them fleeing creditors in the Deep South—began flooding into east Texas, and by 1830 they numbered at least 7,000, more than double the *norteño* population. To make matters worse, the newcomers were making no effort to assimilate, spurning Catholicism and settling away from the *norteño* enclaves around San Antonio and Golidad.

A Mexican general traveling northward to the booming east Texas town of Nacogdoches realized he had crossed into a foreign culture. "As one covers the distance from San Antonio to [Nacogdoches] he will note that Mexican influence is proportionately diminished until, arriving in this place, he will see that it is almost nothing," he wrote his superiors. The Nacogdoches area had been granted to a hotheaded Appalachia-born slave planter, Haden Edwards, who'd tried to rid the area of *norteños* and squatters alike, to make way for "respectable" Deep Southern planters. When his illegal expropriations led authorities to withdraw his grant in 1826, Edwards declared independence, appointing himself the head of the "Republic of Fredonia." Mexican troops drove him back across the border, but the event alarmed the establishment. American immigrants were undermining the region's Mexicanness, flouting laws, languages, and customs. Something had to be done.[5]

In 1830 Mexico reversed policy and banned American immigration altogether, for fear that otherwise "Texas will be lost to this Republic." Many *norteños* opposed the move, with several leading Texas officials petitioning Mexico City for it to be reversed. In any case the law failed to stem the tide. American immigration actually increased, reaching 1,000 a month by 1835, at which point *Tejanos* were outnumbered by American immigrants by more than ten to one. The general in charge of the region reported in 1831 that "there is no physical force that can stop the entrance of the norteamericanos, who are exclusive owners of the coast and the borders of Texas." (In New Mexico and California—much more difficult to reach from the United States—immigrants came in small numbers and did not present an immediate cultural challenge.) Authorities in central Mexico feared that if the region was inundated with Deep Southerners, rebellion and U.S. annexation might soon follow. Ironically, when rebellion did come, *norteños* themselves played a leading role.[6]

El Norte—which has a more individualistic, self-sufficient, and commercial attitude than central Mexico—is often said to be at the forefront of Mexican reform and revolution. That reputation began with the region's armed resistance to Mexico's first military dictator, General Antonio López de Santa Anna, who seized power in 1833, suspended the constitution, and expelled his political opponents. Santa Anna was forced to put down a series of revolts in El Norte, first in Coahuila, then in Texas, New Mexico, and California. *Californio* legislators in Monterey actually declared their province independent until such a time as the constitution was restored; when a new governor arrived from Mexico City, he and his guards were disarmed and sent packing. Meanwhile, Pueblo Indians in New Mexico captured Santa Fe, beheaded Santa Anna's governor, and put a mestizo buffalo hunter in his place; the rebellion was put down a few months later by Santa Anna's troops. In 1839 opposition politicians in the northern states of Tamaulipas, Nuevo León, and Coahuila declared their independence and loyalty to the old constitution; their Republic of the Rio Grande was crushed a few months later, and its leaders took refuge in neighboring Texas.[7]

The Texas Revolution of 1835–36 was the most successful and decisive of the revolts. Offended by Santa Anna's dictatorship, much of the *Tejano* political establishment joined the rebellion, including the bilingual mayor of San Antonio, Juan Seguín, an ally of Stephen Austin. Initially, moderates like Austin and Seguín sought merely to separate from Coahuila but remain a part of Mexico, a position that earned them the epithet "Tories" from east Texas's Appalachian and Deep Southern settlers, who wanted outright independence. Most *Tejanos* appear to have been neutral on the matter, wishing only to survive the conflict with a minimum of disruption. But when Santa Anna's forces invaded the renegade province, Seguín and other *Tejano* leaders joined the secessionists in proclaiming an independent Republic of Texas. Seguín served as an officer in the revolutionary army and was later elected to the republic's senate; another *Tejano*, Lorenzo de Zavala, served as Texas's vice president. Seven *Tejanos* died for Texas at the Battle of the Alamo, where Seguín served as one of Austin's scouts and, later, supervised the burial of the dead. Deep Southern newspapers covered the war intensively, casting it as a racial struggle between barbarous Hispanics and virtuous whites, inspiring thousands of Southern adventurers to cross into Texas to join the fighting. Ultimately Santa Anna's troops were drawn into east Texas, where they were surprised during their siesta by a rebel army led by an Appalachian slave owner, Sam Houston. Santa Anna was captured and, to save his life, agreed to withdraw beyond the Rio Grande. While the war continued for several years, Texas was effectively independent.[8]

Unfortunately for the *Tejanos* their Appalachian and Deep Southern neighbors had no intention of giving them a place in the new order. Most Americans of English descent had deep-seated prejudices against Latin Americans, dating back to the Spanish monarchy's sixteenth-century crusades to rid the world of Protestants. Mexicans offered an additional affront to Anglo-American norms: most were, in the language of the times, racial "half-breeds"—part European, part Native American—and therefore supposedly degraded and lazy. Such racial mixing was particular offensive to Deep Southerners, but it played badly in Indian-fighting Appalachia as well. Even the moderate Stephen Austin characterized Texans' struggle for independence as "a war of barbarism and of despotic principles, waged by the mongrel Spanish-Indian and Negro race against civilization and the Anglo-American race."[9]

Norteño landowners quickly found themselves strangers in their own country as tens of thousands of additional Appalachian and Deep Southern immigrants poured into the country. (Census records show that Appalachian people settled the north-central tier of the state, while Deep Southerners colonized east Texas, concentrating their slave plantations in the Brazos River valley.) The invaders regarded *norteños* as inferiors and enemies to be dispossessed, just as the Cherokee had been. Over the next decade *norteños* were robbed of their livestock and landholdings by force, threats, and fraud, then relegated to the lower ranks of society. All *norteños* were denied citizenship and property rights unless they could prove they had supported the revolution, while a bill to forbid nonwhites from voting was only narrowly defeated. Even Juan Seguín, hero of the Texas Revolution and the elected mayor of San Antonio, was driven into exile after a local hoodlum claimed he was a Mexican sympathizer. "Some envied my position, as held by a *Mexican*; others found me an obstacle to the accomplishment of their villainous [property-seizing] plans," Seguín lamented. "I had been tried by a rabble, condemned without a hearing, and consequently was [forced] to provide for my own safety." He would return to Texas years later to discover that no "Mexican" could rise to a leadership position, and very few retained property.[10]

In effect the Texas Revolution pushed the northeastern border of El Norte back to its current location: just north of San Antonio and just south of Corpus Christi. Northeast, north-central, and central Texas—areas never really populated by *norteños*—were absorbed into Appalachia, while the northern half of the Gulf Coast was annexed into the Deep South, creating the state's classic divides between Houston and Dallas, the Hill Country and the coastal plain, the Hispanic south and the Anglo-dominated north. The northern panhandle would later emerge as a land apart, settled as it was by Midlanders.[11]

But the revolution was only the first phase in the rolling back of El Norte's cultural sphere. Pressured by the Deep South and its "Golden Circle" lobby, in 1845 the U.S. Congress took up a bill to grant statehood to the Texas Republic as a slave state. Predictably the vote passed along clear national lines: Yankeedom and the Midlands against; Appalachia, Tidewater, New Netherland, and the Deep South in favor. Mexico refused to recognize the new border, which included disputed territory in the Rio Grande Valley. U.S. forces were dispatched to the area, where they blockaded river access to the undisputedly Mexican city of Matamoros. After the resulting skirmish was disingenuously cast by President James K. Polk (of Appalachia) as "Mexican aggression," the U.S. House declared war by a vote of 174–14, with all of the dissenters coming from Yankeedom.

As in many future conflicts, opposition to the Mexican-American War was concentrated in Yankeedom, which viewed it as an imperial war of conquest and a betrayal of republican values and pietistic Christian morality. "Who believes that a score of victories over Mexico, the 'annexation' of half her provinces, will give us more Liberty, a purer Morality, a more prosperous industry, than we now have?" asked one prominent critic, the Yankee-born newspaperman Horace Greeley. "Murder [cannot] be hid from the sight of God by a few flimsy rags called banners. . . . Awake and arrest the work of butchery ere it shall be too late to preserve your souls from the guilt of wholesale slaughter!" The Massachusetts legislature, for its part, denounced it as a "war against freedom, against humanity, against justice" because it had "the triple object of extending slavery, of strengthening slave power, and of obtaining the control of the Free States."[12]

The war indeed proved to be a slaughter. U.S. forces drove across Mexico conquering Alta California, New Mexico, and much of the rest of El Norte. By the early fall of 1847, they occupied Mexico City and Veracruz.

For policy makers the question was not how to win the war but rather how much of Mexico they should appropriate. Again, the debate broke largely along national lines. Yankees generally opposed any territorial annexations, fearing they would add more slave states and make the country too large for them to ever hope to assimilate it all into the New England Way. Midlanders took a pacifistic stance. Appalachians enthusiastically backed military conquest and the imperial project, arguing for the total annihilation of Mexico. Tidewater and New Netherland were ambivalent.[13]

In the end, the United States seized only the sparsely populated northern half of Mexico, an area that included the modern states of Arizona, New Mexico, California, Nevada, and Utah. Curiously, further annexations were rejected because of the opposition of Deep Southern leaders, who feared being unable to assimilate the more densely populated, racially mixed central and southern states of Mexico. "More than half of the Mexicans are Indians, and the other is composed chiefly of mixed tribes," warned Senator John Calhoun. "I protest against such a union as that! Ours, sir, is the Government of a white race."[14]

The war, which ended in 1848, and the subsequent Gadsden Purchase split ownership of El Norte between two countries. Sparsely populated southern California and southern Arizona joined more heavily settled New Mexico and south Texas as occupied territories within the United States. *Norteños* in all of these places would be subjected to discrimination, disenfranchisement, and a massive cultural challenge from their new overlords yet would survive a century of occupation to challenge their subjugation in the late twentieth century. El Norte's southern section—the states of Tamaulipas, Nuevo León, Coahuila, Chihuahua, Sonora, and Baja California—would remain in Mexico but would continue to be subject to, and often embrace, the influences of their American neighbors; these northern states remained at odds with central Mexico, serving as the core of support in the Mexican Revolution and the electoral overthrow of the corrupt Revolutionary Institutional Party in the early 1990s.[15]

But large parts of the annexed Mexican territory had never really been colonized and, culturally speaking, had never truly been a part of El Norte: northern California, Nevada, Utah, and most of Colorado and

Arizona. These enormous regions were about to become the birthplace of two new ethnocultural nations, built with staggering speed on lands seized from their native inhabitants. Amazingly the Left Coast and Far West would evolve in complete opposition to each other, and to the occupied Spanish-speaking nation to their south.

CHAPTER 20

Founding the Left Coast

Why is it that the coastal zone in northern California, Oregon, and Washington seems to have so much more in common with New England than it does with other parts of those states? From voting behavior to culture wars to foreign policy, why has the Left Coast found itself allied with Yankeedom—and at odds with its neighbors to the south and east—since its foundation?

The primary reason is that the majority of the Left Coast's early colonists were Yankees who arrived by sea in the hopes of founding a second New England on the shores of the Pacific. And while they didn't fully succeed in this mission—the Left Coast has always had fundamental temperamental differences from its eastern ally—they left a stamp of utopian idealism that put this young nation on a collision course with its neighbors in deferential El Norte and the libertarian Far West.

In the early nineteenth century the Pacific coast of North America was still largely under Native American control. Spain theoretically claimed all of what is now California, but for practical purposes, *norteño* influence began petering out to the north at Monterey, and ceased altogether at San Francisco. Britain and the United States had yet to resolve who controlled the Pacific Northwest, agreeing only that it would eventually be divided between them. On their maps there was just an enormous mass of land called the Oregon Territory, which encompassed what is now British Columbia, Washington, Oregon, and Idaho. Prior to this, the struggle in the region pitted New France against Yankeedom. The New French dominated the local staff of the Hudson's Bay Company, the British fur trading conglomerate that was, in effect, the government of much of what is now western and northern Canada. On the ground, the New French manned most of the company's fortified fur trading posts in the area, and when they retired, some settled down with their Native American wives in the familiar métis pattern. Until the 1830s their primary rivals were ship-borne fur traders from New England, who made no attempt to set up permanent outposts.[1] For the next century or more, the Chinook Indians called all British people "King George Men" and referred to Americans simply as "Bostons."[2]

As a result of this very long-distance fur trade, New Englanders had better intelligence and greater knowledge of the Pacific coast than anyone else in the United States. Not surprisingly, their intellectual and religious leaders soon added this new "wilderness" to the list of places in need of Yankee salvation. In the 1830s Lyman Beecher was calling on his followers to save the West from the cruel machinations of the Pope and his obedient Catholic immigrant followers. "The rapid influx of foreign emigrants, unacquainted with our institutions, unaccustomed to self-government, inaccessible to education . . . and easily embodied and wielded by sinister design," he wrote, threatened "the safety of our republic." The solution, Beecher argued, was to educate and assimilate the newcomers "under the full action of our schools and republican institutions." Beecher, who was then training missionaries in Cincinnati, had German and Irish Catholic immigrants in the Great Lakes and upper Mississippi Valley foremost in his mind. But for those familiar with the Pacific, Beecher's warnings were equally applicable to Catholic New French traders on the Columbia River or, soon thereafter, the *norteños* of California. That Franciscan missionaries were already schooling Indian children in San Jose only increased the urgency of the mission.[3]

This new Yankee "errand in the wilderness" got underway in fits and starts in the late 1820s. A delusional New Hampshire schoolmaster, Hall Jackson Kelley, tirelessly promoted an ambitious colonization scheme for the Pacific Northwest, a region he'd never seen. His elaborate plans for a civic and religious republic never got off the ground, but his marketing effort—he plastered posters across New England, published books, and petitioned Congress for aid—did inspire others. Jason Lee, a northern Methodist preacher from Vermont, traveled overland across the continent to found a mission near what is now Salem, Oregon, in 1834. Working first with Native Americans, Lee recruited teachers and settlers from New England and eventually added an institute that would become the first college in the western United States (now Willamette University).

A Presbyterian missionary named Samuel Parker of Massachusetts spent much of 1835 and 1836 preaching and selecting future mission sites in the Oregon Territory; his book, *The Far West*, drew more Yankees to the territory, most of them clustering near Reverend Lee's Willamette Valley mission in what is now Oregon State. In May 1843 Yankee settlers in the territory held a meeting at which they set up their own provisional government, drafted laws prohibiting slavery, and elected officers; three-quarters of those elected were from New England. The document would later form the basis for Oregon's state constitution.[4]

While the Yankees dominated the political and intellectual scene, they were not to form a majority of the population. Within a few months of the creation of the provisional government, a wagon train arrived bearing over 700 new settlers, doubling the Willamette Valley's non-Indian population. The vast majority of the newcomers were farmers from the Appalachian Midwest. As one historian put it, the Borderlanders "carried to Oregon an allegiance to . . . local sovereignty, grass-roots organization, an independent producer ethic and the 'doctrine of the negative [i.e., weak] state.'" The Borderlanders tended to settle on farms in the countryside, leaving the towns and government to the Yankees. This settlement pattern continued throughout the 1840s and 1850s, leaving New England–born Yankees outnumbered fifteen to one but still in control of most civic institutions.[5]

In Oregon, which split from what became British Columbia in 1846 and from Washington in 1853, the Yankees dominated the scene to a remarkable degree. Salem and Portland were founded by New Englanders, the latter named by a native of Portland, Maine, after winning a coin toss with a Bostonian. The state's first and most influential newspaper, the *Oregon Statesman*, was founded, owned, and operated by Yankees, as was its rival, *The Oregonian*, which promoted a Beecher-like fear of Catholic immigrants. Yankees ran most of the public schools, colleges, and seminaries and dominated debate at the Constitutional Convention of 1857, which produced a document championing communities of independent family farmers and the very Yankee notion that individual interests must be subsumed for the common good. Six of the first eight state governors and six of the first eight U.S senators were Yankees from New England, New York, or the Wyoming Valley of Pennsylvania.[6]

North of the Columbia River, the Washington Territory was much more sparsely populated, the territorial dispute with Britain having discouraged potential settlers, who had no assurances that their land titles would be respected if the area changed sovereignty. Still, the cultural pattern was similar. Attracted by the lumber resources of Puget Sound and the Olympic Peninsula, Yankees from the forests of eastern Maine, northern Vermont, and the Great Lakes arrived in considerable numbers in the 1840s and 1850s. The East Machias, Maine, lumber firm of Pope & Talbot founded the towns of Port Gamble and Port Ludlow and transported both sawmills and workers from the eastern Maine coast in an organized migration that continued for seventy years. ("It seemed everybody there came from East Machias or his father did," one Port Gamble veteran recalled a half century later. "We always had baked beans and Johnny bread at Gamble and plenty of codfish.") When Puget Sound became desperate for women in the 1860s—white men outnumbered white women by a nine-to-one ratio—local leaders recruited 100 single New England women and shipped them to Seattle; to be a descendant of one of these settlers still has *Mayflower*-like cachet there. Mainer Alden Blethen arrived to found the region's principal newspaper, the *Seattle Times*, and Massachusetts' Isaac Stevens was Washington's first territorial governor and U.S. representative. But, as in Oregon, the region was not to have a Yankee majority, as large numbers of Scandinavian, Irish, and Japanese immigrants settled there after the Civil War. Coastal British Columbia developed even later, populated in large part by immigrants from Seattle, Oregon, and northern California who brought their Congregational and Presbyterian churches with them.[7]

The Yankee mission in California was complicated by the fact that parts of the region had already been colonized. El Norte's culture was well rooted south of Monterey, and Yankee traders and travelers who decided to move to southern California prior to the U.S. annexation generally assimilated to *Californio* ways. Arriving by sea, the Yankees congregated in Santa Barbara and Monterey, learned Spanish, converted to Catholicism, took Mexican citizenship and spouses, adopted Spanish versions of their names, and respected and participated in local politics. Some were very successful. Abel Stearns, a shipboard agent from Massachusetts, settled in Los Angeles in 1829, married well, ran a lucrative trading company, and died a spectacularly wealthy cattle rancher. Thomas Larkin, a carpenter and failed businessman from Charlestown, Massachusetts, hoped the province's people would secede from Mexico and join the United States on its own terms; the home he built in Monterey blended New England proportions and roofing with Spanish full-length balconies and adobe construction, yielding the popular hybrid now called the Monterey Style. By the time of the American conquest in 1846, such Mexicanized Yankees comprised around a tenth of California's non-Indian population of 4,000.[8]

But El Norte's cultural influence vanished when one moved away from the coast or north of Monterey. In the San Francisco Bay and Sacramento regions, *norteños* were few and far between, and the immigrants were of a very different sort. At the time of conquest, a tenth of California's population lived on the Bay or along a branch of the Sacramento River that soon became known as the *Rio Americano*, or American River. As in the Oregon Territory, these settlers were a mix of Yankees (who typically arrived by sea and congregated in the towns) and Appalachian people (who arrived overland, fanning out to farms, ranches, and mills). Whatever their differences, the two groups did share a resentment of southern California, Mexican rule, and *norteño* culture. They generally refused to take up Mexican citizenship, occupied land without permission, and openly agitated for American annexation.[9]

If California's north-south split was already apparent by 1845, the 1848 discovery of gold in the American River Valley helped divide the Left Coast from the until-then unpopulated interior. This division—presaging that which would soon divide the older, coastal Pacific Northwest from the arid lands over the Cascades—was largely due to the Yankee presence around San Francisco Bay and adjacent sections of the Pacific seaboard. Even more than their counterparts in Oregon, these Yankees were compelled by a particular mission: they had to save California from the barbarians.

The barbarians, in this case, were the Forty-niners, whose Gold Rush mentality was completely at odds with the Yankee Puritan ethos. "Never was there such a gold-thirsty race of men brought together," one resident said of the hordes that came to California in 1848–50. "The principle is to get all of the wealth of the land possible in the shortest possible time, and then go *elsewhere to enjoy it.*"[10] In what was one of the largest spontaneous migrations in human history to that point, 300,000 arrived in California in just five years, increasing the new American territory's non-Indian population twentyfold. Within twenty-four months San Francisco grew from a village of 800 to a city of 20,000. Its harbor was filled with derelict ships abandoned by their gold-hungry crews, and the pubs, gambling houses, brothels, knife fights, criminal gangs, and drunken parties that followed in their wake were worthy of Port Royal in the time of the buccaneers.

All of this deeply offended Yankees on both coasts, prompting yet another moral crusade, this time to save California. The Reverend Joseph Bendon, a Yale-educated descendant of Puritan preacher John Eliot, proclaimed the Gold Rush a challenge to Protestants to complete the civilizing effort that had been begun by the Franciscan missions. The Congregationalists' American Home Missionary Society immediately dispatched missionaries by steamship, seeing an opportunity not just to save California but to create a Protestant beachhead for taking on the "strong holds of Paganism" in Asia. "If we can plant [in California] a people with our civilization, our Bible, our Puritanism, our zeal for spreading what we know and believe to others, it will be a direct means of pouring light upon the Isles of the Sea and the land of Sinim [Sin] that lies beyond," the society's journal proclaimed on the eve of the great enterprise. "It is the will of God to make some great use of the new movement towards Oregon and California."[11]

The missionaries and their Yankee followers regarded their journey as yet another Pilgrim-like errand to the wilderness, a chance to erect a second City on the Hill. "Sons and daughters of New England, you are the representatives of a land which is the model for every other," Presbyterian minister Timothy Dwight Hunt told San Francisco's New England Society in 1852. "Here is our colony. No higher ambition could urge us to noble deeds than, on the basis of the colony of Plymouth, to make California the Massachusetts of the Pacific."[12]

Large numbers of Yankees joined the migration: 10,000 in 1849 alone, or a quarter of all those arriving by sea. Some were undoubtedly headed straight to the "diggings," but a remarkable number lent support to the effort to create a Yankee California. Some donated land, money, and materials for the missionaries to build their churches and schoolhouses in San Francisco, Sacramento, and Monterey. Graduates of Amherst, Bowdoin, Harvard, Yale, and other Congregational colleges traveled into the mountains to set up outdoor schools among the miners. John Pelton of Andover, Massachusetts, arrived with school supplies, teaching materials, and a bell to found California's first free public school. By 1853 the San Francisco school board was entirely staffed by New Englanders, who made the Boston curriculum mandatory in the city. Sherman Day, the son of the president of Yale, joined a group of New England lawyers and clergymen to help transform a Congregational preparatory school into the College of California, which is now the University of California at Berkeley; most of the professors at the "Yale of the West" were New Englanders. Even the Boston and California Joint Stock Mining and Trading Company brought a staff pastor and divinity students with them in 1849, and required in company rules that they preach sermons on Sunday and host prayer meetings at midweek. Members of the Bunker Hill Mining and Trading Company pledged to "abstain from all the vices and intimidations" of California.[13]

However well funded and organized they were, the Yankees had little luck with their efforts beyond their coastal beachheads. They successfully lobbied to get the state legislature to pass laws protecting the Sabbath, but the California Supreme Court was by then dominated by Borderlanders from the mining districts, who declared the law invalid. San Franciscans on the whole rejected Puritan morality. "In California, the Sabbath is ignored by the masses," the *San Francisco Bulletin* reported in 1860. "The more abandoned resort to gambling saloons where, with drugged whisky and logwood wines they manage to stake their previous week's earnings on a throw of dice or a doubtful game of pasteboard." Yankees had influenced the Left Coast, but they could not make it a commonwealth of saints.[14]

The central problem, of course, was that from 1850 onward the overwhelming majority of California's Left Coast residents—and those of the state as a whole—weren't Yankees. The Gold Rush had drawn people from all over the world: Appalachian farmers, Chilean and Australian miners, Irish and Italian adventurers, and hopeful Chinese laborers. In a land whose colonial culture was yet to be defined, few were willing to simply follow the Yankees' lead. Catholics rejected it altogether in favor of their own dreams that California, on account of its relative isolation and Spanish heritage, might serve as a refuge from Protestant America. They, too, had their schools, missions, orphanages, and colleges: Italian Jesuits were issuing degrees at Santa Clara while Berkeley was still a prep school. When voters elected delegates to the territory's constitutional convention in 1849, Yankees were a distinct minority, outnumbered by Borderlanders and *norteños*. California's first two governors were San Francisco residents, but both were from Appalachia.[15]

While the Yankees failed in their broad mission, they did have a lasting effect on coastal California from Monterey north. The coast blended the moral, intellectual, and utopian impulses of a Yankee elite with the self-sufficient individualism of its Appalachian and immigrant majority. The culture that formed—idealistic but individualistic—was unlike that of the gold-digging lands in the interior but very similar to those in western Oregon and Washington. It would take nearly a century for its people to recognize it, but it was a new regional culture, one that would ally with Yankeedom to change the federation.

CHAPTER 21

War for the West

The Civil War era has long been portrayed as a struggle between "the North" and "the South," two regions that, culturally and politically, didn't actually exist. Historians have danced around the problem, offering a variety of terms to try to support the flawed paradigm: Border South, Middle South, Upper South, Lower South, Cotton South, Border North, or Upper North. They've agonized over the deep internal divisions in Maryland and Missouri, Tennessee and Louisiana, Indiana, Virginia, and Texas. They've argued over whether or not the war was fought for slavery or whether it was a struggle between Celts and their Anglo and Teutonic rivals. Any state-by-state analysis inevitably produces results that are confusing and unsatisfactory.

Seen through the lens of the continent's ethnoregional nations, the parties' motivations, allegiances, and behaviors become clearer. The Civil War was ultimately a conflict between two coalitions. On one side was the Deep South and its satellite, Tidewater; on the other, Yankeedom. The other nations wanted to remain neutral, and considered breaking off to form their own confederations, freed from slave lords and Yankees alike. Had cooler heads prevailed, the United States would likely have split into four confederations in 1861, with dramatic consequences for world history. But hostilities could not be avoided, and the unstable Union would be held together by force of arms.

The first half of the nineteenth century saw a four-way competition for control of the western two-thirds of North America, with Yankeedom, the Midlands, Appalachia, and the Deep South extending their cultures over discrete swaths of the Trans-Appalachian West. At stake, all parties knew, was control of the federal government. Whoever won the largest parcel of territory might hope to dominate the others, defining the norms of social, economic, and political behavior for the rest, much as Russians,

Austrians, Spanish, or Turks were doing in their respective multicultural empires.

But by midcentury this demographic and diplomatic struggle was becoming a violent conflict between the continent's two emerging superpowers: Yankeedom and the Deep South, far and away the wealthiest and most nationally self-aware of the four contestants. Neither could abide living in an empire run on the other's terms.

For fifty years the Deep South had been winning the race. The cotton and sugar booms had encouraged the rapid westward expansion of slave culture and made the region fabulously rich. It had eclipsed Tidewater as the dominant force in the South and enlisted the support of Appalachian presidents and politicians in a white supremacy campaign that had cleared the South and Southwest of Indian nations and Mexican officials. Their southern coalition had dominated the federal government since the War of 1812, pushing the empire-averse Yankees and pacifist Midlanders aside to engage in a series of expansionistic wars. With U.S. troops in control of Mexico City in 1848, Deep Southerners could imagine completing their proposed Golden Circle, adding enough slave states to ensure their permanent control over federal policy and hemispheric affairs. Victory, it seemed, was at hand.

Then things began to come apart. While the plantation slave state was winning few hearts and minds in the wider world, the Yankee and Midland Midwest was filling with foreign immigrants who correctly saw fewer opportunities for themselves in the Deep South and Tidewater; many had already suffered under aristocratic feudal systems at home and were determined to stay far away from their North American equivalents. In 1850 the free states had eight foreign-born inhabitants for every one living in a slave state. With each passing year, Yankeedom, the Midlands, and New Netherland held a greater proportion of the nation's population and therefore a greater number of seats in the House of Representatives. Yankee influence over the Left Coast compounded the problem, ensuring California, Oregon, and Washington would join the United States as free states even as federal authorities declined to seize new territories in the Caribbean. By 1860 the leaders of the Deep South and Tidewater realized the rest of the nations had the political strength to control federal institutions and policy without them. The Deep Southern way of life was in jeopardy. To save it, they would have to leave the Union.[1]

Whatever qualms Americans had about slavery in the 1850s, most people living outside of Yankeedom were willing to overlook it and the issues it raised. Spurred by their mission to improve the world, however, Yankees were not about to ignore it and the moral affront it presented and became the undisputed center of the abolitionist movement. A Massachusetts Yankee, William Lloyd Garrison, founded and published the leading antislavery journal, *The Liberator.* Lyman Beecher's daughter, Harriet Beecher Stowe, wrote the hugely popular *Uncle Tom's Cabin*, which mobilized the public against federal laws requiring U.S. citizens to return runaway slaves to their masters. Frederick Douglass, an escaped Tidewater slave, found refuge in Massachusetts, where he became one of the American federation's most powerful abolitionist voices. When the federal government decided to allow the citizens of the new Kansas Territory to decide whether they would allow local slavery, Bostonians created the New England Emigrant Society, which founded the Kansas towns of Lawrence and Manhattan and helped populate the territory with Yankees. When Appalachian-born residents sacked and burned Lawrence in 1856, another Connecticut-born Yankee, John Brown, slaughtered five men in retaliation; he later tried to provoke a slave rebellion by seizing a federal arsenal in western Virginia in an operation that established him among Yankees as a martyred freedom fighter and as a notorious terrorist to Deep Southern and Tidewater people.

Yankee abolitionists argued that the Deep South and Tidewater were autocratic despotisms. Slave lords' absolute power over those under them, they argued, led to corruption of the family and Christian virtue. "The slave states are one vast brothel," declared English-born Congregational minister George Bourne, in a pamphlet published in Boston. Slave masters and their sons raped their slaves, he and others charged, accounting for the large number of mixed-race children born to slave mothers. "It is so common for the female slaves to have white children that little or nothing is ever said about it," Connecticut minister Francis Hawley reported from the Deep South in Theodore Dwight Weld's *American Slavery as It Is*, a best-selling abolitionist anthology published in 1839. Another contributor, a Connecticut justice of the peace, described how a Tidewater North Carolina planter offered a friend of his $20 for each slave he impregnated. "This offer was no doubt made for the purpose of improving the stock," he added, "on the same principle that farmers endeavor to improve their cattle by crossing the breed." Southern newspaper classifieds were reprinted in abolitionist publications to publicize the fact that slave families were regularly broken up to pay debts, often by selling off toddlers or even a spouse. The "domestic institution," they argued, was a threat to domesticity itself.[2]

In 1860 Yankeedom voted overwhelmingly for the Republican presidential candidate, Abraham Lincoln, an Illinoisan of mixed Yankee, Midland, and Appalachian ancestry who opposed the creation of additional slave states. Lincoln won every single county in New England, the Western Reserve of Ohio, and the Yankee-settled Wyoming Valley of Pennsylvania; he won all but a handful of counties in the entirety of upstate New York and the Yankee Midwest.[3]

Yankee politicians advocated the use of force to prevent the Deep South from seceding and represented the only national caucus to do so prior to the South Carolinian attack on Fort Sumter. During the war Yankeedom was the center of the Union cause, contributing the lion's share of troops, arms, and materiel, including the most decorated black regiment in the Union Army, the Fifty-fourth Massachusetts Infantry.

There is no question that the Deep South seceded and fought the Civil War to defend slavery, and its leaders made no secret of this motive. Slavery, they argued ad nauseam, was the foundation for a virtuous, biblically sanctioned social system superior to that of the free states. When nineteenth-century Deep Southerners spoke of defending their "traditions," "heritage," and "way of life," they proudly identified the enslavement of others as the centerpiece of all three. Indeed, many of their leaders even argued that all lower-class people should be enslaved, regardless of race, for their own good.

In response to Yankee and Midland abolitionists, the Deep South's leaders developed an elaborate defense for human bondage. James Henry Hammond, former governor of South Carolina, published a seminal book arguing that enslaved laborers were happier, fitter, and better looked after than their "free" counterparts in Britain and the North, who were ruthlessly exploited by industrial capitalists. Free societies were therefore unstable, as there was always a danger that the exploited would rise up, creating "a fearful crisis in Republican institutions." Slaves, by contrast, were kept in their place by violent means and denied the right to vote, resist, or testify, ensuring the "foundation of every well-designed and durable" republic. Enslavement of the white working class would be, in his words, "a most glorious act of emancipation." Jefferson's notion that "all men are created equal," he wrote, was "ridiculously absurd." In the Deep Southern tradition, Hammond's republic was modeled on those of ancient Greece and Rome, featuring rights and democracy for the elite, slavery and submission for inferiors. It was sanctioned by the Christian God, whose son never denounced the practice in his documented teachings. It was a perfect aristocratic republic, one that should be a model for the world.[4]

Hammond mocked his Puritan critics as "learned old maids" who liked to "linger with such an insatiable relish" on bizarre and pornographic fantasies of masters raping slaves. The "proportion" of mulattos in the Deep South, he argued, was vanishingly small, and could be accounted for by the presence of Yankee perverts in the region's larger towns. He called the sexual charges—an existential threat to the Deep South's racially based caste system—"ridiculously false," the product of "a game played too often on Tourists in this country." But the charges were true, as Hammond well knew. Scholars later discovered in his private papers that in 1839 Hammond had purchased an eighteen-year-old slave and her two-year-old daughter, commencing sexual relationships first with the mother and later with the daughter, and sharing both with his son. His wife—Hammond noted she could not satisfy "his appetites"—eventually learned of the affairs and left the household for many years. The children and/or grandchildren sired by the enslaved mother and daughter were kept on the estate, because Hammond could not tolerate the idea that "any of my children or possible children [would be] slaves of strangers. Slavery *in the family* will be their happiest earthly condition."[5]

The planters celebrated slavery because it ensured the stability and perpetuation of a republican aristocracy. "The planters are a genuine aristocracy, who cultivate themselves in a leisure founded on slavery," *London Times* correspondent William Russell reported from South Carolina on the eve of war. "The admiration for monarchical institutions on the English model, for privileged classes and for a landed aristocracy and gentry is undisguised and apparently genuine." One planter told Russell: "If we could only get one of the Royal race of England to rule over us, we should be content." Many others expressed regret for the revolution, noting they "would go back tomorrow if they could."[6]

The planters' loathing of Yankees startled outsiders. "South Carolina, I am told, was founded by gentlemen, [not by] witch-burning Puritans, by cruel persecuting fanatics who implanted in the north . . . [and her] newly-born colonies all the ferocity, bloodthirstiness, and rabid intolerance of the Inquisition," Russell reported. "There is nothing in all the dark caves of human passion so cruel and deadly as the hatred the South Carolinians profess for the Yankees," he continued. "New England is to [them] the incarnation of moral and political wickedness and social corruption . . . the source of everything which South Carolina hates." Another planter told him that if the *Mayflower* had sunk, "we should never have been driven to these extremes."[7]

Most people in the South shared the Deep Southerners' credo of white supremacy and their distrust of Yankees, but many disagreed with their ideal of an aristocratic republic. Before the 1860 election the Democratic Party split over slavery at its annual convention, with South Carolina's delegates leading their Deep Southern colleagues out of the convention hall. ("Slavery is our King; Slavery is our truth; Slavery is our divine right," planter William Preston explained in his parting speech.) They were joined only by the Tidewater-dominated Maryland and Delaware delegations; Borderlander and northern delegations (most representing Catholic immigrants) remained in their places. Across "the South" there was considerable dissent, which broke not on state, class, or occupational lines but on ethnoregional ones. Appalachian sections—whether in northern Alabama, eastern Tennessee, or northeastern Texas—resisted secession. Deep Southern–settled ones—southern Alabama, western Tennessee, Gulf Coast Texas—were enthusiastically in favor of it. The Texas struggle pit South Carolinian Louis Wigfall against Borderlanders John Regan and Sam Houston. In Mississippi, Kentucky Borderlander James Alcorn led resistance to radical secessionist politicos under another South Carolina native, Albert Gallatin Brown. The richest planters in Louisiana were the most ardent Unionists; they were not Deep Southerners but rather members of the New French enclave around

New Orleans. ("New Orleans is almost Free Soil in its opinions," one observer remarked. "Creoles . . . cannot be made to comprehend their danger until their Negroes are being taken from their fields.") Running for the Mississippi senate in 1850, Deep Southerner (and future Confederate president) Jefferson Davis was rejected by the Appalachian-settled north of the state, which supported his rival, Knoxville native Roger Barton. By 1860 Appalachian districts in the Gulf States had elected Unionist representatives, who clashed with their lowland counterparts.[8]

Deep Southerners, where they were allowed to vote, overwhelmingly cast their ballots for the hard-line secessionist John C. Breckinridge. (So did South Carolina's legislators, who did not deign to grant the populace a role in choosing their chief executive.) Breckinridge won every state under Deep Southern control, while moderates like John Bell and Stephen Douglas won only a scattering of counties, most of them around Atlanta, a city with a large number of residents from outside the region. Lincoln did not even appear on the ballot in Deep Southern–controlled states.

After Lincoln's victory, South Carolina was the first to secede from the Union. The only states to join it prior to Lincoln's inauguration were those controlled by Deep Southerners: Mississippi, Alabama, Georgia, Florida, Louisiana, and Texas. On February 8, 1861, this Deep Southern coalition met in Alabama to form a new government. Tidewater and Appalachian states did not join them—preferring, as we will see, to form a confederation of their own.

Had Deep Southerners not started attacking federal post offices, mints, customs vessels, arsenals, and military bases in April 1861, they very well might have negotiated a peaceful secession from the Union. Indeed, prior to the South Carolinian militia's assault of Fort Sumter, Yankeedom was isolated, lacking a single national ally in its desire to put down the Deep Southern rebellion by force. President Lincoln pledged not to provoke open warfare, even as he declined to surrender U.S. military bases in the region. When Fort Sumter, which guarded Charleston's harbor, ran low on supplies, Lincoln took a cautious approach: he sent food but not weapons and ammunition, and informed South Carolina in advance. If the Deep Southern Confederates attacked the fort or relief shipment, they stood to alienate supporters of a negotiated settlement in Appalachia, the Midlands, and New Netherland, a fact well known within the Confederate government. "There will be no compromise with Secession if war is forced upon the north," Confederate secretary of state Richard Lathers warned President Davis. "The first armed demonstration against the integrity of the Union or the dignity of the flag will find these antagonistic partisans enrolled in the same patriotic ranks for the defense of both [and] bring every man at the North, irrespective of his party or sectional affiliations, to the support of the government and the flag of his country." Davis, confident that the three aforementioned nations would side with the Confederacy in time of war, ignored Lathers's advice. It would prove one of the worst miscalculations in North American history.[9]

Prior to the attack on Fort Sumter, New Netherland was eagerly supportive of the Deep South's position. Recall that New Netherland had introduced the continent to slavery and relied on slave labor right into the early nineteenth century. In 1790 the region's farming counties—Kings, Queens, and Richmond—had a higher proportion of white slaveholding families than South Carolina. Tolerance—not morality—was at the core of its culture, including tolerance for slaveholding, and left to its own devices, it probably never would have banned the practice. Unfortunately for New Netherlanders, by the nineteenth century they had lost control of New York state government to the Yankees, who by 1827 had eliminated slavery. (New Netherlanders clung to power narrowly in New Jersey, where there were still seventy-five enslaved people at midcentury.) But while the state as a whole was abolitionist, its biggest metropolis was not. Runaway slaves and free blacks were constantly being kidnapped by New York City's many "Blackbirders," slave-catching bounty hunters who deported their captures to the plantations. The city's merchants and bankers had extensive ties with Deep Southern and Tidewater slave lords, and were loath to see them disrupted. As the local *Evening Post* reported in 1860, "The City of New York belongs almost as much to the South as to the North."[10]

In the 1860 election every single county in New Netherland went for Lincoln's opponent, Stephen Douglas, including northern New Jersey, western Long Island, and the southern Hudson Valley. In the aftermath, most New Netherlanders wanted to see the Confederate states leave the Union in peace. Some—including their senior political leadership—advocated seizing the opportunity to secede themselves to form an independent city-state modeled on the Hanseatic League, a collection of free cities in Germany. "While other parts of our state have unfortunately been imbued with the fanatical spirit which actuates a portion of the people of New England," Mayor Fernando Wood told the city council after South Carolina's secession, the city had not "participated in the warfare upon [the slave state's] constitutional rights or their domestic institutions." The city, he continued, "may have more cause of apprehension from our own State than from external dangers" and should escape "this odious and oppressive connection" by leaving the United States and, together with its suburbs on Long Island, becoming an independent, low-tax city-state. The proposal had the support of prominent bankers and merchants, at least one of the city's Democratic congressmen, and at least three of its newspapers. A fourth, the influential *New York Herald*, published details of the governmental structure of Hanseatic city-states "for a better understanding" of how an independent New York City might organize itself. Had the Deep Southerners not attacked Fort Sumter, New Netherland might conceivably have gained its independence as well.[11]

In the run-up to the war, New Netherland's six U.S congressmen had voted with their Deep Southern counterparts on most important issues—the only New York representatives to do so. After South Carolina's secession, Congressman Daniel Stickles continued to support the Deep South, telling his colleagues at the U.S. Capitol that "no man will ever pass the boundaries of the city of New York for the purpose of waging war against any state of this Union." The city, he added, "will never consent to remain an appendage and a slave of a Puritan province."

The attack on Fort Sumter changed opinion overnight. As Lathers had predicted, New Netherland sections of both New York and New Jersey erupted in extreme U.S. patriotism. Mayor Wood, Congressman Stickles, the New York Chamber of Commerce, and the *Herald* immediately rallied to Lincoln and the Union. "The attack on Fort Sumter has made the North a unit," Stickles wrote the federal secretary of war. "We are at war with a foreign power." He himself would raise volunteer regiments and lead them into battle against the Confederates.[12]

Despite a long history of abolitionist sentiment, the Midlands had been ambivalent about Southern secession prior to the attack on Sumter. The

Quaker/Anabaptist commitment to pacifism trumped moral qualms about slavery. Newspapers and politicians from Midland areas of Pennsylvania advocated allowing the Deep South to secede peacefully. Midland-controlled northern Delaware found itself at odds with the Tidewater-dominated south of the state, with some fearing violence might break out between the sections. Midland southern New Jersey had no intention of joining a slave-trading Gotham city-state, even if northern Jersey did.

In the 1860 presidential election the Midlands voted overwhelmingly for Lincoln, except for northern Maryland and Delaware, where he did not appear on the ballot. (In those places, Midlanders voted for the moderate Bell instead.) Lincoln easily won most of the Midland Midwest from central Ohio to southern Iowa, tipping Illinois and Indiana into his column. While Midlanders voted with their Yankee neighbors, they had no desire to be governed by them. Faced with the possibility of a national dissolution, most Midland political and opinion leaders hoped to join the Appalachian-controlled states to create a Central Confederacy stretching from New Jersey to Arkansas. The proposed nation would serve as a neutral buffer area between Yankeedom and the Deep South, preventing the antagonists from going to war with each other. John Pendleton Kennedy, a Baltimore publisher and former congressman, championed this "Confederacy of Border States," which opposed both the Deep South's program of expansion by conquest and the Yankee plans to preserve the Union by force. It was, he argued, the "natural and appropriate medium through which the settlement of all differences is eventually to be obtained." Maryland's governor, Thomas Hicks, saw merit in the proposal, which could preserve the peace in a state split between Midland, Appalachian, and Tidewater sections; he corresponded with governors of Pennsylvania, New Jersey, Delaware, Ohio, and Missouri (all of which had substantial Midland sections) plus New York and Virginia to lay the groundwork for such an alliance should the Union break up.[13]

But the Deep South lost all Midland support after Sumter. In Philadelphia, Easton, and West Chester—Pennsylvania communities that had previously been centers of secessionist sympathy—mobs destroyed pro-Southern newspaper offices, drove pro-Southern politicians from their homes, assaulted secessionists in the streets, and forced homes and businesses to display Union flags. In Maryland the Central Confederacy proposal became obsolete overnight; Midland and Appalachian sections rallied to the Union, Tidewater ones to the Southern Confederacy. Their flag attacked, Midland sections of Indiana, Illinois, and Missouri threw in their lot with the Yankees.[14]

By midcentury, Tidewater had effectively been politically neutered, its people a minority in Maryland, Delaware, North Carolina, and even Virginia (until 1861, when West Virginia's secession tipped the balance back into their favor). As friction increased over slavery, Tidewater found itself forced into the Deep Southern orbit for protection, despite their cultural differences. Unlike that of sugar and cotton, tobacco's global market had weakened, and the Tidewater gentry had sold many of their slaves to Deep Southerners or simply moved their operations to the Gulf. The region's elite felt besieged, and many embraced Deep Southern ideologies, even if they could not carry them out in their own states.

George Fitzhugh, scion of one of Virginia's oldest families, became the region's proslavery standard-bearer. In his voluminous writings, Fitzhugh endorsed and expanded upon Hammond's argument to enslave all poor people. Aristocrats, he explained, were really "the nation's magna carta" because they owned so much and had the "affection which all men feel for what belongs to them," which naturally led them to protect and provide for "wives, children, and slaves." Fitzhugh, whose books were enormously popular, declared he was "quite as intent on abolishing Free Society as you [Northerners] are on abolishing slavery."[15]

As the conflict with the Yankees loomed, there was renewed interest in the old Tidewater theory that racial differences were to blame. In wartime propaganda, the Deep Southern elite was explicitly included in the allegedly superior Norman/Cavalier race in an effort to increase the bonds between the two regions, with the (decidedly un-Norman) Appalachian districts often embraced for good measure. For Tidewater in particular, casting the conflict as a war for Norman liberation from Anglo-Saxon tyranny neatly sidestepped the more problematic slavery issue. The *Southern Literary Messenger*, Tidewater's leading journal, conceded in 1861 that "the Round-heads[16] may gain many victories in view of their superior strength and their better condition" but assured "they will loose the last [battle] and then sink down to their normal position of relative inferiority." The journal argued the Confederate aim was to create "a sort of Patrician Republic" ruled by a people "superior to all other races on this continent."

This propaganda was embraced in the Deep South as well. In an 1862 speech, Jefferson Davis told Mississippi legislators that their enemies were "a traditionless and homeless race . . . gathered by Cromwell from the bogs and fens of the north of Ireland and of England" to be "disturbers of peace in the world." The war, *DeBow's Review* declared, was a struggle to reverse the ill-conceived American Revolution, which had been contrary to "the natural reverence of the Cavalier for the authority of established forms over mere speculative ideas." By throwing off monarchy, slaveholders endangered the wondrous "domestic institution" that rested "on the principle of inequality and subordination, and favor[ed] a public policy embodying the ideas of social status." Democracy "threw political influence into the hands of inorganic masses" and caused "the subjection of the Cavalier to the intellectual thralldom of the Puritan." Other Tidewater and Deep Southern thinkers came to agree that the struggle was really between respect for established aristocratic order and the dangerous Puritan notion that "the individual man was . . . of higher worth than any system of polity." As Fitzhugh put it, it was a war "between conservatives and revolutionists; between Christians and infidels . . . the chaste and the libidinous; between marriage and free-love." Some even championed the dubious notion that the Confederacy was fighting a Huguenot-Anglican counterreformation against Puritan excess. Slavery was not the issue, they argued—defeating democracy was.[17]

In the 1860 presidential election, Tidewater was split between moderate Bell and secessionist Breckinridge, with Bell's support concentrated on the eastern shore of Maryland and in Tidewater North Carolina. After South Carolina seceded, Tidewater wished to follow but was thwarted by other nations' control over Maryland, Virginia, and North Carolina's state governments. Only after Fort Sumter and Lincoln's call to arms did Virginia and North Carolina secede; Maryland and Delaware never did. In all four cases, the attitude of Borderlanders, not Tidewater folk, was the decisive factor.

Greater Appalachia had the most ambivalent reaction to Deep Southern secession and the Yankee call to war. From central Pennsylvania to southern Illinois and northern Alabama, Borderlanders were torn between their disgust with Yankees and their hatred of Deep Southern planters. Both regions represented a threat to Borderlander ideals, but in different ways. The Yankees' emphasis on the need to subsume one's personal desires and interests to the "greater good" was anathema to the Appalachian quest for individual freedom; their moral crusades to change the behavior of others were extremely distasteful, especially their endless harping about racial equality. On the other hand, Borderlanders had already suffered generations of oppression at the hands of aristocratic slave lords and knew that they were the people the planters had in mind when they talked about enslaving inferior whites.[18]

In the run-up to the conflict, many Borderlanders were hostile toward abolitionists, breaking up their lectures, destroying their presses, and egging their politicians. Illinois governor John Reynolds likened abolitionists to the fanatical witch hunters of early New England, as did Indiana's Hoosier press. At the same time, Borderlanders condemned the Fugitive Slave Law, which was, as one Hoosier put it, "converting the Freemen of the North into a gang of slave catchers for the South." Kentucky-born James G. Birney, a slaveholder turned abolitionist, spoke for many Borderlanders when he denounced the Deep Southern system "by which the majority are to be made poor and miserable that the few may spend their useless lives in indolent voluptuousness." Indeed, it sought to make ordinary people "lie down at the foot of the Southern Slaveholders 'like whipt and trembling Spaniels.'"[19]

Caught between these threats to their freedom, Borderlanders became strong supporters of the notion of "popular sovereignty," the principle by which local residents would decide if a new territory would have slaves or not. When this compromise failed to hold the Union together, many Borderlanders wished to either remain neutral or join the proposed Central Confederacy. When South Carolina seceded, Virginia's Borderlander governor, John Letcher, told state legislators that the Union would split into four separate nations, with Virginia, Pennsylvania, New Jersey, and other border and Midwestern states becoming "a mighty fourth force." Appalachia's leading political figure, former president James Buchanan of Pennsylvania, maintained the South should be allowed to go in peace but that the Union should defend itself if attacked. The region was deeply divided in the 1860 election, with the moderate Bell winning narrow majorities in four Appalachian-controlled states (Kentucky, Virginia, Tennessee, and Texas), Lincoln taking the Appalachian vote in Pennsylvania, and Douglas capturing much of the Appalachian Midwest.

When the Gulf states voted for delegates to their respective January 1861 secession conferences, their Appalachian districts were opposed to the exercise. Kentucky refused to call a conference at all and remained neutral in the ensuing war. In February Appalachian-dominated North Carolina and Tennessee held popular referendums on whether to hold secessionist conventions. In both states the proposals were defeated. In Arkansas, Deep Southerners in the state's lowland southeast threatened to secede after delegates from the Appalachian northwest blocked their proposal to leave the Union. When Virginia seceded in April, the Appalachian northwest of the state rebelled against the rebellion, seizing control of the strategically vital Baltimore and Ohio Railroad.[20]

Once again Fort Sumter and Lincoln's subsequent call for troops proved decisive, forcing Appalachian people to choose between two cultures they despised. Deep Southerners assumed Appalachia would rally to the Confederacy because of a shared doctrine of white supremacy. Instead, Borderlanders did as they always had: they took up arms against whatever enemy they felt was the greatest threat, and fought ferociously against them. To the planters' shock, most Appalachian people regarded them as a greater threat to their liberty than the Yankees. Western Virginians set up a Union government in Wheeling, volunteered in large numbers for the Union army, and became a separate state in 1863. Voters in eastern Tennessee rejected the state's secession referendum by more than two to one and tried to set up a Union government of their own; failing that, thousands fled to Kentucky to don blue uniforms while others sabotaged railway bridges. Residents of Appalachian northern Alabama established the Unionist Free State of Winston and fought as Alabama units in the Union army. Altogether a quarter-million men from Appalachian sections of the Confederacy volunteered for Union service, with regiments representing every state save South Carolina. In Pennsylvania, Buchanan declared for the Union, while tens of thousands of Scots-Irish volunteered to punish the Deep Southern traitors. In the Appalachian Midwest most Borderlanders regarded the attack on Sumter as treason and rallied to the

Stars and Stripes. "I was a Kentuckian," one Hoosier told a reporter, "but now I am an American."[21]

The attack on Sumter pushed the Appalachian majority in Pennsylvania, Missouri, Indiana, and western Virginia into the Union camp. Other parts of Appalachia rallied to the Confederacy, regarding Lincoln's call for troops as a direct attack on their communities. This sentiment was especially strong in lower-lying areas where Appalachian slaveholding was more common: central and western North Carolina, middle Tennessee, southwestern Virginia, and northern Arkansas. In the aftermath of Sumter, these regions supported secession ballot measures, causing their states to join the Confederacy three to four months after the Deep South had created it.[22]

The Confederacy, of course, went down in defeat in 1865, its cities occupied by "foreign" troops, its slaves emancipated by presidential decree. Yankees hoped that out of the Union's costly military victory, its occupying forces might carry out a massive project in state building, an effort to democratize the Deep South, Tidewater, and Confederate Appalachia along Yankee and Midlander lines. With its soldiers maintaining order, thousands of Yankee and Midland schoolteachers, missionaries, businessmen, and government officials were deployed to the three regions. They introduced public education, creating segregated elementary schools and black colleges (many of which exist today). They eliminated laws and practices that enforced the Deep Southern caste system. They ensured that newly freed slaves could vote and stand for office and that former top Confederate officials could not. Fifteen African Americans were elected to the U.S. House of Representatives from the former Confederacy between 1870 and 1877, and two represented black-majority Mississippi in the U.S. Senate.[23]

But foreign occupiers have always found it difficult to fundamentally change a culture. The people of Tidewater, the Deep South, and Confederate Appalachia resisted the Yankee reforms as determinedly as they could, and after Union troops withdrew in 1876, whites in the "reconstructed" regions undid the measures. Yankee public schools were abolished. Imposed state constitutions were rewritten, restoring white supremacy and adopting poll taxes, "literacy tests," and other instruments that allowed white officials to deprive African Americans of the right to vote. (As a result, the total presidential vote in South Carolina fell from 182,600 in 1876 to 50,000 in 1900, even as the state's population increased.) Ku Klux Klansmen murdered "uppity" blacks who ran for office or violated the rules of the traditional caste system. Despite a war and a concerted occupation, Deep Southern and Tidewater culture retained their essential characters, setting the stage for future culture clashes in the century to follow.[24]

PART FOUR

CULTURE WARS

1878 to 2010

CHAPTER 22

Founding the Far West

The Far West was the last region of North America to be colonized, and for good reason: it was remarkably inhospitable for Euro-Atlantic civilizations, with their emphasis on cropland agriculture, water-dependent plants and animals, and fixed settlements. It began at the ninety-eighth meridian, which bisects the Dakotas, Nebraska, Kansas, and Oklahoma. West of that point, only twenty inches of rain reached the parched earth each year, less than a third of the amount that fell in Mobile, Alabama. From the arid brown prairies of western Nebraska and eastern Colorado to the deserts of Nevada and interior California and the dry, scrubby mountains of interior Oregon and Washington, there were few places where agriculture could survive without the help of extensive irrigation projects. The altitude was so high—even the plains and mountain valleys stood above the tallest summits of the Appalachians—that many familiar crops wouldn't grow at all, particularly in soils poisoned by alkali salts. Most of the vast region's rivers were too shallow for navigation, isolating settlers from potential markets for anything they did grow. Its Native American tribes had had two centuries to perfect mounted warfare (after the introduction of horses from El Norte), enabling them to better keep interlopers in check. In the Far West the technologies and techniques of the Appalachian frontiersman were as useless as Yankee and Midlands farming practices. Deep Southern plantation crops couldn't be grown at all.

As a result, settlers from the other nations passed over this region in their rush to the lush Left Coast or the gold mining districts on its far western fringe. In 1860 there were more non-Indians living in San Francisco than in the entirety of the Far West. Few who transited the region saw much reason to linger. Before irrigation, trains, or air-conditioning, the High Plains and Western deserts were frightening places where travelers faced blinding sun, staggering heat, and mind-numbing monotony.

Transcontinental trails were littered with the bodies of livestock and people whose water ran out or who were overwhelmed by outlaws or Indian patrols. "After swimming streams and wading sloughs we go to bed at night wet and tired," an emigrant reported from northeastern Nevada in 1850. "In the morning we get up with stiffened limbs and examine ourselves for ticks, and if any are on us they will be as large as a grain of corn. We traveled all day through swarms of mosquitoes and gnats and had to hunt for grass and water until a late hour."[1]

The sheer extremity of the Far Western conditions made it impossible for the other national cultures to take hold here. Greater Appalachia, Yankeedom, and the Midlands each succeeded in adapting to and colonizing the well-watered plains of the Midwest. But as they approached the ninety-eighth meridian, each nation came to a halt, its respective social adaptations no longer able to ensure individual or community survival. There were only two ways for Euro-Americans to expand further into the interior. One was to adopt the nomadic ways of most of the Native American peoples in the region, a practice that worked well for the early fur traders dispatched by the Hudson's Bay Company. The other was to attach themselves to one of the nation's new industrial corporations as it lumbered into the vast interior, deploying capital, machines, mercenaries, and laborers with ruthless single-mindedness. Almost everyone coming to the Far West came in service of the latter model, or found themselves beholden to it.

The Far West, uniquely in North America, is a nation defined not by ethnoregional cultural forces but by the demands of external institutions. It is the one place where environment really did trump the cultural heritage of settlers, imposing challenges that Euro-Americans tried to solve through the deployment of capital-intensive technologies: hard rock mines, railroads, telegraphs, Gatling guns, barbed wire, and hydroelectric dams. As a result, the Far West has long been an internal colony of the continent's older nations and federal government, which possessed the necessary capital. Its people are still often deeply resentful of their dependent status but have generally backed policies guaranteed to preserve the status quo.

The Far West's first settlers were the exception to the aforementioned pattern. Arriving in two geographically separate waves in 1847–50, the earliest Euro-American colonists arrived just ahead of industrial capital. One group—the Yankee Mormons of Utah—would found a distinct subculture of independent farmers in Utah and southern Idaho. The other—the gold-hungry Forty-niners—were highly individualistic frontiersmen in the Appalachian mold. Neither would achieve cultural dominance over the Western interior.

The Mormons—followers of a Yankee-led utopian movement with its origins in Vermont and New York's Burnt-over District—began arriving on the shores of Utah's Great Salt Lake in the late 1840s. Fleeing persecution in the Midwest in 1847, they originally intended to settle outside the United States, but their plans were frustrated by the United States–Mexico War and, shortly thereafter, the U.S. annexation of their promised land in the desert. Their leader, Vermont-born Brigham Young, was made the first governor of the Utah Territory in 1850, and two years later 20,000 Mormons were living there. Almost all were from Yankeedom, which explains why in 2000, Utah had the highest percentage of English Americans of any state in the Union, edging out Vermont and Maine.

With a communal mind-set and intense group cohesion, the Mormons were able to build and maintain irrigation projects that enabled small farmers to survive in Far Western conditions. In the process they created an enclave of independent producers in a region otherwise controlled by absentee owners and other external forces. While at odds with Yankeedom over many issues, the Far West's Mormon enclave betrays its Yankee origins in its communitarianism, its emphasis on morality and good works, and its desire to assimilate others. Today the area's influence can be felt across Utah, southern Idaho, and eastern Nevada, and it is the most politically influential homegrown force in the Far West.

The Forty-niners who rushed into California's central valley and eastern mountains in pursuit of gold, in contrast, were atomized, heterogeneous, and hedonistic. They were drawn from all over the world but particularly from Appalachian sections of the East. Consistent with this demographic, the initial emphasis of the settlers was on individual effort and competition, with small producers working surface deposits and holding on to the proceeds. In those early years the size of a claim was limited to what an individual could work himself, and little capital was required to do so. "The life of a miner is one of labor, peril, and exposure," one journalist wrote of the era, "but it possesses the fascinating element of liberty and the promise of unlimited reward."[2]

Unfortunately those compensations were not to last. Within a few years California's surface deposits were depleted, and the mining moved underground, where capital and labor requirements could be met only by companies and bankers. Mining quickly became a corporate affair, with the miners reduced to wage labor and the "unlimited reward" accruing to the owners. When, in 1859, the silver Comstock Lode was discovered over the mountains in what is now Nevada, thousands headed east to work in the hills surrounding Virginia City, Nevada's boomtown, where improvised crushing mills processed what was carted to them. Nevada's territorial legislature was dominated by these "old Californians" who championed independent prospectors and small businessmen as boisterous crowds rallied outside their meeting hall to make the public will known. But this boom, too, was not to last.

The corporate takeover of Nevada's mines and political system followed a pattern that would continue in the Far West for nearly a century. By early 1864 the Comstock's surface deposits had run out. When delegates gathered that summer to write Nevada's first constitution, mining interests introduced a bill that effectively exempted mines from taxation, even though they represented most of the territory's economic activity. Delegates linked with the mining industry claimed taxes would prompt the corporations to leave the region, imperiling the jobs of their hired miners and, by extension, demand for farm goods, cattle, lumber, and other supplies and services provided by locals. The frightened delegates passed the bill, effectively transferring the tax burden to everyone else in Nevada. It was a ruse that would be repeated again and again across the Far West.[3]

Within a few years it was no longer necessary for big firms to use fearmongering to work their will; they simply owned Nevada's legislators and congressional delegation. By 1870 Nevada politics was no longer a struggle between individual producers and corporate interests but simply a clash between competing cartels. The Bank of California—which had repossessed huge numbers of mining claims during a recession—owned processing facilities, the timber and water supplies, and the key railroad for the Comstock region. Thereafter a rival conglomerate, the Sacramento-based Central Pacific Railroad, bought up most of the bank's competitors in these sectors while monopolizing transportation between Nevada and the rest of the continent and controlling settlement of the 100-mile-wide strip surrounding most of its rail corridor. Both of these competing cartels spent lavishly to put their own associates in office and to build political machines to cultivate new generations of company men for placement in state and federal positions. From 1865 to 1900 every U.S. senator from Nevada save one was closely associated with one or another of the cartels. Eventually the cartels agreed to divide control of Nevada between them. The Bank of California group focused on paying state legislators to pass industry-friendly laws and regulations, while the Central Pacific Railroad bought the congressional delegations. Local offices were left to the labor unions, which focused not on advocating for their constituents but on keeping nonwhites (especially Chinese) out of the mines and other workplaces, sometimes by use of mob violence. The era of the independent producer was over, and not just in Nevada.[4]

Outside the mining districts, the colonization of the Far West was led by railroad companies, which effectively controlled the development of much of the vast territory. The Union Pacific, Central Pacific, Kansas Pacific, and Northern Pacific had effective monopolies over access to their respective slices of the area, setting fares for passengers and freight. None of them was based in the region.

The railroads also served as the Far West's primary real estate and colonization agents. To encourage the construction of these staggeringly expensive transcontinental projects, the federal government had given these railroads 60- to 100-mile swaths of land around their respective lines. Taken together, the railroads were awarded over 150 million acres of the region in the second half of the nineteenth century, an area the size of Montana and Idaho combined. The companies could sell parcels to settlers who, in turn, became entirely dependent on the railroad for transport of goods and people in or out of the region. First, however, they had to attract the settlers.[5]

Elsewhere on the continent railroads followed in the wake of colonization, extending their lines in response to demand. In much of the Far West, however, the railroads came first and supervised colonization themselves.

They invested in huge marketing campaigns, publishing newspapers, maps, and magazines extolling the arid West. Wyoming's Laramie Plain was comparable to the "fertile prairies of Illinois" even though it was 5,000 feet higher and had a third as much rain and a growing season two months shorter. The Great Salt Lake region was arranged with "striking similarity" to the Holy Land, and the railroads had comparison maps published to prove it. Kansas was "the garden spot of the world."[6] The Northern Pacific set up colonization offices in London, Liverpool, Germany, the Netherlands, Norway, and Sweden, issuing brochures in local languages and arranging for discounted "emigration tickets" with the steamship companies. The Union Pacific and Burlington railroads spent $1 million in advertising for Nebraska alone at a time when you could build a house for $700. The Northern Pacific advertised its lands in 200 North American newspapers and 100 European ones. The railroad companies built or contributed to the construction of churches and schools to anchor newly founded prairie towns, and encouraged settlement even in lands outside the swath they controlled, confident that the settlers would still depend on the rails.

The fraudulent ad campaigns benefited from a climatological fluke that delivered record rainfalls in the late 1860s, just as the first big wave of colonists were settling the High Plains. Americans, caught up in the notion of Manifest Destiny, thought they saw the hand of God at work as the brown prairies turned green. Leading scientists of the day encouraged such thinking, endorsing the crackpot theory that "rain follows the plow." Cyrus Thomas, a noted climatologist, proclaimed, "As population increases, the moisture will increase." Rain was said to be triggered by smoke from locomotives, by the planting of trees and the plowing of land, even by the vibrations generated by humans and their livestock. Government bureaucrats incorporated the assumptions of this New Meteorology into the assignment of land grants, which presumed a family could survive on 160 acres of unirrigated Colorado prairie just as well as their counterparts had on 160 acres of lush Illinois or Indiana grassland. Hundreds of thousands of independent yeoman farmers rode the rails to the middle of nowhere and sank their precious capital into a land that older maps had labeled the Great American Desert.[7]

The renowned explorer and geologist John Wesley Powell—a native of Yankee New York—tried to get the truth out in a book-length report to

Congress. Much of the Far West could not support farming, he told the nation, and even if all the streams and rivers were diverted into irrigation projects, it would redeem only 1 to 3 percent of the land. The government land grants—based on eastern precedents—were ill conceived, as 160 acres of irrigated land would be too much for one family to farm, and 160 acres of unirrigated land was far too small; the latter could be used only for ranching, and in that case would require 2,500 acres to succeed. The "rain follows the plow" theory was bunk, Powell insisted. The country could "expect a speedy return to extreme aridity," he warned, "in which case a large portion of the agricultural industries . . . now growing up would be destroyed." He recommended a series of watershed-based federal irrigation districts and communal pasturelands, and a slow, cautious settling of the Far West by individual producers assisted by prudent public investment. Needless to say, Powell's suggestions were ignored.[8]

The fantasy ended in the winter of 1886, when much of the Far West endured arctic conditions: weeks of subzero temperatures that killed somewhere between a third and three-quarters of the High Plains's cattle and not a few of its yeoman farmers. The following year the rains failed to appear, and in the year after that. By 1890, independent farmers were fleeing the drought-stricken region in droves, reducing the populations of Kansas and Nebraska by nearly half. Sixty percent of the million or so farmers on the plains gave up. The winter also put an end to the cattlemen who'd been overgrazing public lands beyond the railway zones, destroying the topsoil, which then eroded away into the tributaries of the Missouri River, changing it from clear to deep brown. The drought drove the cattlemen away, but the damage was permanent. "Since those high and far-off days the range has never been capable of supporting anything like the number of cattle it could have supported if the cattle barons had not maimed it," Far West native Bernard DeVoto wrote in 1947. "It never will be capable of supporting a proper number again during the geological epoch in which civilization exists." The Dust Bowl years of the 1930s only made matters worse. As DeVoto would later write, the Far West had "caused the collapse of the frontier culture, thus also set the full stop to the American dream."[9]

What groups did survive the nineteenth century in the Far West—the Mormon enclave excepted—did so only by associating with massive external corporations or even larger federal infrastructure projects built by massive external corporations. The U.S. government dammed rivers and streams, built aqueducts to move water from one basin to another, and underwrote the construction and maintenance of extensive irrigation systems, all to enable a few farmers to grow crops in the desert. Mining companies expanded to new territories and states, often running them as their own feudal preserves. The railroads, having no competitors, continued to charge whatever they pleased, developing a system by which rail fares into or out of the Far West were many times more expensive per mile than fares in or between the Eastern nations and the Left Coast. As late as the twentieth century one could ship goods from Chicago to Seattle via Helena cheaper than from Chicago to Helena on the very same train. Raw goods could be shipped out of the Far West more cheaply than finished goods, in an intentional scheme concocted by the railroads to prevent manufacturing industries from taking hold in the region and to keep it dependent on the cities of the Left Coast, Yankeedom, the Midlands, and New Netherland.[10]

Internally, corporate control over Far Western politics and society was disturbingly thorough. In the late nineteenth and early twentieth centuries, Anaconda Copper literally ran Montana, buying off judges, local officials, and politicians in both parties and, via the "cemetery vote," controlling the state's elections. Its politicians in turn delivered rules, regulations, and tax policies that enriched Anaconda and its executives. Founded by the ruthless Marcus Daly, an Irish immigrant and veteran of the Nevada silver boom, and supported by San Francisco mining magnate George Hearst, Anaconda owned the mines, the smelters that processed the ore, the coal mines that fueled the smelters, the forests that supplied the timber needed in the mines, the power plants that powered the facility, the railroad that connected the parts, and even the banks that financed them. On Daly's death in 1900 his company employed three-fourths of all wage earners in Montana. As late as 1959 it owned five of the state's six daily newspapers, which repressed news unfavorable to the company (like stories regarding the fines it paid for sending faulty wire to Allied troops in World War II). Until the 1970s it maintained "hospitality rooms" for friendly legislators at the state capitol in Helena, where women and drink were available to the compliant. Notoriously stingy, Anaconda never gave anything to its hometown of Butte save a small workers' park; this was subsequently destroyed along with much of the town itself to make way for a gigantic Anaconda pit mine and future Superfund site.[11]

Meanwhile much of the land in the Far West that hadn't been turned over to the railroad companies, seized by mining interests, or granted to Indians as reservations remained in the hands of the federal government. Even today the federation owns about a third of Montana and Colorado; half of Utah, Wyoming, and Idaho; two-thirds of Far Western Oregon; and 85 percent of Nevada. Far Westerners have had little control over this land, which the federal government has often turned over for exploitation by the same corporate interests that have dominated the rest of the region. Lumber giants logged national forests for next to nothing. Ranching companies grazed on public lands. Oil and gas companies prospected on federally administered Indian reservations, with federal agencies often neglecting to require them to pay their royalties. Morris Garnsey of the University of Colorado summarized the other nations' attitudes toward the Far West in 1945. "Get control of the raw material, get it out as cheaply as possible, and haul it away as fast as possible," he wrote. "The interests of the local area are a secondary consideration. The region becomes a colonial dependency of an industrial empire."[12]

The result of these formative experiences is that by the early twentieth century, the people of the Far West would come to resent both the corporations and the federal government, seeing them as joint oppressors. By allying with the Deep South, their political leaders have managed to weaken federal stewardship of Far Western resources. Ironically, this has merely served to increase corporate dominance over their nation.

Far Westerners have long agitated for greater local control of their economic future. Despite the considerable influence of railroads, banks, and mining companies, they managed to write state constitutions that protected laborers via eight-hour work laws, banned private militias (which were often used to break strikes), and prohibited employers from including clauses in employment contracts that absolved them of responsibility for accidents, even those resulting from gross corporate negligence. The Far West was a hotbed of economic populism, labor unionism, and even socialism right up until World War II. Its people elected progressives like

Montana senator Burton Wheeler (a Massachusetts native who sided with workers against Anaconda) or Senator William Borah of Idaho (who sponsored the bill creating the federal Department of Labor). FDR swept the Far West in 1932, propelled by the region's hostility to the Wall Street financiers they believed had caused the Great Depression. But the cultural revolution of the 1960s drove a wedge between the Far Westerners and left-wing forces in Yankeedom, New Netherland, and the Left Coast. "Liberalism was turning away from the popular economic progressivism with which Mountain states support had been forged," Republican strategist Kevin Phillips would write at the end of the decade, "and was shifting into a welfare establishmentarianism lacking in appeal to the old radical Mountain states (where Northeastern causes are suspect, whether liberal or conservative)."[13]

The cartels have since made a comeback, in large part by backing political candidates who serve their interests while attacking the Far Westerners' other historical enemy: the federal government. Where the government was concerned, the popular majority long ago developed a concise agenda: get out, leave us alone, and give us more money. They want dams maintained on the upper Columbia but no regulations protecting salmon. They want Washington to keep providing $2 billion in irrigation subsidies but not to try to prevent them being used to exhaust the last of the region's great ancient aquifers. Many of the Far West's senators and congressmen receive most of their campaign donations from interests outside the region and have become among the most reliable champions of the external industrial corporations at work there. But they do so through the libertarian rhetoric of individual freedom from governmental tyranny. "We oppose the federal intrusion in the everyday lives of the people of our great country," Wyoming senator John Barrasso explained in announcing the 2009 creation of a Western Caucus of senators. "The government should get out of the way of prosperity and liberty [and] . . . cannot legislate economic progress by spending billions in taxpayer dollars or imposing strict environmental regulations." Utah senator Orrin Hatch added that "one of the aims of the Senate Western Caucus is to thwart the anti-oil agenda of the Washington elite and their extreme environmentalist allies." Added his Utah colleague Robert Bennett, "It's time for us to recognize the tremendous treasure trove that the American West represents and move ahead in an intelligent fashion to exploit it," noting that the energy resources extended "up on into Canada." The senators did not propose increasing the self-reliance of their corporate donors by raising timber-cutting royalties or grazing fees on public lands to market rates, or making large agribusinesses compensate taxpayers for the real cost of operating the dams and water projects that allow them to grow cotton in the desert.[14]

Indeed, the Far West's hostility to federal power has been the glue that's held this authority-averse region in an otherwise unlikely alliance with the continent's most authoritarian nation, with lasting repercussions for North America and the world.

CHAPTER 23

Immigration and Identity

If the existence of the American nations seems persuasive enough for the seventeenth and eighteenth centuries and the first three-quarters of the nineteenth century, one might still ask how they could possibly have survived to the present day. After all, isn't the United States a nation of immigrants, and Canada, too, for that matter? In the late nineteenth and early twentieth centuries, did we not welcome to our shores tens of millions of people from all over the world, those tired, poor, huddled masses yearning to breathe free who flowed through Ellis and Angel Islands on their way to create the wondrously diverse America of today? Surely the cultures of the regional nations were subsumed by the great multicultural tide of 1830 to 1924, surviving only in the imaginations of a few old-money white Anglo-Saxon Protestants still hiding out in their last scraps of habitat: Nantucket, Harvard Yard, and Skull and Bones reunions. Did not the arrival of millions of Irish, Germans, Italians, Slavs, Jews, Greeks, and Chinese in the course of a single lifetime herald the birth of a genuinely "American" (or, for that matter, "Canadian") identity that cemented the country together to fight two world wars?

The short answer is no.

These great immigration waves enriched and empowered these two North American federations, but they did not displace their preexisting regional nations. These remained the "dominant cultures" which nineteenth- and early-twentieth-century immigrants' children and grandchildren either assimilated into or reacted against. Immigrant communities might achieve political dominance over a city or state (as the Irish did in Boston or the Italians in New York), but the system they controlled was the product of the regional culture. They might retain, share, and promote their own cultural legacies, introducing foods, religions, fashions, and ideas, but they would find them modified over time by adaptations to local conditions and mores. They might encounter prejudice and hostility from the "native" population, but the nature and manifestation of this opposition varied depending on which nation the natives belonged to. Immigrants didn't alter "American culture," they altered America's respective regional cultures. Indeed, in many ways the immigrations of 1830–1924 actually accentuated the differences among them.

A few words on this era of mass immigration. Between 1830 and 1924 some 36 million people emigrated to the United States. They arrived in three distinct waves. The first—the arrival of some 4.5 million Irish, Germans, and British people between 1830 and 1860—has already been touched on; it triggered Yankee fears that those immigrants who were Catholic would undermine the republic through slavish obedience to the Pope, and it motivated New England's mission to "save the west" by assimilating newcomers to the Yankee Way. The second, between 1860 and 1890, saw twice as many immigrants, largely from the same countries, plus Scandinavia and China. The third wave, from 1890 to 1924, was the largest of all, with some 18 million new arrivals, mostly from southern and eastern Europe (particularly Italy, Greece, and Poland), three-quarters of whom were either Catholic or Jewish; this wave also included many Chinese and caused some alarm among native-born North Americans who feared these new foreigners would be unable to assimilate to local ways. This third wave was cut short in 1924, when the U.S. Congress imposed quotas designed to protect the federation from the taint of "inferior races," including Italians, Jews, and immigrants from the Balkans and East Europe. Immigration remained restricted—and heavily biased toward northern Europeans—until the early 1950s. Despite the scale of immigration, newcomers were always a small minority. The proportion of foreign-born remained at about 10 percent of the U.S. population throughout the period, peaking at 14 percent in 1914. Its cumulative effect was important but not overwhelming. Even after adding together all immigrants between 1790 and 2000—66 million altogether—and their descendants, demographers have calculated that immigration accounts for only about half the early-twenty-first-century population of the United States. In other words, if the United States had sealed its borders in 1790, in the year 2000 it would still have had a population of about 125 million instead of 250 million. The 1820–1924 immigration was enormous, but it was never truly overpowering.[1]

Another key point to note is that these "great wave" immigrants didn't spread out evenly across the federation but rather concentrated in a few locations. Throughout the period, the majority of immigrants lived in New Netherland, the Midlands, and Yankeedom and most of the rest on the Left Coast. They settled in a handful of gateway cities, especially New York, Philadelphia, Boston, Chicago, and San Francisco. Virtually none of them came to Tidewater, Appalachia, the Deep South, or El Norte. (The Far West, which was still being colonized, attracted only small numbers of immigrants, but they accounted for a significant share of the region's population—about a quarter in 1870, and almost a fifth in 1910.) New York City alone had more foreign-born residents in 1870 than the entirety of Tidewater, Appalachia, and the Deep South combined. Scholars have shown that immigrant communities tended to fan out to the suburbs as they gained wealth and influence; this kept the influence of "ethnic" communities concentrated in immigration's "have" nations, and left the "have-not" nations almost untouched.[2]

It's not difficult to understand why immigrants avoided the three southern nations. Most were fleeing countries with repressive feudal systems controlled by entrenched aristocracies; until 1866 the Deep South and Tidewater were repressive, near-feudal systems with entrenched aristocracies, and after Reconstruction ended in 1877 they returned to form. With little industry and an agricultural sector dominated by large landholdings, the two lowland southern nations had little to attract newly arrived immigrants. Greater Appalachia remained poor, with few cities and jobs. In the three southern nations, strict adherence to local customs and practices remained key to being accepted as "American," which made them less attractive to foreigners.

In El Norte an "American" was pretty much anyone who wasn't a *norteño*; even a German-speaking Catholic was considered an "Anglo." But because it lacked major ports or cities, El Norte was simply too remote for large numbers of immigrants to settle there.

By contrast, New Netherland and the Midlands had been explicitly multicultural since their foundation and so were places where it was viewed as normal for people of many languages, religions, and cultures to live side by side. Nearly all of these nations' major cities—New York, Trenton, Philadelphia, Baltimore, Pittsburgh, Cincinnati, and the Midland border cities of Chicago and St. Louis—had attracted huge numbers of immigrants and "ethnic" majorities. New York City had an Irish majority in the 1850s, was run by Irish in the 1870s, attracted a quarter of all Italian immigrants in the federation in 1880, and was 25 percent Jewish in 1910. Slavs congregated in and around Pittsburgh, while ethnic enclaves of all sorts formed in Chicago and Philadelphia. Cultural diversity was entirely in keeping with the Midlander worldview. For both these nations, being "American" had nothing to do with one's ethnicity, religion, or language but was rather a spirit or state of mind. When pundits speak today of America always having been multicultural, multiethnic, and multilingual, they're really referring to New Netherland and the Midlands. In these nations it's almost impossible to describe immigrant groups as having acculturated, as it's not at all clear what they would be acculturating to, beyond an ethic of toleration, individual achievement (in New Netherland) and, possibly, the use of English. The American model of cultural pluralism originates in the traditions of these two nations.[3]

The Great Wave came at a time when the Left Coast and Far West were still in their infancy, so in these areas many immigrant groups had as much cultural leverage as their native competitors. Here *everything* was new, and cultural groups competed with one another to shape society. There were limits, of course. On the Left Coast, the Yankee elite worked hard to assimilate settlers from nations foreign and domestic. In the Far West, however, the banks and cartels that dominated the economy were not above using violence against those who threatened their interests. In both nations blacks, Asians, and Hispanics encountered considerable hostility, with Chinese and Japanese treated as an inferior people to be used much like slaves. Japanese children were kept out of California classrooms as late as 1907 on the theory that they lacked the aptitude for higher learning.[4] But most other immigrant groups were able to take advantage of the fact that these Western nations were still defining their values and power structures, and many were able to play an essential role in that enterprise. On the Left Coast and in the Far West, being "American" was never about being Protestant or being descended from English or British "stock"; rather, it was about embracing individual achievement and pursuing "the American Dream." When pundits start waxing poetic about how becoming "American" is about embracing the "free-market" mentality and pursuing one's potential, they are on sound footing in these two nations.

Yankeedom presented a far more complicated situation. Before 1830 this region was remarkably homogeneous, with a well-earned reputation for intolerance. Yankeedom had rejected immigrants for much of the colonial period, but by the mid-nineteenth century its rapidly expanding industrial centers and the forests, farms, and mines on its Midwestern frontier attracted large numbers of foreigners, many of whom were neither English nor Protestant. We've already seen how Yankees sought to save not only their own frontier but even the Pacific Coast from the "dangerous influences" of Catholic immigrants, slaveholding Southerners, and German brewers. But as the Great Wave crashed over the United States in the late nineteenth century, Yankees redoubled their efforts to conform newcomers to "American" norms, by which they really meant New England ones.

This crusade focused on educating immigrants and their children. Schools had always been seen as institutions of acculturation in New England and its colonies. Until the twentieth century most people's "job prospects" as farmers, laborers, or industrial workers were in no way enhanced by knowing how to read, write, and do arithmetic. Rather, children were schooled in order to acculturate them to Yankee ways and to build the community bonds considered essential to preventing the formation of an aristocracy and, thus, the collapse of the republic. The Great Wave only increased the Yankees' sense of urgency. "It is fatal for a democracy to permit the formation of fixed classes," the influential educational philosopher (and Vermont native) John Dewey argued in 1915. "The democracy which proclaims equality of opportunity as its ideal requires an education in which learning and social application, ideas, practice, work, and recognition of the meaning of what is done are united from the beginning and for all." Everyone should be educated together in common schools according to a common curriculum, Yankees had long argued, to ensure social and cultural continuity. From the mid-nineteenth century New England governments required towns to maintain tuition-free schools, and by century's end many Yankee-controlled states had made attendance mandatory. (By contrast, the Deep

South had no effective public education system and actively discouraged the mixing of classes and castes.)[5]

Immigrants presented additional challenges. "A foreign people, born and bred and dwarfed under the despotisms of the Old World, cannot be transformed into the full stature of American citizens merely by a voyage across the Atlantic, or by subscribing the oath of naturalization," Horace Mann, the Yankee reformer widely credited as "the father of American public education," told fellow educators in 1845. Schools, he argued, had to train children to "self-government, self-control," and "a voluntary compliance with the laws of reason and duty" lest they "retain the servility in which they have been trained" or fall into "the evils of anarchy and lawlessness." By 1914 that mission had been expanded to include adult immigrants, who were offered free evening classes in English, mathematics, U.S. history, and "hygiene and good behavior." In Massachusetts and Connecticut, towns were required to maintain these programs, and attendance was compulsory for every illiterate person between sixteen and twenty-one years of age. The programs were also adopted in New Netherland and the Midlands (usually through the efforts of transplanted Yankees) but generally on a voluntary basis. They received little official support in the Deep South, Appalachia, and the Far West, where most state constitutions actually forbade legislators from spending tax dollars on adult education.[6]

The notion of America having been a "melting pot" in which immigrants were transmuted into "Anglo-Protestant Americans" really refers to a Yankee remedy intimately tied to the folkways of a covenanted, utopia-building people who were themselves almost entirely English in origin. Perhaps the greatest popularizing institution for this school of assimilation was the Henry Ford English School, founded in 1914 in the heart of the Yankee Midwest. There, Ford's immigrant workers were taught not just English but history and the Yankee values of thrift, cleanliness, and punctuality. At their graduation ceremony students dressed in the fashions of their home countries paraded down the gangway of a mock ship and into a gigantic cauldron labeled "melting pot," which their teachers began stirring with giant spoons; a few minutes later, the graduates marched out of the pot wearing "American" suits and ties and waving the American flag. Meanwhile, historians at Harvard, Yale, and other

Yankee institutions were crafting a mythic "national" history for students to celebrate, which emphasized the centrality of the (previously neglected) Pilgrim voyage, the Boston Tea Party, and Yankee figures such as the minutemen, Paul Revere, and Johnny Appleseed. (The Puritans were recast as champions of religious freedom, which would have surprised them, while Jamestown, New Amsterdam, and the early Anglican settlements of Maine were ignored.) In the Yankee paradigm, immigrants were to assimilate into the dominant culture which, from their point of view, was indeed characterized by the "Protestant" (i.e., Calvinist) work ethic, self-restraint, a commitment to "common good," and hostility to aristocratic institutions. Cultural pluralism, individualism, or the acceptance of an Anglo-British class system was not on the Yankees' agenda.[7]

In the early twenty-first century, a new wave of immigration has prompted a heated debate about what it means to be "American" and what should and shouldn't be expected of a person who wishes to count himself as one. Conservatives like the late Harvard political scientist Samuel Huntington assert that America is now weakly held together by just two factors: the "continuing centrality" of a dominant "Anglo-Protestant" culture (with special emphasis on the English language and the "Protestant" work ethic) and the shared ideology of a two-century-old "American Creed" championing equality, individualism, liberty, personal prosperity, and representative government. Huntington's followers fear these precious unifiers are being broken down by their opponents, the foolhardy champions of multiculturalism and ethnic pluralism. In contrast, the multiculturalists argue that America's true genius is to have created the possibility of a place where people of different cultures, religions, races, and language groups can coexist, each maintaining its own values and identity. Both schools argue a historical basis for their definition of American identity, and find weaknesses in the historical examples their opponents raise in defense of their views.[8]

In fact, both sides are evoking characteristics that were true of only a subset of North America's ethnoregional nations rather than "America" as a whole. Certainly the Calvinist work ethic has always been central to the Yankee identity at the same time that it was anathema to that of the Deep South or Tidewater, where a leisurely "pace of life" has long been seen as virtuous. (No Deep Southern aristocrat feared he would be kept from Heaven on account of idleness; much of the Yankee elite was haunted by this notion.) "Englishness," language and all, was absolutely *not* at the heart of the Midlands and New Netherland identity, where multiculturalism was indeed the norm; applied to El Norte, theories of "Anglo-Protestant" cultural origins look comical. Extreme individualism is central to the Appalachian and Far Western identities but has always been frowned upon in communitarian New England and New France. "Liberty" in the sense Huntington thought of it was absolutely not part of the Deep Southern or Tidewater vision of the American identity, while representative government was championed by their slaveholding elite only to the extent that they themselves did all the representing. Far from embracing multiculturalism, Yankees have spent their history either keeping outsiders away or trying to assimilate them (and the rest of the country) to New England norms. It is fruitless to search for the characteristics of an "American" identity, because each nation has its own notion of what being American should mean.

Failing to recognize this, Huntington's disciples have done a great deal of hand-wringing about the supposedly exceptional nature of the dominant Mexican stream of the current "fourth wave" of mass immigration. In 1970, 760,000 Mexican-born individuals were living in the United States, or about 1.4 percent of Mexico's population. In 2008, that number had jumped seventeenfold to 12.7 million, or 11 percent of all native Mexicans on the planet. They comprised 32 percent of the foreign-born population of the United States in 2008, the same proportion as the Irish did in the third quarter of the nineteenth century. The vast majority live in El Norte, where they now constitute an overwhelming majority of the population and see no reason to "assimilate" to some Anglo-Protestant norm. This was enormously alarming to Huntington and to others living outside El Norte, who fear a *reconquista* is taking place. In a sense they're correct: Mexicans have retaken control of the American portion of El Norte, and large numbers of immigrants from southern Mexico are becoming assimilated into *norteño* culture. But this isn't so much a threat to the "dominant culture" of the region as a return to its origins.[9]

There is not, however, any chance of Mexico's annexing El Norte:

norteños on both sides of the present border would sooner break off from both countries and form their own republic. After all, even the Mexican portion of El Norte is three times wealthier than southern Mexico, where it is forced to export tax dollars. As Harvard fellow Juan Enriquez has noted, there's very little binding the region to Mexico City, which doesn't provide it with technology, basic services, security, or a market for its products. If El Norte's Mexican sections—Baja California, Nuevo León, Coahuila, Chihuahua, Sonora, and Tamaulipas—had their choice, Enriquez notes, they'd probably prefer some European Union–style relationship with the United States rather than to remain in Mexico; they have more in common with the American section of El Norte than they do with the rest of their own country. "Southwest Chicanos and *Norteño* Mexicanos are becoming one people again," University of New Mexico Chicano Studies professor Charles Truxillo told the Associated Press in 2000, adding that the creation of a separate state was inevitable. His suggested name for the new country: the República del Norte.[10]

CHAPTER 24

Gods and Missions

While immigration reinforced the distinctions between the nations in the decades after the Civil War, differences in fundamental values polarized them into two hostile blocs separated by buffer states. The result was a cultural Cold War pitting an angry, humiliated, and salvation-minded Dixie bloc against a triumphant, social-reform-minded alliance of Yankeedom, New Netherland, and the Left Coast. This culture war would simmer for a century after Appomattox before breaking into open conflict in the 1960s. This chapter traces the formation of these two blocs in the Reconstruction era and the divergent worldviews and cosmology that have kept them in opposition ever since.

The roots of the conflict began in the aftermath of the Confederate defeat, when the Deep South, Tidewater, and much of Greater Appalachia were occupied by a Yankee-dominated army. With over half a million deaths, the war triggered lasting resentment all around, but the occupation made these sentiments worse in the Deep South and Tidewater. As a result, these nations would create a strong Dixie coalition that would eventually include all of Greater Appalachia and come to dominate continental politics at the turn of the millennium.

Midlanders, New Netherlanders, and Yankees seized control of much of the former Confederacy in the aftermath of the Civil War and attempted to reformat the region on Yankee lines. The occupiers set up military districts, appointed governors, and deployed troops to enforce their decisions. Union-backed governors were seen by locals as puppets, with the exception of Tennessee's William Brownlow, a Unionist Borderlander from Knoxville.[1] The occupiers banned leading Confederates from public office and the voting booth, allowed outside business interests to seize control of important segments of the regional economy, and rewrote laws to reflect their own values. The northern forces were confident that the region's people would quickly embrace their institutions, values, and political structures once their bloodthirsty leaders were deposed. They set up racially integrated, New England–style school systems, imported Yankee schoolteachers to run them, and imposed local taxes to pay for them. They "freed" an oppressed people—the region's enslaved blacks—but failed to provide the security or economic environment in which they might thrive. They assumed their natural allies in one region—the Unionist-minded strongholds of Appalachia—would support their effort to remake the zone of occupation in an essentially Yankee image. But despite the backing of military units, the control of broad sectors of government, education, and the economy, and a massive civilian outreach program, not only did the occupation fail to achieve most of its goals, it unified the three southern nations against them to a degree never before seen.

Scholars have long recognized that "the South" as a unified entity didn't really come into existence until *after* the Civil War. It was the resistance to Yankee-led Reconstruction that brought this Dixie bloc together to ultimately include even Appalachian people who'd fought against the Confederacy during the war.

Their institutions and racial caste system under attack, Deep Southerners and Tidewaterites organized their resistance struggle around the one civic institution they still controlled: their churches. The evangelical churches that dominated the three southern nations proved excellent vehicles for those wishing to protect the region's prewar social system. Unlike the dominant denominations in Yankeedom, Southern Baptists and other southern evangelicals were becoming what religious scholars have termed "Private Protestants" as opposed to the "Public Protestants" that dominated the northern nations, and whom we'll get to in a moment. Private Protestants—Southern Baptists, Southern Methodists, and Southern Episcopalians among them—believed the world was inherently corrupt and sinful, particularly after the shocks of the Civil War. Their emphasis wasn't on the social gospel—an effort to transform the world in preparation for Christ's coming—but rather on *personal* salvation, pulling individual souls into the lifeboat of right thinking before the Rapture swept the damned away. Private Protestants had no interest in changing society but rather emphasized the need to maintain order and obedience.

Slavery, aristocratic rule, and the grinding poverty of most ordinary people in the southern nations weren't evils to be confronted but rather the reflection of a divinely sanctioned hierarchy to be maintained at all costs against the Yankee heretics. By opposing slavery, one Southern Methodist minister declared, the Yankee "was disloyal to the laws of God and man"—"a wild fanatic, an insane anarchist, a law breaker, [and] a wicked intermeddler in other men's matters." Since biblical passages tacitly endorsed slavery, abolitionists were proclaimed guilty of being "more humane than God." The Episcopal bishop of Alabama, Richard Wilmer, proclaimed his church had been right to support the Confederacy in order "to maintain the supremacy of the Word of God and the teachings of universal tradition." It was no accident that hard-core resisters of the northern occupation called themselves Redeemers, and that the end of the Union occupation in 1877 was labeled "The Redemption."[2]

The southern clergy helped foster a new civil religion in the former Confederacy, a myth scholars have come to call the Lost Cause. Following its credo, whites in the Deep South, Tidewater, and, ultimately, Appalachia came to believe that God had allowed the Confederacy to be bathed in blood, its cities destroyed, and its enemies ruling over it in order to test and sanctify His favored people. Defeat of God's chosen on the battlefield, Nashville Presbyterian preacher and wartime chaplain James H. McNeilly noted, "did not prove the heathen to be right in the cause, nor that the Israelites were upholding a bad cause." Confederate soldiers may have "poured their blood like festal wine," McNeilly added, but it was not in vain, as "questions of right and wrong are not settled before God by force of arms." Instead, a Deep Southern theologian would argue, the righteous would "by steadfastness to principle" defeat the federal government, which he had determined to be akin to the "beast having seven heads and ten horns" in the Book of Revelation. The righteous cause was, conveniently enough, to promote the folkways of the Deep South to the greatest degree possible, upholding the classical Roman idea of the slaveholding republic, prescribing democracy for the elite and obedience for everyone else.[3]

While the Lost Cause fostered a powerful Dixie alliance in this time period, there were distinct differences in the three member nations' goals. In the Deep South and Tidewater, the planter elite generally maintained effective control over their formerly enslaved workforce and so weren't opposed to having them vote, so long as they cast ballots as they were told to. The great planters weren't particularly interested in "white empowerment" if that meant empowering the poor whites of their region. The goal was to maintain the class and caste systems, making sure that neither blacks nor the white underclass got any Yankee or Midlander ideas about the "common good" or the virtues of a more egalitarian society.

In Appalachia, however, such rigid hierarchies had never existed, and free blacks initially had more room to maneuver. Ironically this relative social dynamism triggered a particularly gruesome counterattack in the borderlands. Appalachia's staggering poverty—made worse by war and economic dislocation—created a situation in which many white Borderlanders found themselves in direct competition with newly freed blacks, who tended to be less deferential than those in the lowlands. The response was the creation of a secret society of homicidal vigilantes called the Ku Klux Klan. The original Reconstruction-era Klan was founded in Pulaski, Tennessee, and remained almost entirely an Appalachian phenomenon, a warrior order committed to crushing that nation's enemies. Klansmen tortured and killed "uppity" blacks, terrorized or murdered Yankee schoolteachers, burned schoolhouses, and assaulted judges and other officials associated with the occupation. Revealingly, it was disbanded on the orders of its own Grand Wizard in 1869 because the Dixie bloc's white elite had become concerned that it was encouraging the lower white orders to think and act on their own.[4]

In all three nations the resistance to Reconstruction was largely successful. There could be no return to formal slavery, but the racial caste system was restored, backed by laws and practices that effectively prevented blacks from voting, running for office, or asserting their common humanity. In the Deep South and Tidewater, single-party rule became the norm and was exercised to resist change, social reform, or wide citizen participation in politics. The caste system became so secure that when sociologists from the University of Chicago came to study it in the 1930s, citizens openly bragged of participating in the torture and murder of blacks who failed to show "proper respect" for whites. ("When a nigger gets ideas," a government official in Mississippi told the researchers, "the best thing to do is to get him under ground as quick as possible.") In Appalachia, Scots-Irish historian and U.S. senator Jim Webb has noted,

"Fresh or divergent opinions were stifled from above, sometimes violently . . . and resulted in the eventual diminishment not only of blacks but also of many whites." Education levels fell. Economic isolation from the rest of the federation grew. As other parts of the United States expanded and developed through the late nineteenth century, Appalachia fell backward, its people caught in a life not much removed from that of their immigrant ancestors in the colonial era.[5]

While a Dixie bloc was coalescing around individual salvation and the defense of traditional social values, a Northern alliance was forming around a very different set of religious priorities. It was spearheaded by the clergy and intellectual elite of Yankeedom, but it found a ready audience across the Midlands, the Left Coast, and New Netherland.

From the time of the Puritans, the Yankee religious ethos focused on the salvation of society, not of the individual. Indeed, the Puritans believed every soul's status had already been determined. All that was left to do was to carry out God's work and try to make the world a more perfect and less sinful place. As we've already seen, this led Yankees to embrace all sorts of utopian missions, from building a "City on the Hill" in Massachusetts to creating a model society in Utah based on the Book of Mormon to "saving" other parts of the continent by assimilating them into enlightened Yankee culture. The Yankees represent an extreme example of Public Protestantism, a religious heritage that emphasizes collective salvation and the social gospel. Whereas late-nineteenth- and early-twentieth-century Southern Baptists and other salvation-minded denominations generally judged alcoholism as an individual failing of character, Yankee Congregationalists, Northern Methodists, Unitarians, and Anglicans viewed it as a social ill in need of legislative redress. While Salvationists concentrated on saving the souls of the poor, champions of the Social Gospel fought for labor protections, the minimum wage, and other collective solutions intended to reduce poverty itself. Whereas Private Protestants emphasized individual responsibility for one's lot in life, Public Protestants tried to harness government to improve society and the quality of life. These conflicting worldviews put the two blocs on a political collision course.[6]

Reconstruction was but the first large-scale social engineering effort by the Northern coalition. When Yankee teachers became disillusioned with the slow pace of their efforts to educate and uplift former slaves in the Deep South and Tidewater, many turned their attention to Appalachian whites, who were seen as people much like their "forefathers on the bleak New England shore." Borderlanders began to enter popular consciousness in the North in the 1880s and 1890s, when a series of literary and scholarly articles appeared painting them as a people marooned in an eighteenth-century time warp, consumed by feuds and fixated on witchcraft and other superstitions. Studies falsely proclaimed that the Appalachian people spoke Elizabethan English and were "uncontaminated with slavery." The Yankee-born president of Kentucky's Berea College, Congregational minister William Goodell Frost, committed to bringing the "saving elements" of modern civilization to Appalachia, which would turn it into "the New England of the South." Hundreds of Yankee-run freedmen's schools were constructed across the region through the 1930s. By the eve of World War II the effort had lost its momentum—and had been forced out of parts of the southern mountains—but the region remained a place of abject poverty.[7]

Reformers in the Northern coalition had by then turned to other projects. Temperance and Prohibition were driven almost entirely by Yankees and Midlanders. Maine was the first state to ban the manufacture and sale of liquor (from 1851 to 1856), while the influential Women's Christian Temperance Union was founded in Yankee-settled Evanston, Illinois, and led by early feminist Frances Willard, the daughter of a Congregational schoolteacher from upstate New York. The lobbying group that won a constitutional amendment criminalizing alcohol, the Anti-Saloon League, was founded in Ohio's Western Reserve in 1893 by a Congregational minister; its most powerful leader, William Wheeler, was an Oberlin-educated native of the Western Reserve descended from Massachusetts Puritans. Deep Southerners would later embrace Prohibition (Mississippi didn't legalize drinking until 1966), but the crusade was conceived and spearheaded by Yankees.[8]

Yankees and New Netherlanders also led the turn-of-the-century crusades to ensure the welfare of children. These two groups were responsible for a radical reduction in infant mortality (by the development, in Rochester, N.Y., Massachusetts, and New York City, of a system to distribute hygienic, subsidized milk supplies to mothers); for the advent and expansion of playgrounds for urban children (Massachusetts *required* citizens of its forty-two largest towns to vote on whether to pay for them, and forty-one voted affirmatively); for the first concerted effort to help orphaned street children (the New York City–based Children's Aid Society, founded by Yale-educated Connecticut Congregationalist Charles Loring Brace); the first laws regulating child labor and adoption (both in Massachusetts); and the first organizations devoted to preventing child abuse (the Massachusetts and New York City Societies for the Prevention of Cruelty to Children). The primary organization devoted to ending child labor, the National Child Labor Committee, was a union of New Netherland– and Appalachian Arkansas–based movements that fought to secure state laws against the practice; the effort met success in the Northern bloc but was resisted in the southern nations, which eventually had reform forced upon them via the federal government.[9]

The struggle for women's suffrage was conceived and fought by reformers in Yankeedom and the two nations with the deepest attachment to liberty of conscience: New Netherland and the Midlands. The historic initial meeting of women's rights advocates was held in Yankee Seneca Falls, New York, in 1848. It was followed two years later by the first National Women's Rights Convention, staged in Worcester, Massachusetts, and backed by a broad pantheon of male Yankee luminaries, from newspaperman Horace Mann and abolitionist William Lloyd Garrison to the writer Wendell Phillips and Unitarian philosopher William Henry Channing; it was no coincidence that every one of its next ten conventions was held in one of the three aforementioned nations. When the Nineteenth Amendment finally passed in 1919, state legislators representing these nations and the Left Coast quickly ratified it; those in the Dixie bloc did not. The women who led the long struggle were also from the three northeastern nations, including Susan B. Anthony (daughter of Massachusetts Quakers), Lucy Stone (Massachusetts-born, Oberlin-educated), Elizabeth Cady Stanton (descended from early Dutch settlers and born, raised, and educated in Yankee upstate New York), and Carrie Chapman Catt (born in Yankee Ripon, Wisconsin, educated in Midland Ames, Iowa).[10]

While the Dixie bloc fought to keep things as they were or return them to the way they used to be, Yankeedom and especially New Netherland and the Left Coast were becoming increasingly tolerant of unusual social experiments and countercultural movements. Appropriately enough, it was the old New Netherland hamlet of Groenwijck—its erratic country roads absorbed into the expanding city and renamed "Greenwich Village"—that became the federation's first and foremost bohemian district. From approximately 1910 to 1960, this enclave was a magnet for cultural revolutionaries of all sorts: anarchist philosophers, free-verse poets, Cubist painters, feminists, gays, Freudian thinkers, hard-drinking writers, free-love playwrights, and idiosyncratic musicians. Flaunting poverty and eccentricity, they shocked the middle classes, perplexed their Midland and Deep Southern parents, and, in the words of historian Ross Wetzsteon, created "a cult of carefree irresponsibility . . . in the service of transcendental ideas." From that single square mile tucked inside the tolerant cocoon of New Netherland would spring much of what the religious conservatives of the Dixie bloc would later mobilize against: the gay rights movement, modern art, the beatniks and their hippie successors, left-wing intellectualism, and the antiwar movement. Like seventeenth-century Amsterdam, New Netherland provided a sanctuary for heretics and freethinkers from more rigid nations, consolidating its position as the continent's cultural capital. While bohemia would start moving to the Left Coast in the 1950s, it got its start in a Dutch-founded village.[11]

In the three northeastern nations, the desire to improve the world frequently took precedence over religious belief itself, especially if the church was standing in the way of progress. Ironically the Puritan mission to purify the world through good works had sown the seeds of its own undoing: over the course of 250 years many descendants of the New England divines came to believe the world couldn't achieve purity if an established church was suppressing dissent, because faith had no meaning if it was coerced. Much of the Yankee elite turned to Unitarianism, an offshoot of the New England church that embraced scientific inquiry and the pursuit of social justice. Under Unitarian president Charles Eliot, Harvard was secularized in the 1870s, while the Yankee-run American Secular Union fought to ban religion from public schools. Midlanders and New Netherlanders—whose societies were founded on religious and cultural pluralism—tended to support such efforts, knowing that if church and state were fused, dissenters would face discrimination. The mainline Public Protestant denominations based in these regions accommodated scientific discoveries about the age and formation of the Earth and the evolution of life by adopting an allegorical rather than a literal interpretation of Scripture. Still, in the early twentieth century, it was not at all uncommon in these nations for educated people to argue that churches should wither away altogether to make way for the triumph of scientific reason. It was a position that would prevail by the end of the century—but in northern Europe, not North America. Within the U.S. federation, strong secularists were destined for defeat by a Private Protestant counterattack of impressive strength, power, and longevity.[12]

Opposition to modernism, liberal theology, and inconvenient scientific discoveries occurred in pockets across the continent in the late nineteenth and early twentieth centuries, but only in the Dixie bloc did it represent the dominant cultural position, backed by governments and defended from criticism by state power. In the cultural wars that have followed, the three southern nations have been the stronghold of biblical inerrancy; the elimination of barriers between church and state; teaching children religious rather than scientific explanations for the origins and nature of the universe; maintaining legal, political, and social restraints against homosexuality, civil rights, and interracial dating; and of preventing the secularization of society.

Christian fundamentalism appeared in North America in reaction to the liberal theologies that were becoming dominant in the northern nations. It took its name from *The Fundamentals*, a twelve-volume attack on liberal theology, evolution, atheism, socialism, Mormons, Catholics, Christian Scientists, and Jehovah's Witnesses edited by Appalachian Baptist preacher A. C. Dixon. Fundamentalism's early organizers gathered around the World Christian Fundamentals Association, founded by another Baptist preacher, William Bell Riley, who was born in Appalachian Indiana, raised in Boone County, Kentucky, and exposed to Yankee heresy while the pastor of a Minnesota church. Inspired also by William Jennings Bryan—a Scots-Irish presidential candidate from the (very Appalachian) Egypt District of Illinois—fundamentalist-minded

Private Protestants went to war against science and its corrosive theory of evolution.[13]

During the 1920s, anti-evolutionary activists afflicted the entire federation, but they found lasting success only in Appalachia and the Deep South. Legislators in Florida, Tennessee, Mississippi, and Arkansas passed laws making it illegal to teach evolution in schools. North Carolina's governor ordered the removal of all textbooks which "in any way intimate an origin of the human race other than that contained in the Bible." Authorities in Louisiana and Texas (states controlled by Deep Southerners and Borderlanders) redacted all references to evolution from school texts. Dozens of Appalachian and Deep Southern university professors were dismissed for criticizing such measures, and many others refused to take a public position for fear of persecution. Newspapers supported the attack on science. "The professors at the state university may believe they are descended from apes and baboons," Breathitt County, Kentucky's *Jackson News* editorialized, "but let it be known that the good people of Breathitt are pure Anglo-Saxon." "Don't disappoint the people of Mississippi, Governor," the Jackson *Clarion-Ledger* pleaded as the executive contemplated a veto of an anti-evolution bill. "Don't do something that may shake the faith of young people in the first book of the Bible." Political candidates often put the suppression of evolution at the center of their campaigns, while a revived KKK bristled against Darwin's theory because it contradicted biblical arguments that God had created blacks as servile and inferior beings. Southern Baptists joined the crusade en masse. The movement reached its high-water mark at the infamous 1925 Scopes Trial, where Tennessee officials prosecuted a high school biology teacher for teaching evolution. The Tennessee Supreme Court found him guilty, but critical national media attention undermined fundamentalism's respectability.[14]

Thereafter, the Public Protestant majorities in Yankeedom, New Netherland, and the Midlands assumed the fire-and-brimstone crowd was ruined, their irrational beliefs exposed as superstition, their authoritarian tactics as violations of American values. But the fundamentalists spent the thirties and forties organizing themselves, building Bible fellowships, Christian colleges, and a network of gospel radio stations. Unnoticed by North America's opinion elite, their numbers grew through the 1950s, while membership in mainline Protestant churches declined. Secularism was in retreat as well, its champions fighting only to keep the state, not the people, free from religion. Behind the veneer of a prosperous and content postwar United States, a full-scale cultural war was quietly brewing. In the 1960s it would finally explode.[15]

CHAPTER 25

Culture Clash

After simmering for the better part of a century, North America's cultural Cold War broke into open conflict in the late 1950s and the 1960s.

Each coalition underwent an internal civil war in this period: in the Dixie bloc, African Americans rose up against segregation and the caste system, while the four nations of the Northern alliance faced a youth-led cultural uprising. Both of these destabilizing events started as homegrown phenomena led by disaffected people from within each bloc but soon drew intervention from outside their respective regions. In the first uprising—the civil rights movement—the northern nations' assistance proved decisive, as it marshaled federal power and troops to force whites in Tidewater, Appalachia, and especially the Deep South to dismantle their cherished racial caste system. In the second "uprising"—the sixties cultural revolution—Dixie-based political leaders intervened in the Northern alliance–based cultural shift by opposing the young revolutionaries from the Left Coast, New Netherland, and Yankeedom, whose agenda was diametrically opposed to everything the Deep South and Tidewater stood for. Weakened by revolution at home, Dixie bloc leaders were unable to stop the youth movement in the short term, but they have since spearheaded efforts to roll back much of what the rebellion accomplished. The interbloc resentments stemming from these twin uprisings widened the divide between the nations, poisoning efforts to find common ground and mutually acceptable solutions in early twenty-first-century America.

The civil rights movement has been called the "Second Reconstruction" because of the dramatic effect it had on Southern culture and because of the role of the Yankee- and Midlands-directed federal government in forcing change. Like the first Reconstruction, this remarkably pacifistic uprising[1] by Deep Southern African Americans permanently altered certain aspects of Deep South and Tidewater culture, but it prompted white retrenchment on other issues in these nations and Greater Appalachia.

In 1955 the three nations of the Dixie bloc were still authoritarian states whose citizens—white and black—were required to uphold a rigid, all-pervasive apartheid system. Across the bloc adult blacks were required to refer to even teenage whites as "Mister," "Miss," or "Missus," while whites were forbidden to address blacks of any age with these titles, using "boy," "Auntie," or "Uncle" instead. Blacks and whites were prohibited from dining, dating, worshipping, playing baseball, or attending school together. The caste system required that blacks and whites use separate drinking fountains, rest rooms, waiting rooms, and building entrances; that factories maintain separate production lines, with blacks unable to be promoted into "white" positions regardless of experience, merit, or seniority; and that theaters, lunch counters, restaurants, railroad companies, and public bus systems maintain separate seating by race. In Mississippi it was illegal to print, publish, or distribute "suggestions in favor of social equality or of intermarriage between whites and Negroes," with perpetrators subject to up to six months in prison. Klansmen and other vigilante groups tortured and executed blacks who violated these rules, often with the public approval of elected officials, newspaper editors, preachers, and the region's leading families. White violators faced legal penalties and, worse, the social ostracism that resulted from having one's family branded "nigger lovers." Dixie's white religious leaders, with few exceptions, either bestowed divine endorsement on this system or kept silent.[2]

African Americans in the Deep South led the movement, challenging apartheid policies across the region: the discrimination on Montgomery, Alabama's, public buses (1955–56); the ban on black students at Little Rock Central High School (1957), in Orleans Parish, Louisiana, elementary schools (1960), and at the universities of Georgia (1961) and Mississippi (1962); the denial of voting rights in Mississippi (1962); the segregation of businesses and suppression of the right of assembly in Birmingham, Alabama (1963); and, perhaps most poignantly, the bloody voting-rights protests in Selma, Alabama (1965). The majority of the movement's most famous figures were Deep Southerners, including the Reverend Martin Luther King Jr. (from Atlanta), John Lewis (southern

Alabama), James Meredith (central Mississippi), and Rosa Parks (Tuskegee, Alabama). They were backed by civil rights activists, white and black, from New Netherland (Robert Moses, slain activists Andrew Goodman and Michael Schwerner) and Yankeedom (Malcolm X). President John F. Kennedy and Attorney General Robert Kennedy—icons of Yankeedom—provided crucial support from the White House and a blueprint for the Appalachian Texan Lyndon B. Johnson to follow after the president's assassination.

Across the Dixie bloc white Southerners initially reacted to the movement with disbelief, having been conditioned to think that "our Negroes" were "happy" to be oppressed, patronized, and deprived of basic human and civil rights. Clearly their beloved blacks were being manipulated by what Deep Southern politicians called "outside agitators"—Yankees and New Netherlanders—who were often also believed to be communists. Consistent with the Deep Southern and Tidewater conception of *libertas*, white resisters rallied around the notion that the uprising was about taking away white people's "freedoms," including the freedom to oppress others. When the U.S. Supreme Court ruled that segregation was unconstitutional, Deep Southern legislators set up state antisubversion agencies charged with investigating and destroying efforts to "overthrow our form of government" and armed with wiretapping and subpoena powers. (Mississippi's State Sovereignty Commission declared one civil rights group—the Student Nonviolent Coordinating Committee—to be subverting "Mississippi's way of life" simply for engaging in the entirely legal act of helping to register black voters.)

As blacks challenged the caste system, many in the Dixie bloc pledged "massive resistance." The extreme steps they took to defend their "way of life" laid bare the inhuman, despotic nature of the region's cherished practices. Arkansas governor Orval Faubus called out bayonet-bearing National Guardsmen to prevent nine black students from starting class at Little Rock's Central High School, an act that forced President Dwight D. Eisenhower to deploy the 101st Airborne Division and federalize the entire Arkansas Guard. As school integration proceeded across the Deep South, angry white mobs jeered, taunted, and threatened not only frightened black schoolchildren but also white children and parents who continued to use the nominally integrated public schools. Communities across the Dixie bloc responded by shutting down their entire public school systems, slashing property taxes, and helping set up whites-only private academies in their place. Prince Edward County, Virginia (in Tidewater), went without public schools for years—depriving blacks and poor whites of any education whatsoever—until the Supreme Court ruled that this, too, was unconstitutional. When the pastor of a white Methodist church in Jackson, Mississippi, tried to admit black worshippers, his own deacons formed a "color guard" to turn any away at the door. Klansmen murdered civil rights workers of both races, while city authorities turned fire hoses, attack dogs, and mounted horsemen on peaceful marchers. But faced with a choice between integrated schools or no schools at all, between ending Jim Crow and accepting mob rule, between dropping some aspects of Southern "heritage" and being forced to take troubling measures to defend it, large numbers of whites in the region chose to accept at least token changes.[3]

But the levels of acceptance were uneven across the Dixie bloc, particularly after President Johnson signed the 1964 Civil Rights Act into law. The legislation, which denied federal funds to segregated schools and forced most businesses to integrate, had been opposed by virtually every member of Congress from the Deep South, Tidewater, or Appalachia—even in states that had remained in the Union during the Civil War (West Virginia senator and former Klansman Robert Byrd led the three-month filibuster against it). In the aftermath, journalists from across the federation reported that integration went smoothest in Appalachia and Tidewater, and encountered the greatest resistance in the rural Deep South, especially in Mississippi, Alabama, and southwestern Georgia. Thereafter, the most fiery defenders of segregation on the national stage were Deep Southerners: Georgia governor Lester Maddox (who had declared himself enslaved by the changes), South Carolina governor and senator Strom Thurmond (an arch-segregationist candidate for president who, at age twenty-two, had fathered a child with his family's sixteen-year-old black maid), and Alabama governor and four-time presidential candidate George Wallace (who had tossed a "gauntlet before the feet of tyranny" to pledge "segregation now, segregation tomorrow, segregation forever"). Right into the twenty-first century, Deep Southerners clashed over the display of the Confederate flag and, by extension, the meaning of their heritage. Not surprisingly, the sharpest conflict on this issue has taken place in South Carolina, whose political leaders insist on flying it over the state capitol.[4]

While it forced key social changes, the Second Reconstruction did not alter the Dixie bloc's Private Protestant values. Many whites in Appalachia, Tidewater, and the Deep South became further entrenched in a Southern evangelical worldview that resisted social reform or the lifting of cultural taboos, and increasingly sought to break down the walls between church and state so as to impose *their* values and moral code on everyone else. This counterattack was quiet at first, as Southern evangelicals and fundamentalists concentrated on building the institutional machinery necessary to take on their northern opponents on the national stage. Many of the private academies whites set up to avoid attending school with blacks were transformed into Christian academies providing "faith-based" education, with an emphasis on conservative values, creationism, and obedience to authority. (The financial burdens these schools place on less-affluent whites prompted evangelical leaders to embrace taxpayer support of these institutions via "school vouchers.") Dixie preachers took particular advantage of television, creating powerful media empires such as Pat Robertson's Christian Broadcasting Network, the Billy Graham Evangelistic Association, and Jerry Falwell's PTL Club. They built a network of fundamentalist universities like Robertson's Regent University (which seeks to train "God's representatives on the face of the Earth" until the Second Coming), Falwell's Liberty University (which teaches that dinosaur fossils are 4,000 years old), and Bob Jones University (which didn't admit black students until 1971 and banned interracial dating and marriage until 2000). By the early 1990s, Dixie-bloc religious figures were ready to do battle against the secular, sexually liberated, science-based, "big government" ethos the northern nations had foisted on the federation.[5]

While Dixie reactionaries were struggling to preserve apartheid, conservatives in Yankeedom, New Netherland, and the Left Coast spent the 1960s fighting to contain a youth-driven cultural revolution of a very different sort.

Combining the utopia-seeking moral impulses of secularized

Puritanism, the intellectual freedom of New Netherland, and the tolerant pacifism of the Midlands, the social movement sought to remake and improve the world by breaking down the very sorts of traditional institutions and social taboos Dixie whites were fighting to protect. The Port Huron Statement, a 1962 manifesto considered the founding document of this "youth movement," was an amalgam of core Yankee and Midlander values. It called for universal disarmament, an end to the "permanent war economy," and the cultivation of each person's "infinitely precious and . . . unfulfilled capacities for reason, freedom, and love"—statements that William Penn's early settlers would undoubtedly have endorsed. It demanded an end to "power rooted in possession, privilege, or circumstance" and the establishment of a "participatory democracy" with decisions "carried on by public groupings"—talking points that could have been drafted by the early Puritans. The public sector was seen as a force for good, so long as citizens reclaimed it from the tyranny of corporate and military power. This movement was far removed from the values of the Deep South and Tidewater, and the gap would only grow after the Vietnam War and the 1968 assassinations of Martin Luther King and Robert F. Kennedy radicalized its adherents.[6]

While inspired by the civil rights struggle, the cultural revolution of the 1960s barely touched the Dixie bloc. Its major events, leaders, and lasting results were confined almost entirely to the four northern nations: Yankeedom, New Netherland, the Midlands, and the Left Coast. The hippie movement emerged from the Beats' old lairs in the San Francisco Bay Area and in Manhattan. The youth movement's principal organization, Students for a Democratic Society, was founded in Yankee Michigan and had its strongest following at campuses in Yankeedom (Harvard, Cornell, Minnesota, Wisconsin, Michigan, Oberlin, Binghamton), the Left Coast (Berkeley, Stanford, Reed), New Netherland (Columbia, City University of New York), and the Midlands (Swarthmore, Antioch, Earlham). The Free Speech Movement (1964) and the Summer of Love (1967) were both centered in the San Francisco Bay Area. The Woodstock Festival (1969) and the Kent State massacre (1970) both occurred in Yankeedom. The Stonewall Riots (1969)—a watershed event in the gay rights movement—took place in Greenwich Village, while San Francisco's Castro district emerged as the western capital of gay culture.

Later, more radical groups also sprang from these same nations, like the Black Panthers (founded in Oakland) and all three collectives of the Weather Underground. Earth Day, which launched the modern environmental movement, was conceived by a Wisconsin senator, promoted in a speech in Seattle, and spearheaded by students at the University of Pennsylvania.[7]

The sixties era also experienced uprisings for cultural emancipation in both El Norte and New France. The former was partially successful, while the latter stopped just short of the establishment of an independent Québécois nation-state.

Since the United States' incorporation of much of El Norte, *norteños* had been treated as second-class citizens, especially in south Texas and southern California, where most "Anglos" were from the Deep South or Greater Appalachia. Local governments and school boards were run entirely by Anglos, even in areas with a 60-to-90-percent Hispanic population. Crystal City—a 95 percent *norteño* town in south Texas—was typical: right up to the early 1960s the Anglo minority owned virtually all the land and businesses and ran the town council and school board, ensuring even that *norteño* teens remained a minority on the cheerleading squad. But in the 1960s, young *norteños* began to assert their rights, organizing voter registration drives and citizens' movements. In Crystal City they shocked the Anglo minority by quietly mobilizing voters to take over the city council (1963) and brazenly seizing control of a majority of school board seats (1969), enabling them to appoint a *norteño* superintendent and plenty of teachers and cheerleaders. In San Antonio, *norteño* activists worked with Roman Catholic priests to mobilize voters to seize control of the city council in 1975. Yuma, Arizona, native César Chávez organized agricultural laborers and boycotts to improve labor conditions on farms in southern California and Texas. In Los Angeles, the militant Brown Berets arranged student walkouts, protests against police brutality, and even a short-lived occupation of Santa Catalina Island, which they proclaimed for Mexico. After the 1960s, *norteños* were no longer powerless residents of El Norte; from local school boards to representation in the U.S. Senate to the New Mexico governor's mansion, they had begun running the region again.[8]

The Québécois' "Quiet Revolution" of the 1960s was something of a misnomer. After a century of dominance by Anglo-Canadians and the Catholic hierarchy, the people of Québec elected a liberal reformer, Jean Lesage, to lead the province in 1960. Over the coming decade Lesage and his allies transformed Québec's institutions along the lines of postwar metropolitan France, secularizing public education, founding a strong social welfare state, unionizing the public workforce, and nationalizing energy utilities into a powerful state conglomerate, Hydro-Québec. The people of New France, Lesage's Liberal Party proclaimed, would now be *Maîtres chez nous*—"Masters in Our Own Home." Pierre Vallières, founder of the radical terrorist group Front de libération du Québec (or FLQ), wrote a manifesto called *White Niggers in America*, which compared the Québécois liberation struggle to that of the blacks of the southern United States. But the FLQ did not embrace Reverend King's nonviolent tactics. In 1969–70 they bombed the Montréal Stock Exchange (injuring twenty-seven) and the home of Montréal's mayor, and kidnapped and murdered the province's vice premier, prompting Ottawa to declare martial law in a successful bid to round up its ringleaders. Thereafter, voters put the separatist Parti Québécois into power, which immediately recognized aboriginal rights to self-determination, instituted French as the only state language in the province, and initiated unsuccessful referenda on independence in 1980 and 1995; the latter measure was defeated by only 0.4 percent of the vote. Today, the Québécois are definitely masters in their own home. The question for the future is whether they will accept keeping their home within the Canadian federation at all.[9]

The culture wars of the 1990s and 2000s were in essence a resumption of the sixties-era struggle, with a majority of people in the four northern nations generally supporting social change and an overwhelming majority of those in the Dixie bloc defending the traditional order. (Opinion in El Norte and the Far West varied, based on the issue at hand.) Northern alliance campaigns for civil liberties, sexual freedom, women's rights, gay rights, and environmental protection all became divisive sectional issues, just as Dixie's promotion of creationism, school prayer, abstinence-only sex education, abortion bans, and state's rights did.

Take the environmental movement, for instance. The entire history of the movement prior to Earth Day took place in the four Public Protestant nations, where the spiritual emphasis was on bettering this world rather than preparing for the next. The Sierra Club, the continent's first grassroots environmental group, was founded in San Francisco in 1892 with substantial support from faculty at Stanford and Berkeley. George Bird Grinnell, a Yale-educated New Yorker, fought the mass slaughter of birds by recreational shooters through the foundation of the New York–based Audubon Society (1905). Another New Yorker, President Theodore Roosevelt, pioneered federal government involvement in environmental protection, founding the national forest, park, and wildlife refuge systems. Roosevelt's Yankee cousin, Franklin Delano Roosevelt, created the National Wildlife Federation in 1936. Aldo Leopold, the father of the science of wildlife management and founder of the Wilderness Society, was the Yale-educated son of German immigrants to the Midland Midwest and spent most of his career in Yankee Wisconsin. Environmental writer Rachel Carson (*The Sea Around Us* [1951], *Silent Spring* [1962]) was a Pennsylvania Midlander who analyzed ecosystems in Yankee Maine. Two of the prominent environmental groups that emerged from the sixties—the Natural Resources Defense Council and the Environmental Defense Fund—were based in New Netherland. Greenpeace took shape in the Left Coast city of Vancouver, the militant Sea Shepherd Conservation Society in coastal Washington State, and the Friends of the Earth in San Francisco, under the auspices of Berkeley native David Brower (who also founded the Earth Island Institute and the League of Conservation Voters). The father of the Appalachian Trail, Benton MacKaye, wasn't from Appalachia at all but was rather a Harvard-trained native of Connecticut whose grandparents had been prominent Yankee abolitionists.[10]

Although comprising nearly half the territory of the contiguous United States, the Dixie bloc was conspicuously absent from the green movement until well after the sixties pushed it into world consciousness. Political leaders in El Norte and the Far West often shared Dixie's skepticism about the need to protect natural resources. When, in 2009, the U.S. House narrowly passed a bill to cap and trade carbon emissions to address global warming, the measure received near-unanimous support in New Netherland, the Left Coast, and Yankeedom, including that of every congressman in New England; the Far West offered near-unanimous bipartisan opposition, joined by the overwhelming majority of Appalachian and Deep Southern lawmakers; Tidewater and the Midlands were divided.[11]

Opposition to the 1972 Equal Rights Amendment was also regional, with all state governments controlled by Deep Southerners declining to ratify it, and those dominated by Appalachia opposing or rescinding ratification (with the exception of West Virginia). States dominated by Yankees, Midlanders, and Left Coasters all ratified the amendment, with the exception of Illinois (where majorities ratified it but never by the three-fifths majority required by the state's constitution). Tidewater no longer dominated any single state, but the one state in which the culture remained strongest, Virginia, also opposed ratification. (The Far West was split.)

In 2010 opinion on gay marriage also fell along predictable national lines. Legislatures have passed laws permitting same-sex marriages in the three northern New England states. State courts have mandated same-sex marriages in three others: Yankee Connecticut and both Yankee/Midland Iowa and tri-national California. (Residents of the Far West and El Norte sections of California rebelled, overturning the court decision via a 2008 ballot measure, despite the opposition of voters in nearly every Left Coast county.) By contrast, every single Dixie bloc–controlled state had passed laws or constitutional amendments banning same-sex marriage. On another issue, *USA Today* reported in 2006 that every state controlled by the Deep South could be expected to ban or greatly restrict abortion services if *Roe v. Wade* were to be overturned; every New England state, plus those comprising New Netherland and the Left Coast, were expected to protect women's access.[12]

The following chapter will examine the issues of militarism and national defense, but in regard to corporate behavior, the two blocs were also divided. The northern sixties rebels regarded big business as an oppressive force that despoiled the Earth and dehumanized the individual. By contrast, the nations of the Dixie bloc have continued to promulgate policies that ensure they remain low-wage resource colonies controlled by a one-party political system dedicated to serving the interests of a wealthy elite. To keep wages low, all Dixie-bloc states passed laws making it difficult to organize unions—which their politicians sold as protecting the "right to work"—or to increase the minimum wage. Taxes are kept too low to adequately support public schools and other services.

Urban planning and land-use zoning—commonplace among the four Northern allies—are shunned as a hindrance to business, even in major cities like Houston, which had hundreds of miles of unpaved, unlit streets as recently as the 1980s. From the gas fields of Louisiana to the industrial hog farms of North Carolina, environmental and workplace safety rules are notoriously lax.

These divergent approaches to economic development, tax policy, and social spending have only increased tensions between the cultural blocs. In the aftermath of the civil rights and sixties movements, the Dixie bloc has lured away most of the Yankee and Midland manufacturing sector by offering foreign and domestic corporations substantially lower wages, taxes, and regulations in a deunionized environment. The continent's Yankee automotive industry was all but destroyed in the 1990s and 2000s in favor of foreign-owned factories in the Deep South and Greater Appalachia, just like the textile and forest products industries before it. Some observers fear that the "neo-Confederates" will force the other nations to follow their lead, turning the entire federation into a giant "low-wage export platform" for advanced, highly educated industrial societies in Western Europe and northeast Asia. Meanwhile, innovation and research has become increasingly concentrated in knowledge clusters, most of which lie in the nations that have emphasized education and rationalism. Google, Apple, Microsoft, and Amazon all formed around Left Coast cities, just as the first "Silicon Valley" formed around Boston's Route 128, also known as the Yankee Highway.[13]

But the culture wars haven't been confined to domestic issues. Indeed, they have often raged strongest over issues of war and peace, humanitarian interventions, and the federation's proper role on the world stage.

CHAPTER 26

War, Empire, and the Military

As on cultural issues, the two "superpower" national blocs have traditionally disagreed on the United States' proper role in the world, how it should behave toward other states and federations, and whether internal dissent should be tolerated when "national" honor or security is at stake. Once again, opinion has split along ethnonational grounds, with the three nations of the Dixie bloc steadfastly supporting virtually every war since the 1830s, regardless of its purpose and opponents, while championing the use of force to expand and maintain the United States' power and suppressing dissenting opinions. Opposition to foreign wars—to the extent it has existed—has been concentrated in the four nations of the Northern alliance, although Appalachia is often skeptical of distant imperial undertakings, at least until the fighting starts. As on other issues, the Far West and El Norte are swing nations on foreign policy.

Consider the case of the Spanish-American War of 1898, in which the United States achieved a quick and resounding victory, crushing Spanish forces and seizing control of Cuba, Puerto Rico, Guam, and the Philippines. Initially every nation supported this "splendid little war," which ostensibly was fought to help Cubans achieve independence and to avenge the destruction of the USS *Maine* in Havana, allegedly by Spanish agents. At the time, the federal government was still controlled by the Northern alliance, with Western Reserve–born Yankee William McKinley occupying the Oval Office. But with honor at stake, Dixie residents signed up for federal military duty in large numbers, seeing an opportunity to prove their loyalty to the federation. Several Confederate veterans served as senior generals, one of whom, Major General Joseph Wheeler, reportedly got sufficiently agitated during the fighting in Cuba to yell out, "We've got the damn Yankees on the run!"

However, federal unity collapsed over the question of the disposition of the occupied territories, which included Puerto Rico, Guam, the

Philippines, and the independent kingdom of Hawaii (seized outright during the war on the pretext that somebody else would if the United States did not). Turn-of-the-century opposition to the creation of an American empire was centered in Yankeedom, though it was inspired by very different concerns. For Yankee critics—by no means a majority opinion even in their nation—the subjugation of foreign territories was a flagrant violation of the principles for which New Englanders had fought the American Revolution, particularly the right to representative self-government. Dissenters organized an anti-imperial movement, all of whose most prominent spokespeople were Yankees, including former president Grover Cleveland (who called annexations "dangerous perversions of our national mission"), Massachusetts senator George F. Hoar (who championed Filipino independence, noting that "love of liberty does not depend on the color of the skin"), and John Adams's great-grandson Charles Francis Adams Jr., who approved of the Filipinos' "very gallant resistance" of the U.S. occupation. The Boston-based Anti-Imperialist League was also dominated by Yankees, who accounted for twenty-eight of their forty-three vice presidents. (Only three resided in the Deep South, and none in the Far West.) When the Philippines insurrection turned violent and the U.S. commander ordered his troops to kill everyone in a province of 250,000 (at least 1,000 and possibly as many as 50,000 Filipinos are believed to have perished), the League exposed and condemned the atrocities. Harvard alumni rallied to stop the college from granting an honorary degree to President McKinley. While there were many Yankee imperialists—Massachusetts senator Henry Cabot Lodge was perhaps the best-known of them all—it was the only region that also had a large antiwar movement.[1]

The Dixie bloc was in favor of the unilateral use of military power to vanquish perceived enemies and increase U.S. prestige, but with Reconstruction still in living memory, they were skeptical of the federal government creating and maintaining an overseas empire of subordinate territories. An empire, the Dixie bloc argued, was acceptable only if the territories that were acquired were racially and geographically "suitable" for eventual absorption into the federation as full-fledged states. Such cases held forth the hope of a partial fulfillment of the Deep South's plans for a "Golden Circle" in the tropics. Dixie-bloc leaders were much less enthusiastic about the annexation of territories with "unassimilatable" populations and the large standing armies and navies that would be required to police and subjugate them. An expanded federal military might one day be turned against the Dixie bloc itself, they reasoned, perhaps turning it, too, into a subordinate colony of the northern nations. Offering statehood to places with large numbers of free "inferior" peoples would put further pressure on the bloc's cherished apartheid system. Thus many Dixie-bloc political leaders rejected the annexation of Hawaii, due to the presence of large numbers of Asians and native Hawaiians on the islands. "How can we endure the shame when a Chinese senator from Hawaii with his pigtail hanging down his neck and with his pagan joss in hand shall rise from his curule chair and in pigeon English proceed to chop logic with [senators] George Frisbie Hoar or Henry Cabot Lodge?" asked Appalachian Missouri senator Champ Clark. Others in Dixie cautiously endorsed the annexation, on the promise that a Deep South–style caste system would be imposed on nonwhites in the islands, ensuring white supremacy. The use of brute military force to crush America's enemies was a good thing, so long as it didn't result in any Yankee-inspired efforts to reengineer, "uplift," and assimilate inferior peoples.[2]

The three Dixie nations also emerged as the most enthusiastic supporters of U.S. involvement in World War I and the suppression of dissenters and pacifists. Goaded by the first Southern president since the Civil War—Appalachian Virginian Woodrow Wilson—the southern nations held that God had endorsed the war and that opposition to it was tantamount to treason. Pacifists, Wilson said publicly, were filled with "stupidity," and opponents of the war should face "a firm hand of stiff repression." Any congressman who opposed the war, Alabama representative J. Thomas Heflin proclaimed, "deserves the contempt and scorn of every loyal American citizen." The people of Wisconsin, Senator Thomas Hardwick of Georgia announced, were "false to America [and] the cause of democracy throughout the world" because 100,000 of them had voted for a pacifist candidate in their senate primary. Mississippi's Jackson *Clarion-Ledger* editorialized that antiwar leaders should be "shot or hung," while the Charleston *News and Courier* was satisfied with "repression, stern and absolute." When a small Georgia paper criticized Wilson's warmongering, the president shut the paper down with the enthusiastic approval of the rest of the Deep Southern press. Dixie antiwar leaders such as Mississippi senator James Vardaman appealed to the region's racism, arguing (correctly) that the war was giving black soldiers the idea that they deserved equality; even so, Vardaman was turned out of office with the approval of at least one preacher who'd condemned him for hampering "God's war against the devil." Wilson, for his part, assuaged Dixie fears that his idealistic war for democracy and self-determination in Europe would threaten their own authoritarian caste system. The president oversaw the purging of black administrators at federal agencies and the introduction of racially segregated bathrooms, lavatories, and offices in many government buildings; Wilson also segregated military training camps, forcing the Union's army to adopt Dixie ways. Such moves earned him the loyalty and admiration of Dixie-bloc lawmakers, who later championed his League of Nations plan. When, years after Wilson's death, Midlander senator Gerald Nye criticized his war policies, Texas senator Tom Connally challenged Nye to a fistfight, and Virginia senator Carter Glass became so angry that he wounded himself pounding his desk. The commander in chief, like the Deep Southern and Tidewater oligarchs themselves, was not to be questioned.[3]

Jim Webb, the historian, Marine Corps veteran, and Virginia senator, has pointed out that during World War I, many Borderlanders enlisted in the Marine Corps, imparting "a strong tradition of Scots-Irish and Southern influence on the culture and leadership style of that elite Corps which continues to this day." He argues that the Corps's preference for frontal assaults, its "fire team" system of interlocking unit commanders, and the tradition of having leaders who "led from the front" can all be traced to Borderlander precedents dating back to William Wallace of *Braveheart* fame. Many of our most famous officers, Webb points out, had Scots-Irish ancestors, including John J. Pershing, Douglas MacArthur, George Patton, and a host of Marine commandants.[4]

By contrast, the four leading opponents of intervention in World War I in the U.S. Senate were Yankees or Left Coasters: Harry Lane of Oregon, George W. Norris (a Western Reserve transplant to Nebraska), Asle Gronna (a Minnesotan representing North Dakota), and Robert La Follette of Wisconsin. When the United States entered the war, these four men were joined by three other Wisconsin congressional representatives to form the core of the antiwar caucus on Capitol Hill.[5]

The rise of Adolf Hitler put the Dixie bloc in a potentially awkward position. The Nazis had praised the Deep South's caste system, which they used as a model for their own race laws. Nazi publications approved of lynching as a natural response to the threat of racial mixing. ("It is a hundred times better" for Southern whites, one pro-Nazi intellectual wrote, "if exaggerated racial hatred leads to a hundred lynchings per year than if each year 50,000 mulatto children are born.") But white opinion makers in the Dixie bloc generally did not reciprocate the admiration. Instead they attacked the Nazis for their suppression of Jews while carefully avoiding discussion of the Nazis' vicious propaganda against blacks, the forced sterilization of mixed-race children, and Hitler's calls to exterminate the "Negroid race." The uncomfortable parallels between the two racist regimes were regularly pointed out by African American publications across the federation but got virtually no airing within Dixie's white caste. Dixie-bloc representatives lambasted the Germans and supported every important legislative act in preparation for war, from approving the draft to expanding the Navy. From 1933 onward this bloc's congressmen gave stronger support to military preparedness than any other part of the federation, even as they opposed Roosevelt's domestic policies. The public was behind them. In a national poll conducted two months before Pearl Harbor, 88 percent of Southerners said war was justified to defeat Nazi Germany, compared to 70 percent of the residents of Northeast states and 64 percent of "Midwesterners." During the conflict, the bloc had ninety military volunteers for every one hundred draftees, compared to an average of fifty for the federation as a whole. "They had better start selective service," (Appalachian) Alabama representative Luther Patrick joked, "to keep our boys from filling up the army."[6]

During the 1930s the federation was divided on the necessity of preparing for war. New Netherland congressmen were hawkish on military preparations, perhaps because so many of their constituents had emigrated from countries endangered by Hitler. Their Left Coast, Far West, and El Norte colleagues followed suit, especially as the federal government began situating war industries and military bases in the region. Midlanders generally opposed these measures, in part due to the German Americans' reluctance to go to war with their former countrymen. Opinion in Yankeedom was deeply divided, with the New England core more inclined to prepare for war than the Great Lakes and Yankee Midwest.[7]

After the Japanese attack on Pearl Harbor, the nations banded together to a degree never seen before or since. Borderlanders fought for the traditional Scots-Irish reason: to avenge an attack by defeating their enemies on the field of battle. The Tidewater and Deep Southern elite—still very much in charge of their nations—wished to uphold U.S. "national" honor and to defend their Anglo-Norman brethren across the sea. Pacifist Midlanders backed the war as a struggle against military despotism, while Yankees, New Netherlanders, and Left Coasters emphasized the anti-authoritarian aspect of the struggle. Residents of El Norte and the Far West embraced a war that showered their long-neglected regions with federal largesse.[8]

Indeed, Hitler and Emperor Hirohito did more for the development of the Far West and El Norte than any other agent in those regions' histories. Long exploited as internal colonies, both nations were suddenly given an industrial base to help the Allies win the war. The two nations got shipyards and naval bases (in San Diego and Long Beach), aircraft plants (Los Angeles, San Pedro, and Wichita) and integrated steel mills (in Utah and interior California). There were nuclear weapons labs (Los Alamos) and test sites (White Sands) in New Mexico. Landing strips and modern airports were built throughout the area, reducing its remoteness and creating the first challenge to the transportation monopolies that had kept the Far West in a state of thralldom. The number of military facilities and defense plants in these two nations continued to grow during the Cold War in radical disproportion to their population; today they are dependent on the military-industrial complex, which influences both nations' political priorities.[9]

In addition to these effects, El Norte experienced a profound agricultural labor shortage during the war as farm and railroad laborers migrated to better-paying jobs at the new military plants. The solution: a wartime guest worker program by which 250,000 Mexican citizens were allowed into El Norte, setting the foundation for a far larger and less organized postwar program that would tip the balance of power back to *norteños* a few decades later.[10]

In the 1960s the Dixie bloc was the most hawkish region on the war in Southeast Asia, providing firm support for (Appalachian Texan) President Johnson's escalation of the conflict. Of some thirty-odd Dixie senators, only two consistently opposed the war, and both were from Appalachia. One, Arkansas's J. William Fulbright, was a committed racist who saw parallels between the federal efforts to reshape Vietnam (by propping up the Saigon regime) and the American South (by supporting civil rights activists) and vigorously fought against both. The other was an anomaly: the "patron saint of Texas liberals," Ralph Yarborough, who ultimately was ousted for his antiwar and pro–civil rights views. Only a handful of Dixie congressmen supported a landmark 1970 Senate measure that would have stopped military interventions in Cambodia, ensuring the measure's failure. "Words are fruitless, diplomatic notes are useless," South Carolina representative L. Mendel Rivers said of Vietnam. "There can be only one answer from America: retaliation, retaliation, retaliation, retaliation! They say, quit the bombing, I say, Bomb!" When radical antiwar activists proposed assassinating prowar senators, all the men on their hit list were Deep Southerners. Of the two dozen most significant antiwar events of the period, only one took place in the Dixie bloc: the killing of protesting black students at Jackson State University by white policemen in 1970. Throughout the conflict, most of the dissenting minority in Dixie were Borderlanders who questioned the purpose of intervening in another country's civil war. "If we must fight, let us fight in defense of our homeland and our own hemisphere," Kentucky senator Tim Lee Carter said. "Our sons' lives are too precious to lose on foreign soil. If they must die, let it be in defense of America."[11]

Opposition to the war centered in Yankeedom, New Netherland, and the Left Coast, generally on the grounds that it was an unjust imperial intervention. The antiwar movement started on these nations' campuses, with the first marches on military facilities originating from Berkeley and the first Vietnam "teach-in" held at the University of Michigan in 1965. The first mass demonstration took place in New York City in 1967 with

300,000 participants, while that fall's 400,000-person March on the Pentagon was dominated by students from New York and Boston, with substantial representation from campuses in the Yankee Midwest. Vietnam Veterans Against the War was founded by six returned soldiers in New York City and concentrated its activities in the northeast. The Kent State shootings occurred in Ohio's Yankee-founded Western Reserve, part of a wave of strikes that started at Oberlin (Yankeedom) and Princeton (New Netherland) minutes after President Nixon announced U.S. forces were invading Cambodia; of the hundreds of universities that eventually joined the strike, the vast majority were located in these three nations. They also provided the core of antiwar sentiment in Washington, with the 1970 measure to end operations in Cambodia receiving overwhelming support from their congressional delegations.[12]

The Midlands neither forcefully challenged nor endorsed the controversial conflict, and even its students were ambivalent. At the March on the Pentagon, witnesses noted that students from the Philadelphia and Baltimore areas were noticeably scarce, despite their close proximity to Washington, D.C. True to regional traditions, those Midlanders who did take an active stance against the war often did so on pacifist grounds, with the Philadelphia-based American Friends Service Committee mobilized to discourage violent confrontations at antiwar rallies and to provide relief to both North and South Vietnamese civilians. One Baltimore Quaker, Norman Morrison, killed himself by self-immolation outside Secretary of Defense Robert McNamara's office in solidarity with Vietnamese monks who'd done the same in front of the U.S. Embassy in Saigon.[13]

Far Western political representatives generally supported the war, with most rejecting congressional efforts to stop military operations in Cambodia. The region produced several prominent hawks, including Barry Goldwater (of central Arizona) and Wyoming senator Gale McGee. El Norte representatives were stalemated, with even Hispanic congressmen at odds over Cambodia and other war-related issues. Antiwar protests were relatively rare in both nations, with the exception of student uprisings in Los Angeles and a chain of demonstrations led by the Chicano Moratorium, a *norteño*-led coalition. The protestors repeatedly emphasized that Chicano youths should be fighting not for Vietnam but rather "for social justice right here in the United States." As it was an essentially nationalistic movement, its participants generally did not seek to join forces with non-Hispanic opponents of the war but rather with Puerto Ricans and other Spanish-speaking people within the federation.[14]

After the 2000 election, the Dixie bloc established simultaneous control over the White House, Senate, and House of Representatives for the first time in forty-six years. The White House was led by a Deep Southern president (the Houston-raised, Brazos Valley–based George W. Bush), the House by Deep Southern Texans Dick Armey and Tom DeLay, and the Senate by Borderlander Bill Frist, a member of an elite Nashville family whose ancestors had founded Chattanooga, Tennessee.[15]

The federation's foreign policy took an immediate and radical departure from previous norms, a change in direction that only accelerated after the terrorist attacks on New York and Washington the following September. The new plan was to enhance the United States' position as the world's only superpower through military force: a series of preemptive wars against potential rivals; the sidelining of any inconvenient treaties, international organizations, or diplomatic obligations; and a severing of potentially encumbering relationships with traditional allies, save those with Israel. Bush canceled more international treaties in his first year than any other president in U.S. history. He ended negotiations with the Palestinians, insisting they become a full-scale democracy as a prerequisite to Israel's ending its occupation. Representative Armey advocated ethnic cleansing of the West Bank's three million Palestinians, while DeLay asserted the occupied territories "belonged to Israel," apparently on biblical grounds. But most controversial of the Bush administration's foreign policy decisions was to invade Iraq, a country that had not threatened the United States and whose secular dictatorship was hated by the fanatics who had planned the September 11 attacks.[16]

The Iraq war provided a litmus test of the nations' commitment to internationalism or, alternately, to the unilateral use of U.S. military power. The results fell into a now recognizable pattern: the Dixie bloc gave Bush's Iraq policies a ringing endorsement. An August 2002 Gallup poll found "Southerners" approved of an invasion by 62 to 34 percent, compared to 47 to 44 percent for "Midwesterners." Two months later, Dixie congressional representatives voted to authorize the war by a more than four-to-one ratio, far higher than any other region. Only when the war deteriorated into an ugly occupation did Appalachia and Tidewater enthusiasm begin to falter; congressional representatives from these two nations were divided over whether to condemn Bush's 2006 plan to increase the military commitment. Deep Southerners and Far Westerners, meanwhile, strongly opposed any criticism of the president's strategy. On the other side of the argument, the Left Coast congressional delegation was unanimous in its disapproval of the military "surge," and Yankeedom and El Norte nearly so. As in other wars, opinion in the Midlands and New Netherland was mixed.[17]

U.S. foreign policy has shown a clear national pattern for the past two centuries. Since 1812, the anti-interventionist, anti-imperial Yankees have squared off against the bellicose, unilateralist hawks in the Deep South and Tidewater. Appalachia, while providing the warriors, is often divided on the wisdom of going to war when there is neither the prospect of territorial aggrandizement nor revenge. The Yankees—idealistic, intellectual, and guided by the Public Protestant mission—have sought foreign policies that would civilize the world and, thus, has often dominated the Foreign Affairs Committees on Capitol Hill. The Dixie-bloc—martial and honor-bound—has generally aimed to dominate the world and has traditionally controlled the federation's Armed Services Committee. "U.S. foreign policy," Michael Lind has argued, is merely "civil war by other means."[18]

CHAPTER 27

The Struggle for Power I: The Blue Nations

The nations have been struggling with one another for advantage and influence since they were founded, and from 1790 the biggest prize has been control of federal government institutions: Congress, the White House, the courts, and the military. As the central government has grown in size, scope, and power, so have the nations' efforts to capture and reshape it—and the rest of the continent—in their image. Since 1877 the driving force of American politics hasn't primarily been a class struggle or tension between agrarian and commercial interests, or even between competing partisan ideologies, although each has played a role. Ultimately the determinative political struggle has been a clash between shifting coalitions of ethnoregional nations, one invariably headed by the Deep South, the other by Yankeedom.

Since the end of Reconstruction no one nation has had any hope of dominating the others independently. Instead, each has sought to form alliances with like-minded partners.

The most durable and lasting coalition has been that forged between Yankeedom and the Left Coast in the 1840s, one we've seen in action in both the culture wars and foreign policy. With its crusading utopian agenda, Yankeedom has usually set the tone: a quest for betterment of the "common good," seen as best achieved through the creation of a frugal, competent, and effective government supported by a strong tax base and able to ensure the availability and prudent management of shared assets. The Left Coast's views are nearly identical, though it added environmental quality to the shared agenda during the twentieth century and tempered the Yankees' messianic certainties with the products of its frequent technological experiments, from Monterey-style housing in the mid-nineteenth century to the iPod in the early twenty-first. The world, Left Coasters insisted, can be easily and frequently reinvented.

Between 1877 and 1897 these two nations dominated the federal government with the tacit assistance of their Civil War allies in the Midlands and their colonial minions in the Far West. Together their congressional representatives pushed through policies designed to enrich and empower their societies while weakening their archenemies in the Deep South and Tidewater. First they built a wall of tariffs around the federation, protecting their manufacturing sectors from European competition. The tariffs collected at U.S. Customs Houses accounted for nearly 60 percent of all federal revenue by 1890—far more money, in fact, than the federal government actually needed. Much of this surplus was then pumped back to the citizens of Yankeedom, the Midlands, and the Far West in the form of generous new Civil War pensions, payable in arrears to veterans, their widows, or their children. In the early 1890s these pension payments accounted for more than 37 percent of all federal expenditures, almost double the military budget at the time. Since only Union soldiers qualified for pensions, nearly all of this wealth poured into the northern nations, including the Left Coast and the Far West, which were home to many Union veterans. At the same time, Yankees made a last-ditch attempt to thwart the resurgence of the Deep Southern and Tidewater oligarchs by protecting black and poor white voters. Their tool was the 1890 Force Bill, a piece of legislation introduced by Yankee Brahmin senator Henry Cabot Lodge that allowed federal review and military intervention in disputed federal elections. All save three congressmen from Yankeedom, the Far West, and the Left Coast supported the bill. Although it also received the endorsement of a fair number of Midland and Appalachian congressmen, the Force Bill was ultimately defeated by Dixie and its occasional ally, New Netherland.[1]

The populous, powerful city-state of New Netherland played the superpower blocs off one another until the turn of the century. A nation built on global commerce, it found itself aligned with Dixie's cotton lords in opposition to protective tariffs. Flooded with immigrants, New Netherland was home to only a tiny percentage of Union veterans in the 1880s and so had also opposed the Yankees' pension scheme. Its corrupt political machine, known as Tammany Hall, felt threatened by the Force Bill and mobilized against it on Capitol Hill. Throughout the nineteenth century New Netherland was by no means a reliable member of the Northern alliance.[2]

In the twentieth century, New Netherland found common ground with Yankeedom in its need, as an enormously complex urban center, for effective government and expensive public infrastructure. This was the nation with the fewest qualms about taxation and large-scale public institutions—indeed, New York City could hardly exist without them. New Netherland's bewilderingly diverse population may not have been particularly concerned about the plight of Deep Southern blacks, but it was repelled by Dixie's emphasis on white *Protestant* supremacy, social conformity, and the suppression of dissent. And while New Netherland has never been the most democratically governed of places—again, witness Tammany Hall—it has always valued cultural diversity, freedom of conscience, and freedom of expression. Long the most socially liberal nation on the continent—very much a live-and-let-live place—New Netherland had little choice but to cast its lot with the Yankees and against the zealotry of the Deep South.

With New Netherland on board, the Yankee-led Northern alliance achieved its current three-nation form. Together it has consistently promoted a coherent agenda for more than a century, regardless of which political party was dominant in the region. From the "conservative" administration of Republican Teddy Roosevelt to the "liberal" one of Democrat Barack Obama, these three nations have favored the maintenance of a strong central government, federal checks on corporate power, and the conservation of environmental resources.

During the first half of the twentieth century, the Republican Party was still the "party of the north," and it dominated the federal government until the coming of the Great Depression. Except for Woodrow Wilson's presidency, northern Republicans occupied the White House continuously from 1897 to 1932, and only lost it to Wilson by splitting their vote in a three-way race. Of the six presidents in this period, three were Yankees (McKinley, Taft, and Coolidge), one was a New Netherland plutocrat of Dutch origin (Teddy Roosevelt), and two were Midlanders (Midland Ohioan Warren Harding and German/Canadian Quaker Herbert Hoover). Although they presided over an era of laissez-faire capitalism, all of them save Hoover supported civil rights for African Americans and all (except Coolidge) an expanded reach for the federal government and checks on corporate and plutocratic power. They weren't averse to cutting taxes, but generally did not do so in ways that skewed the benefits to the wealthy.

Teddy Roosevelt broke up the great corporate trusts, intervened in a major strike to secure a solution beneficial to miners, and founded the National Park Service, national wildlife refuges, and the U.S. Forest Service; he also championed the federal regulation and inspection of meat, food, and pharmaceuticals, and made the first Jewish cabinet appointment in U.S. history. Taft, the Yale-educated child of Massachusetts Puritans, furthered Roosevelt's antitrust investigations and backed constitutional amendments instituting the federal income tax and the direct popular election of U.S. senators. Harding did reduce income taxes for corporations and the wealthy but also sought to make government more effective through the creation of the Office of Management and Budget and the General Accounting Office; he also founded what is now the Veterans Administration. Coolidge, famous for his refusal to regulate banks and corporations as president, did so out of a desire to avoid a bloating of the federal government; as governor of Massachusetts, he had promoted labor, wage, and workplace safety protections and the inclusion of labor representatives on corporate boards. As president, Coolidge cut taxes, but in a way unfavorable to the rich. Hoover expanded the national park and veterans' hospital systems, founded the federal Department of Education and the Department of Justice's antitrust division, and fought (unsuccessfully) for low-income tax cuts and universal pensions for senior citizens.[3]

These most conservative of Northern alliance presidents would all probably be considered big-government liberals by the standards of early-twenty-first-century Dixie-bloc political leaders. So, too, would the Northern alliance–led Republican Party of the 1950s. In Eisenhower's first term, the GOP controlled the White House and both branches of Congress but created the Department of Health, Education and Welfare. Eisenhower later sent federal troops to Arkansas to enforce civil rights rulings and, in his farewell address, warned of the threat to democracy posed by the emerging "military-industrial complex."[4]

The three Northern alliance nations have supported the same presidential candidates in nearly every presidential election from 1988 to 2008, always opting for the more progressive choices: Obama over John McCain, John

Kerry and Al Gore over George W. Bush, and Michael Dukakis over George H. W. Bush. (The more liberal New Netherland broke with its allies to reject conservatives Ronald Reagan and Richard Nixon, the only nation to definitively do so.) All supported LBJ over Barry Goldwater in 1964 and the ever-popular Eisenhower over Midlander Adlai Stevenson in the 1950s. While some candidacies failed to generate a clear voter consensus within one or more of these nations,[5] only once in the postwar period have they firmly endorsed rival candidates: when New Netherland chose George McGovern over Richard Nixon in 1972.

In the same period only four men from Northern alliance nations have occupied the White House: Republicans Gerald Ford and George H. W. Bush and Democrats John F. Kennedy and Barack Obama.[6] True to their origins, all four sought to better society through government programs, expanded civil rights protections, and environmental safeguards. Both Republicans represented their party's moderate wing and soon found themselves at odds with their Dixie-bloc constituents. Ford supported the Equal Rights Amendment and the act that created federally funded special education programs across the country, and appointed John Paul Stevens to the Supreme Court. Facing budget deficits inherited from Reagan, Bush raised taxes on the wealthy and refused to lower the capital gains tax, despite knowing it would make him politically unpopular. He supported the extension of civil rights to disabled people and the reauthorization of the Clean Air Act, and increased federal spending on education, research, and child care. Likewise, John F. Kennedy proposed what later became the 1964 Civil Rights Act, dispatched federal troops and agents to force Dixie governors to allow black students into the Universities of Georgia and Alabama, increased the minimum wage and federal funding for affordable housing and mental health services, and launched a watershed investigation of environmental issues that laid the groundwork for the creation of the Environmental Protection Agency. In his first two years in office, Obama supported an overhaul of the federation's health insurance industry, the regulation of the financial services industry, and efforts to reduce greenhouse gas emissions—all against strong Dixie opposition.[7]

When Dixie-bloc conservatives captured control of the GOP in the aftermath of the civil rights struggle, Northern alliance Republicans (and

Dixie blacks) abandoned the party in large numbers. Between 1956 and 1998 the percentage of New Englanders who cast their votes for Republican candidates fell from 55 percent to 33 percent, and those of New Yorkers (both Yankee and New Netherlander) fell from 54 to 43 percent, while the Yankee Midwest also saw declines that accelerated during the first decade of the twenty-first century. By 2010 the Republicans had lost control of the lower house of every single state legislature in the three Northern alliance nations, all but one of the upper houses, and seven of the thirteen governors' mansions in states dominated by the alliance. In a flip-flop of enormous proportions, the Democrats had become the party of the Northern alliance, and the "party of Lincoln" had become the vehicle of Dixie-bloc whites.[8]

During the George W. Bush administration, the Northern alliance's Republican congressional delegation was all but eliminated. Vermont senator Jim Jeffords—who'd voted against Reagan and Bush's tax cuts for the wealthy and in support of gay rights and education spending—abandoned the party after his colleagues stripped funding for a program to help disabled children. Senator Lincoln Chafee of Rhode Island was defeated by a Democratic challenger in 2006, left the party, and was subsequently elected governor as an independent. In 2008 Minnesota senator Norm Coleman lost his seat to liberal comedian Al Franken, while Far Western Mormon Oregonian senator Gordon Smith was unseated by a Democratic challenger from the Left Coast. By 2009 there were only three Republican U.S. senators left in the entire Northern alliance, and two had an American Conservative Union lifetime rating of less than 50 of 100 points; the only conservative, New Hampshire's Judd Gregg, announced in 2010 that he would not seek reelection. The Republican Party was essentially extinct in the region of its birth.[9]

Northern alliance congressional representatives have generally upheld their nations' agendas, regardless of party affiliation. In the late 1970s they voted en masse to prohibit Dixie's "right to work" laws (which forbade union shop contracts) and to change laws that exempted small firms from federal workplace safety inspections and effectively prohibited strikes by workers at large construction sites. (The Dixie bloc opposed these efforts, en masse.) In 1980, when there were still plenty of northern Republicans, every Yankee and New Netherland congressional representative save three supported a measure to allocate federal low-income heating assistance based on how cold it actually was in a given consumer's community; Left Coasters in Washington and Oregon were also unanimously in favor. (Only Californians, with their mild climate, opposed the measure.) By contrast, the Deep South was unanimously opposed to the measure and Appalachia nearly so. (Tidewater, with its cooler winter conditions, defected to the Northern position, regardless of party.)[10]

The divisive 2010 House vote on President Obama's health care overhaul bill illustrates Northern alliance cohesion. Yankee representatives backed the bill 62 to 21, New Netherlanders by 24 to 6, and the Left Coast by a staggering 21 to 2. The results were the same on a vote a few months later to strengthen the financial regulatory system in the aftermath of the near-meltdown of the world banking system. Yankeedom approved the measures by 63 to 19, the Left Coast by 21 to 1, and New Netherland, 26 to 4, despite being the federation's financial capital. Both measures were overwhelmingly opposed by the Dixie-bloc delegation as unwarranted intrusions into the private marketplace.[11]

Even when Congress does vote along strict party lines, Republican defectors are nearly always from the Northern alliance or the Midlands. In 1999 only four Republican House representatives refused to impeach Bill Clinton for lying about an extramarital affair: two Yankees and two Midlanders, one of them a transplant from Massachusetts. Only three Republicans broke ranks to pass Obama's 2010 financial reform overhaul, all of them from New England.[12]

In short, by the early twenty-first century, Northern alliance Democrats and Republicans had far more in common with one another than with their counterparts in the Dixie bloc. Indeed, the southern coalition stood against nearly everything the northerners held dear.

CHAPTER 28

The Struggle for Power II: The Red and the Purple

Contrary to popular opinion, the Dixie bloc has not been a particularly stable coalition. The dominant parties—the Deep South and Greater Appalachia—have been archenemies for much of their history, having taken up arms against one another in both the American Revolution and the Civil War. The junior partner, Tidewater, was always less committed to apartheid and authoritarianism than its southern neighbor and today is increasingly falling under the influence of the Midlands. The Deep Southern oligarchy, whose economic interests the bloc ultimately serves, has had to contend with the enfranchisement of millions of black voters in its own region, a tendency toward gentlemanly moderation among the Tidewater elite, and the powerful populist sentiment of many Borderlanders. All of these forces threaten to undermine the Dixie coalition.

The goal of the Deep Southern oligarchy has been consistent for over four centuries: to control and maintain a one-party state with a colonial-style economy based on large-scale agriculture and the extraction of primary resources by a compliant, poorly educated, low-wage workforce with as few labor, workplace safety, health care, and environmental regulations as possible. On being compelled by force of arms to give up their slave workforce, Deep Southerners developed caste and sharecropper systems to meet their labor needs, as well as a system of poll taxes and literacy tests to keep former slaves and white rabble out of the political process. When these systems were challenged by African Americans and the federal government, they rallied poor whites in their nation, in Tidewater, and in Appalachia to their cause through fearmongering: The races would mix. Daughters would be defiled. Yankees would take away their guns and Bibles and convert their children to secular humanism, environmentalism, communism, and homosexuality. Their political hirelings discussed criminalizing abortion, protecting the flag from flag burners, stopping illegal immigration, and scaling back government spending when on the campaign trail; once in office, they focused on cutting taxes for the wealthy, funneling massive subsidies to the oligarchs' agribusinesses and oil companies, eliminating labor and environmental regulations, creating "guest worker" programs to secure cheap farm labor from the developing world, and poaching manufacturing jobs from higher-wage unionized industries in Yankeedom, New Netherland, or the Midlands. It's a strategy financial analyst Stephen Cummings has likened to "a high-technology version of the plantation economy of the Old South," with the working and middle classes playing the role of sharecroppers.[1]

For the oligarchs the greatest challenge has been getting Greater Appalachia into their coalition and keeping it there. Appalachia has relatively few African Americans, a demographic fact that undermined the alleged economic and sexual "threat" raised by black empowerment. Borderlanders have always prized egalitarianism and freedom (at least for white individuals) and detested aristocracy in all its forms (except its homegrown elite, who generally have the good sense not to *act* as if they're better than anyone else). There was—and still is—a powerful populist tradition in Appalachia that runs counter to the Deep Southern oligarchs' wishes. Most of the great Southern populists have been self-made men from the borderlands, including Lyndon Johnson (from Texas Hill Country), Ross Perot (Texarkana), Sam Rayburn (eastern Tennessee), Ralph Yarborough (born in Northeast Texas, based near Austin), Mike Huckabee (Hope, Arkansas), or Zell Miller (of the North Georgia mountains) in the first half of his political career. Appalachia also gave Dixie many of its most successful progressives, including Bill Clinton (also from Hope), Al Gore (from an elite Nashville-area Scots-Irish family), and Cordell Hull (born in a log cabin in north-central Tennessee). Further complicating the oligarchy's strategy, much of Appalachia fought against the Confederacy in the Civil War, which always made the Lost Cause story line a bit harder to sell.[2]

Two factors worked in the oligarchs' favor, however: racism and religion. During the Civil War, Borderlanders fought to maintain the Union, not to help African Americans, and they were deeply offended by the Yankee drive to liberate and enfranchise blacks during Reconstruction. ("It is hard to say who they hate the most," Tennessee governor William

Brownlow said of his fellow Appalachian Unionists in 1865, "the rebels or the Negroes.")[3] Second, Borderlanders and poor whites in Tidewater and the Deep South shared a common religious tradition: a form of Private Protestantism that rejected social reform, found biblical justification for slavery, and denounced secularism, feminism, environmentalism, and many key discoveries of modern science as contrary to God's will. After 1877 this suite of "social issues" bonded together ordinary people across the Dixie bloc. It's much the same dynamic that Thomas Frank described in *What's the Matter with Kansas?* which revealed how the oligarchs of his native state used social and "moral" issues to rally ordinary people to support the architects of their economic destruction. "The trick never ages; the illusion never wears off," Frank writes:

> *Vote* to stop abortion, *receive* a rollback in capital gains taxes. *Vote* to make our country strong again; *receive* deindustrialization. *Vote* to screw those politically correct college professors; *receive* electricity deregulation. *Vote* to get government off our backs; *receive* conglomeration and monopoly everywhere from media to meatpacking. *Vote* to stand tall against terrorists; *receive* Social Security privatization. *Vote* to strike a blow against elitism; *receive* a social order in which wealth is more concentrated than ever before in our lifetimes, in which workers have been stripped of power and CEOs are rewarded in a manner beyond imagining.[4]

Mr. Frank was writing about developments over the past forty years in a state straddling the Midlands and Far West, but the strategy he describes was originally developed a century earlier in Greater Appalachia and used to great effect.

For the first few decades after 1877, the federal government was in the hands of the Yankee–Left Coast axis. During that time Dixie-bloc representatives voted en masse against nineteenth-century Yankee tariffs and pensions, African American voting rights, and Senator Lodge's Force Bill. Dixie arguments against civil rights and free elections were explicitly racist. "We will never surrender our government to an inferior race," argued (Appalachian) Georgia representative Allen Candler, who was later elected governor. "We wrested our State government from negro supremacy when the Federal drum-beat rolled closer to the ballot-box and Federal bayonets hedged it deeper about than will ever again be permitted in this free Government." In solid Borderlander tradition, Representative William Breckinridge of Kentucky likened the Force Bill to those "passed by an English Parliament for Irish constituencies and defended on precisely the same grounds." Rarely mentioned was the fact that so long as blacks and poor whites were disenfranchised, the oligarchs would retain power in the Deep South and Tidewater. Even as the Force Bill was being debated, Dixie governments were imposing new poll taxes and other measures to suppress democratic participation. In Mississippi voter participation fell from 70 percent in 1877 to less than 10 percent in 1920. "The results were everywhere the same," historian Richard Franklin Bensel found. "Almost all blacks and most poor whites were disfranchised and the plantation elite achieved hegemonic control over the region."[5]

Dixie's effect on federal politics was minimal, however. In the early twentieth century the coalition secured the White House only once, when Teddy Roosevelt founded the Progressive Party, split the Northern alliance vote, and gave the presidency to Woodrow Wilson. Wilson, as we've already seen, was a committed segregationist who persecuted dissenters during World War I. But he was also an Appalachian Southerner, born in Staunton, Virginia, to a Borderlander family of mixed Scots-Irish, Scots, and north English origin. In accord with national stereotype, he combined racism and intolerance of dissent with attempts to curb corporate power: namely, the creation of the Federal Reserve system, the Federal Trade Commission, and programs to channel credit and innovations to small farmers of the sort who dominated his home region. The oligarchs of the Deep South had not yet had their day.

The dynamic changed in the 1960s, when Democrats JFK and LBJ backed up civil rights activists against extralegal resistance in Dixie. "I think we just delivered the South to the Republican Party for a long time to come," Johnson told an aide hours after signing the 1964 Civil Rights Act into law. Indeed, much of the Dixie coalition promptly abandoned the Democratic Party and the populist Appalachian president who'd dared betray the caste system. In 1968 their presidential nominee was the radical Deep Southern racist George Wallace, who ran as a third-party candidate on a promise to demonstrate that "there sure are a lot of rednecks in this country." They might have backed him in 1972 as well had he not been shot and paralyzed by a deranged fame seeker while campaigning in Midland Maryland. They rallied instead to a new cohort of Dixie-style Republicans from El Norte's Anglo minority—Richard Nixon and Ronald Reagan—who succeeded in overthrowing the Northern alliance's control of the GOP.[6]

Since the mid-1960s these three nations have always endorsed the more conservative presidential candidates, except when faced with a choice between a Dixie Southern Baptist and a more conservative Yankee. They all endorsed McCain over Obama, George W. Bush over Kerry, George H. W. Bush over Dukakis, Reagan over Mondale, Nixon over McGovern, and Nixon and Wallace over Humphrey in 1968. Defections came when the more liberal candidate was from the Dixie bloc: Appalachia and the Deep South went for Carter (a Georgian Baptist) over Ford (raised in Yankee Michigan) in 1976, while Tidewater split; Appalachia and the Deep South chose Arkansas Borderlander Bill Clinton in 1992 while Tidewater went for more conservative (but Yankee-bred) George H. W. Bush. Appalachia also defected to Clinton in 1996 (over Midlander Bob Dole) and was divided by the candidacies of liberal Borderlander Al Gore (against the younger Bush) and Carter (against Reagan).

Dixie-bloc voters back ultraconservatives with remarkable consistency. As of 2009 eighteen serving U.S. senators had earned a lifetime rating of 90 or above (out of 100) from the American Conservative Society. Every single one came from the Far West or the Dixie bloc. White representatives in the Dixie coalition voted en masse against the civil rights and voting acts of the 1960s; for bans on union shop contracts in the 1970s; for lowering taxes on the wealthy and eliminating taxes on inherited wealth in the 1980s, 1990s, and 2000s; for invading Iraq in 2003; and for blocking health care and financial regulatory reform and increases in minimum wages in 2010.

Dixie's congressional leadership has consistently advocated policies and positions that are often shocking to public opinion in the Northern alliance. The 1984 Republican Party platform, Deep Southern senator Trent Lott declared, was a good document because it was full of "things that Jefferson Davis and his people believed in." Tidewater senator Jesse

Helms tried to block the creation of the Martin Luther King holiday on the grounds that the civil rights leader had been a "Marxist-Leninist" who associated with "Communists and sex perverts." Deep Southern House majority leader Tom DeLay proclaimed in the early 2000s, "The causes of youth violence are working parents who put their kids into daycare, the teaching of evolution in the schools, and working mothers who take birth control pills." "Nothing," DeLay told bankers in 2003, "is more important in the face of war than cutting taxes." As the U.S. economy unraveled in 2008, former Deep Southern senator and Swiss bank vice chairman Phil Gramm told the *Washington Times* the country was in "a mental recession" and that its people had "become a nation of whiners . . . complaining about a loss of competitiveness, America in decline." After the 2010 BP oil spill, Representative Joe Barton (from Deep Southern Texas) publicly apologized to the company for having been pressured to create a fund to compensate its victims, calling the initiative—but not the spill—"a tragedy of the first proportion."[7]

From the 1990s, the Dixie bloc's influence over the federal government has been enormous. In 1994 the Dixie-led Republican Party took control of both houses of Congress for the first time in forty years. The Republicans maintained their majority in the U.S. House until 2006 and controlled the Senate for many of those years as well. While perhaps disappointed with the progressivism of Jimmy Carter's presidency, Deep Southern oligarchs finally got one of their own in the White House in 2000, for the first time since 1850. George W. Bush may have been the son of a Yankee president and raised in far western Texas, but he was a creature of east Texas, where he lived, built his political career, found God, and cultivated his business interests and political alliances. His domestic policy priorities as president were those of the Deep Southern oligarchy: cut taxes for the wealthy, privatize Social Security, deregulate energy markets (to benefit family allies at Houston-based Enron), stop enforcing environmental and safety regulations for offshore drilling rigs (like BP's *Deepwater Horizon*), turn a blind eye to offshore tax havens, block the regulation of carbon emissions or tougher fuel efficiency standards for automobiles, block health care benefits for low-income children, open protected areas to oil exploration, appoint industry executives to run the federal agencies meant to regulate their industries, and inaugurate a massive new foreign guest-worker program to ensure a low-wage labor supply. Meanwhile, Bush garnered support among ordinary Dixie residents by advertising his fundamentalist Christian beliefs, banning embryonic stem cell research and late-term abortions, and attempting to transfer government welfare programs to religious institutions. By the end of his presidency—and the sixteen-year run of Dixie dominance in Washington—income inequality and the concentration of wealth in the federation had reached the highest levels in its history, exceeding even the Gilded Age and Great Depression. In 2007 the richest tenth of Americans accounted for half of all income, while the richest 1 percent had seen their share nearly triple since 1994.[8]

But if the Northern alliance and Dixie bloc have stood in near-constant monolithic opposition to each other, what accounts for the shift in power over the years? The answer: the behavior of the three "swing" nations.

Neither of the continent's superpower blocs has ever truly dominated the U.S. government without first winning the backing of at least two of the swing nations: the Midlands, El Norte, and the Far West. From 1877 to 1933 the Northern alliance controlled the federation with the support of the Far West and the Midlands. The era of Dixie ascendancy and dominance—1980 to 2008—was founded upon an alliance with the Far West and the Midlands, and on the presidential bids of conservative Anglos from El Norte: Barry Goldwater, Richard Nixon, and Ronald Reagan. Even in periods when neither bloc was truly dominant, governing majorities were created through intranational alliances: between Dixie, New Netherland, and the Midlands in the New Deal Era; between the northern nations and Appalachian progressives in the 1960s; and between El Norte, Tidewater, and the Northern alliance in the election of Barack Obama.

What, then, are the three swing nations' priorities?

The Midlands is the most philosophically autonomous of the nations, for centuries leery of both meddlesome, messianic Yankees and authoritarian Dixie zealots. Midlanders share the Yankees' identification with middle-class society, the Borderlanders' distrust of government intrusion, the New Netherlanders' commitment to cultural pluralism, and the Deep South's aversion to strident activism. It's truly a middle-of-the-road American society and, as such, has rarely sided unambiguously with one coalition, candidate, or movement. When it has—for FDR in the 1930s,

Reagan in the 1980s, or Obama in 2008—it has been at a time of profound national stress and in reaction to perceived excess. It's no accident that the Midlands straddle—but do not control—many of the key "battleground states" at the turn of the millennium: Pennsylvania, Ohio, Illinois, and Missouri. Its modern presidents, Truman and Eisenhower, were both "compromise candidates" who were able to defuse intrabloc rivalries to win the White House for one party or the other.

By contrast, the Far West's agenda has been clear: to escape the colonial domination of the Northern alliance while maintaining the stream of federal subsidies upon which its way of life was built. In the late nineteenth century, Far Western congressional representatives voted in lockstep with the Northern alliance because they were bought and paid for by Yankee- , New York–, or San Francisco–based railroad, mining, ranching, and timber interests. But during the New Deal, World War II, and the Cold War, federal government spending transformed the region via the creation of airports, highways, dams, irrigation and water transfer projects, research laboratories, military bases, academies, research institutes, and a profusion of defense industry plants. The nation developed homegrown industrial and agricultural interests, senators with local power bases, and an agenda set in Las Vegas, Phoenix, and Denver rather than New York, Cleveland, and Chicago.[9]

As a result, since 1968 it has aligned itself with the Dixie bloc out of a shared interest in gelding federal regulatory power for the benefit of large corporate interests. From its emergence in the 1880s until 1968, the Far West's presidential vote reflected that of the Northern alliance in nearly every election. From 1968 to 2004 it almost always voted for the candidate favored by the Dixie bloc, except when Dixie has spurned a conservative in favor of a liberal Southerner. In the same period, its congressional representatives sided with their Deep Southern counterparts to pass tax cuts, oppose health care and financial reform, and roll back environmental regulations. Its affinity with Dixie is limited, however, as its people have a strong libertarian streak that balks at restrictions on dissent and civil liberties. In the 2008 election, fault lines began to appear in the Dixie–Far West partnership, with Colorado and Nevada voting for the northern candidate (Obama) over a Far Western native son who chose to run on a Dixie platform (John McCain); Republican support had ebbed in nearly every county in the region, leaving McCain with a thin margin of victory even in "ultraconservative" Montana.

In the future, however, the balance of power will be largely shaped by the affinities of the rapidly growing, increasingly assertive Hispanics of El Norte. Until the second half of the twentieth century, the other nations generally ignored El Norte, a national culture that controlled no state governments and was assumed to be on the road to extinction, its various elements absorbed into the Far West, Greater Appalachia, and the Deep South. *Norteños*—isolated in enclaves in the Far West and marginalized by the racial caste system in the border states under Dixie control—were expected to go quietly the way of the American Indians.

But *norteños* began reasserting control over the political and cultural life of New Mexico, south Texas, and southern Arizona, and making deep inroads in Southern California. They've elected their own to city halls from San Antonio to Los Angeles, the governorship of New Mexico, the U.S. Congress, and the U.S. Senate seats for New Mexico and Colorado. As discussed in chapter 23, their numbers have increased rapidly both in raw totals and percentage of the federation's population, triggering talk of a *reconquista* of land lost after the Mexican-American War. Already the largest U.S. minority, Hispanics of all origins are expected to account for a quarter of the federation's population by 2025. In 2010, *norteños* already constituted a majority in Los Angeles, San Antonio, and El Paso and a plurality in the state of New Mexico. Some observers believe that, if Mexico were to break up, several of its northern states might seek annexation or political affiliation with the United States, further increasing El Norte's influence and prestige within the federation. The bloc that wins the allegiance of El Norte stands to control American affairs.[10]

For 150 years the Dixie bloc has done itself few favors in neglecting to win *norteño* hearts and minds. The Deep South's caste system and Appalachia's commitment to white supremacy led to the oppression and alienation of *Tejanos* and New Mexico Hispanos. Anglo colonists in Arizona and southern California—a majority of whom hailed from Dixie and have voted for Dixie candidates—didn't go out of their way to integrate Spanish-speaking people into politics and society while they were in power. As a result, El Norte's activists and political leaders have aligned themselves with northerners while its electorate has voted with

Yankeedom in every presidential election since 1988. With Dixie and Far Western populists railing against the dangers of Mexican immigration, El Norte can be expected to back the Northern bloc for some time to come.

Finally, let's step back for a little perspective.

Consider for a moment what U.S. politics and society might be like if the Dixie bloc never existed, or if the Confederacy had peacefully seceded in 1861. You don't have to stretch your imagination, because this very scenario has been playing out north of the U.S. border.

Canada, created in 1867, is a federation composed of a slightly different mix of nations than the United States. To the east are Canada's older English-speaking societies—the Yankee Maritimes—and New France. In the center are Midland-settled southern Ontario and Manitoba, with their pluralistic and pacifistic leanings, home to both the federal capital, Ottawa, and Canada's most important city, Toronto. Beyond the 100th meridian the Far West spreads across the border, carrying libertarian thought and the extractive economy through much of Saskatchewan, Alberta, and interior British Columbia, and on into southern parts of the Yukon and Northwest Territories. British Columbia's Pacific coast is an extension of the Left Coast, with environmentally conscious, socially liberal Vancouver and Victoria identifying more closely with their neighbors on Puget Sound and the Olympic Peninsula than with the right-leaning energy magnates over the mountains in Calgary.

Anglo Canadians often complain that they lack a shared cultural identity other than "not being American," and there is some basis for that. English-speaking Canada is really four nations—five, if you count the British Isles' lost colony of Newfoundland, whose people still say they are "going to Canada" when they board ferries to the mainland. As in the United States, the Yanks, Midlanders, and Left Coasters get along fairly well, supporting national health care, gun control, and multiculturalism. All experience friction with the Far West, which was the stronghold of the Reform Party, which sought to reduce taxes, regulations, and the size and scope of federal services while championing agribusiness, free trade, and the oil, gas, and oil shale industries. (It merged with the Conservatives in 2000, and at this writing has one of its own, Stephen Harper of Calgary, leading the country as prime minister.) After the divisive 2000 U.S. election, a map started circulating on the Internet dividing the continent into two countries, "the United States of Canada" and "Jesusland." Within days, a Canadian wag had added a third country, "Alberta," suggesting the depth of the philosophical divide between the Far West and other parts of Canada.

As discussed in chapter 13, the nations in Canada had limited control over their own destinies during the century after the American Revolution, a period when British aristocrats in imperial service governed. This altered the course of their development, preventing the spread of strong town governments in the Maritimes, for example. But what has really made Canada fundamentally different from the United States is that the four Anglo nations squared off not against an authoritarian, white supremacist Dixie bloc but rather against an extremely open-minded, socially relaxed, socialist-minded society founded on unusually enlightened ideas about race and multiculturalism.

Comparative early-twenty-first-century sociological surveys have found that New France is the most postmodern nation in North America. It is the region with the lowest proportion of people who believe in the devil (29 percent) and hell (26 percent). Asked if they agreed that the "father of the family must be master in his own house," only 15 percent of Québécois said yes, compared with 21 percent of Far Western Canadians, 29 percent of New Englanders, and 71 percent of respondents in Alabama, Mississippi, and Tennessee. Another academic pollster found them to be more tolerant of homosexuality, extramarital affairs, prostitution, abortion, divorce, and having neighbors with AIDS, large families, drug problems, or emotional instability. Québec, one scholar found, was the region of North America with the highest degree of enlightened individualism and the least respect for traditional forms of authority. (British Columbia and New England were its closest rivals in this regard, Dixie states its polar opposite.) Montréal, New France's metropolis, reflects many of these attitudes, combining "the tolerance of Amsterdam, the élan of Paris, and the fine dining of the San Francisco Bay" with a large bohemian quarter (the Plateau) reminiscent of the Greenwich Village of old. While the Dixie bloc pulls the U.S. federation hard to the right, New France pulls Canada well to the left.[11]

Champlain's legacy has also, via New France, enabled Canada to build a remarkably successful multicultural society since the cultural revolution of the 1960s. French and English have equal standing in the federation, of course, and Québec has been recognized as a "separate society" and allowed to conduct its affairs entirely in French. But its multiculturalism extends beyond that to the Canadians' attitudes toward its Native American peoples, many of whom have been able to maintain their cultural distinctiveness, language, and customs, even passing some on to Canadian society at large. Due to New France's benign attitude toward Indians, many northern tribes are now reclaiming sovereignty over what amounts to a majority of the Canadian landmass and spurring the emergence of the largest nation of them all.

Epilogue

If the power struggles among the nations have profoundly shaped North America's history over the past four centuries, what might they hold for us in the future? Will the political map of the continent in the year 2100 look the same as it did in 1900 or 2000? Will it still be divided into three enormous political federations, or will it have morphed into something else: a Balkanized collection of nation-states along the lines of twentieth-century Europe; a loose E.U.-style confederation of sovereign nation-states stretching from Monterrey, Mexico, to the Canadian Arctic; a unitary state run according to biblical law as interpreted by the spiritual heirs of Jerry Falwell; a postmodernist utopian network of semisovereign, self-sustaining agricultural villages freed by technological innovations from the need to maintain larger governments at all? No one, if he or she is being both thoughtful and honest, has any idea.

What can be said is this: given the challenges facing the United States, Mexico, and, to a lesser extent, Canada, to assume that the continent's political boundaries will remain as they were in 2010 seems as farfetched as any of these other scenarios.

At this writing the United States appears to be losing its global preeminence and has been exhibiting the classic symptoms of an empire in decline. Kevin Phillips—the political strategist who, back in 1969, used regional ethnography to accurately predict the following forty years of American political development—has pointed out the parallels between late imperial Holland, Britain, and the present-day United States. Like its superpower predecessors, the United States has built up a staggering external trade deficit and sovereign debt while overreaching itself militarily and greatly increasing both the share of financial services in national output and the role of religious extremists in national political life. Once the great exporter of innovations, products, and financial capital, the United States is now deeply indebted to China, on which it relies for much of what its people consume and, increasingly, for the scientists and engineers needed by research and development firms and institutions. Its citizenry is deeply divided along regional lines, with some in the "Tea Party" movement adopting the rhetoric of the eighteenth-century Yankee minutemen, only with the British Parliament replaced by the federal Congress, and George III by their duly elected president. Its military has been mired in expensive and frustrating counterinsurgency wars in Mesopotamia and Central Asia, while barbarians have stormed the gates of its political and financial capitals, killing thousands in the surprise attacks of September 2001. Add in the damage to public confidence in the electoral system caused by the 2000 election, the near-total meltdown of the financial sector in 2008, and extreme political dysfunction in the Capitol, and it's clear the United States has not started the century auspiciously.

As of this writing the Mexican federation is in even worse shape. For years, leading foreign policy experts have been openly describing it as a failed state. Narcotics traffickers have bought the loyalty of state governors, police chiefs, and border guards while killing uncooperative judges, journalists, and officials; the situation has gotten so bad that the national army has been deployed to put down the drug cartels but doesn't appear to be winning. Ethnic Maya are fighting an ongoing independence struggle in Chiapas and other southern provinces. Northern Mexicans openly question what benefits they derive from their association with Mexico City, which takes their taxes and gives little in return. The capital region, in the words of political analyst Juan Enriquez, "continues to govern as if it were the old Aztec empire, extracting a tribute and expecting its wishes and demands to be catered to." It's not hard to imagine Mexico shattering in a time of crisis—a climate-change-related disaster, a global financial collapse, a major act of terrorism—freeing the Mexican half of El Norte to orient itself northward.[1]

Canada's national fractures have been obvious for some time, with New France pushing for outright independence right up through 1995. In that year 60 percent of Québec's Francophones voted in support of an independence referendum. The measure was narrowly defeated by the overwhelming opposition not only of the province's English-speaking minority but of its First Nation sections, which voted 9 to 1 against. It was probably the Native people of Canada, ironically enough, who saved the federation from breaking up entirely. Independence has been tabled as a key issue ever since, with most Québécois recognizing that if they left Canada, they would probably have to leave the northern two-thirds of their province behind, as the people there aren't part of the New French nation and have occupied the land since before the existence of France itself. The other nations have also made substantial concessions to New France since the 1970s. The federal government is officially bilingual, even as the province of Québec is allowed to be officially French only. New Brunswick—long dominated by its Yankee core—is now the only officially bilingual province in Canada, in recognition of the fact that its northern and eastern reaches are part of New France. The lower house of the federal parliament has recognized Québec as a "distinct society," while New French–style multiculturalism has become the civic religion of Canadians everywhere. Today, Canada is perhaps the most stable of the three North American federations, largely because the four Anglo nations, New France, and First Nation have made important compromises with one another. Canada has in effect rejected any illusion of being a nation-state with a single dominant culture. Whether that proves enough to preserve the federation in the long term remains to be seen.

One scenario that might preserve the status quo for the United States would be for its nations to follow the Canadian example and compromise on their respective cultural agendas for the sake of unity. Unfortunately, neither the Dixie bloc nor the Northern alliance is likely to agree to major concessions to the other. The majority of Yankees, New Netherlanders, and Left Coasters simply aren't going to accept living in an evangelical Christian theocracy with weak or nonexistent social, labor, or environmental protections, public school systems, and checks on corporate power in politics. Most Deep Southerners will resist paying higher taxes to underwrite the creation of a public health insurance system; a universal network of well-resourced, unionized, and avowedly secular public schools; tuition-free public universities where science—not the King James Bible—guides inquiry; taxpayer-subsidized public transportation, high-speed railroad networks, and renewable energy projects; or vigorous regulatory bodies to ensure compliance with strict financial, food safety, environmental, and campaign finance laws. Instead, the "red" and "blue" nations will continue to wrestle with one another for control over federal policy, each doing what it can to woo the "purple" ones to their cause, just as they have since they gathered at the First Continental Congress.

Another outside possibility is that, faced with a major crisis, the federation's leaders will betray their oath to uphold the U.S. Constitution, the primary adhesive holding the union together. In the midst of, say, a deadly pandemic outbreak or the destruction of several cities by terrorists, a fearful public might condone the suspension of civil rights, the dissolution of Congress, or the incarceration of Supreme Court justices. One can easily imagine circumstances in which some nations are happy with the new order and others deeply opposed to it. With the Constitution abandoned, the federation could well disintegrate, forming one or more confederations of like-minded regions. Chances are these new sovereign entities would be based on state boundaries, because state governors and legislators would be the most politically legitimate actors in such a scenario. States dominated by the three Northern alliance nations—New York, New Jersey, and the New England, Great Lakes, and Pacific Northwest states—might form one or more confederations. States controlled by the Deep South—South Carolina, Georgia, Alabama, Mississippi, and Louisiana—might form another. The mountain and High Plains states of the Far West would constitute an obvious third. The situation might be more complicated within often-divided Greater Appalachia or the "nationally mixed" states of Texas, California, Pennsylvania, Ohio, and Arizona. It's not impossible to imagine some of the resulting coalitions extending into Canada or, in the case of El Norte, Mexico. If this extreme scenario were to come to pass, North America would likely be a far more dangerous, volatile, and unstable place, inviting meddling from imperial powers overseas. If this scenario of crisis and breakup seems far-fetched, consider the fact that, forty years ago, the leaders of the Soviet Union would have thought the same thing about their continent-spanning federation.

Or perhaps the federation will simply reach accommodation over time as its component nations come to agree that the status quo isn't serving anyone well. A time might come when the only issue on which the nations find common ground is the need to free themselves from one another's veto power. Perhaps they'd join together on Capitol Hill to pass laws and constitutional amendments granting more powers to the states or liquidating many of the functions of the central government. The United States might continue to exist, but its powers might be limited to national defense, foreign policy, and the negotiation of interstate trade agreements. It would, in other words, resemble the European Union or the original Confederation of 1781. If that were to happen, its component states could be counted on to behave in accordance with their respective national heritages. Yankee New Englanders might cooperate closely with one another, much as the Scandinavian countries do within Europe. Texans might finally utilize their constitutional right (under the terms of their annexation to the United States) to split into as many as five individual states. Illinoisans might agree to divide downstate from Chicagoland. Southern, northern, and interior California might each become a separate state. The external borders of this retooled United States might remain in place, or perhaps some Canadian or Mexican provinces might apply for membership in this looser, more decentralized federation. Throughout history far stranger things than this have happened.

But one thing is certain: if Americans seriously want the United States to continue to exist in something like its current form, they had best respect the fundamental tenets of our unlikely union. It cannot survive if we end the separation of church and state or institute the Baptist equivalent of Sharia law. We won't hold together if presidents appoint political ideologues to the Justice Department or the Supreme Court of the United States, or if party loyalists try to win elections by trying to stop people from voting rather than winning them over with their ideas. The union can't function if national coalitions continue to use House and Senate rules to prevent important issues from being debated in the open because members know their positions wouldn't withstand public scrutiny. Other sovereign democratic states have central governments more corrupted than our own, but most can fall back on unifying elements we lack: common ethnicity, a shared religion, or near-universal consensus on many fundamental political issues. The United States needs its central government to function cleanly, openly, and efficiently because it's one of the few things binding us together.

What might North America have been like if none of the ten Euro-Atlantic nations had ever been established? If the original Indian nations—the First Nations in Canadian parlance—had avoided the devastating epidemics of the sixteenth and seventeenth centuries and continued to develop on their own terms, what might they have been like today?

Actually, it seems we're about to find out.

In the far north a very old nation is reemerging after centuries in the cold. Across the northern third of the continent, aboriginal people have been reclaiming sovereignty over traditional territories from northern Alaska to Greenland and nearly everywhere in between. In this sprawling region of dense boreal forests, Arctic tundra, and treeless, glaciated islands, many native peoples never signed away the rights to their land, which they still occupy and, to a surprising degree, continue to live off using the techniques of their forefathers. They've won key legal decisions in Canada and Greenland that give them considerable leverage over what happens in their territories, forcing energy, mining, and timber companies to come to them, hat in hand, for permission to move forward on resource extraction projects. In 1999 Canada's Inuit—they don't want to be called "Eskimos"—won their own Canadian territory, Nunavut, which is larger than Alaska. The Inuit of Greenland control their own affairs as an autonomous, self-governing unit of the Kingdom of Denmark and are moving aggressively toward full independence.

Together with the Innu, Kaska, Dene, Cree, and dozens of other tribes, the northern aboriginal people have cultural dominance over much of Alaska, the Yukon, Northwest Territories, and Labrador, all of Nunavut and Greenland, northwestern interior British Columbia, and the northern swaths of Alberta, Saskatchewan, Manitoba, Ontario, and Québec. This eleventh nation—First Nation—is far and away the largest of all by geography (much bigger than the continental United States), but the smallest by population (less than 300,000, all told).

First Nation is a highly communalistic society. Most tribal land in the far north is owned in common under a form of title that prevents it from ever being sold to an individual or exploited in such a way that diminishes its value to future generations. In Greenland there is no private property at all: everyone is allowed to responsibly use the people's shared land, but it is thought the height of absurdity that any one person should "own" it, which would be comparable to someone's asserting ownership of the wind. Inuit—whether dwelling in Labrador, Nunavut, Greenland, or Alaska—still hunt, fish, and gather a substantial amount of their food, and all of those "home foods" and the implements associated with them are generally regarded as common property as well. If a hunter kills a seal, it's handed over to whoever needs it. Villages have communal freezers that anyone can access—free of charge or accounting—because food cannot belong to one person. If the tribe engages in an industrial enterprise, the proceeds belong to everyone.[2]

Not surprisingly, First Nation has an extremely strong environmental ethic. In Canada—where a revolutionary 1999 supreme court decision recognized Indian oral histories as legitimate evidence in establishing precolonial territories—aboriginal people are setting the terms by which oil, gas, mining, and timber companies have to abide. The 2,000-person Innu nation in Labrador has created a top-notch, ecosystem-based forestry management plan for their ancestral lands in Labrador, which at 17.5 million acres, are larger than West Virginia. They hired professional forest ecologists to identify areas that shouldn't be cut for the good of wildlife and water quality and added their own hunting, fishing, and trapping grounds. In the end, 60 percent of their territory was placed off-limits to loggers; the rest is sustainably harvested for the good of the collective nation. Similar interventions have resulted in a 57.6-million-acre forestry plan for Kaska lands in northern British Columbia and the Yukon and a new national park and wildlife refuge in the Northwest Territories that is eleven times the size of Yellowstone. "There's a new game in town where First Nations are driving outcomes across the board and trying to achieve a balance between their land, history, the modern economy, and the future," says Larry Innes, who has worked with tribes across the Canadian north as director of the Canadian Boreal Initiative, an environmental initiative financed by the Pew Charitable Trusts. "Canada is really one of the last, best places where we can get the balance right."[3]

In both Canada and Greenland the Inuit have been at the forefront of the climate change battle, as warmer temperatures are already disrupting their way of life. In Ilulissat and other northern Greenland settlements, hunters are reluctantly giving up their sled dog teams because sea ice no longer forms in winter. (You can't travel by "land" in Greenland because rugged mountains and mile-tall glacial fronts block every route.) Alaskan villages have already had to be moved to escape the advancing sea and melting permafrost. Polar bears and other game are vanishing. Meanwhile drug abuse, alcoholism, and teen suicide have become endemic. "In one lifetime, our way of life has been transformed," says Sheila Watt-Cloutier of Nunavut, whose climate change work as chair of the Inuit Circumpolar Council earned her a 2007 Nobel Peace Prize nomination. "We've been seeing the breakdown of our society."[4]

Greenlanders, for one, have decided the best way to move forward is to be masters of their own destiny. In 2009 they achieved a state of near-independence from Denmark following a self-rule referendum supported by 76 percent of voters. Greenlanders now control the criminal justice, social welfare, and health care systems, land-use planning, fisheries management, and environmental regulations, education, transportation, and even the issuance of offshore oil exploration contracts. "It's a natural thing for a population to run their own country," says the island's foreign minister, Aleqa Hammond. "We don't think like Europeans, we don't look like Europeans, and we're not in Europe. It's not that we have bad feelings about Denmark, but it's a natural thing for a population with its own race and identity to want to cut its strings to foreign rule." Securing independence won't be easy, she admits, given that the country is still dependent on Danish government subsidies to maintain its government, hospitals, and generous social welfare system. But she believes Greenlanders have a secret weapon: women like herself. "You'll notice here in Greenland that the women are very strong, not only physically strong, but in all respects: in politics, business, education level and everything," she says, adding that roughly half the island's parliament is female. "Our bishop is a woman, most mayors are women and so forth. There's never been a fight for gender equality in Greenland. Women have always been powerful in our society. Our God was female, and when the Christians came to Greenland [in the eighteenth century] and said 'our God is mighty and great and he looks like us,' our first reaction was: a *He*? Because not only are our women smarter and more pretty than men, they also give birth, they give life, and when there are problems in society, the women are the ones who are fighting to be sure the society survives. The Inuit language has no difference between he or she, or between mankind and animal," she adds. "They're all equal."[5]

Communalistic, environmentally minded, and female-dominated, the people of First Nation will have a very different approach to the global challenges of the twenty-first century from that of the other nations of the continent and the world. And starting in Greenland, First Nation is building a series of nation-states of its own, giving North America's indigenous peoples a chance to show the rest of the world how they would blend post-modern life with premodern folkways.

ACKNOWLEDGMENTS AND SUGGESTED READING

American Nations is largely a work of synthesis and, as such, has many intellectual forebears, informants, and godparents. A few works were especially helpful to me in thinking about North America's regional cultures, and I recommend them heartily for those wishing to further explore their development, expansion, and characteristics.

Joel Garreau first advanced the notion that North America was defined by international rivalries in *The Nine Nations of North America*, which appeared in 1981 and came into my hands as a junior high school student shortly thereafter. As I mentioned at the outset, Garreau's argument was ahistorical, and so, to my thinking, couldn't quite hit the nail on the head. However, his overall point—that the continent's real, meaningful fissures did not correspond to official political boundaries—was spot-on and helped inspire my own inquiry nearly three decades later.

Some of my favorite works on regionalism are also among the most accessible to the general reader. David Hackett Fischer's *Albion's Seed* (1989) posits that four "British folkways" were transposed to British North America in the colonial period that roughly correspond to Yankeedom, the Midlands, Tidewater, and Greater Appalachia. Fischer's focus is on demonstrating continuities between specific regional cultures in the British Isles and their North American splinters, a thesis that's taken some knocks from other academics. I think his most important contribution is to have substantiated the presence, origins, and salient characteristics of distinct regional cultures on this side of the pond. One of Fischer's more recent works, *Champlain's Dream* (2008), did much the same for New France. Russell Shorto's excellent *Island at the Center of the World* (2004) brought the Dutch period of New York's history alive and argued for its lasting impact on the culture of the Big Apple—a thesis I heartily endorse. Kevin Phillips's prophetic 1969 study *The Emerging Republican Majority* identified many of the key fault lines between regional cultures and used them to predict four decades of American political developments; two of his later works—*The Cousins' Wars* (1999) and *American Theocracy* (2006)—draw on regional differences in exploring Anglo-American relations and the decline of American power respectively. In *Made in Texas* (2004), a scathing attack on the Dixification of American politics, Michael Lind identifies regional tensions between what I would call the Appalachian and Deep Southern sections of his home state, and some of their salient policy differences in the late twentieth and early twenty-first centuries.

Among the more technical scholarly works, a few stand out. Wilbur Zelinsky's *The Cultural Geography of the United States* (1973) developed useful concepts for mapping and analyzing regional cultures. Raymond Gastil's *Cultural Regions of the United States* (1975) fleshed out regional variations in a variety of subjects and social indicators. *Imperial Texas: An Interpretive Essay in Cultural Geography* (1969) by Donald W. Meinig used similar approaches to examine the oft-discussed cultural fissures in Texas. Frederick Merk's *History of the Westward Movement* (1978) and Henry Glassie's *Pattern in the Material Folk Culture of the Eastern United States* (1968) are invaluable in tracing settlement flows.

Another set of works shed light on important aspects of particular nations. E. Digby Baltzell—scholar of the American elite—compared and contrasted the cultures of the leading families of the intellectual capitals of Yankeedom and the Midlands in his exhaustive 1979 study, *Puritan Boston and Quaker Philadelphia*. For understanding El Norte's Spanish heritage, David J. Weber's *Spanish Frontier in North America* (1992) and *The Mexican Frontier, 1821–1846: The American Southwest Under Mexico* (1982) provide essential background. Rhys Issac's *The Transformation of Virginia 1740–1790* (1982) describes the Tidewater gentry's world at its apogee in wonderful detail. For New Netherland in the Dutch era, I recommend Oliver A. Rink's 1986 study *Holland on the Hudson: An Economic and Social History of Dutch New York*. On the Deep South and the Barbadian system on which it was first modeled, turn to Richard S. Dunn's 1972 study *Sugar and Slaves: The Rise of the Planter Class in the English West Indies, 1624–1713* and his April 1971 paper "English Sugar Islands and the Founding of South Carolina" in the *South Carolina Historical Magazine*. The classic—and very chilling—academic examination of Deep

Southern culture in the early twentieth century is *Deep South: A Social Anthropological Study of Case and Class*, published by a team of researchers at the University of Chicago in 1941. On the spread of the nations into the Midwest and the implications thereof see especially Richard Power, *Planting Corn Belt Culture: The Impress of The Upland Southerner and Yankee in the Old Northwest* (1953); Paul Kleppner, *The Cross of Culture: A Social Analysis of Midwestern Politics, 1850–1900* (1970); and Nicole Etcheson, *The Emerging Midwest: Upland Southerners and the Political Culture of the Old Northwest, 1787–1861* (1996). For the Far West and Left Coast, start with Marc Reisner's *Cadillac Desert* (1986), David Alan Johnson's *Founding the Far West: California, Oregon, and Nevada, 1840–1890* (1992), and Kevin Starr's, *Americans and the California Dream, 1850–1915* (1973). My thanks to all of these authors—and to many others whose works appear in the endnotes—for creating so many fine ingredients.

My greatest debt is to my wife, Sarah Skillin Woodard, who shared in this project's many stresses while in graduate school and, much of the time, pregnant. As fate would have it, *American Nations* and our first child wound up being due at the same time, and Sarah continued editing the manuscript and offering me active support and assistance at a time when these roles should have been reversed. Thank you, my love; you know this would never have been finished without your many contributions and sacrifices. Our son, Henry, who ultimately beat this book into the world, has been a joy and inspiration, even if his editorial advice is sometimes difficult to interpret.

My friend and journalistic colleague Samuel Loewenberg—who splits his time between Berlin, Geneva, and the relief camps of Africa—took the time to read sections of *American Nations* and offered invaluable advice at a time when it was needed; thanks much, Sam, I owe you yet another one. My agent, Jill Grinberg, not only continued to provide me with stellar representation, but at a critical juncture, provided assistance that went far beyond the call of duty; no author could ask for a better person in his corner. At Viking, I am grateful to my editor, Rick Kot, for his support and sound advice on both this book and *The Lobster Coast*. Thanks also to designers Paul Buckley at Viking and Oliver Munday in Washington, D.C. (for the cover); to Viking's Francesca Belanger (for designing the book itself); to Sean Wilkinson of Portland, Maine (for creating the maps and patiently revising them); and to copy editor Cathy Dexter (wherever you are).

And thanks to you, the reader, for taking this journey with me. If you enjoyed the trip, do tell your friends.

April 2011
Portland, Maine

NOTES

Introduction

1. Miriam Horn, "How the West Was Really Won," *U.S. News & World Report*, 21 May 1990, p. 56; Samuel L. Huntington, *Who Are We? The Challenges to America's National Identity*, New York: Simon & Schuster, 2004, pp. 67–70; James Allen Smith, *The Idea Brokers: Think Tanks and the Rise of the New Policy Elite*, New York: Free Press, 1991, pp. 179–181; Barack Obama, "Remarks on Iowa Caucus Night," Des Moines, IA, 3 January 2008.
2. Jim Webb, *Born Fighting*, New York: Broadway Books, 2004, pp. 13, 255; Angela Brittingham and C. Patricia de la Cruz, *Ancestry: 2000*, Washington, D.C.: U.S. Census Bureau, 2004, p. 8.
3. Michael Adams, *Fire and Ice: The United States, Canada, and the Myth of Converging Values*, Toronto: Penguin Canada, 2003, pp. 81–83.
4. Oscar J. Martinez, *Troublesome Border*, Tucson: University of Arizona Press, 1988, pp. 107–108.
5. Haya El Nasser, "U.S. Hispanic Population to Triple by 2050," *USA Today*, 12 February 2008; Sebastian Rotella, "Eyewitness: Carlos Fuentes," *Los Angeles Times*, 28 September 1994.
6. Hans Kurath, *A Word Geography of the Eastern United States*, Ann Arbor, MI: University of Michigan Press, 1949, p. 91; Henry Glassie, *Pattern in the Material Folk Culture of the Eastern United States*, Philadelphia: University of Pennsylvania Press, 1968, p. 39; Raymond D. Gastil, *Cultural Regions of the United States*, Seattle: University of Washington Press, 1975, pp. 11, 49, 83, 107, 139; Wilbur Zelinsky, "An Approach to the Religious Geography of the United States," *Annals of the Association of American Geographers*, Vol. 51, No. 2, 1961, p. 193; Kevin Phillips, *The Emerging Republican Majority*, New Rochelle, NY: Arlington House, 1969, pp. 47, 209, 299; Frederick Jackson Turner, *The United States: 1830–1850*, New York: Holt, Rinehart & Winston, 1935 (appended map); Frank Newport, "State of the States: Importance of Religion" (press release), Gallup Inc., 28 January 2009, available at http://www.gallup.com/poll/114022/State-States-Importance-Religion.aspx; U.S. Census Bureau, "Table 228: Educational Attainment by State: 1990 to 2007" in *Statistical Abstract of the United States 2010*, available online via http://www.census.gov/compendia/statab/2010/tables/10s0228.pdf.
7. U.S. Census Bureau, *Profile of General Demographic Characteristics: 2000, Geographic Area: New York, N.Y.*, Table DP-1, p. 2, online at http://censtats.census.gov/data/NY/1603651000.pdf.
8. Wilbur Zelinsky, *The Cultural Geography of the United States*, Englewood Cliffs, NJ: Prentice-Hall, 1973, pp. 13–14.

9. Bill Bishop, *The Big Sort*, New York: Houghton Mifflin Harcourt, 2008, pp. 9–10, 45.
10. Donald W. Meinig, *Imperial Texas: An Interpretive Essay in Cultural Geography*, Austin: University of Texas Press, 1969, pp. 110–124; Zelinsky (1973), pp. 114–115.
11. Serge Schmemann, "The New French President's Roots Are Worth Remembering," *New York Times*, 15 May 2007.

Chapter 1: Founding El Norte

1. John H. Burns, "The Present Status of the Spanish-Americans of New Mexico," *Social Forces*, December 1949, pp. 133–138.
2. Charles C. Mann, *1491: New Revelations of the Americas Before Columbus*, New York: Knopf, 2005, pp. 102–103.
3. Alan Taylor, *American Colonies: The Settling of North America*, New York: Penguin, 2001, p. 53–54; Mann, pp. 102–103.
4. Mann (2005), pp. 140–141; Taylor (2001), p. 57.
5. Thomas Campanella, *A Discourse Touching the Spanish Monarchy* [1598], London: William Prynne, 1659, pp. 9, 223.
6. David J. Weber, *The Mexican Frontier, 1821–1846*, Albuquerque: University of New Mexico Press, 1982, p. 232; David J. Weber, *The Spanish Frontier in North America*, New Haven, CT: Yale University Press, 1992, p. 322.
7. Taylor (2001), pp. 460–461; Weber (1992), pp. 306–308; Weber (1982), pp. 45–46.
8. Taylor (2001), p. 61.
9. James D. Kornwolf and Georgiana Kornwolf, *Architecture and Town Planning in Colonial North America, Vol. 1*, Baltimore: Johns Hopkins University, 2002, pp. 122, 140; Robert E. Wright, "Spanish Missions," in *Handbook of Texas Online* at http://www.tshaonline.org/handbook/online/ articles/SS/its2.html.
10. Weber (1992), p. 306; Jean Francois Galaup de La Perouse (1786) as quoted in James J. Rawls, "The California Mission as Symbol and Myth," *California History*, Fall 1992, p. 344.
11. Russell K. Skowronek, "Sifting the Evidence: Perceptions of Life at the Ohlone (Costanoan) Missions of Alta California," *Ethnohistory*, Fall 1998, pp. 697–699.
12. Weber (1982), pp. 123–124, 279.
13. Weber (1992), pp. 15, 324.
14. Clark S. Knowlton, "Patron-Peon Pattern among the Spanish Americans of New Mexico," *Social Forces*, October 1962, pp. 12–17; Gastil (1975), p. 249.
15. Phillips (1969), pp. 282–283; Andrew Gumbel, *Steal This Vote: Dirty Elections and the Rotten History of Democracy in America*, New York: Nation Books, 2005, pp. 17–22.
16. Weber (1982), pp. 243, 284; Martinez (1988), pp. 107–111.
17. Taylor (2001), pp. 82, 458–460; Paul Horgan, *Great River: The Rio Grande in North American History*, Vol. I, New York: Holt, Rinehart & Winston, 1954, pp. 225–226; Weber (1982), pp. 92, 123.
18. Weber (1992), pp. 326–328; Manuel G. Gonzalez, *Mexicanos: A History of Mexicans in the United States*, Bloomington: Indiana University Press, 1999, p. 53; Martinez (1988), p. 107.

19. Edward Larocque Tinker, "The Horsemen of the Americas," *Hispanic American Historical Review*, May 1962, p. 191; Odie B. Faulk, "Ranching in Spanish Texas," *Hispanic American Historical Review*, May 1965, pp. 257, 166; C. Allan Jones, *Texas Roots: Agricultural and Rural Life Before the Civil War*, College Station: Texas A&M University, 2005, pp. 12–16; Peter Tamony, "The Ten-Gallon or Texas Hat," *Western Folklore*, April 1965, pp. 116–117.
20. Hubert Howe Bancroft, *The Works of Hubert Howe Bancroft*, Vol. 19, San Francisco: The History Company, 1886, p. 162; C. Wayne Hanselka and D. E. Kilgore, "The Nueces Valley: The Cradle of the Western Livestock Industry," *Rangelands*, October 1987, p. 196.

Chapter 2: Founding New France

1. Samuel Eliot Morison, *Samuel de Champlain: Father of New France*, Boston: Little, Brown & Co., 1972, p. 41.
2. David Hackett Fischer, *Champlain's Dream*, New York: Simon & Schuster, 2008, pp. 21, 37–45, 134.
3. Ibid., pp. 118, 134, 342, 528–529.
4. Samuel de Champlain, *Voyages of Samuel de Champlain, 1604-1618*, Vol. 4, New York: Scribner & Sons, 1907, pp. 54–55; Helena Katz, "Where New France Was Forged," *The Globe & Mail* (Toronto), 26 July 2004.
5. Fischer (2008), pp. 210–217.
6. Morison (1972), pp. 94–95; Fischer (2008), pp. 212–219. The teens were Charles de Biencourt (future governor and vice admiral of Acadia), Charles La Tour (future governor of Acadia), and Robert du Pont-Grave (who became a leading fur trader in the St. John Valley).
7. Fischer (2008), pp. 380, 401, 457; Cornelius J. Jaenan, "Problems of Assimilation in New France, 1603–1645," *French Historical Studies*, Spring 1966, p. 275.
8. Sigmund Diamond, "An Experiment in 'Feudalism': French Canada in the Seventeenth Century," *William and Mary Quarterly*, January 1961, pp. 5–13.
9. One was my eighth-great-grandmother, who came to Québec in 1671, married another recent immigrant, and bore at least four children.
10. Peter N. Moogk, "Reluctant Exiles: Emigrants from France in Canada before 1760," *William and Mary Quarterly*, July 1989, pp. 471, 477–484, 488; Stanislas A. Lortie and Adjutor Rivard, *L'Origine et le parler de Canadiens-français*, Paris: Honoré Champion, 1903, p. 11; Fischer (2008), pp. 472–488.
11. Moogk (1989), pp. 497; John Ralston Saul, *A Fair Country: Telling Truths About Canada*, Toronto: Penguin Canada, 2008, pp. 9, 11; Diamond (1961), pp. 25, 30.
12. Diamond (1961), p. 30; Saul (2008), pp. 10–11; Alaric and Gretchen F. Faulkner, "Acadian Settlement 1604–1674," in Richard W. Judd et al., eds., *Maine: The Pine Tree State from Prehistory to the Present*, Orono: University of Maine Press, 1994, p. 93; Owen Stanwood, "Unlikely Imperialist: The Baron of Saint-Castin and the Transformation of the Northeastern Borderlands," *French Colonial History*, Vol. 5, 2004, pp. 48–49.
13. Diamond (1961), pp. 21–23.

14. Ibid., pp. 22–23, 28–29; Robert Forster, "France in America," *French Historical Studies*, Spring 2000, pp. 242–243.
15. Moogk (1989), p. 464.

Chapter 3: Founding Tidewater

1. Taylor (2001), pp. 129–131; John Smith, "A True Relation (1608)" in Lyon Gardiner Tyler, ed., *Narratives of Early Virginia*, New York: Scribner & Sons, 1907, pp. 136–137; Cary Carson et al., "New World, Real World: Improvising English Culture in Seventeenth-Century Virginia," *Journal of Southern History*, February 2008, p. 40.
2. Carson et al., pp. 40, 68; Jack P. Greene, *Pursuits of Happiness: The Social Development of Early Modern British Colonies and the Formation of American Culture*, Chapel Hill: University of North Carolina Press, 1988, p. 9.
3. Carson et al., p. 69.
4. Taylor (2001), pp. 125–136.
5. Greene (1988), p. 12.
6. Oscar and Mary F. Handlin, "Origins of the Southern Labor System," *William and Mary Quarterly*, April 1950, p. 202; Bernard Bailyn, *Voyagers to the West: A Passage in the Peopling of America on the Eve of the Revolution*, New York: Knopf, 1986, pp. 345–348; David Hackett Fischer, *Albion's Seed: Four British Folkways in America*, New York: Oxford University Press, 1989, pp. 401–402.
7. Greene (1988), p. 84; Handlin & Handlin, pp. 202–204; James H. Brewer, "Negro Property Owners in Seventeenth-Century Virginia," *William and Mary Quarterly*, October 1955, pp. 576, 578.
8. Taylor (2001), pp. 136–137; Robert D. Mitchell, "American Origins and Regional Institutions: The Seventeenth Century Chesapeake," *Annals of the Association of American Geographers*, Vol. 73, No. 3, 1983, pp. 411–412.
9. Warren M. Billings, *Sir William Berkeley and the Forging of Colonial Virginia*, Baton Rouge: Louisiana State University Press, 2004, pp. 97–109; Kevin Phillips, *The Cousins' Wars: Religion, Politics, and the Triumph of Anglo-America*, New York: Basic Books, 1999, pp. 58–59.
10. Billings (2004), p. 107; Douglas Southall Freeman, *Robert E. Lee: A Biography*, New York: Charles Scribner, 1934, p. 160; Fischer (1989), pp. 212–219; David Hackett Fischer, "Albion and the Critics: Further Evidence and Reflection," *William and Mary Quarterly*, April 1991, p. 287; Willard Sterne Randall, *George Washington: A Life*, New York: Holt, 1998, pp. 9–13.
11. Wallace Notestein, *The English People on the Eve of Colonization*, New York: Harper & Row, 1954, pp. 45–60; John Toland, ed., *The Oceana and other works of James Harrington, with an account of his life*, London: T. Becket & T. Cadell, 1737, p. 100.
12. Martin H. Quitt, "Immigrant Origins of the Virginia Gentry: A Study of Cultural Transmission and Innovation," *William and Mary Quarterly*, October 1988, pp. 646–648.
13. Daniel J. Boorstin, *The Americans: The Colonial Experience*, New York: Vintage, 1958, pp. 106–107.

14. Carson et al., p. 84.
15. Fischer (1989), pp. 220–224.
16. Ibid., pp. 398–405; Rhys Isaac, *The Transformation of Virginia*, New York: W. W. Norton, 1982, pp. 134–135.
17. David Hackett Fischer, *Liberty and Freedom*, New York: Oxford University Press, 2005, pp. 5–9.
18. Isaac (1982), pp. 35–39, 66; Kornwolf and Kornwolf (2002), Vol. 2, pp. 578–588, 725; Fischer (1989), p. 412.
19. Fischer (1989), p. 388; Greene (1988), pp. 82–84.

Chapter 4: Founding Yankeedom

1. Boorstin (1958), pp. 1–9; Greene (1988), p. 19; William D. Williamson, *The History of the State of Maine,* Vol. 1, Hallowell, ME: Glazier, Masters & Co., 1839, pp. 380–381; Fischer (1989), p. 55; Alice Morse Earle, *The Sabbath in Puritan New England*, New York: Charles Scribner & Sons, 1902, pp. 246–247.
2. Greene (1988), pp. 20–21.
3. Alexis de Tocqueville, *Democracy in America* [1835], *Vol. 1*, New York: Knopf, 1945, pp. 32–33.
4. Thomas Jefferson Wertenbaker, *The Puritan Oligarchy*, New York: Charles Scribner's Sons, 1947, pp. 44–47; Fischer (1989), p. 38n.
5. Fischer (1989), pp. 130–131.
6. Taylor (2001), pp. 195, 202.
7. Emerson W. Baker, *The Devil of Great Island: Witchcraft and Conflict in Early New England*, New York: Palgrave MacMillan, 2007, pp. 134–139.
8. Richard Baxter, *Life and Times*, London: M. Sylvester, 1696, p. 51; D. E. Kennedy, *The English Revolution, 1642–1649*, New York: St. Martin's Press, 2000, p. 75 (quoting John Wildman).

Chapter 5: Founding New Netherland

1. Robert C. Ritchie, *The Duke's Province: A Study of New York Politics and Society, 1664–1691*, Chapel Hill: University of North Carolina Press, 1977, pp. 26–29; H. L. Mencken, *The American Language*, New York: Alfred Knopf, 1921, p. 348.
2. "Relation of 1647" in Reuben Gold Thwaites, ed., *The Jesuit Relations and Allied Documents*, Vol. 31, Cleveland: Burrows Brothers, 1898, p. 99
3. R. R. Palmer and Joel Colton, *A History of the Modern World to 1815*, New York: Alfred Knopf, 1983, pp. 159–163; Els M. Jacobs, *In Pursuit of Pepper and Tea: The Story of the Dutch East India Company*, Amsterdam: Netherlands Maritime Museum, 1991, pp. 11–18.
4. Russell Shorto, *Island at the Center of the World*, New York: Doubleday, 2004, pp. 94–100; James H. Tully, ed., *A Letter Concerning Toleration* [1689], Indianapolis, IN: Hackett Publishing, 1983, p. 1.
5. Joep de Koning, "Governors Island: Lifeblood of American Liberty," paper given at the AANS/NNS Conference, Albany, NY, 9 June 2006, pp. 3–4, 8–10; Shorto, (2004) pp. 94–96; William Bradford, "History of Plymouth Plantation [1648]" in

William T. Davis, ed., *Bradford's History of Plymouth Plantation 1606–1646*, New York: Charles Scribner's & Sons, 1920, p. 46.

6. Oliver A. Rink, *Holland on the Hudson: An Economic and Social History of Dutch New York*, Ithaca, NY: Cornell University Press, 1986, p. 156.
7. Ibid., pp. 98–115; Taylor (2001), p. 255.
8. Rink (1986), pp.233–235; Koning (2006), pp. 12–14; Thomas J. Archdeacon, *New York City, 1664–1710: Conquest and Change*, Ithaca, NY: Cornell University Press, 1979, p. 45.
9. Rink (1986), p. 227; p. 169; Laurence M. Hauptman and Ronald G. Knapp, "Dutch-Aboriginal interaction in New Netherland and Formosa: An historical geography of empire," *Proceedings of the American Philosophical Society*, April 1977, pp. 166–175; Shorto (2004), p. 124.
10. Ritchie (1977), pp. 150–151; William S. Pelletreau, *Genealogical and Family History of New York*, Vol. 1, New York: Lewis Publishing Co., 1907, pp. 147–153; Cuyler Reynolds, *Genealogical and Family History of Southern New York*, Vol. 3, New York: Lewis Publishing Co., 1914, p. 1371; Lyon Gardiner Tyler, *Encyclopedia of Virginia Biography*, Vol. 4, New York: Lewis Historical, 1915, p. 5.
11. Rink (1986), pp. 160–164, 169; Archdeacon (1979), p. 34.
12. Taylor (2001), pp. 259–60.
13. Shorto (2004), pp. 293–296; Ritchie (1977), pp. 31–33; Taylor (2001), p. 260.

Chapter 6: The Colonies' First Revolt

1. Chief Justice Joseph Dudley, quoted in John Gorham Palfrey, *History of New England*, Vol. 3, Boston: Little, Brown & Co, 1882, pp. 514–531.
2. Quote on troops from Palfrey, pp. 517n, 521–522; David S. Lovejoy, *The Glorious Revolution in America*, New York: Harper & Row, 1972, pp. 180–181, 189–193; "Declaration of the Gentlemen, Merchants, and Inhabitants of Boston and the Country adjacent, April 18, 1689," in Nathanael Byfield, *An Account of the Late Revolution in New England*, London: Richard Chitwell, 1689, pp. 12–24.
3. "Declaration," in Byfield, pp. 11–12.
4. Lovejoy (1972), p. 182; Increase Mather, "Narrative of the Miseries of New England, By Reason of an Arbitrary Government Erected There" (December 1688), in *Collections of the Massachusetts Historical Society*, 4th series, Vol. 9, Boston: Massachusetts Historical Society, 1871, p. 194.
5. Byfield (1689), p. 24.
6. Palfrey (1882), pp. 576–583; Lovejoy (1972), 240; David Lyon, *The Sailing Navy List*, London: Conway, 1993, p. 13.
7. "Depositions of Charles Lodowyck, New York: 25 July 1689," in J. W. Fortescue, ed., *Calendar of State Papers, Colonial Series, America and West Indies: 1689–1692*, London: His Majesty's Stationery Office, 1901, p. 108.
8. "Letter from members of the Dutch Church in New York to the Classis of Amsterdam," 21 October 1698, in *Collections of the New York Historical Society for the Year 1868*, New York: Trow-Smith, 1873, p. 399; Adrian Howe, "The Bayard Treason Trial: Dramatizing Anglo-Dutch Politics in Early Eighteenth-

Century New York City," *William and Mary Quarterly*, Third Series, 47:1 (January 1990), p. 63.

9. "Declarations of the freeholders of Suffolk, Long Island," in Fortescue, p. 35; "Lt. Governor Nicholson to the Lords of Trade, New York, 15 May 1689," in Fortescue, p. 38; Stephen Saunders Webb, *Lord Churchill's Coup: The Anglo-American Empire and the Glorious Revolution of 1688 Reconsidered*, Syracuse, NY: Syracuse University Press, 1998, pp. 199–200.
10. "Address of the Militia of New York to the King and Queen, June 1689," in Fortescue, p. 76; "Letter from members of the Dutch Church . . . ," pp. 399–400; "Deposition of Lt. Henry Cuyler, New York: 10 June 1689," in Fortescue, p. 65.
11. "Stephen van Cortland to Governor Andros, New York: 9 July 1689," in Fortescue, pp. 80–81; David W. Vorhees, "The 'Fervent Zeal' of Jacob Leisler," *William and Mary Quarterly*, Vol. 51, No. 3, 1994, p. 471.
12. "Minutes of the Council of Maryland, 24 March 1689," in Fortescue, p. 18; "Minutes of the Council of Virginia, 26 April 1689," in Fortescue, p. 32; Thomas Condit Miller and Hu Maxwell, *West Virginia and Its People, Vol. 3*, New York: Lewis Historical Publishing Co., 1913, p. 843; "Nicholas Spencer to William Blatwayt, Jamestown, Va.: 27 April 1689," in Fortescue, p. 32; "Nicholas Spencer to Lord of Board and Plantations, Jamestown, Va.: 29 April 1689," in Fortescue, p. 33.
13. Lovejoy (1972), pp. 266–267; "Declaration of the reasons and motives for appearing in arms on behalf of the Protestant subjects of Maryland, 25 July 1689," in Fortescue, pp. 108–109; Michael Graham, "Popish Plots: Protestant Fears in Early Colonial Maryland, 1676–1689," *Catholic Historical Review*, Vol. 75, No. 2, April 1993, pp. 197–199, 203; Beverly McAnear, "Mariland's Grevances Wiy the Have taken Op Arms," *Journal of Southern History*, Vol. 8, No. 3, August 1942, pp. 405–407.
14. Lovejoy (1972), pp. 256–257; Howe (1990), p. 64; Taylor (2001), pp. 284–285.
15. "The case of Massachusetts colony considered in a letter to a friend at Boston, 18 May 1689," in Fortescue, p. 40; Taylor (2001), pp. 283–284.

Chapter 7: Founding the Deep South

1. Richard S. Dunn, *Sugar and Slaves: The Rise of the Planter Class in the English West Indies 1624–1713*, Chapel Hill: University of North Carolina Press, 1972, p. 77; Taylor (2001), pp. 215–216; David Robertson, *Denmark Vesey*, New York: Alfred Knopf, 1999, p. 15.
2. Dunn (1972), pp. 69, 72.
3. Ibid., pp. 73; Richard S. Dunn, "English Sugar Islands and the Founding of South Carolina," *South Carolina Historical Magazine*, Vol. 101, No. 2 (April 1971), pp. 145–146.
4. Robertson (1999), p. 14; Greene (1988), p. 147; Robert Olwell, *Masters, Slaves and Subjects: The Culture of Power in the South Carolina Low Country, 1740–1790*. Ithaca, NY: Cornell University Press, 1998, pp. 34–35, 37.
5. Olwell (1998), pp. 79, 81; Dunn (2000), p. 153.
6. Fischer (2005), pp. 70–71.

7. Maurie D. McInnis, *The Politics of Taste in Antebellum Charleston*, Chapel Hill: University of North Carolina Press, 2005, p. 324; Taylor (2001), p. 226; Kurath (1949), p. 5.
8. M. Eugene Sirmans, "The Legal Status of the Slave in South Carolina, 1670–1740," *Journal of Southern History*, Vol. 28, No. 4, November 1962, pp. 465–467; "An Act for the Better Ordering and Governing of Negroes and Slaves" [1712 reenactment of the 1698 law] in David J. McCord, *The Statutes at Large of South Carolina, Vol. 7*, Columbia, SC: A. B. Johnston, 1840, pp. 352–365.
9. For an excellent discussion of the distinct slave systems, see Ira Berlin, "Time, Space, and the Evolution of Afro-American Society on British Mainland North America," *American Historical Review*, Vol. 85, No. 1, February 1980, pp. 44–78.
10. Greene (1998), pp. 191–192; Berlin (1980), pp. 68–69, 72, 74.
11. Greene (1998), pp. 191–192; Berlin (1980), p. 56, 66; Robertson (1999), p. 18.
12. Allison Davis et al., *Deep South: A Social Anthropological Study of Caste and Class*, Chicago: University of Chicago Press, 1941, pp. 15–44.
13. Ibid., pp. 244–250; Martha Elizabeth Hodes, *Sex, Love, Race: Crossing Boundaries in North American History*, New York: New York University Press, 1999, p. 119; Caryn E. Neumann, *Sexual Crime: A Reference Book*, Santa Barbara, CA: ABC-Clio, 2010, p. 6; Josiah Quincy quoted in Olwell (1998), p. 50.
14. Olwell (1998), pp. 21–25.
15. Greene (1988), p. 142; Betty Smith, *Slavery in Colonial Georgia, 1730–1775*, Athens: University of Georgia Press, 1984, p. 5; Taylor (2001), pp. 241–242.
16. Taylor (2001), pp. 243–244; Allan Gallay, "Jonathan Bryan's Plantation Empire: Law, Politics and the Formation of a Ruling Class in Colonial Georgia," *William and Mary Quarterly*, Vol. 45, No. 2, April 1988, pp. 253–279.

Chapter 8: Founding the Midlands

1. Cara Gardina Pestana, "The Quaker Executions as Myth and History," *Journal of American History*, Vol. 80, No. 2, September 1993, pp. 441, 460–461; Taylor (2001), pp. 264–265; Theophilus Evans, *The History of Modern Enthusiasm, from the Reformation to the Present Times*, London: W. Owen, 1757, p. 84; Boorstin (1958), pp. 35–39.
2. E. Digby Baltzell, *Puritan Boston and Quaker Philadelphia*, New York: Free Press, 1979, pp. 94–106.
3. Samuel Pepys, journal entry of 30 August 1664; "Sir William Penn" and "William Penn," in Hugh Chisholm, ed., *Encyclopedia Britannica*, 11th edition, Vol. 21, New York: Encylopaedia Britannica Co., 1911, pp. 99–104; Richard S. Dunn, "An Odd Couple: John Winthrop and William Penn," *Proceedings of the Massachusetts Historical Society*, 3rd Series Vol. 99, 1987, pp. 7–8.
4. Dunn (1987), p. 3.
5. Ibid., pp. 3–4; Fischer (1989), pp. 453–455, 461; Kornwolf and Kornwolf, Vol. 2, pp. 1175–1177.
6. Taylor (2001), p. 267; Dunn (1987), pp. 10–12; John Alexander Dickinson and Brian J. Young, *A Short History of Quebec*, Montreal: McGill-Queen's University Press, 2003, pp. 65–66.

7. Walter Allen Knittle, *Early Eighteenth Century Palatine Emigration*, Philadelphia: Dorrance & Co., 1936, pp. 1–81; Dunn (1987), p. 16; Charles R. Haller, *Across the Atlantic and Beyond: The Migration of German and Swiss Immigrants to America*, Westminster, MD: Heritage Books, 1993, p. 200; Oscar Kuhns, *The German and Swiss Settlements of Colonial Pennsylvania*, New York: Abingdon Press, 1914, p. 57.
8. Fischer (1989), p. 432; Richard H. Shryock, "British Versus German Traditions in Colonial Agriculture," *Mississippi Valley Historical Review*, Vol. 26, No. 1, June 1939, pp. 46–49.
9. Shryock, pp. 49–50; Fischer (1989), pp. 601–602; "The German Protest Against Slavery, 1688," *The Penn Monthly*, February 1875, p. 117.
10. Baltzell (1979), pp. 127–132; Boorstin (1958), p. 68; John Fanning Watson, *Annals of Philadelphia and Pennsylvania, in the Olden Time*, Vol. 1, Philadelphia: Elijah Thomas, 1857, p. 106.
11. R. J. Dickson, *Ulster Emigration to Colonial America, 1718–1775*, Belfast, U.K.: Ulster Historical Foundation, 1976, p. 225; James Leyburn, *The Scotch-Irish: A Social History*, Chapel Hill: University of North Carolina Press, 1962, pp. 175, 180, 192.
12. Boorstin (1958), pp. 51–53.
13. Ibid., pp. 54–66; Taylor (2001), p. 430.

Chapter 9: Founding Greater Appalachia

1. "State of the Commonwealth of Scotland" in William K. Boyd, ed., *Calendar of State Papers, Scotland, 1547–1603: Vol. 5, 1574–1581*, Edinburgh: H. M. General Register House, 1907, p. 564; Fischer (1989), p. 628; Jonathan Swift, *Proposal for Universal Use of Irish Manufacture*, Dublin: E. Waters, 1720.
2. Phillips (1999), p. 179.
3. Charles Knowles Bolton, *Scotch Irish Pioneers in Ulster and America*, Boston: Bacon & Brown, 1910, pp. 44–45.
4. "Abstract of the receipts on the hereditary and additional duties [in Ireland]," in Richard Arthur Roberts, ed., *Calendar of Home Papers, 1773–1775*, London: Her Majesty's Stationery Office, 1899, pp. 513–514; Bailyn (1986), pp. 36–42.
5. Patrick Griffin, *The People with No Name*, Princeton, NJ: Princeton University Press, 2001, pp. 102–105.
6. Ibid., pp. 593–596; Warren R. Hofstra, "The Virginia Backcountry in the Eighteenth Century," *Virginia Magazine of History and Biography*, Vol. 101, No. 4, October 1993, pp. 490, 493–494; Fischer (1989), pp. 740–741.
7. Grady McWhiney, *Cracker Culture: Celtic Ways in the Old South*, Tuscaloosa: University of Alabama Press, 1988, pp. 52–57; Charles Woodmason, *The Carolina Backcountry on the Eve of the Revolution* [1768], Chapel Hill: University of North Carolina Press, 1953, p. 52.
8. Hofstra (1993), p. 499; Fischer (1989), pp. 765–771; Griffin (2001), p. 112.
9. Fischer (1989), pp. 749–757, 772–774; Leyburn (1962), pp. 261–269.
10. Bailyn (1986), pp. 13–29.
11. Joanna Brooks, "Held Captive by the Irish: Quaker Captivity Narratives in Frontier Pennsylvania," *New Hibernia Review*, Autumn 2004, p. 32; Rachel N. Klein,

"Ordering the Backcountry: the South Carolina Regulation," *William and Mary Quarterly*, Vol. 38, No. 4, October 1981, pp. 668–672.

12. Brooke Hindle, "March of the Paxton Boys," *William and Mary Quarterly*, Third Series, Vol. 3, No. 4, October 1946, pp. 461–486.
13. Ibid.; Merrill Jensen, *The Founding of a Nation: A History of the American Revolution*, New York: Oxford University Press, 1968, p. 27.
14. Charles Desmond Dutrizac, "Local Identity and Authority in a Disputed Hinterland: The Pennsylvania-Maryland Border in the 1730s," *Pennsylvania Magazine of History and Biography*, Vol. 115, No. 1, January 1991, pp. 35–61; Taylor (2001), p. 434; Klein (1981), pp. 671–680.
15. Klein (1981), pp. 671–679; Robert F. Sayre, ed., *American Lives: An Anthology of Autobiographical Writing*, Madison: University of Wisconsin, 1994, p. 171.
16. Walter B. Edgar, *South Carolina: A History*, Columbia: University of South Carolina Press, 1998, pp. 212–216; Klein (1981), p. 680.
17. Robert D. W. Connor, *History of North Carolina*, Vol. 1, Chicago: Lewis Publishing Co., 1919, pp. 302–320.
18. George D. Wolf, *The Fair Play Settlers of the West Branch Valley, 1769–1784*, Harrisburg, PA: BiblioBazaar, 1969, pp. 27–28, 46–48, 88.
19. Bailyn (1986), pp. 21–22, 536–541.

Chapter 10: A Common Struggle

1. Linda Colley, *Britons: Forging the Nation, 1707–1737*, New Haven, CT: Yale University Press, 1994, p. 167; Fischer (1989), pp. 823–824.
2. Taylor (2001), pp. 438–442; Fischer (1989), pp. 824–826; Marshall Delancey Haywood, "The Story of Queen's College or Liberty Hall in the Province of North Carolina," *North Carolina Booklet*, Vol. 11, No. 1, July 1911, p. 171; Phillips (1999), pp. 86–88, 93; Joseph C. Morton, *The American Revolution*, Westport, CT: Greenwood Press, 2003, p. 31.
3. Even so, Massachusetts has a town and a college named in his honor.
4. Bernhard Knollenberg, "General Amherst and Germ Warfare," *Mississippi Valley Historical Review*, Vol. 41, No. 3, December 1954, pp. 489–494; Taylor (2001), pp. 433–437.
5. Phillips (1999), pp. 171–173; Edmund S. Morgan, "The Puritan Ethic and the American Revolution," *William and Mary Quarterly*, Vol. 24, No. 1, January 1967, pp. 3–43; Fischer (1989), p. 827; Capt. Levi Preston quoted in David Hackett Fischer, *Paul Revere's Ride*, New York: Oxford University Press, 1995, pp. 163–164.
6. John M. Murrin et al., eds., *Liberty, Equality, Power: A History of the American People*, Belmont, CA: Thompson Learning, 2009, pp. 148–149.
7. Marc Engal, "The Origins of the Revolution in Virginia: A Reinterpretation," *William and Mary Quarterly*, Vol. 37, No. 3, July 1980, pp. 401–428; Thad W. Tate, "The Coming of the Revolution in Virginia: Britain's Challenge to Virginia's Ruling Class, 1763–1776," *William and Mary Quarterly*, Third Series, Vol. 19, No. 3, July 1962, pp. 324–343.
8. A. Roger Ekirch, "Whig Authority and Public Order in Backcountry North Carolina, 1776–1783," in Ronald Hoffman et al., eds., *An Uncivil War: The*

Southern Backcountry During the American Revolution, Charlottesville: University Press of Virginia, 1985, pp. 99–103.

9. Phillips (1999), pp. 211–219; Baltzell (1979), p. 181.
10. Edward Countryman, "Consolidating Power in Revolutionary America: The Case of New York, 1775–1783," *Journal of Interdisciplinary History*, Vol. 6, No. 4, Spring 1976, pp. 650–670.
11. Robert A. Olwell, "'Domestic Enemies': Slavery and Political Independence in South Carolina, May 1775–March 1776," *Journal of Southern History*, Vol. 55, No. 1, Feb. 1989, pp. 21–22, 27–28.
12. Ibid., pp. 29–30.
13. Karen Northrop Barzilay, "Fifty Gentlemen Total Strangers: A Portrait of the First Continental Congress," doctoral dissertation, The College of William and Mary, January 2009, pp. 17–20.
14. John Adams quoted in Boorstin (1958), p. 404.
15. John E. Ferling, *A Leap in the Dark: The Struggle to Create the American Republic*, New York: Oxford University Press, 2003, p. 116.
16. "Letter of Noble Wimberly Jones, Archibald Bulloch, and John Houstoun to the President of the First Continental Congress, Savannah, Ga.: 6 April 1775," in Allen Candler, ed., *Revolutionary Records of the State of Georgia*, Vol. 1, Atlanta: Franklin Turner, 1908.
17. George Wilson, *Portrait Gallery of the Chamber of Commerce of the State of New York*, New York: Chamber of Commerce, 1890, pp. 30–32; Barzilay (2009), pp. 182–183; Carl Lotus Becker, *The History of Political Parties in the Province of New York, 1670–1776*, Madison: University of Wisconsin, 1907, pp. 143–146.
18. Barzilay (2009), pp. 291–295; "Plan of Union," in Worthington C. Ford et al., eds., *Journals of the Continental Congress, 1774–1789*, Vol. 1, Washington, D.C.: Government Printing Office, 1904, pp. 49–51; Becker, p. 143, n. 149.
19. Henry Laurens quoted in Olwell (1989), p. 29.

Chapter 11: Six Wars of Liberation

1. David Hackett Fischer, *Paul Revere's Ride*, New York: Oxford University Press, 1995, p. 151–154; Max M. Mintz, *The Generals of Saratoga*, New Haven, CT: Yale University Press, 1990, pp. 82–84; Joseph Ellis, *American Creation: Triumphs and Tragedies at the Founding of the Republic*, New York: Knopf, 2007, pp. 32–34.
2. Robert McCluer Calhoon, *The Loyalists in Revolutionary America, 1760–1781*, New York: Harcourt Brace, 1973, pp. 371–372; Oscar Barck, *New York City During the War for Independence*, Port Washington, NY: Ira J. Friedman Inc., 1931, pp. 41–44; Judith L. Van Buskirk, *Generous Enemies: Patriots and Loyalists in Revolutionary New York*, Philadelphia: University of Pennsylvania Press, 2002, p. 16.
3. Bart McDowell, *The Revolutionary War: America's Fight for Freedom*, Washington, D.C.: National Geographic Society, 1977, pp. 58–60; Calhoon, pp. 373–377; Countryman (1976), p. 657; Christopher Moore, *The Loyalists: Revolution, Exile, Settlement*, Toronto: Macmillan of Canada, 1984, pp. 93–101; Reverend Ewald Schaukirk quoted in Van Buskirk, p. 21; Barck, pp. 78, 192–195; Calhoon,

pp. 362–363; Edwin G. Burrows and Mike Wallace, *Gotham: A History of New York City to 1898*, New York: Oxford University Press, 2000, p. 194.

4. Calhoon (1973), pp. 356–358; Piers Mackesy, "British Strategy in the War of American Independence," in David L. Jacobson, ed., *Essays on the American Revolution*, New York: Holt, Rinehart and Winston, 1970, pp. 174–6.
5. Moore (1984), pp. 107–109; Buskirk (2002), pp. 179, 193.
6. Calhoon (1973), pp. 360, 382–390.
7. Ibid., pp. 390–395; McDowell (1977), pp. 66–81.
8. Anne M. Ousterhout, "Controlling the Opposition in Pennsylvania during the American Revolution," *Pennsylvania Magazine of History and Biography*, Vol. 105, No. 1, January 1981, pp. 4–5, 16–17, 30.
9. Olwell (1989), pp. 30–32, 38.
10. Ibid., pp. 37–48.
11. Zubly quoted in Gordon S. Wood, *The Creation of the American Republic, 1776–1787*, Chapel Hill: University of North Carolina Press, 1969, p. 95; Olwell (1989), p. 36; W. W. Abbot, "Lowcountry, Backcountry: A View of Georgia in the American Revolution," in Hoffman et al., (1985), pp. 326–328.
12. Spain surrendered Florida to the British under the terms of the 1763 Peace of Paris, which ended the Seven Years' (or "French and Indian") War.
13. Calhoon (1973), p. 474.
14. Leyburn (1962), p. 305.
15. Richard R. Beeman, "The Political Response to Social Conflict in the Southern Backcountry" in Hoffman et al., (1985), p. 231; Ekrich in Hoffman et al., pp. 99–100, 103–111; Crow in Hoffman et al., pp. 162, 168–169; Fischer (2005), pp. 82–84.
16. Olwell (1989), pp. 32, 37; British Maj. George Hanger quoted in Robert M. Weir, "The Violent Spirit: the Reestablishment of Order and the Continuity of Leadership in Post-Revolutionary South Carolina," in Hoffman et al., (1985), p. 74; Henry Lee to Gen. Greene, 4 June 1781, in Richard K. Showman, ed., *The Papers of General Nathanael Greene,* Vol. 8, Chapel Hill: University of North Carolina Press, 2005, pp. 300–311.
17. Weir in Hoffman et al., (1985), p. 71–78; Calhoon, pp. 491–495.
18. Weir in Hoffman et al., (1985), pp. 76–77.
19. Olwell (1989), pp. 36, 40–41.
20. Gary B. Nash, *The Unknown American Revolution: The Unruly Birth of Democracy and the Struggle to Create America*, New York: Penguin, 2006, pp. 335–339.

Chapter 12: Independence or Revolution?

1. Jack P. Greene, "The Background of the Articles of Confederation," *Publius*, Vol. 12, No. 4, Autumn 1982, pp. 32, 35–36.
2. Jack Rakove, "The Legacy of the Articles of Confederation," *Publius*, Vol. 12, No. 4, Autumn 1982, pp. 45–54; Greene (1982), pp. 37–40, 42.
3. Calvin C. Jillson, "Political Culture and the Pattern of Congressional Politics Under the Articles of Confederation," *Publius*, Vol. 18, No. 1, Winter 1988, pp. 8–10; H. James Henderson, "Factional relationships between the Continental

Congress and State Legislatures; a new slant on the politics of the American Revolution," *Proceedings of the Oklahoma Academy of Sciences for 1966* [Vol. 47], Oklahoma Academy of Sciences, 1967, pp. 326–327.

4. Jillson, pp. 11–12, 17.
5. Paul Wentworth, "Minutes respecting political Parties in America and Sketches of the leading Persons in each Province [1778]" in B. F. Stevens, ed., *Facsimiles of Manuscripts in European Archives*, London: Malby & Sons, 1889; "London, January 6," *South-Carolina Weekly Gazette*, 10 April 1784, p. 2; Bancroft quoted in Joseph Davis, *Sectionalism in American Politics, 1774–1787*, Madison: University of Wisconsin Press, 1977, p. 67.
6. J. R. Pole, "Historians and the Problem of Early American Democracy" in Jacobson (1970), pp. 236–237.
7. Merrill Jensen, "Democracy and the American Revolution" in Jacobson, pp. 219–225.
8. Jensen in Jacobson, pp. 218, 226–227; quotes from Howard Zinn, *A People's History of the United States*, New York: HarperCollins, 1999, pp. 70, 75, 81, 83, 85, 88–89; J. R. Pole, "Historians and the Problem of Early American Democracy" in Jacobson (1970), p. 238; Phillips (1999), p. 324.
9. Alexander Hamilton, "Federalist No. 8" and "Federalist No. 15," in Clinton Rossiter, ed., *The Federalist Papers*, New York: Penguin, 1961, pp. 66–71, 107; Washington quoted in Richard B. Morris, "The Confederation Period and the American Historian," *William and Mary Quarterly*, 3rd Series, Vol. 13, No. 2, April 1956, p. 139.
10. John P. Roche, "The Founding Fathers: A Reform Caucus in Action," in Jacobson (1970), pp. 267–271; Calvin Jillson and Thornton Anderson, "Voting Bloc Analysis in the Constitutional Convention: Implications for an Interpretation of the Connecticut Compromise," *Western Political Quarterly*, Vol. 31, No. 4, December 1978, pp. 537–547.
11. Shorto (1983), pp. 304–305, 315–316.
12. See Orin Grant Libby, "The Geographical Distribution of the Vote of the Thirteen States on the Federal Constitution, 1787–8," *Bulletin of the University of Wisconsin*, Vol. 1, No. 1, June 1894, pp. 1–116.
13. Roche in Jacobson (1970), pp. 267–275; Jillson and Anderson (1978), pp. 542–545.

Chapter 13: Nations in the North

1. John Bartlett Brebner, *The Neutral Yankees of Nova Scotia*, New York: Russell & Russell, 1970, pp. 24–29, 54–57, 312–319; Ann Gorman Condon, *The Envy of the American States: The Loyalist Dream for New Brunswick*, Fredericton, NB: New Ireland Press, 1984, p. 78; Worthington Chauncey Ford, ed., *Journals of the Continental Congress 1774–1789*, Vol. 3, Washington, D.C.: Government Printing Office, 1905, p. 315; Phillips (1999), pp. 141–145.
2. Jack P. Greene, "The Cultural Dimensions of Political Transfers," *Early American Studies*, Spring 2008, pp. 12–15.
3. Justin H. Smith, *Our Struggle for the Fourteenth Colony: Canada and the American Revolution*, Vol. 1, New York: G. P. Putnam's Sons, 1907, p. 474.

4. "Thomas Dundas to the Earl Cornwallis, Saint John, N.B., 28 December 1786," in Charles Ross, ed., *Correspondence of Charles, first Marquis Cornwallis,* Vol. 1, London: John Murray, 1859, p. 279; Condon (1984), pp. 85–89.
5. Condon (1984), pp. 85–89, 190–192; Stephen Kimber, *Loyalists and Layabouts: The Rapid Rise and Faster Fall of Shelburne, Nova Scotia*, Scarborough, Ont.: Doubleday Canada, 2008, pp. 3, 10, 291–295, 301.
6. Alan Taylor, "The Late Loyalists: Northern Reflections of the Early American Republic," *Journal of the Early Republic*, Vol. 27, Spring 2007, p. 23.
7. Ibid., pp. 3–31.
8. Ibid.

Chapter 14: First Secessionists

1. Terry Bouton, *Taming Democracy: "The People," The Founders, and the Troubled Ending of the American Revolution*, New York: Oxford University Press, 2007, pp. 178–179.
2. Ibid., pp. 181–183.
3. Ibid., pp. 76–77, 83–87.
4. Ibid., pp. 83–87.
5. On Franklin see Samuel Cole Williams. *History of the Lost State of Franklin*, Johnson City, TN: Watauga Press, 1933; John C. Fitzpatrick, *Journals of the Continental Congress*, Vol. 28, Washington, D.C.: Government Printing Office, 1933, pp. 384–385.
6. Bouton, pp. 197–215.
7. Ibid., pp. 224–226.
8. William Hogeland, *The Whiskey Rebellion*, New York: Scribner, 2006, pp. 172–176, 181–183, 205–208; Bouton (2007), pp. 234–241.
9. James M. Banner Jr., *To the Hartford Convention: The Federalists and the Origins of Party Politics in Massachusetts, 1789–1815*, New York: Alfred A. Knopf, 1970, pp. 89–92.
10. David McCullough, *John Adams*, New York: Simon & Schuster, 2001, pp. 504–505; *Courier of New Hampshire*, 22 August 1797.
11. McCullough, pp. 505–506; Vanessa Beasley, *Who Belongs in America?*, College Station, TX: Texas A&M University Press, 2006, pp. 45–46, 53; H. Jefferson Powell, "The Principles of '98: An Essay in Historical Retrieval," *Virginia Law Review*, Vol. 80, No. 3, April 1994, p. 704.
12. James P. Martin, "When Repression Is Democratic and Constitutional: The Federalist Theory of Representation in the Sedition Act of 1798," *University of Chicago Law Review*, Vol. 66, No. 1, Winter 1999, pp. 146–148; *The Patriotick Proceedings of the Legislature of Massachusetts*, Boston: Joshua Cushing, 1809, p. 116.
13. Beasley (2006), p. 47; Kevin R. Gutzman, "A Troublesome Legacy: James Madison and 'The Principles of '98,'" *Journal of the Early Republic*, Vol. 15, No. 4, Winter 1995, pp. 580–581; Birte Pflegler, "'Miserable Germans' and Fries's Rebellion," *Early American Studies*, Fall 2004, pp. 343–361.
14. McCullough (2001), p. 521; Fischer (1989), p. 843.
15. McCullough (2001), pp. 521–525.

16. Donald W. Meinig, "Continental America, 1800–1915: The View of a Historical Geographer," *The History Teacher*, Vol. 22, No. 2, February 1989, p. 192; Edmund Quincy, *Life of Josiah Quincy*, Boston: Ticknor & Fields, p. 91; Banner (1970), p. 100.
17. Banner (1970), pp. 13–14, 34–35, 37; *Patriotick Proceedings*, p. 90; Alison LaCroix, "A Singular and Awkward War: The Transatlantic Context of the Hartford Convention," *American Nineteenth Century History*, Vol. 6, No. 1, March 2005, p. 10.
18. Banner (1970), pp. 41–42; J. S. Martell, "A Side Light on Federalist Strategy During the War of 1812," *American Historical Review*, Vol. 43, No. 3, April 1938, pp. 555–556; Samuel Eliot Morison, ed., *The Life and Letters of Harrison Gray Otis*, Vol. 2, Boston: Houghton Mifflin, 1913, pp. 5–8; "Federal Project of Secession from the Union," *The Democrat* [Boston], 1 February 1809, p. 3.
19. Maine, the sixth New England state, didn't regain its independence from Massachusetts until 1820; Samuel Eliot Morison, "Our Most Unpopular War," *Proceedings of the Massachusetts Historical Society*, Third Series, Vol. 80 (1968), pp. 39–43.
20. Donald R. Hickey, *The War of 1812: A Forgotten Conflict*, Urbana: University of Illinois Press, p. 256; Martell (1938), pp. 559–564; Meinig (1989), p. 199.
21. Morison (1968), pp. 47–52; "The Crisis," *Columbian Centinel* [Boston], 17 December 1814, p. 1.
22. Morison (1968), pp. 52–54; "Report and the Resolutions of the Hartford Convention," *Public Documents Containing the Proceedings of the Hartford Convention*, Boston: Massachusetts Senate, 1815.

Chapter 15: Yankeedom Spreads West

1. Frederick Merk, *History of the Westward Movement*, New York: Knopf, 1978, pp. 112–114; Howard Allen Bridgman, *New England in the Life of the World*, Boston: Pilgrim Press, 1920, pp. 30, 34–35.
2. Bridgman, pp. 49, 51, 64–66; Lois Kimball Matthews, *The Expansion of New England*, Boston: Houghton Mifflin, 1909, p. 180.
3. "Marietta College," in James J. Burns, *The Educational History of Ohio*, Columbus: Historical Publishing Co., 1905, p. 370; Albert E. E. Dunning, *The Congregationalists in America*, New York: J. A. Hill, 1894, pp. 368–377.
4. Matthews (1909), pp. 207, 231; Ellis B. Usher, "The Puritan Influence in Wisconsin," *Proceedings of the State Historical Society of Wisconsin* [for 1898], Madison, WI, 1899, pp. 119, 122; *Portrait and Biographical Record of Sheboygan County, Wisconsin*, Chicago: Excelsior, 1894, pp. 125–184; Bridgman (1920), p. 112.
5. Phillips (1969), pp. 331–332.
6. Rev. M. W. Montgomery, "The Work Among the Scandinavians," *Home Missionary*, March 1886, p. 400.
7. Paul Kleppner, *The Third Electoral System, 1853–1892*, Chapel Hill: University of North Carolina Press, 1979, p. 48; John H. Fenton, *Midwest Politics*, New York: Holt, Rinehart & Winston, 1966, p. 77; Paul Kleppner, *The Cross of Culture: A Social Analysis of Midwestern Politics, 1850–1900*, New York: Free Press, 1970, pp. 76–78.

8. The classic study is Kleppner (1979). See also Phillips (1969); Fenton; Kleppner (1970).
9. Stewart H. Holbrook, *The Yankee Exodus*, Seattle: University of Washington Press, 1950, pp. 68–72.
10. Merk (1978), p. 119.
11. Kevin Phillips, *American Theocracy*, New York: Viking, 2006, pp. 110–111; D. Michael Quinn, *Early Mormonism and the Magic World View*, Salt Lake City: Signature Books, 1998, pp. 64–128.
12. Phillips (2006), p. 109.

Chapter 16: The Midlands Spread West

1. Albert Bernhardt Faust, *The German Element in America*, Vol. 1, Boston: Houghton-Mifflin, 1901, p. 421–422; Robert Swierenga, "The Settlement of the Old Northwest: Ethnic Pluralism in a Featureless Plain," *Journal of the Early Republic*, Vol. 9, No. 1, Spring 1989, pp. 82–85.
2. *Federal Gazette* [Philadelphia], 5 March 1789, p. 2; Kleppner (1979), pp. 57–59.
3. Swierenga, pp. 89–90, 93; Faust, Vol. 1, pp. 447–448, 461; Richard Sisson et al., eds., *The American Midwest: An Interpretive Encyclopedia*, Bloomington: Indiana University Press, 2007, p. 741.
4. Faust, Vol. 1, pp. 90–104; John A. Hawgood, *The Tragedy of German America*, New York: G. P. Putnam & Sons, 1950, p. 219.
5. Thomas D. Hamm, *The Quakers in America*, New York: Columbia University Press, 2003, pp. 38–39, 50.
6. Richard Pillsbury, "The Urban Street Pattern as a Culture Indicator: Pennsylvania, 1682–1815," *Annals of the Association of American Geographers*, Vol. 60, No. 3, September 1970, p. 437; Faust, Vol. 2, pp. 28–30.
7. Krista O'Donnell et al., *The Heimat Abroad: The Boundaries of Germanness*, Ann Arbor: University of Michigan Press, 2005, pp. 144–145; Hawgood (1950), p. 41.
8. Kleppner (1979), pp. 180–187; Phillips (1999), p. 436.
9. Phillips (1999), pp. 434–436.

Chapter 17: Appalachia Spreads West

1. Robert E. Chaddock, *Ohio Before 1815*, New York: Columbia University, 1908, p. 240; p. 173; David Walker Howe, *What Hath God Wrought?: The Transformation of America, 1815–1848:* New York: Oxford University Press, 2007, p. 239; Richard Power, *Planting Corn Belt Culture: The Impress of the Upland Southerner and Yankee in the Old Northwest*, Indianapolis: Indiana Historical Society, 1953, p. 41.
2. *Narrative of Richard Lee Mason in the Pioneer West*, 1819, New York: C. F. Heartman, 1915, p. 35; Frederick Law Olmsted, *The Cotton Kingdom*, Vol. 2, New York: Mason Brothers, 1862, p. 309; Nicole Etcheson, *The Emerging Midwest: Upland Southerners and the Political Culture of the Old Northwest, 1787–1861*, Bloomington: Indiana University Press, 1996, p. 5; Howe (2007), p. 137.
3. Merk (1978), pp. 125–126; Allan Kulikoff, *Agrarian Origins of American Capitalism*, Charlottesville: University Press of Virginia, 1992, p. 218.

4. *Journal of the Senate of Illinois*, Springfield: Illinois Journal, 1869, p. 373; Etcheson (1996), pp. 6, 12; Howe (2007), p. 139.
5. Power (1953), pp. 35–36.
6. Ibid., pp. 115–119.
7. Ibid., pp. 112–115.
8. Ibid., pp. 97–124.
9. Frank L. Klement, "Middle Western Copperheadism and the Genesis of the Granger Movement," *Mississippi Valley Historical Review*, Vol. 38, No. 4, March 1952, p. 682; Etcheson (1996), p. 7.
10. Etcheson (1996), pp. 36, 44.
11. Phillips (1969), p. 293; Clement Vallandigham, *Speeches, Arguments, Addresses, and Letters*, New York: J. Walter, 1864, pp. 101, 104; Kleppner (1979), pp. 235–236; Merk (1978), p. 120–122, 408–409.
12. C. C. Royce, *Map of the Territorial Limits of the Cherokee Nation of Indians [and] Cessions*, Washington, D.C.: Smithsonian Institution, 1884; Jeff Biggers, *The United States of Appalachia*, Emeryville, CA: Shoemaker & Hoard, 2006, pp. 34–35.
13. Biggers, pp. 29–44; Patrick Minges, "Are You Kituwah's Son? Cherokee Nationalism and the Civil War," paper presented at the American Academy of Religion Annual Meeting, Philadelphia: November 1995; Howe (2007), pp. 343–346.
14. Andrew Jackson, *Fifth Annual Address to Congress*, 3 December 1833.
15. Merk (1978), p. 121; Fischer (1989), pp. 849–850; Margaret Bayard Smith, *The First Forty Years of Washington Society*, New York: Scribner, 1906, pp. 295–296; Edward L. Ayers, Lewis L. Gould, David M. Oshinsky, and Jean R. Soderlund, *American Passages: A History of the United States*, Boston: Wadsworth Cengage, 2009, pp. 282–283.
16. Howe (2007), pp. 344–357, 414–416.
17. Elliott J. Gorn, "Gouge and Bite, Pull Hair and Scratch: The Social Significance of Fighting in the Southern Backcountry," *American Historical Review*, Vol. 90, No. 1, February 1985, pp. 18–43.
18. Phillips (2006), pp. 108–113.

Chapter 18: The Deep South Spreads West

1. Merk (1978), pp. 205–207.
2. Howe (2007), pp. 127–129; Frank L. Owsley, "The Pattern of Migration and Settlement on the Southern Frontier," *Journal of Southern History*, Vol. 11, No. 2, March 1945, pp. 147–176; Merk (1978), p. 199.
3. Howe (2007), p. 130.
4. Francis Butler Simkins, "The South," in Merrill Jensen, ed., *Regionalism in America*, Madison: University of Wisconsin Press, 1951, pp. 150–151; Missouri Deep Southerner William P. Napton quoted in Robert E. Shalope, "Race, Class, Slavery and the Antebellum Southern Mind," *Journal of Southern History*, Vol. 37, No. 4, Nov. 1971, pp. 565–566; Peter Kolchin, "In Defense of Servitude," *American Historical Review*, Vol. 85, No. 4, October 1980, p. 815; William Peterfield Trent, *Cambridge History of American Literature*, Vol. 17, Cambridge, UK: Cambridge University Press, 1907–1921, p. 389; Alexander H. Stephens, "Cornerstone

Address, March 21, 1861," in Frank Moore, ed., *The Rebellion Record*, Vol. 1, New York: G. P. Putnam, 1862, pp. 44–46.

5. Fred A. Ross, *Slavery Ordained of God*, Philadelphia: J. B. Lippincott, 1857, pp. 5, 29–30.
6. "The Message, the Constitution, and the Times" *DeBow's Review*, Vol. 30, Issue 2, February 1861, pp. 162, 164; "What Secession Means," *Liberator*, 11 July 1862, p. 1.
7. William W. Freehling, *The Road to Disunion*, Vol. 2: *Secessionists Triumphant, 1854–1861*, New York: Oxford University Press, 2007, pp. 149–151; Thomas N. Ingersoll, "Free Blacks in a Slave Society: New Orleans, 1718–1812," *William and Mary Quarterly*, 3rd Series, Vol. 48, No. 2 , April 1991, pp. 173–200.
8. Lewis William Newton, "Americanization of Louisiana," doctoral thesis, University of Chicago, 1929, pp. 122, 163, 170–173.
9. Phillips (1999), pp. 341–349.
10. Robert E. May, *The Southern Dream of a Caribbean Empire: 1854–1861*, Baton Rouge: Louisiana State University Press, 1973, pp. 15–65.
11. Ibid., pp. 27–33, 60–62, 70–71, 75, 168–196; Freehling (2007), pp. 153–155.
12. May, pp. 78–133.
13. Ibid.
14. Ibid., pp. 149–154.

Chapter 19: Conquering El Norte

1. Weber (1982), pp. 20–32.
2. Ibid., pp. 34, 44, 47, 63, 124–125, 157, 188–189.
3. Ibid., pp. 158–162.
4. Ibid.; Howe (2007), pp. 658–9; Merk (1978), p. 267.
5. Weber (1982), pp. 162–172; T. R. Fehrenbach, *Lone Star: A History of Texas and the Texans*, New York: Da Capo Press, 2000, pp. 163–164.
6. Weber (1982), pp. 170–177, 184.
7. Ibid., pp. 255–272, 266; Howe (2007), p. 661.
8. Weber (1982), pp. 247–254; Howe (2007), pp. 661–667; Merk (1978), p. 275; Jordan (1969), pp. 88–103.
9. Weber (1992), p. 339.
10. Juan Nepomuceno Seguín, *Personal Memoirs of John N. Seguín*, San Antonio, TX: Ledger Book and Job Office, 1858, pp. 29–32; Leobardo F. Estrada et al., "Chicanos in the United States: A History of Exploitation and Resistance," *Daedalus*, Vol. 110, No. 2, pp. 105–109; Martinez (1988), pp. 88–91; D. W. Meinig, *Imperial Texas: An Interpretive Essay in Cultural Geography*, Austin: University of Texas Press, 1969, pp. 44.
11. Terry G. Jordan, "Population Origins in Texas, 1850," *Geographical Review*, Vol. 59, No. 1, January 1969, pp. 83–103.
12. Frederick Merk, "Dissent in the Mexican War," in Samuel Eliot Morison et al., eds., *Dissent in Three American Wars*, Cambridge, MA: Harvard University Press, 1970, pp. 35–44, 49.

13. Louise A. Mayo, *President James K. Polk: The Dark Horse President*, New York: Nova Science Publishers, 2006, pp. 110–133; Merk (1978).
14. Day, p. 15; Merk (1970), pp. 51–52.
15. Martinez (1988), p. 108–109.

Chapter 20: Founding the Left Coast

1. Astoria, Oregon, the first "American" settlement on the Pacific coast, was the creation of New Netherlander John Jacob Astor but manned by Scots and French Canadian hirelings. In 1813, after just two years in operation, it was sold to a British company, which in turn merged with the Hudson's Bay Company. Culturally speaking, Astor's outpost was of little consequence.
2. W. H. Gray, *History of Oregon, 1792–1849*, Portland, OR: Harris & Holman, 1870, p. 19; Samuel Eliot Morison, *The Maritime History of Massachusetts*, Boston: Houghton Mifflin, 1921, pp. 52–53.
3. Lyman Beecher, *A Plea for the West*, Cincinnati: Truman and Smith, 1835, pp. 30, 37, 48–61; Kevin Starr, *Americans and the California Dream, 1850–1915*, New York: Oxford University Press, 1973, p. 93.
4. Gray (1870), pp. 312–318; Holbrook (1950), pp. 226–227; Bridgman (1920), pp. 208–215.
5. David Alan Johnson, *Founding the Far West: California, Oregon, and Nevada, 1840–1890*, Berkeley: University of California Press (1950), 1992, pp. 56–57.
6. D. A. Johnson, pp. 64, 139–149, 162–163; Holbrook (1950), pp. 227–230.
7. Holbrook (1950), pp. 235, 237, 252–253; Phillips (1969), p. 418; *Japanese Immigration: An Exposition of Its Real Status*, Seattle: Japanese Association of the Pacific Northwest, 1907, pp. 11, 46; Alexander Rattray, *Vancouver Island and British Columbia*, London: Smith, Elder & Co.: 1863, pp. 9, 16, 159, 171–173; Merk (1978), pp. 327, 417.
8. Starr (1973), pp. 26–27; D. A. Johnson (1992), pp. 20–22; Gerald Foster, *American Houses*, Boston: Houghton Mifflin, 2004, pp. 212–215.
9. D. A. Johnson (1992), pp. 20–22.
10. "Missionary Correspondence: California, August 1st, 1849," *The Home Missionary*, Vol. 22, No. 7, November 1849, pp. 163–168; Malcolm J. Rohrbough, *Days of Gold: The California Gold Rush and the American Nation*, Berkeley: University of California Press, 1997, p. 156; Kevin Starr and Richard J. Orsi, *Rooted in Barbarous Soil: People, Culture, and Community in Gold Rush California*, Berkeley: University of California Press, 2000, pp. 25, 50.
11. "Mission to California," *The Home Missionary*, Vol. 21, No. 9, January 1849, pp. 193–196.
12. Starr (1973), p. 86.
13. Bridgman (1920), pp. 180–195; Starr (1973), p. 87; Holbrook (1950), pp. 151–156.
14. Starr (1973), p. 87; D. A. Johnson (1992), pp. 35–36; S. R. Rockwell, "Sabbath in New England and California," *San Francisco Bulletin*, 1 September 1860, p. 1.
15. Starr, pp. 93–94; D. A. Johnson, pp. 104–108. California's first governor, Peter Hardeman Burnett, was born to a poor family in Nashville; his successor, John McDougall, was a war veteran and native of Appalachian Ross County, Ohio.

Chapter 21: War for the West

1. Edith Abbott, *Historical Aspects of the Immigration Problem: Select Documents*, Chicago: University of Chicago Press, 1926, p. 330.
2. *American Slavery as It Is*, New York: American Anti-Slavery Society, 1839, pp. 16, 97, 169–170.
3. See http://atlas.lib.niu.edu/Website/Election_1860/; Fischer (1989), p. 857.
4. Freehling (2007), pp. 27–30; John Henry Hammond, *Two Letters on Slavery in the United States*, Columbia, SC: Allen, McCarter & Co., 1845, p. 10.
5. Freehling (2007), pp. 30–32; Hammond (1845), p. 15.
6. *London Times*, 28 May 1851, p. 10.
7. Ibid.
8. Phillips (1999), p. 372; Marc Engal, "Rethinking the Secession of the Lower South: The Clash of Two Groups," *Civil War History*, Vol. 50, No. 3, 2004, pp. 261–290; Dunbar Rowland, *Encyclopedia of Mississippi History*, Vol. 1, Madison, WI: Selwyn A. Brant, 1907, pp. 216–217.
9. William C. Wright, *The Secession Movement in the Middle Atlantic States*, Rutherford, NJ: Fairleigh Dickinson University Press, 1973, pp. 210–212.
10. Phillips (1999), pp. 424–427; Burrows and Wallace (2000), pp. 560–562.
11. Wright (1973), pp. 176–178; "Mayor Wood's Recommendation on the Secession of New York City," 6 January 1861; "The Position of New York," *New York Herald*, 3 April 1861, p. 1.
12. Wright (1973), pp. 191, 203–205.
13. Phillips (1999), pp. 435–436; Wright (1973), pp. 34–46.
14. Wright (1973), pp. 40, 161–162.
15. Freehling (2007), pp. 35–38.
16. In the time of the English Civil War, supporters of Parliament had been called "Roundheads" on account of their then unusual preference for short-cropped hair.
17. Robert B. Bonner, "Roundheaded Cavaliers? The Context and Limits of a Confederate Racial Project," *Civil War History*, Vol. 58, No. 1, 2002, pp. 34–35, 42, 44–45, 49; "A Contest for the Supremacy of Race, as between the Saxon Puritan of the North and the Norman of the South," *Southern Literary Messenger*, Vol. 33, July 1861, pp. 23–24; J. Quitman Moore, "Southern Civilization, or the Norman in America," *DeBow's Review*, Vol. 32, January 1862, pp. 11–13; Jan C. Dawson, "The Puritan and the Cavalier: The South's Perceptions of Contrasting Traditions," *Journal of Southern History*, Vol. 64, No. 4, November 1978, pp. 600, 609–612.
18. Etcheson (1996), pp. 109–110.
19. Ibid., pp. 110–111, 115–117.
20. Engal (2004), pp. 262, 285–286; Freehling (2007), pp. 501–506; Richard Nelson Current, *Lincoln's Loyalists: Union Soldiers from the Confederacy*, Boston: Northeastern University Press, 1992, pp. 1–8.
21. Current, pp. 14–20, 29–60; Etcheson (1996), pp. 137–129.
22. Freehling (2007), pp. 527–541.

23. Eric Foner, *Reconstruction: America's Unfinished Revolution, 1863–1877*, New York: Harper & Row, 1988, pp. 354–355; Fischer (1989), pp. 862–863.
24. Fischer (1989), p. 863.

Chapter 22: Founding the Far West

1. Walter Griffith quoted in John Phillip Reid, "Punishing the Elephant: Malfeasance and Organized Criminality on the Overland Trail," *Montana: The Magazine of Western History*, Vol. 47, No. 1, Spring 1997, p. 8.
2. D. A. Johnson (1992), pp. 72–76.
3. Ibid., pp. 223–225.
4. Ibid., pp. 313–331.
5. Marc Reisner, *Cadillac Desert: The American West and Its Disappearing Water*, New York: Viking, 1987, p. 37; James B. Hedges, "The Colonization Work of the Northern Pacific Railroad," *Mississippi Valley Historical Review*, Vol. 13, No. 3, December 1926, p. 313.
6. Hedges (1926), pp. 311–312, 329–331, 337; Reisner, pp. 37–39.
7. Reisner (1987), pp. 35–43.
8. Ibid., pp. 46–48.
9. Ibid., pp. 105–110; Bernard DeVoto, "The West Against Itself," *Harper's Magazine*, January 1947, pp. 2–3; DeVoto (1934), p. 364.
10. John Gunther, *Inside USA*, New York: Harper, 1947, p. 152.
11. Tom Kenworthy, "Mining Industry Labors to Drown Montana Water Quality Initiative," *Washington Post*, 30 October 1996, p. A3; Gunther, pp. 166–174; Carl B. Glasscock. *The War of the Copper Kings*, New York: Bobbs-Merrill Co., 1935.
12. Morris E. Garnsey, "The Future of the Mountain States," *Harper's Magazine*, October 1945, pp. 329–336.
13. Amy Bridges, "Managing the Periphery in the Gilded Age: Writing Constitutions for the Western States," *Studies in American Political Development*, Vol. 22, Spring 2008, pp. 48–56; Phillips (1969), pp. 399–402.
14. Michael Lind, "The New Continental Divide," *The Atlantic*, January 2003, pp. 87–88; Thomas Burr, "Senators Form New Western Caucus," *Salt Lake Tribune*, 24 June 2009; Transcript of Republican Senator's News Conference, Washington, D.C., 24 June 2009, *CQ Transcripts*, 24 June 2009; Tom Kenworthy, "'Self-Reliant' Westerners Love Federal Handouts," *Salt Lake Tribune*, 4 July 2009.

Chapter 23: Immigration and Identity

1. Phillips (1999), pp. 588–589; Peter D. Salins, *Assimilation, American Style*, New York: Basic Books, 1997, pp. 22–30; Huntington (2004), pp. 45, 57.
2. Howard Odum and Harry Estill Moore, *American Regionalism*, New York: Henry Holt, 1938, p. 438; Salins, p. 148; U.S. Bureau of the Census, "Nativity of the Population, for Regions, Divisions, and States: 1850 to 1990," Internet Release: 9 March 1999.

3. Nathan Glazer and Daniel Patrick Moynihan, *Beyond the Melting Pot*, Cambridge, MA: MIT Press and Harvard University Press, 1964, pp. 138–139, 185, 217–219; Leonard Dinnerstein and David M. Reimers, *Ethnic Americans: A History of Immigration and Assimilation*, New York: Dodd, Mead & Co., 1977, pp. 41–45.
4. Salins (1997), p. 69.
5. Maris A. Vinovskis, *Education, Society, and Economic Opportunity*, New Haven, CT: Yale University Press, 1995, pp. 109–110; John Dewey, *Schools of Tomorrow*, New York: E. P. Dutton, 1915, pp. 313–316; Salins (1997), pp. 64–66.
6. Horace Mann, *Annual Reports of the Secretary of the Board of Education of Massachusetts for the Years 1845–1848*, Boston: Lee and Shepard, 1891, pp. 36–37; H. H. Wheaton, "Education of Immigrants," in Winthrop Talbot, ed., *Americanization*, 2nd ed., New York: H. W. Wilson Company, 1920, pp. 207–208.
7. Salins (1997), pp. 46–48; Huntington (2004), pp. 129–135; Stephen Mayer, "Adapting the Immigrant to the Line: Americanization in the Ford Factory, 1914–1921," *Journal of Social History*, Vol. 14, No. 1 (Autumn 1980), pp. 67–82.
8. Huntington (2004), pp. 11–20, 30–42.
9. Ibid., pp. 221–255; Pew Hispanic Center, *Mexican Immigrants in the United States, 2008* [fact sheet], 15 April 2009.
10. Juan Enriquez, *The Untied States of America*, New York: Crown, 2002, pp. 171–191; Associated Press, "Professor Predicts Hispanic Homeland," 31 January 2000.

Chapter 24: Gods and Missions

1. David M. Chalmers, *Hooded Americans: The History of the Ku Klux Klan*, Durham, NC: Duke University Press, 1987, p. 16.
2. Clifford J. Clarke, "The Bible Belt Thesis: An Empirical Test of the Hypothesis of Clergy Overrepresentation," *Journal for the Scientific Study of Religion*, Vol. 29, No. 2, June 1990, pp. 213–216; Martin E. Marty, *Righteous Empire: The Protestant Experience in America*, New York: Dial Press, 1970, pp. 178–206; Phillips (2006), pp. 142–148; Charles Reagan Wilson, *Baptized in Blood: The Religion of the Lost Cause, 1865–1920*, Athens, GA: University of Georgia Press, 1980, pp. 64–65, 71.
3. Wilson, pp. 41–43.
4. Chalmers, pp. 16–21.
5. Davis et al., (1941), p. 392–400; Webb (2004), pp. 238–252.
6. Marty (1970), pp. 178–206.
7. James C. Klotter, "The Black South and White Appalachia," *Journal of American History*, Vol. 66, No. 4, March 1980, pp. 832–849.
8. K. Austin Kerr, "Organizing for Reform: The Anti-Saloon League and Innovation in Politics," *American Quarterly*, Vol. 32, No. 1, 1980, pp. 37–53; Ruth B. A. Bordin, *Frances Willard: A Biography*, Chapel Hill: University of North Carolina Press, 1986, pp. 14–27; Harold Underwood Faulkner, *The Quest for Social Justice: 1898–1914*, New York: Macmillan, 1931, pp. 222–227.
9. Faulkner, pp. 178–184; Herbert J. Doherty Jr., "Alexander J. McKelway: Preacher to Progressive," *Journal of Southern History*, Vol. 24, No. 2 (May 1958), pp. 177–190.
10. Fischer (2004), p. 451; Alma Lutz, *Susan B. Anthony: Rebel, Crusader, Humanitarian*, Washington, D.C., Zenger Publications, 1976, pp. 21–40; Elisabeth

Griffith, *In Her Own Right: The Life of Elizabeth Cady Stanton*, New York: Oxford University Press; 1985, pp. 4–7; 227–228; Andrea Moore Kerr, *Lucy Stone: Speaking Out for Equality*, New Brunswick, NJ: Rutgers University Press, 1992, pp. 20–28; Nate Levin, *Carrie Chapman Catt: A Life of Leadership*, Seattle: BookSurge, 2006.

11. Ross Wetzsteon, *Republic of Dreams*, New York: Simon & Schuster, 2002, pp. 1–14.
12. Noah Feldman, *Divided by God: America's Church-State Problem and What We Should Do About It*, New York: Farrar, Straus and Giroux, 2005, pp. 52, 115–117, 127–132, 138.
13. Marty (1970), pp. 215–226.
14. R. Halliburton Jr., "Reasons for Anti-Evolutionism Succeeding in the South," *Proceedings of the Oklahoma Academy of Sciences*, Vol. 46 (1965), pp. 155–158.
15. Feldman (2005), pp. 146–149, Phillips (2006), pp. 113–119.

Chapter 25: Culture Clash

1. While the movement against Jim Crow in Dixie was Gandhi-esque, frustrations with informal racism in the Northern alliance triggered an armed uprising in Detroit and violent riots in many other cities, particularly after MLK's assassination.
2. Jason Sokol, *There Goes My Everything: White Southerners in the Age of Civil Rights, 1945–1975*, New York: Knopf, 2006, pp. 97, 100–103, 293; Jim Crow examples from the website of the National Park Service's Martin Luther King Jr. National Historic Site at http://www.nps.gov/malu/forteachers/ jim_crow_laws.htm.
3. Sokol, pp. 58–59, 86–88, 104, 116–123, 163–171, 196–197, 213, 243.
4. Ibid., pp. 204–205; Claude Sitton, "Civil Rights Act: How South Responds," *New York Times*, 12 July 1964, p. E7; Comer Vann Woodward, *The Strange Career of Jim Crow*, New York: Oxford University Press, 2002, pp. 175–176; Nikitta A. Foston, "Strom Thurmond's Black Family," *Ebony*, March 2004, pp. 162–164; Rick Perlstein, *Nixonland*, New York: Scribner, 2008, p. 131; Charles Joyner et al., "The flag controversy and the causes of the Civil War—A statement by historians," *Callaloo*, Vol. 24, No. 1, 2001, pp. 196–198.
5. John C. Jeffries and James E. Ryan, "A Political History of the Establishment Clause," *Michigan Law Review*, Vol. 100, No. 2, November 2001, pp. 282–283, 328–338; Phillips (2006), p. 215; Daniel K. Williams, "Jerry Falwell's Sunbelt Politics: The Regional Origins of the Moral Majority," *Journal of Policy History*, Vol. 22, No. 2, 2010, pp. 129–140; Robert D. Woodberry and Christian S. Smith, "Fundamentalists et al.: Conservative Protestants in America," *Annual Review of Sociology*, Vol. 24, 1998, pp. 31, 44, 47.
6. Tom Hayden, *The Port Huron Statement*, New York: Thunder's Mouth Press, 2005, pp. 44–180; Tom Hayden and Dick Flacks, "The Port Huron Statement at 40," *The Nation*, 5 August 2002.
7. John Robert Howard, "The Flowering of the Hippie Movement," *Annals of the American Academy of Political and Social Science*, Vol. 382, March 1969, pp. 43–47, 54; James P. O'Brien, "The Development of the New Left," *Annals of*

the American Academy of Political and Social Science, Vol. 395, May 1971, pp. 17–20; Maurice Isserman and Michael Kazin, *America Divided: The Civil War of the 1960s*, New York: Oxford University Press, 2000, pp. 168–172.

8. Calvin Trillin, "U.S. Journal: Crystal City, Texas," *New Yorker*, 17 April 1971, pp. 102–107; Calvin Trillin, "U.S. Journal: San Antonio," *New Yorker*, 2 May 1977, pp. 92–100; Joel Garreau, *The Nine Nations of North America*, Boston: Houghton Mifflin, 1981, pp. 240–244; Matt S. Meir, *The Chicanos: A History of Mexican Americans*, New York: Hill & Wang, 1972, pp. 249–250.
9. John Dickinson and Brian Young, *A Short History of Quebec*. Montreal: McGill–Queen's University Press, 2003, pp. 305–360; Garreau (1981), pp. 371–384.
10. D. T. Kuzimak, "The American Environmental Movement," *Geographical Journal*, Vol. 157, No. 3, November 1991, pp. 265–278; Curt Meine, *Aldo Leopold: His Life and Work*, Madison: University of Wisconsin Press, pp. 1–20.
11. See http://politics.nytimes.com/congress/votes/111/house/1/477.
12. Summary of same-sex marriage laws as of mid-2010 as per information at the website of the National Conference of State Legislatures: www.ncsl.org; http://www.latimes.com/news/local/la-2008election-california-results,0,3304898.htmlstory; National Conference of State Legislatures, "Same Sex Marriage, Civil Unions and Domestic Partnerships," April 2010, Web document accessed 2 July 2010 via http://www.ncsl.org/IssuesResearch/HumanServices/SameSexMarriage/tabid/16430/Default.aspx; Susan Page, "*Roe v. Wade*: The Divided States of America," *USA Today*, 17 April 2006.
13. Michael Lind, "The Southern Coup," *New Republic*, 19 June 1995; Michael Lind, "The Economic Civil War," Salon.com, 18 December 2008.

Chapter 26: War, Empire, and the Military

1. Frank Friedel, "Dissent in the Spanish-American War and the Philippine Insurrection," in Samuel Eliot Morison et al., *Dissent in Three American Wars*, Cambridge: Harvard University Press, 1970, pp. 67–68, 76–93; E. Berkeley Tompkins, *Anti-Imperialism in the United States: The Great Debate, 1890–1920*, Philadelphia: University of Pennsylvania Press, 1970, pp. 2–3, 115–116, 124–133, 144–147; Robert L. Beisner, *Twelve Against Empire: The Anti-Imperialists, 1898–1900*, New York: McGraw-Hill, 1968, pp. 107–108, 160; Colin Woodard, "The War Over Plunder: Who Owns Art Stolen in War?," *MHQ: The Quarterly Journal of Military History*, Summer 2010, pp. 48–51.
2. Beisner, p. 160; Tompkins, pp. 107–113.
3. Anthony Gaughan, "Woodrow Wilson and the Rise of Militant Interventionism in the South," *Journal of Southern History*, Vol. 65, No. 4, November 1999, pp. 789–808; Henry Blumenthal, "Woodrow Wilson and the Race Question," *Journal of Negro History*, Vol. 48, No. 1, January 1963, pp. 5–7.
4. Jim Webb (2004), pp. 48, 192, 254–255.
5. Michael Lind, "Civil War by Other Means," *Foreign Affairs*, Vol. 78, No. 5, September 1999, pp. 126–127.
6. John Peter, Horst Grill, and Robert L. Jenkins, "The Nazis and the American South in the 1930s: A Mirror Image?" *Journal of Southern History*, Vol. 58, No. 4,

November 1922, pp. 667–694; George L. Grassmuck, *Sectional Biases in Congress on Foreign Policy*, Baltimore: Johns Hopkins University Press, 1951, pp. 36–41, 122–127; Gaughan (1999), p. 772; Carl N. Degler, "Thesis, Antithesis, Synthesis: The South, The North, and the Nation," *Journal of Southern History*, Vol. 53, No. 1, February 1987, p. 17; Lind (1999), p. 128.

7. Grassmuck, pp. 36–41, 122–127.
8. Jim Webb (2004), p. 300; Fischer (1989), p. 877.
9. DeVoto (1947), pp. 6–7; Fred M. Shelley, *Political Geography of the United States*, New York: Guilford Press, 1996, pp. 219–222.
10. Matt S. Meier and Feliciano Rivera, *The Chicanos: A History of Mexican Americans*, New York: Hill & Wang, 1972, pp. 202–221.
11. Randall Bennett Woods, "Dixie's Dove: J. William Fulbright, the Vietnam War, and the American South," *Journal of Southern History*, Vol. 60, No. 3, August 1994, pp. 533–552; A. J. Bauer, "Ralph Yarborough's Ghost," *Texas Observer*, 21 September 2007; Phillips (1969), p. 259; Lind (1999), p. 131; Roy Reed, "F.B.I. Investigating Killing of 2 Negroes in Jackson," *New York Times*, 16 May 1970.
12. Clark Akatiff, "The March on the Pentagon," *Annals of the Association of American Geographers*, Vol. 61, No. 1, March 1974, pp. 29–30; Mitchell K. Hall, "The Vietnam Era Antiwar Movement," *OAH Magazine of History*, Vol. 18, No. 5, October 2004, pp. 13–17; Robert E. Lester, ed., *A Guide to the Microfilm Edition of the President's Commission on Campus Unrest*, Bethesda, MD.: Congressional Information Service, 2003, pp. v–vi, 10–24.
13. Akatiff, pp. 29–30; http://afsc.org/story/peoples-park-berkeley.
14. Vote on stopping operations in Cambodia as per: http://www.govtrack.us/congress/vote.xpd?vote=h1970-294]; Ernesto Chávez, *"Mi raza primero!" Nationalism, Identity, and Insurgency in the Chicano Movement in Los Angeles, 1966–1978*, Los Angeles: University of California Press, 2002, pp. 64–71.
15. Sandy Maisel and Mark D. Brewer, *Parties and Elections in America*, Lanham, MD: Rowman & Littlefield, 2008, p. 426.
16. Michael Lind, *Made in Texas: George W. Bush and the Southern Takeover of American Politics*, New York: Basic Books, 2003, pp. 147–148.
17. John B. Judis, "The War Resisters," *The American Prospect*, 6 October 2002; Congressional votes (H Conf 63 and 2002 Iraq War Resolution) as per http://www.govtrack.us/congress/vote.xpd?vote=h2002-455.
18. Lind (1999), pp. 133, 142.

Chapter 27: The Struggle for Power I: The Blue Nations

1. Richard Franklin Bensel, *Sectionalism and American Political Development, 1880–1980*, Madison: University of Wisconsin Press, 1984, pp. 63–67.
2. Ibid., p. 119.
3. Robert Sobel, "Coolidge and American Business," [online document] at http://web.archive.org/web/20060308075125/http://www.jfklibrary.org/coolidge_sobel.html.
4. Alan Greenblat, "The Changing U.S. Electorate," *CQ Researcher*, 30 May 2008, p. 469.
5. In 1960 and 1976, Yankeedom was divided over whether to support (Irish Catholic) John F. Kennedy over Richard Nixon or (Deep Southern Baptist) Jimmy

Carter over Gerald Ford, qualms not shared by its allies. In 1968, Yankeedom and the Left Coast were split over Hubert Humphrey and Nixon, while New Netherland supported Humphrey. All three nations—and much of the country—split in the 1948 race between Harry Truman and John Dewey.

6. Obama was born and raised outside "the nations" (in Hawaii and, later, Indonesia) but has spent almost his entire pre-presidential adult life in the Northern alliance. He attended Columbia and Harvard Law School, lived in New York City, and then moved to Chicago, where he taught at the (decidedly Yankee) University of Chicago and started his family and political career.
7. Bensel (1984), pp. 300–301.
8. Jerold G. Rusk, *A Statistical History of the American Electorate*, Washington, D.C.: CQ Press, 2001, pp. 230–231, 305, 315; http://en.wikipedia.org/wiki/Political_party_strength_in_U.S._states.
9. Jessica Reaves, "James Jeffords," *Time*, 24 May 2001.
10. Bensel (1984), pp. 296–297, 300–301.
11. See http://politics.nytimes.com/congress/votes/111/house/1/887 and http://politics.nytimes.com/congress/ votes/111/house/2/413.
12. Calculated after reviewing http://www.washingtonpost.com/wp-srv/politics/special/clinton/ housevote/all.htm and http://politics.nytimes.com/congress/votes/111/senate/2/206.

Chapter 28: The Struggle for Power II: The Red and the Purple

1. Stephen D. Cummings, *The Dixification of America: The American Odyssey into the Conservative Economic Trap*, Westport, CT: Praeger, 1998, p. 193.
2. Doug Monroe, "Losing Hope," *Atlanta Magazine*, September 2003, p. 259; Richard B. Drake, *A History of Appalachia*, Lexington: University of Kentucky Press, 2001, pp. 158–161.
3. Foner (1988), pp. 178–187.
4. Thomas Frank, *What's the Matter with Kansas?*, New York: Henry Holt, 2004, p. 7.
5. Bensel (1984), pp. 74–82.
6. Robert Dallek, *Lyndon B. Johnson: Portrait of a President*, New York: Oxford University Press, 2004, p. 170; http://www.pbs.org/wgbh/amex/wallace/sfeature/quotes.html; Arthur Bremer, *An Assassin's Diary*, New York: Pocket Books, 1973.
7. Peter Applebome, *Dixie Rising*, New York: New York Times Books, 1996, p. 121; Todd J. Gillman, "McCain Campaign Co-chairman Phil Gramm Says America in 'Mental Recession,'" *Dallas Morning News*, 11 July 2008; Bob Dart, "Helms: True Believer to Some, Senator 'No' to Others," Cox News Service, 21 August 2001.
8. Lind (2003), pp. 1–8, 92–108, 118; Emmanuel Saez, "Striking It Richer: The Evolution of Top Incomes in the United States," unpublished manuscript, 17 July 2010.
9. Garreau (1981), pp. 301–327.
10. John M. Broder, "L.A. Elects Hispanic Mayor for First Time in Over 100 Years," *New York Times*, 18 May 2005; Huntington (2004), pp. 242–246; Enriquez (2000), pp. 183–189.

11. Michael Adams, (2003), pp. 79–85; Edward Grabb and James Curtis, *Regions Apart: The Four Societies of Canada and the United States*, Toronto: Oxford University Press, 2004, pp. 146, 212.

Epilogue

1. Enriquez (2000), p. 171.
2. Author interview, Aleqa Hammond, foreign minister of Greenland, Nuuk, Greenland, 11 September 2007; Edmund Searles, "Food and the Making of the Inuit Identity," *Food & Foodways*, Vol. 10, No. 1–2, 2002, pp. 55–78.
3. Doug Struck, "Canada Sets Aside Vast Northern Wilderness," *Washington Post*, 22 November 2007, p. A30; Canadian Boreal Initiative, press release, 7 April 2008; author telephone interview, Larry Innes, Canadian Boreal Initiative, Portland, ME, and Ottawa, 20 May 2008; author telephone interview, Valerie Courtois, environmental planner, Innu Nation, 22 May 2008, Portland, ME, and Sheshatshiu, Labrador.
4. Author interview, Sheila Watt-Cloutier, Ilulissat, Greenland, 9 September 2007; Randy Boswell, "Canadian a Favorite for Nobel Peace Prize," *Ottawa Citizen*, 6 October 2007, p. A6.
5. Author interview, Aleqa Hammond; Sarah Lyall, "Fondly, Greenland Loosens Danish Rule," *New York Times*, 22 June 2009, p. 4; Colin Woodard, "As Land Thaws, So Do Greenland's Aspirations for Independence," *Christian Science Monitor*, 16 October 2007; Greenland Home Rule Act, Kingdom of Denmark Act No. 577 of 29 November 1978.

INDEX

Page numbers in *Italics* refer to maps.